The Wisdom of
Earnest Shurtleff Holmes

The Wisdom of Earnest Shurtleff Holmes

By Ernest Shurtleff Holmes

The Science of Mind
Creative Mind and Success
Creative Mind

Wilder Publications, LLC.
PO Box 3005
Radford VA 24143-3005

ISBN 10: 1-60459-071-8
ISBN 13: 978-1-60459-071-5
First Edition
10 9 8 7 6 5 4 3 2 1

The Science of Mind

TABLE OF CONTENTS

Part III: SPECIAL ARTICLES

PEACE BE UNTO THEE, STRANGER

Peace be unto thee, stranger, enter and be not afraid.
I have left the gate open and thou art welcome to my home.
There is room in my house for all.
I have swept the hearth and lighted the fire.
The room is warm and cheerful and you will find comfort and rest within.
The table is laid and the fruits of Life are spread before thee.
The wine is here also, it sparkles in the light.
I have set a chair for you where the sunbeams dance through the shade.
Sit and rest and refresh your soul.
Eat of the fruit and drink the wine.
All, all is yours, and you are welcome.

FOREWORD

In presenting these lessons on Mental Science, I do not claim to have discovered any new Truth. The Truth has been known in every age by a few; but the great mass of people has never even dreamed that we live in a mental and spiritual world. To-day, however, there is a great inquiry into the deeper meaning of life because the race has reached a state of unfoldment where a broader scope is possible.

These lessons are an attempt to put into the spoken word and into print some of those great truths known to the enlightened of all ages.

To suppose that the Creative Intelligence of the world would create man in bondage and leave him bound would be to dishonor that Creative Power which we call God. On the other hand, to suppose that God could make man as an individual, without leaving him to discover himself, would be to suppose an impossibility. Individuality must be spontaneous and can never be automatic. The seed of freedom must be hid within the shell of the human. But, like the Prodigal of old, man must make the great discovery for himself. Although the journey may at times seem hard and the burden too great to bear, man still feels within a subtle sense, a mystical presence, a divine Reality. Thus, the inherent nature of himself is forever seeking to express itself in terms of freedom. We will do well to listen to this inner voice, for it tells us of a life wonderful in its scope, of a love beyond our fondest dreams, of a freedom which the soul craves.

But the great love of the universe must be one with the great law of Its own Being, and we must approach love through the law.

This, then, is the teaching, Love and Law. As the love of God is perfect, so the law of God is also perfect. We must understand both. "Who hath ears to hear, let him hear."

I wish to express my appreciation to the authors whose names are mentioned following the different lessons in this course of instruction, as well as to many others whose names are not mentioned. The Truth comes to us from all sources, and our understanding of it is the result of the time, thought and effort of thousands of people who have given their lives to its study.

I wish to express special appreciation to Miss Anne Shipman, of Boston, Mass., without whose untiring efforts it is not probable that these manuscripts would have ever been gotten in shape for publication; and to my mother whose great faith in these teachings has inspired me with the hope and the belief that they may be of benefit to those who study them.

E.S.H.

YOURSELF

Oh, weary heart, laden with earth's weight and care,
Oh, feet, stumbling on the way, bleeding and bare,
Oh, arms outstretched, and hands upheld in prayer,
Oh, back, which so oft has felt the lash and rod,
Oh, soul, which cries aloud for the living God,
Oh, life, struggling to free itself from the clod;
Know this: there is no power from without,
Yourself must answer every fear and meet all doubt
With some divine, indwelling power
Which you yourself, upon yourself, shall shower;
And giving, take, and taking, give
Unto that life which you, yourself, shall live.

PART I: THE EVOLUTION OF MAN'S THOUGHT

INSTINCTIVE MAN

If we traced man's history back into the dim past we should come to a place where he did not consciously know himself. We should come to a place where Instinctive Man alone existed; for the self-conscious man had not yet evolved.

Nothing can be more apparent than that man, as he now appears, is the result of growth and unfoldment. But in order to unfold, he had to have something from which to unfold, and since he is intelligent, he must have unfolded from an intelligent cause.

Instinctive Man, then, means that Inner Something, or Life, which we do not see but which is, of course, there. We might say that Instinctive Life is God in man, or the idea of God, working through man. But if Instinctive Man is an idea of God, why is he not perfect? The answer is that he is perfect, but that as soon as individuality is evolved he must be left alone to discover himself. Even God could not make a mechanical Individuality. If man is created with the attributes of self-choice and free will, he must be let alone to make the great discovery for himself.

NATURE WAITS ON MAN'S SELF-RECOGNITION

We note, that from the day when Instinctive Life brought man to the point of self-choice, it let him alone, and from that day Instinctive Life has waited on man's unfoldment. It is true that during all this time it has carried on the automatic functions of the body and has even silently told man what to do; but it has let him alone in all other ways. It may, and must, hold man as a perfect being, but it also must let him discover this fact for himself. During all of this time, however, Instinctive Life, or God, must be silently waiting for the great discovery to be made and must always be ready to respond to man's advancement. We note this to be true along the line of man's progress. For instance, consider the discovery of any of nature's forces; we know that they must have always existed; but, so far as man is concerned, they exist to him only after he has discovered, and learned how to make use of them. Electricity was a reality in the universe when Moses led the Children of Israel from the land of Egypt, but neither Moses nor any of his followers knew anything about it, and so they did not receive any benefits from its use. This is true of any and all of the natural laws; they always existed, and as soon as understood may be used. In this way, Instinctive Life waits upon man's discovery of the natural laws and his discovery of himself and his relationship to the great Whole.

If this is so evidently true of all the forces in the natural world we must expect to find the same thing to be true of those inner and finer forces within man. The unfoldment of these inner and finer forces through man is what we call his evolution.

THE FIRST GREAT DISCOVERY

The first great discovery that man made was that he could think. This was the day when he rose from the ground and said, "I AM." This marked the first great day of personal attainment; and from that day man became an individual and had to make all further progress himself; any compulsory evolution stopped when man became an individual, and from that day he had to work in conscious union with Nature and Her forces; but he did not have to work alone, for Instinctive Life has always been with him and will never depart from him. Instinctive Life desires that man shall express more, and yet more, of its own limitless possibilities.

Man is evolving from an Infinite basis; behind him is the great Unknown but not the great unknowable; for the unknown becomes known through man, and whatever more Instinctive Life is to do for him must be done through him. Nature must work through man in order to work for him. This is true all along the line of life and endeavor.

The first great discovery of man was that he could think, plan and execute. As the result of this discovery he has built up a great civilization and all that goes with it. He has harnessed electricity to his inventions, tied steam and compelled it to do his bidding. He has laid waste forests, built cities, made the desert to bloom, and has thrown the lines of his commerce around the globe; indeed, he has seemed to possess the earth.

THE INNER SENSE AWAKENS

But with all of man's powers he has still felt a vague sense of something more, something greater, something further along; a sort of mystical inner sense of things, an instinctive urge, a blind groping after a greater light. Disregarding all of his apparent power, man has still been unhappy, sick, lonely and afraid. The cities which he built have crumbled into dust, the nations which he fostered have, one by one, fallen into ruin, and history alone remains to tell the tale of most of his endeavors.

In spite of man's apparent power he has suffered greatly, and death has crowned his life and work with a pall of darkness and uncertainty.

THE GREAT QUESTION "WHY"

The great question "Why" has forever been upon his lips. Few indeed have been able to answer this question; and these few have been passed by, unheeded, in the struggle for existence.

Man has struggled along the weary road with a heavy heart and bleeding feet, only to be met by the grave. The lack of a sense of completion has beset his every pathway; and in his blind groping he has held up his hands in speechless anguish, and his broken cries have rent the air with supplications to an apparently unheeding Deity.

Why the suffering, the sorrow, the sin, the sickness and a lifetime of trouble, only to be met at last by the grim and sinister tomb?

Why, why, why? Man has sought the wise only to discover their foolishness; he has sought the learned only to find a lack of wisdom. Why, why, why? His cry has appeared to go forth into an empty nothingness. But hark! from somewhere a vague answer has come, some subtle inner sense of things; some unknown presence has given answer and a still small voice has said to him, "Man, know thyself." The Instinctive Man has again spoken and told him to search more deeply into his own nature; to look deep within himself for the answer to life. The hour has struck in the evolution of man when he can understand this voice and do its bidding.

THE GREATEST DISCOVERY OF ALL TIME—MIND

Man's response to this inner Instinctive Voice has caused him to start on the greatest adventure of his career, the discovery of Mind.

Man's first discovery of his ability to think was set aside as being too evident to take any notice of; he could think, but what of it! Of course, it was a proof that he was, but that was all; he had always been able to think; this simply gave him the ability to know his needs and try to supply them. This he had always done.

The ability to think seemed to be an automatic thing; it came with him and would doubtless die when he died; the brain seemed to be the organ of thought; and, of course, when death stilled the brain it would no longer operate—this was self-evident.

THE BRAIN DOES NOT THINK

But the day came when some wise man said that it is not the brain that thinks at all; for if the brain, of itself, could think, then one could cut it out and it would keep right on thinking. No, the brain of itself could not think; and yet, without a brain man could not think; which simply means that man needs a brain while here, but that the brain, of itself, does not think. The brain does not think and yet man thinks; so behind the brain there must be a thinker. But where is this thinker? We do not see him. Have we a right to say that there is a thinker when no one has ever seen him? Yes; for can we name a single force of nature that we can see? Have we ever seen electricity or any of the other forces of nature? No; and the only evidence we have of their existence is that we see what they do. We have light and motive power, so we have a right to suppose that there is a force which we call electricity. This is true all along the line, for we see effects and not causes.

WE DO NOT SEE THE THINKER

But to return to the thinker; we do not see him, but the proof of his reality is in the evidence of his works. We know that the legs do not walk; for, if severed from the body, they could not carry any one very far. Cut off the hand and see if it could still hold anything in its grasp! Pluck out the eye and it cannot see; and so it is with all the organs of the body. There is a thinker and doer back of the organism who is using it for a conscious purpose.

THE BODY UNCONSCIOUS WITHOUT THE THINKER

This is a great discovery; for it means that the body without the thinker could neither be sick nor suffer; for without the thinker there could be no movement of the body. Why then are we sick? This inquiry will not be answered until every form of disease is swept from the face of the earth and numbered with the things that were once thought necessary. For man has discovered that the body, of itself, has no life nor power to act.

Let us follow the course of man's thought since he first made this discovery about the body and began to apply his knowledge. He first realized that Instinctive Man built up the body through evolution; and, after having created and evolved a perfect body, left it in man's keeping to do with as he willed. At first, man was ignorant of this, thinking that the body was self-operating; but as soon as he discovered that such was not the case he began to formulate certain new theories about himself. He discovered that while he could consciously think and decide, something happened to his thoughts after he had thought them. They went somewhere; for soon they would come back as remembrance. Man had now discovered that he could consciously think and that his thought would come back to him again. This led to the conclusion that memory is an active thing, an inner mental action. He said, "Memory is the storehouse of all my conscious thoughts and it is active. My body is not conscious of life, but my thought is conscious of my body; my body is operated upon by my thought; and it must also be operated upon by my memory, since memory is active. But, since memory is only the result of conscious thought, memory, of itself, is an unconscious operation of what was once a conscious thought."

THE CONSCIOUS AND THE UNCONSCIOUS THOUGHT

Since man always has had the habit of naming things, he named his memory his "unconscious thought," and his conscious thought he called his "objective mind." He now came to the conclusion that he had two minds, one conscious and one unconscious, or sub-conscious. The conscious mind being the one that he used all of the time in his self-conscious state and the sub-conscious mind being the storehouse of all his conscious thoughts, as well as the seat of his memory. It follows, that as conscious thought acts, unconscious thought must also operate. This conclusion led to the discovery that the sub-conscious mind is the builder of the body; not that it really made the body in the first place, for Instinctive Man did that; but that the sub-conscious mind keeps the body going and is always acting on the thoughts of the conscious mind. After carefully watching this process, man discovered that he could consciously think and, by so doing, make such an impression on his unconscious thought that it would do what he directed. From these observations he deduced the law of suggestion to be one of action and reaction. Thus he found how habits are formed; that they are conscious ideas fallen into the inner thought and carried out to logical conclusions.

A NEW BASIS OF THOUGHT

Therefore, he began to reason: "Instinctive Man within me is perfect and yet I appear to be imperfect. My apparent imperfection must be the result of an imperfect thinking; in reality I am, and always have been, perfect. I will now begin to think differently about myself and see what happens." And as he began to think from the new basis he found that the body responded and was healed. So he came to this conclusion: "God made me perfect but He also made me an individual, which means that I can do with myself as I will. I cannot really destroy my body but I can make it most uncomfortable. Since God made me and made me perfect, each one of the organs of my body represents a perfect idea."

Realizing this to be true, he began to think from this basis, and the organs of the body responded. He found that thoughts of peace produced a peaceful condition while thoughts of fear produced a disturbed condition; that confidence made him strong while fear made him weak. In fact, he was able to trace each mental attitude to its physical correspondent. He discovered that, asleep or awake, the inner mind works all the time. He also found that by analyzing his thought he could discover what ailed him. This he called psycho-analysis.

THE LAW OF MIND

Then another idea came to him: the whole thing was in accordance with law. He had discovered a law of mind just as he, at another time, discovered a law of electricity. If it were law, then he could always use it and it would always respond. From this he gradually built up a definite technique for the practice of right thinking.

He found that if he always thought of himself as being perfect he would always feel better. But what should he do with his body when it appeared sick? How was he to think of himself when he was sick? Could he deny that he was sick when he was suffering? Yes; for his sickness was the result of thought, and by changing the thought he could change the effect. He learned to turn away from the body when it was sick and go back into mind and think of the body as being perfect; for his thought worked independently of the body. He turned from the image of sickness to the idea of health and said, "I am perfect, no matter what the appearance may be."

UNCONSCIOUS MIND AT WORK

But some kinds of sickness had never entered his mind at all; that is, he had never consciously thought of them. How was he to reconcile this fact with his new theory? For a while this was a hard problem to solve; but by a still more careful study of his inner self, he discovered that what he called his subjective mind took all of his thoughts and did something with them. He found that there were certain combinations of thought which, brought to their logical conclusions, would produce certain kinds of diseases. He did not have to consciously think of a certain disease to have it; but if he thought certain kinds of thoughts they would produce their logical results. For instance, if he were excited all the time it would produce nervousness; if he became angry it would secrete poison in his system, and so on through the whole category of the human ailments; somewhere in mind they had their reason for being. Perhaps he could not always tell exactly where, but, by knowing that his body was perfect, he could still heal himself. He knew that as time went on and his knowledge grew he would find out more and more about himself and so be better able to heal himself. He was glad that he had started on the right track; he believed that he would know all in time and never be sick again.

ANOTHER GREAT DISCOVERY—THOUGHT REACHED OTHERS

Then a new discovery came, which was that he could think of others and heal them. It seemed to make no difference where they were; he could think of them and heal them. This was a most astounding fact, for it meant that there was a common mind somewhere through which his thought operated; for he could not reach another unless there were a medium between himself and the other person. This seemed strange; for what he had learned to think of as his individual subjective mind, was, after all, only the personal use that he was making of something which was around every one. He began to think for others, and found that mind responded to his thinking for them and caused some action to take place in their bodies. He called this medium "Universal Mind," or "the Law of God." It seemed to be as omnipresent as the law of electricity or any of the other forces of nature.

THE DISCOVERY OF RACE-THOUGHT

In this way he discovered how it was possible that the whole race might have held certain kinds of thoughts and how they might have operated through any one who was receptive to them. That is, if any one should feel discouraged, other thoughts of discouragement might gain entrance also and make him feel worse. This he called race-suggestion. But how was he to protect himself from it? By knowing that it could not operate through him; that he was a perfect idea and could not be affected by suggestion; for, after all, it was nothing but thought. He learned to build a mental wall around himself which could not be entered unless he chose. This he called "Divine Protection."

A UNIVERSAL MEDIUM WHICH ALL MUST COME TO BELIEVE IN

Man had now discovered that he could help and heal himself and others by thinking into some kind of a Universal Law of Mind. He found that, like all other forces of nature, it was a great Impersonal Law and could be consciously used whenever he wished to use It and that the use of It was through right thinking. He realized that the time must come when the race would be healed by knowing the Truth about itself. But because the Law was mental it could only work for those who believed in It, and since many did not believe, the thing to do was to heal himself and others who wished to be healed, waiting for the rest of the world to realize the fact.

ANOTHER QUESTION COMES UP—WHY ARE PEOPLE POOR?

But another thought came to him. If he could think into some kind of a Universal Medium of Mind and heal himself and others; if this Mind could produce such a physical effect on the body, why could it not also produce the same kind of an effect on conditions and the affairs of life? Why was it that some were rich and some poor? Was this fate, or was it because there was not enough for all? If the One Mind made bodies, why did It not also create conditions? And if It did, why did it not give to all alike?

Why were some people happy and prosperous and others unhappy, weak and poor? Could the answer to this also be in Mind? Could it be that just as man had thought of himself as sick, and so made sickness, he had thought of poverty and made this condition possible in his experience?

Questions like these and many others came into the mind of man and caused him to search even more deeply into the nature of things. Looking about, he saw some succeed and some fail, though all was taking place in the same world and under common conditions. So he knew that it must be something in man, and not outside of him, that made all these things possible. He realized that conditions did not make themselves. Everything in man's life was run by man himself.

MAN BEGINS TO REALIZE THAT HIS CONDITIONS ARE CONTROLLED BY THOUGHT

In this way man realized that even his affairs were controlled by thought working through the avenue of the One Mind. He discovered that by changing his thought he could remold his affairs, and that by right thinking he could bring into his life new conditions. But would there be enough to go around should every one become prosperous? Yes, for Instinctive Life is Limitless.

REALIZES THAT HE MUST THINK CORRECTLY

So man discovered that he could control his affairs by right thinking; he could bring into his experience the things he wished to enjoy if he thought correctly; and since this was all in accordance with law he could do so consciously. He realized that the time would come when every one would think correctly; and poverty, unhappiness, and all that goes with them, would be swept from the face of the earth. They were never intended to be, but man had misused his power; now that he understood, he would change his whole manner of thinking and consequently he would become happy and have plenty. But every one did not believe this. Many said that it was a foolish idea, while others said that it was too good to be true. However, it was soon proven that whoever would believe and comply with the Law could prove it to be true. If some did not wish to believe, that was all right; there were plenty who would, and the direct proofs of their lives would in time convince others. In this way, eventually, all would be saved from unbearable conditions. The thing to do was to teach the Law to those who did believe.

And so the lessons which follow are for this purpose, to teach those who believe in the Law how to use It.

The race is made up of individuals, and the place to begin is with the person who believes in the greater possibility. Each one, for himself, must work out the law of his own being. It is within the power of every man to completely change his environment and completely heal his body. Whether or not he will do this depends entirely upon his own conviction and his own determination. Nature attends him on the way and is always ready to serve; but he is an individual and nothing will ever be forced upon him. Let any one follow the Law, comply with Its nature, and consistently apply himself to right thinking and living, and he will prove to himself that life holds all and more than he has ever imagined.

PART II: THE LESSONS

Lesson One: Introduction

In presenting these lessons in Mental Science to the public, it is my desire to make it possible for any one, who cares to take the time to study them, to demonstrate the truths that will be discussed. It is, perhaps, hard to set down in writing a complete teaching in Mental Science that will not appear difficult to understand; but this could be said as well of any science, and the Science of Mind is no exception to the general rule.

SCIENCE

Science is knowledge of facts built around some proven principle. All that we know about any science is that certain things happen under certain conditions. Take electricity as an example; we know that there is such a thing as electricity; we have never seen it, but we know that it exists because we can use it; we know that it operates in a certain way and we have discovered the way it works. From this knowledge we go ahead and deduce certain facts about electricity; and, applying them to the general principle, we receive definite results. No one has ever seen the power or the energy that we call electricity; and the only proof we have that it really exists is that from it we receive light, heat and motive power.

No one has ever seen any of the great causes that lie back of the manifestations of life, and perhaps no one ever will; but we know that such principles exist because we can use them.

HOW LAWS ARE DISCOVERED

The discovery of a law is generally made more or less by accident, or by some one who, after careful thought and observation, has come to the conclusion that such a principle must exist. As soon as a law is discovered experiments are made with it, certain facts are proved to be true, and in this way a science is gradually formulated; for any science consists of the number of known facts about any given principle. As more and more facts are gathered and proven, the science expands and gradually becomes accepted by all and used by those who understand it. In this way all of our sciences have been evolved until to-day we have the use of powers and unseen forces of which our ancestors never even dreamed.

PROOF OF MIND

This is true of the Science of Mind. No one has ever seen Mind or Spirit, but who could possibly doubt their existence? Nothing is more self-evident than that we live; and since we live, we must have life; yet who has ever seen this life? The only proof of life we have is that we live; and the only proof we have of Mind is that we can think; so we are perfectly justified in believing that we have a mind and that we live.

WHERE OUR THOUGHTS GO

As we watch the processes of thought we find that we think consciously, and we also find that something happens to our thoughts after we have thought them; for instance, they become memory. This proves that we have a deeper aspect of mind, which is called subjective, lying just below the threshold of the conscious. This subjective mind is the place where our thoughts go and from whence they eventually return to us again as memory. Observation proves this to be true; for it always happens this way.

Observation has proven that the subjective mind is the seat of memory and that it contains mental pictures, or impressions, of all that has ever happened to the individual. As these mental impressions come to the surface of the conscious mind they are called memories.

Moreover observation has shown that the subjective mind is the builder of the body. It has proven that it is not only the seat of memory; it is also the avenue through which Instinctive Man works. We mean by Instinctive Man that part of the individual which came with him when he was born—that inner something which makes him what he is. For instance, we do not have to consciously think to make the body function; so we say that the inner, or the Instinctive, Man, does this for us. This is true of most of the functions of the body; they appear to be automatic; they came with us and are nature's way of working through us. So we say that in the unconscious or the sub-conscious or the subjective, there is a silent process forever working away and always doing its duty, carrying on all of the unconscious activities of the body without effort on our part.

SUGGESTION BECOMES MEMORY

It has been observed that suggestions, planted in the subconscious, become memories, and eventually tend to externalize in the body. From this it has been deduced that the sub-conscious mind is the builder of the body and is the creative factor in man. It has also been proven that certain types of thought produce certain kinds of results. This shows that the subjective mind takes our suggestions and tends to act upon them, no matter what the suggestion may be.

While the Instinctive Man, or the Natural Man, must be perfect, it is known that the thoughts of the conscious man may hinder instinctive action, through adverse suggestion. That is, conscious thought, acting as memory, may build a false condition in the body, which condition we call disease. Conscious thought may also erase this memory and thereby heal the disease.

Through observations such as these, a science of the subjective mind has gradually been formulated, many facts have been put together; and, to-day, these facts constitute what we call the science of the subjective life in its relationship to mental healing.

MENTAL MEDIUM THROUGH ALL

It has also been proven that thought operates in such a manner as to make it possible to convey mental impressions from one person to another, showing that there is a mental medium between all people. When we think of it, how could we talk with each other unless there were some kind of a medium through which we talked? We could not; and so we know that there really is such a medium. While there is a place where our bodies begin and leave off, as form, there does not appear to be a place where our thought leaves off. Indeed, the observations made and the facts gathered show that the medium between men's minds is omnipresent; that is, it seems to be everywhere present. Radio also shows this, for messages are sent out through some kind of a universal medium, and all that we can say of it is that we know the medium is there. So it is with Mind; all that we can say is that everything happens just as though it were there. We have a perfect right, then, to say that such a medium exists.

This opens up a far-reaching theory, for it leads to the conclusion that we are surrounded by a Universal Mind which is the Medium of the communication of our thoughts. Perhaps this is the Mind of God! Who knows? That It is there, we cannot doubt.

READING THOUGHT

Other observations have shown even more wonderful possibilities. It is known that certain people can read our thoughts, even when we are not aware of the fact, showing that thought operates through a medium which is universal, or always present. This also shows that the medium is subjective; for it retains our thoughts and transmits them to others. This leads to the conclusion that what we call our subjective mind is really the use that we, as individuals, make of something which is universal. Perhaps, just as radio messages are operative through a universal medium, our thoughts are operative through the medium of a Universal Mind. Indeed, this has been believed for thousands of years by some of the deepest thinkers.

MENTAL LAW

As we think of the medium of radio transmission in terms of law, so we should think of the Mental Medium in terms of law; for it must be the law of mental action. While we might think of it as the Mind of God, we surely could not think of it as the Spirit of God; for the Mental Medium is automatic, while the Spirit must be Self-Knowing. We could not call the Universal Medium of Mind God, any more than we could call electricity God. It is but one of the many attributes of God or the Universe of Life. It is the avenue through which God operates as Law.

THE WORD OF GOD AS LAW

Since man has a self-conscious mind, a subconscious mind and a body, we know that he is threefold in his nature. First, he is conscious mind or spirit; next, he is subconscious mind or mental law; and then, he is body. The conscious mind controls the subconscious; and in its turn, the subconscious controls the body.

It is evident that man comes from God, Life or Nature, whichever we choose to call It. It is also evident that we can get from Life only that which is in It. Man must partake of the Divine Nature if he comes from It or is made out of It; for what is true of the Whole must also be true of any of Its parts. Something cannot come from nothing; something must come from something; for nothing comes from nothing and nothing is the result; but man is something, else he could not declare himself; and since he is something, he must be made from, or come out of, something; and that something must be what we call God.

THREEFOLD NATURE OF GOD

If we study the true nature of man, then, we shall have delved into the real nature of God, or First Cause, from which man springs; and as we have found that man is threefold in his nature, so we must also deduce that God is threefold in His Nature; that is, God is Spirit, or Self-Knowingness; God is Law and action; and God is Result or Body. This is the inner meaning of the teaching of "the Trinity." But let us elaborate: God, as Self-Knowing Spirit, means the Divine Being Whom we have always thought of and believed in; the Being to Whom we have prayed and Whom we have adored. God, as Law, means the way in which the Spirit works; and Law in this sense, would be the servant of the Spirit. God, as Body, means the manifestation of the Spirit. We might put it in another form and say, there is the Thing, the way that It works and the result of Its work. Still another form would be to say, Cause, Medium and Effect.

TRINITY OF BEING

A trinity of being appears to run through all Nature and all Life; for instance, there is electricity, the way it works and its result, which is light or motive power. There is the seed, the creative medium of the soil and the plant. Turn it as we may, we are confronted with the necessity of a trinity of being. There must always be the thing, what it does and the way that it operates. Always a trinity runs through life and through everything in it. But through the Trinity of God and man there runs a Self-Conscious Spirit, and this is what distinguishes man from the brute, or from a purely mechanical creation; and is the only thing that could make God a Self-Knowing Power.

CONSCIOUS MIND IN GOD AND MAN

In God and in man there is a power that, while it may not transcend law, yet consciously uses it for definite purposes. In God this knowledge must be complete, but in man it is, of course, but dimly perceived. Jesus, the wisest Man who ever lived, said that God and man are One in real nature, and no doubt this understanding was what gave Him His marvelous power.

UNITY

It is well to remember that the enlightened in every age have taught that back of all things there is One Unseen Cause: In studying the teachings of the great thinkers we find that a common thread runs through all—the thread of Unity. There is no record of any deep thinker, of any age, who taught duality.

One of the great teachings of Moses was, "Hear, O Israel, the Lord our God is One Lord"; 1 and the saying, "*I am* that *I am*," 2 was old when Moses was yet unborn; for it had been inscribed over the temple entrances for generations. We may go back much farther than Moses and find the same teaching, for it crops out from the literatures and sayings of the wise of all ages. Jesus taught this when He said, "I and the Father are One," 3 and in the saying, "The Father that dwelleth in me." 4

This teaching of Unity is the chief cornerstone of the Sacred Scriptures of the East as well as of our own Sacred Writings. It is to-day the mainspring of the teachings of the modern philosophies, such as Christian Science, Divine Science, The Unity Teachings, The New Thought Movement, The Occult Teachings, The Esoteric or Inner Teachings, and even of much that is taught under the name of Psychology. Without this basic teaching of Unity these movements would have but little to offer. Science has found nothing to contradict this teaching, and it never will, for the teaching is self-evident.

WORSHIP OF GOD

That there is a God or First Cause no one can doubt. That the Being Whom we call God really exists from eternity to eternity is self-evident. In every age people have worshipped some kind of Deity. It is true that as the evolution of man has progressed the idea of God has expanded, and the more that people have realized of life, and of nature and her laws, the clearer has been the concept of Deity, for this is the logical result of an unfolding mentality.

MANY GODS

The first stages of human thought brought out the idea that there were many gods, the natural outcome of a life which experienced many kinds of misfortune and difficulties. As there were many gods so there were many devils or evil powers; but as the understanding of man grew he began to realize that there could not be so many powers, since the Cause back of everything must be a Unity, else It could not exist. More than one power would indicate a universe divided against itself, and this kind of a universe could not hold together. However, it has taken a long time to come to this conclusion, and in the stages between many weird ideas have been formulated and believed in. At first there were many gods and many devils; but as thought progressed, this was narrowed down to One God and one devil or evil power. Duality has been believed in since time immemorial, and, indeed, is still believed in by many. By duality we mean a belief in more than One Power back of all things.

BELIEF IN DUALITY—ITS RESULTS

The belief in duality has robbed theology of power and has polluted philosophy with untruths; it has divided science against itself and has made countless thousands go through life with saddened hearts.

DUALITY IN THEOLOGY

The belief in duality has given rise in theology to the idea of a God and a devil, each with equal power to impose upon man a blessing or a curse, and

men have worshiped a devil just as truly as they ever worshiped God. Even
to-day this monstrous thought is robbing men of their birthright to happiness
and a sense of security. Even to-day, and openly, men still teach that there is
an evil power in the universe, that there is damnation to the souls of those
who do not fall down and worship—they know not what. But the time is
rapidly coming when such teachings will be thrown on the scrap heap and
numbered among the delusions of a frantic mentality. It has been the habit
of many religious teachers of all times to hold the crowd in awe before a
mighty throne of condemnation and utter destruction, till the poor, ignorant
population have rent the air with their lamentations of complete despair.
This, indeed, was a good method to compel the attention with the hope of
salvation through some sacred rites to be performed by those whom God had
appointed. In justice to such an awful performance, we would better give to
these religious teachers the benefit of the doubt and say that they themselves
have believed in the atrocious teachings which they have so unhesitatingly
given out.

Be this as it may, the time has now come for a clearer understanding of the
true nature of the Deity, in Whom we all believe, and Whom we all seek to
know and to understand. That there is a God no sane person would deny; that
there could be a God of vengeance and hate, having all the characteristics of
a huge man in a terrible rage, no person can well believe and keep his sanity.
We will say, then, and without mincing matters in the least, that the most we
had better believe about such a God is that there is no such being.

DUALITY IN PHILOSOPHY

As the belief in duality has robbed theology of its greater message, so it has
robbed much of the philosophy of the ages of a greater truth; for in philosophy
the belief in duality has created a confusion that is almost as great as that in
theology. It has made a philosophy of good and evil in which men have come
to believe. True philosophy in every age, however, has perceived that the
Power back of all things must be One Power; and the clearer the thought of
Unity, the greater has been the philosophy. It has shone forth as a beacon
light toward which weary souls have traveled, hoping to find reality. To the
great philosophers of all times we owe the advancement of the world; for they
have been the great way-showers and helpers of mankind. In reverence, we
humbly bow before them as Messengers of the Most High; for God has spoken
through their lips and has told us that we are not creatures of the dust but
that we are Divine Beings, made in the image of Perfection and with an
endless destiny.

DUALITY AND SCIENCE

The belief in duality has robbed science, in that it has created Spirit and
matter; i.e., a dual universe. However, modern science is rapidly giving out a
different idea of the universe; for with the passing of matter into a
hypothetical and theoretical ether there is but little left on which to hang any
belief in materialism. We now are told that all matter is in a constant state of
flow; that it all comes from one source; and that it will eventually return to
that source.

AN AWAKENING

The world is waking up to the fact that things are not at all what they appear to be; that matter and form are but the one substance appearing and disappearing; and that form is simply used to express something which is formless, but self-conscious life. What this life is, science does not attempt to explain. This has been left to theology, and whether or not it has been delegated to those competent to handle the problem time alone will tell.

PHILOSOPHY LEADS MAN'S THOUGHT

Philosophy has always transcended science and always will; for philosophy deals with causes while science deals with effects. A scientist observes the result of nature's work while a philosopher speculates as to its cause. Many things which philosophy has taught for thousands of years are to-day being demonstrated by science. The two should really go hand in hand; for one deals with causes and the other with effects. True philosophy and true science will some day meet on a common basis; and, working together, will give to the world a theology of reality. Then, indeed, will "God go forth anew into Creation."

A DEEP INQUIRY

The deep thinkers of antiquity as well as the philosophers of all ages have meditated long and earnestly on the nature of the Divine Being. Knowing that there could be but One Ultimate Reality back of all things, they have pondered deeply upon the nature of that Reality; and it is a significant fact that all of the greatest thinkers have come to about the same conclusion.

THE GREAT DIFFICULTY

The difficulty that has beset the path of true philosophy has been the necessity of explaining a multiplied Creation with a Unitary Cause. Nothing is more evident than that we live in a world of constant change. Things and forms come and go continuously; forms appear only to disappear; things happen only to stop happening; and it is no wonder that the average person, unused to trying to discover causes, is led to feel and to believe that there is a multiple cause back of the world of things.

The philosophers of all times have had to meet the difficulty of explaining how One Cause could manifest Itself in a multiplicity of forms without dividing or breaking up the One. This has not been easy, yet, when understood, the explanation becomes very apparent.

THE VOICE OF GOD IN CREATION

The argument has been something after this manner: The Ultimate Cause back of all things must be One, since Life cannot be divided against Itself; the Infinite must be One, for there could not be two Infinites. Whatever change takes place must take place within the One; but the One must be Changeless; for, being One and Only, It cannot change into anything but Itself. All seeming change, then, is really only the play of Life upon Itself; and all that happens must happen by and through It. How do these things happen through It? By some inner action upon Itself. What would be the nature of this inner action? It could not be physical, as we understand physics, but would have to be by the power of the inner Word of Life; that is, the Voice of God, God standing for the First great and Only Cause of all that Is.

THE WORD OF GOD

It is impossible to conceive of anything other than the Word of God being that which sets power in motion. This is why the Scriptures announce that, "In the beginning was the Word, and the Word was with God and the Word was God. All things were made by Him, and without Him was not anything made that was made." 5 God speaks and it is done.

It is evident that First Cause must be Self-Existent; that is, It must be Causeless. Nothing came before That Which was First; and, while it may be a little hard to understand this, yet we can all grasp the fact that whatever the Being is Whom we call God, It must be Self-Existent.

SPIRIT KNOWS ITSELF

God speaks and it is done; but if God speaks, His Word must be Law. The Word of God is also the Law of God. God is Word, God is Law and God is Spirit; this is self-evident. We arrive at the conclusion that God, as Spirit, is Self-Conscious Life. That Spirit is conscious is proven by the fact that we have evidence of this consciousness strewn through all time and space. God must know that God Is. This is the inner meaning of the teaching of the "I AM," handed down from antiquity. "The Spirit is the Power that knows Itself," is one of the oldest sayings of time.

LAW, SERVANT OF THE WORD

Spirit knows Itself, but the Law is the servant of the Spirit and is set in motion through Its Word. It is known that all law is some form of universal force or energy. Law does not know itself; law only knows to do; it is, therefore, the servant of the Spirit. It is the way that the Spirit works; and is the medium through which It operates to fulfill Its purpose.

Did God make law? As it is not possible to conceive a time when law did not operate, it is impossible to conceive that it was ever created; therefore, law must be coexistent and coeternal with Spirit. We might say that law is one of the attributes of Spirit.

The Spirit operated through law which is some part of Its own Nature; therefore, all action must be some action of Spirit as Law. The Word of Spirit sets Its purposes in motion through the law; and since the law must be as Infinite as the Spirit, we could not think of a time when it was not, or a time when it would cease to be; neither can we imagine the law ever failing to operate when set in motion.

We have, then, an Infinite Spirit and an Infinite Law; Intelligence and the way that It works; God, working through Law, which is unfailing and certain.

FORMS OF SPIRIT OR CREATION

Next, we come to the forms of Spirit, which forms we call matter. But what is matter? Science tells us that matter is eternal and indestructible; that, at first, it is an invisible cosmic stuff; and that it gradually takes form through some law working within it. The worlds were formed by the power of His Word. We know that right now worlds are being formed in the vast reaches of space, and worlds are also ceasing to be; that is, they are gradually losing their form. In this way Creation is eternally going on. This proves a definite purposefulness, a definite law set in motion to work out this purposefulness, and a definite form as the result of the operation of this purposefulness. In other words, it shows that there is an Intelligence inherent in the universe which knows what It is doing, and how to do it, and which knows why It does it; and that there is a law obeying Its will. It also shows that there is something upon which It operates. This "something" we will call matter in its unformed state. Perhaps this is "the ether" of science; it is impossible to say; but surely there is something upon which the Spirit works.

The teaching of the great thinkers of all times is that we live in a threefold universe of Spirit, Soul and Body—of Intelligence, Substance and Form.

MEANING OF CREATION

With this in mind, we shall be better able to realize that Creation does not mean making something out of nothing, but means the passing of Substance into form through a law which is set in motion by the Word of Spirit. Creation is eternally going on; for we could not imagine a time when the activity of Spirit would cease. It is "the same yesterday, to-day and forever." 6

The whole action of Spirit must be within Itself, upon the Law, which is also within Itself, and upon the Universal Stuff, or matter, which is also within Itself. The three must in reality be One; hence, "The Trinity."

THE WORD ALONE IS CONSCIOUS

One of the main facts to bear in mind is, that, of the three attributes of Spirit, the Word alone is conscious of Itself. The Law is force, and matter is simply stuff ready to take form. Since law or energy is proven to be timeless, that is, not added to or taken from; and since matter is known to be of the same nature, we have a right to suppose that both matter and law are coexistent and coeternal with Spirit. But Spirit alone is Conscious. Law, of itself, is only a force, and matter has no mind of its own. Law is not a thinker but is a doer, while matter cannot think but is thought upon.

THE THOUGHT OF GOD

Just what is meant by the Word of God? This must mean the Inner Consciousness, or Self-Knowingness, of Spirit; the Thought of God. The word "thought" seems to mean more to us than any other word; it seems to cover the meaning better, for we know that thought is an inner process or consciousness.

The Thought of God must be back of all that really exists, and, as there are many things that really exist, there must be many thoughts in the Mind of the Infinite. This is logical to suppose; for an Infinite Mind can think of an infinite number of ideas. Hence the world of multiplicity or many things. But the world of multiplicity does not contradict the world of Unity; for the many live in the One.

ETERNAL CREATION

There may be confusion in the minds of men but not in the Thought of God; and so we have a universe expressing the limitless Ideas of a Limitless Mind, and without confusion. We have, then, a Cosmic World, and an infinite and endless Creation. This is the inner meaning of those mystic words, "World without end." Creation always was and always will be. Things may come and things may go, but Creation goes on forever; for It is the Thought of God coming into expression. This is, indeed, a wonderful concept, for it means that there will always be a manifestation of the Divine Ideas. We need not worry about whether it will ever cease; it cannot cease so long as God exists; and since God will be forever, there will forever be some kind of manifestation.

THE UNIVERSE IS ALIVE

The universe is alive with action and power, with energy and life. We touch it only in parts, but from these parts we do catch a glimpse of the nature of the Whole. "He hath not left Himself without a witness." 7 Modern science is revealing many things that the great thinkers of the ages have announced. One of them is that matter is in a constant state of flow; it is like a river flowing in, out and on; it is operated upon by an unseen force or law and takes its form through some agency which science supposes to be the Will and Purpose of Spirit. This we call the Word. All things were made by the Word.

CONCLUSION

To sum up: There is a power in the universe which acts as though It were Intelligent and we may assume that It is. There is an activity in the universe which acts as law. We know this to be true. And there is a formless stuff in the universe, forever taking form, and forever changing its form; this also is self-evident. We have every right, then, to assume that there is a threefold nature of Being which we will call Spirit, Soul and Body. We will think of the Spirit as the great Actor, the Soul as the medium of Its action, and the Body as the result of this action. We will think of Spirit as the only Conscious Actor, the only Power that knows Itself. We will think of Soul as a blind force, obeying the Will of Spirit; and we will think of Body as the effect of the Spirit, working through law, thus producing form. We will say that neither the Law nor the stuff from which form comes has any conscious intelligence, but must, because of its nature, take the form of the Word. This simplifies the whole matter and enables us to see that in the entire universe One Power Alone really acts, the Power of the Word of God.

The chart in lesson one of this series is an attempt to portray the Threefold Nature of the Universe; to show how the Spirit, acting through Law, becomes Form; for this is the inner meaning of Creation.

FOOTNOTES

1 Deut 6:4.
2 Exodus 3:14.
3 John 10:30.
4 John 14:10.
5 John 1:1, 3
6 Heb. 13:8.
7 Acts. 14:17

LESSON ONE: METAPHYSICAL MEANING OF WORDS USED IN UNIVERSAL CHART

UPPER SECTION

SPIRIT.—The Intelligent Power back of and through everything; the First Person of The Trinity.

Absolute.—The Unconditioned, that which nothing can limit.

FIRST CAUSE.—That from Which everything comes. The Cause of all that is made manifest on any plane. That Which comes first. The first in any creative series. The Life back of Things.

GOD.—The same as Spirit. The Self-Knowing Mind back of everything. The Heavenly Father and the Eternal Mother of all. The Being Whom we worship and adore. The One and Only Conscious Mind in the Universe, personal to all who believe in Him. It is impossible to conceive of such a vast idea as God, and the only way that we can conceive of the Divine Being is through our own nature, for His Spirit is Our Spirit.

THE GREAT "I AM."—Revealed to Moses as the One and Only Real Mind or Power in the Universe. That beside Which there is no other. I Am is another way of saying God. The "I AM" in man is the Life of man; without this "I AM," man could not be.

CONSCIOUS MIND.—That Power of Consciousness which knows Itself. That which is conscious of Its Own Being. "The Spirit is the power Which knows Itself." The Self-Knowing God. The Intelligence in the Universe which reveals Itself in all of Its Creation. If God were not Self-Conscious, then man could not be self-conscious. It is impossible for us to conceive of such a Universal Consciousness. We touch It only in spots, but the evidence of this Conscious Mind is strewn throughout all time and space; and the eternal activity of the Cosmos is proof enough that such a Conscious Mind really exists. In short, it is the entire manifestation of Spirit on any and all planes. "In my Father's House are many Mansions." 15 We do not, of course, see all these mansions, but science has revealed to us that many exist which we do not see, and revelation has shown that the Universe is Infinite. "For we know in part." 16

Lesson One: Metaphysical Chart No. I.

This chart, which is called the Universal Chart, shows the Universe as a Trinity of Being. The upper section designates those attributes of Spirit which are Self-Conscious. The middle section shows the subconscious aspect of Law; and the lowest section shows the effect of Spirit working through the medium of Universal Mind. Read and carefully study the full explanation and meaning of the words used in this chart.

UPPER SECTION

PURPOSEFULNESS.—When we speak of the purposefulness of Spirit we mean that Conscious Mind has the ability to know what It wishes to express and the power to express it. Dean Inge says that there can be no such thing as an infinite purpose because this would be a contradiction of the meaning of Infinite. This is probably true; but it does not follow that there could be no such thing as an element of purposefulness running through the Eternal Mind. Indeed, the evidence of this quality of being is so complete in the Universe that we cannot deny it. The evolution of creation on this planet alone would presuppose some kind of a purposefulness.

SELF-PROPELLING.—The Spirit must be Its own propelling power, Its own motive power. To suppose that Spirit had to go somewhere to get energy with which to energize Itself would be to suppose Spirit is not First Cause. Whatever the nature of that which comes first is, It must have within Itself all that It needs with which to express Itself. We must realize that, in dealing with Causation, we are dealing with That which is the First of everything and is absolutely Unconditioned. It does not need to be energized, but is the energy back of all form and all manifestation of Life.

SELF-EXISTENT.—It is difficult to grasp the idea of self-existence; but we can do so to a degree at least. For instance, we might ask the question, "Why is water wet?" There is no reason why; it is wet simply because it is its nature to be wet. If we were to ask the question, "Who made Life?", it could not be answered; because if we were to assume that some power made Life we would not be supposing that Life is First Cause. We must grasp the fact that, in dealing with Real Being, we are dealing with that which was never created. When did two times two begin to make four? Never, of course. It is a self-existent truth. God did not make God; God is. This is the meaning of the saying, "*I am that I am.*" All inquiry into Truth must begin with the self-evident fact that Life Is. The Truth is that which Is and so is Self-Existent.

"Never The Spirit was born;
The Spirit shall cease to be never;
Never was time It was not;
End and beginning are dreams."

VOLITION.—Volition means the power of conscious choice.

CHOICE.—Choice means the ability to choose consciously.

WILL.—Will means decision coming into execution.

Volition, choice and will must be attributes of Spirit. They mean practically the same thing. We must be careful, however, not to think of these qualities of Spirit in terms of human or limited thought. When we choose, we choose between different things; but when Spirit chooses, It simply announces that It is a certain thing. The Spirit does not have to will to make things happen; things happen because it is the will of Spirit that they should be. This will, then, is simply the execution of a purpose; and since Spirit is Absolute, there can be nothing to deny Its Will. Choice, volition and will are necessary and real attributes of Self-Existent Power; for without them there would be no channel through which the Ideas of God could be expressed. In man these qualities of mentality are limited but in God they are limitless.

POWER.—The energy by which everything lives.

LIFE.—Life means that Inner Something that makes everything live. Life and Power are necessary attributes of a Limitless Being, and go hand in hand to complete a Perfect Being. Life is That Which Lives, and Power is the Energy with which It operates. Considering Life and Power as a combined quality of Causation, we see that they combine to make the underlying basis of all manifestation visible and invisible. In the objective world, Life is the Power that binds everything together; It is the Intelligent Basis of all that exists. For instance, in the material world, It is the Power that holds the atoms together that they may produce form. In the mental world, It is the

Power that enables us to think; and in the Spiritual World, It is the Power that enables us to live at all.

It appears that Life manifests on different levels. In the mineral world, and in the world of all material form, It seems to be unconscious; that is, It is not manifesting in a self-conscious state. We know, however, that a certain degree of intelligence runs through all Creation. Chemical Affinity is a manifestation of Life as the attraction of Itself to Itself. In plant life It seems to have a more developed degree of consciousness. That is, It manifests in the vegetable world as a power to express in one spot, but without volition to move about. This, however, does not limit The Spirit but is simply one of the ways that It works. In the animal world, we see different degrees of Life's manifestation, from the first cell life up to Man. For instance, a dog is more intelligent than a fish, yet each has the power to move about. The fish seems to move by instinct alone; the dog appears to have some degree of conscious being, although there is a difference of opinion on this score. At least, in most animal life, we find the ability to move about and, either from instinct or self-choice, the ability to express a certain degree of freedom. In man, Life expresses in terms of Volition and Self-Will; It is manifesting at the level of Self-Consciousness. While The Spirit, of Itself, must always know Itself, yet we are perfectly justified in saying that It manifests on different levels. This does not limit The Spirit, but on the other hand proves that It is really Limitless. For if It had to manifest on one level only, It would then be limited, but because It can manifest on as many levels as It wishes It is Limitless.

When Spirit manifests in the purely mechanical and material world we say that It is Unconscious Life; when It manifests in the animal world we say that It is manifesting in a state of simple consciousness; and when It manifests in and through man we say that It is in a Self-Conscious State. As this Self-Conscious state of man's mentality reaches a larger world of realization and comprehends something of Its Unity with the Whole, we say that It is in a Cosmic State. We now know of four different levels upon which Spirit manifests:—Unconscious State, Simple-Consciousness, Self-Consciousness and Cosmic-Consciousness. All of these are but different ways through which the One Power operates. Life, then, is that quality of Being, running through all, which enables anything to be what It is.

TRUTH.—The Truth is That which Is. It is the Reason, Cause and Power in and through everything. It is Birthless, Deathless, Changeless, Complete, Perfect, Whole, Self-Existent, Causeless, Almighty, God, Spirit, Law, Mind, Intelligence, and anything and everything that implies Reality.

FREE SPIRIT.—Means that which cannot be bound; It is free to do as It chooses, but cannot, of course, do anything that denies Its own Nature.

PEACE.—An inner calm so complete that nothing can disturb it. The Peace which comes only from the knowledge that It is All. Fathomless Peace is meant by the Peace of the Spirit. This is the peace to which Jesus referred when He said, "Peace I leave with you, My peace I give unto you." 8 The Infinite is always at peace because there is nothing to disturb It.

POISE.—That perfect balance which maintains everything in its proper place without effort. It is the law of equilibrium without which nothing could be maintained. It is the law of balance that must exist in the Infinite Mind, since there is nothing to disturb It. Poise or balance is the law back of what we call "the Law of Compensation." It is Life perfectly balancing Itself. Self-Existent Life alone could produce complete poise. We cannot fathom the full meaning of poise as it exists in Spirit; but we can understand that it means an Eternal Power, unruffled by conflicting emotions, always sure of Itself, unhurried and certain.

THE WORD.—The Word means, of course, the ability of Spirit to declare Itself into manifestation, into form. The Word of God means the Self-Contemplation of Spirit. The Manifest Universe, as we see It, as well as the Invisible Universe that must also exist, is the result of the Self-Contemplation of the Lord. "He spake and it was done." "The Word was with God and the Word was God. All things were made by Him and without Him was not anything made that was made." 9 The starting point of all Creation is in the Word of Spirit. The Word is the Concept, Idea, Image or Thought of God. It is the Self-Knowing Mind Speaking Itself into manifestation. Everything has a Word back of it as its Initial Cause.

THE PERFECT LOGOS.—"The Divine Creative Word." The Perfect Word of God.

ONLY—ALL.—Beside Which there is none other. That Which has within Itself all that really is. The Life of everything and the Love through everything. The One Presence and the One Infinite Person Whom we call God or Spirit. Within This One all Live.

KNOWING NO OTHER.—The Spirit could know nothing outside Itself. It is The Center and Circumference of everything that exists. It has no enemies, no differences, no otherness, no apartness, no separation from Itself; is Undivided. Complete and Perfect within Itself. It has no opposites and no oppositions. It knows only of Its own ability to do; and, since It is All, It cannot be hindered in any way, shape or manner. It is not possible to conceive of such a complete Life and Power; but we do catch glimpses in moments of real inspiration when we realize, to a degree, at least, that God is All.

FATHER-MOTHER GOD.—The Spirit contains within Itself the Life Principle of both the masculine and feminine. It is both combined in One.

UNITY.—The Axioms of Reason declare that that Which is Infinite cannot be divided against Itself. The Infinite is, therefore, Indivisible and consequently a Perfect Unit. "Hear, O Israel, the Lord our God is One Lord." 10 It is also, "That Whose Center is everywhere and Whose Circumference is nowhere." All of It is present at any and every point within It. It is not approaching a point nor receding from it, but is always at it. The Whole of God is present at any and every point within God. It was to this Indwelling Spirit that Jesus prayed; for God is within man as well as throughout all Creation. It is, "That thread of the All-Sustaining Beauty Which runs through all and doth all unite." "His lines have gone out into all places." 11 "There is no place where God is not." This concept enabled Job to say, "In my flesh shall I see God." 12 All Life is bound together by One common law of Love, and Love is the Self-Givingness of Spirit, manifested in and through all that is visible and invisible. It was the realization of this One Presence that illumined the saints and sages of the past. "I and the Father are One." 13 "The Father dwelleth in

Me, He doeth the works." 14 We must come to sense this Marvelous Presence; for It is the secret of metaphysical work; God in all and through all.

MACROCOSM.—Means the Universal World. It is another word for the Whole.

THE GREAT HOUSE.—Another way of saying The Universal.

MASCULINE.—The Assertive Principle of Being. The Self-Conscious, Self-Propelling Power of Spirit. The Projective Principle of Life, impregnating the Universal Soul with its ideas and concepts.

ACTIVE.—The Self-Realizations of Spirit constitute Its Active Being. It acts upon Itself. Since we could not conceive of an unconscious consciousness, we could not imagine an inactive consciousness. The Spirit, by reason of Its Infinite Capacity to know Itself, must always be acting upon Itself. This action is what we call Creation. Creation is eternally going on. It may stop in one place and begin in another, but It is always going on; and, as we know that God will always be God, we know that Creation will never cease. This is the meaning of those mystical words, "World without end." This point must not be overlooked, for there are people who believe that some day Creation will cease. No more unphilosophical position could be taken than to suppose that the activity of Spirit would ever cease. There is another philosophical delusion that many believe in, namely, that there are periods when Spirit does not create. This is impossible, since we cannot conceive of a time when Spirit will cease to be conscious of Itself. *It's self-consciousness is its action.* We might imagine that It would not create more worlds like the one in which we live; but to suppose that It could stop creating would be to suppose that It could stop Being.

PERSONALNESS.—We do not think of God as a tremendous Person, but we do think of the Spirit as the Infinite Personalness in and through all Life. We must remember that Infinite as Spirit is, It is still Self-Conscious; and Infinite Self-Knowingness is the Infinite Essence of Personalness, or the Abstract Essence of all personality. To think of God simply as an Infinite Principle would be to resolve the Divine Being into an Infinite It, a cold Impersonal Law containing no warmth or color, and certainly no responsiveness. Such a concept of God would rob man of his Divine Birthright and throw him, empty-handed, into an abyss of Law and Action without motive or direction. No worse state of mentality could be imagined than one in which man thought of God simply as a Principle. The very fact that man comes from the Universe in a self-conscious state proves that behind all manifestation there is a Power that knows Itself; and a Power that knows Itself must be Personal. It is not, of course, limited but must be Infinite. As wonderful as the concept may be, God is Personal to all who believe in Him. God is responsive to all who approach Him, and God is the Element of Personalness back of all personality.

CONSCIOUS IDEA.—No two ideas are alike. The Creative Mind of the Universe, being Infinite, thinks of a limitless number of things, and each thing is, therefore, separate and distinct in the great Whole. Just as the atoms of science are cemented together by the ether, so each idea of Divine Mind is united in One Spirit. No two things are alike; no two roses are alike; no two people are alike. All come from One Life; all are in One Life and all live by It; but each forever maintains its identity in the Perfect Whole.

CHANGELESS.—The One cannot change by reason of the fact that, being All, there is nothing for It to change into but Itself. It, therefore, remains Changeless. The One Cause back of all never changes, but It does constantly remain active; and so we perceive a changing form within that which is Changeless. Nothing changes, however, but the form. We know that matter and energy are indestructible and eternal, but we also know that within them a change is forever taking place. If we realize that nothing changes but form we will not become confused over the idea of the Changeless. Water may turn into ice and ice may be melted and again become water. Where was the water when it was ice? Where was the ice when it was water? Nothing really happened, except that a form took shape and again became formless. The Principle back of it did not change.

OMNISCIENCE.—The All-Knowing, All-Perceiving Mind of God.

OMNIPOTENCE.—The All-Powerful One.

OMNIPRESENCE.—The Constant Presence of the Undivided Whole. Read again the explanation of Unity.

REASON DEDUCTIVE ONLY.—The Spirit does not reason as man reasons; that is, It makes no inquiry into Truth, but Itself is the Truth. It knows intuitively; therefore, It simply announces Itself to be That which It is. If we were to ascribe to It any reasoning power, we should be compelled to say that It reasons deductively only, or from the Whole to a part.

MIDDLE SECTION

SOUL.—Used in the sense of the World-Soul, or Medium through which Spirit operates. It is the Holy Ghost or Third Person of the Trinity.

CREATIVE MEDIUM.—Like the creative soil in which seeds are planted and from which plant life grows, the Soul of the Universe is the Creative Medium into which the Word of Spirit falls and from which Creation arises. We must be careful not to think of Soul and Spirit as separate; for they are really two parts, or aspects of the same thing, each being Self-Existent and Coeternal with the other. The simplest way to think of the World-Soul is to think of It as we would the soil in which we plant seeds.

SUBJECTIVE.—The dictionary defines subjective as "the impression which an object makes on the mind." The external object is a percept while the impression is a concept. The concept, or idea, would be subjective; for it would be the impression which the mind receives.

In the above chart we are interpreting the word subjective as meaning the receptacle of the thought forms of Spirit. The Soul is Subjective to the Spirit; that is, It receives impressions from It. Subjective always means something that receives.

SUBCONSCIOUS MIND.—The same as Subjective. The Spirit is Conscious Mind; the Soul is Subconscious Mind; It is like the soil or ground; It receives and acts. It is not a Knower as Spirit is, but is a Doer, or Executor, of the Will of the Spirit.

UNCHOOSING.—Unlike Spirit, the Soul has no choice of Its own. Being subjective, It is bound to receive but cannot choose. We must always bear in mind that Soul simply reflects the images that the Spirit casts into It.

IMMATERIAL.—The Soul is immaterial, as we think of matter; but It is the substance of Spirit and might be considered to be the Matter of Spirit. As all matter in the physical world is supposed to finally resolve into the ether from which it came, so we may think of the Substance of Soul as we think about the ether and realize that everything in form finally becomes Soul-Stuff again. Perhaps the simplest way to think of It, however, would be to think of It as the last and final analysis of matter. We know that matter comes from somewhere, and the teaching is that Soul-Stuff is the thing from which it comes. We must, however, distinguish Soul-Stuff from Soul. Soul is Subjective Intelligence; for, while It may not have the ability to choose, It certainly has the ability to intelligently work out the commands of Spirit. We must never think of the subconscious as though it were unconscious. The Soul of the Universe is next in Principle to Spirit and but little lower than Spirit. Subconscious means subjective consciousness but not unconsciousness. While the Soul may not choose, having no self-knowing consciousness of Its own, yet It has an intelligence of Its own, which is Infinite compared to the power of intelligence which we exhibit. For instance, the whole intelligence of the race could not create a buttercup or a pansy; yet the Intelligence in the creative soil in the earth will produce as many for us as we ask it to; that is, of course, if we plant the seeds. This same idea holds good in that greater Creative Medium of the Spirit which we call the Soul of the Universe. It has the intelligence and the power to produce things but no choice as to what It is to produce.

Soul and Soul-Stuff are two different things; but they belong together and must be placed in the category of the Creative Medium. Soul is Subconscious Mind working on Immaterial Stuff and creating from It the many forms which we see. Think of It as a seed working in the soil and the soil working on the seed.

ILLUSION OF MIND.—This does not mean that Subjective Mind is an illusion, but it does mean that forms could be projected into It which were not really true. For a more complete explanation of this, see chart in the lesson on Psychic Phenomena.

IMPERSONAL.—The Creative Medium is Impersonal, having no personality of Its own as the Spirit has. It neither knows nor cares who uses It, but is always ready to work for any or all alike. Remember this.

FEMININE.—The Universal Medium or Soul has been called the "Womb of Nature" and "The Holy Mother," because It is receptive to the Spirit and is impregnated with the Divine Ideas. It gives birth to the Ideas of the Spirit and is, therefore, the Feminine Principle of Nature.

NEUTRAL.—Soul is neutral. Like the soil it will produce any or all kinds of plants. Having no conscious mind of Its own, It receives all ideas and works them out into form. We must always remember that the Creative Medium is neutral. If It could choose, It could reject, and this is just what It cannot do. It is bound to accept and act, just as the soil does when we plant cabbages in the ground. It does not argue, but at once goes to work to produce cabbages. When we plant potatoes it does the same thing. We may plant cabbages and potatoes with roses and pansies; and we shall receive all four plants from the one neutral creative medium which knows neither good nor bad, but is conscious only of its ability to do.

PLASTIC.—This refers to Soul-Stuff, either formed or unformed. It is entirely an indeterminate stuff; that is, it has no mind of its own. Matter has no intelligence at all, but is the material which is formed by the power of the Word.

MAYA.—Refers to the illusion of mind.

BLIND FORCE.—Some of the early philosophers referred to the Soul or Creative Medium as a "Blind force not knowing, only doing." This we know to be true of all law. Law knows only to do but has no conscious volition of its own.

LAW.—It will be apparent by now that the Creative Medium of Spirit is the great Mental Law of the Universe. It is the Law obeying the Will of the Spirit. It is the Universal Law of Mind. All law is Mind in action.

MEDIUM OF ALL THOUGHT, POWER AND ACTION.—It is the one Medium through which all Law and all Power operate. It is the One Law within which all the lesser laws work.

CINEMA PICTURES.—Means that It is the Medium of all thought forms. See explanation of chart covering the lesson on Psychic Phenomena.

PASSIVE AND RECEPTIVE.—Means neutral and feminine.

REASON DEDUCTIVE ONLY.—Being subjective, the Creative Medium cannot analyze, dissect nor deny. Because of Its nature, It must always accept. Consequently, It is always deductive in Its reasoning powers.

KARMIC LAW.—Karmic Law means the law of cause and effect. The Karmic Law works through the Medium of the World-Soul.

THE SERVANT OF THE SPIRIT THROUGHOUT THE AGES.—The Universal Soul, being the Creative Principle of Nature and the Law of Spirit, has been called "The Holy Ghost or The Servant of the Eternal Spirit throughout the Ages."

Let us realize that neither the Soul of the Universe nor the Spirit were ever created. Each is Eternal.

LOWEST SECTION

BODY.—The entire manifestation of Spirit, both visible and invisible, is the Body of God. Within this One Body of God is included all lesser bodies. This One Body, coupled with the Intelligence running through it, is called the Son, or the Second Person of the Trinity. This, of course, includes man, both visible and invisible. It also includes every gradation of consciousness from the simple to the complex, from a cell to an archangel.

"All are but parts of One stupendous Whole,
Whose body Nature is, and God the Soul."

EFFECT.—That which follows cause. Effect is that which did not make itself, but which must have a power back of it causing it to be. All manifestation is effect and all effect is subject to its cause. The Creator is greater than His Creation. Everything that we see, touch, taste, feel, hear or sense with the physical senses is an effect. "Things which are seen are not made of things which do appear." 17 This means that what we see comes from what we do not see.

FORM.—Form is definite, the result of a definite idea. Form is real as form, but is not self-conscious; it is subjective to the power that created it. Forms come and go, but the power back of them remains forever and is changeless. Form is temporary, but Mind is Eternal. It is necessary that Spirit should manifest in *some kind of form* in order that It may come into Self-Expression through Self-Realization. This is the meaning of that Creation which is eternally going on.

OBJECTIVE.—Means the object, the external, the effect.

CONDITIONS.—The result of causes, another word for effect.

RESULTS.—What happens as a necessary result of the law of cause and effect. Results follow causes mathematically.

TIME.—Dean Inge says that "Time is a sequence of events in a Unitary Whole." This is an excellent definition; for, of course, time is not a thing of itself; it is simply a measure of experience in eternity. Time does not contradict Eternity, but allows It to become expressed in terms of definite experience. Time is necessary since it allows experience to take place within the One, but time is never a thing of itself. It is really impossible to measure time; for yesterday is gone and to-morrow has not come, and to-day is rapidly slipping into the past. If we were to attempt to put a finger on any period of time it would be gone before we could point to it. But, illusive as time is, it is still necessary to experience.

SPACE.—Space, like time, is not a thing of itself, but is only the outline of form. It is a relative distance within the Absolute. Space, also, is necessary to the expression of Spirit; for without it no definite form could be produced. We must not be confused over the ideas of time and space, as they are not things of themselves. They are entirely relative, but none the less necessary.

THINGS.—Mean forms in time and space. Things are always results and never make themselves; they are the objectifications of Spirit. Things are necessary to the manifestation of Spirit. They are the result of the Self-Knowingness of the Word of God. Things vary in size and shape, in time and duration, from the planet to the peanut, from a moment to an eternity.

REFLECTION.—The world of matter reflects the Thoughts of God.

ILLUSION OF MATTER.—Refers to false forms.

MULTIPLICITY, MANY.—From One come many. From Unity comes multiplicity, but multiplicity does not contradict Unity. It is like the soil from which come many plants. We grow many plants from one soil, but the Unity of the soil is never disturbed in the least. So the One Mind, working through the Creative Medium of the Universe, produces many things.

RELATIVE MIRROR.—Both the Absolute and the relative are reflected in the mirror of matter.

EMANATION.—Projection of Spirit into form.

FOOTNOTES

8 John 14:27.
9 John 1:1, 3.

10 Deut 6:4.
11 Ps. 19:4.
12 Job 19:26.
13 John 10:30.
14 John 14:10.
15 John 14:2.
16 1 Cor. 13:9.
17 Heb. 11:3.

LESSON ONE: THE NATURE OF BEING

The circle in Chart No. I signifies Universal Life, because it is without beginning and without end. We have divided it into three parts, calling one Spirit, one Soul and the other Body; not because the nature of Being is three distinct things, but because It is a Unity with three distinct attributes, i.e., Spirit, Soul and Body.

SPIRIT

We treat of Spirit as the Active and the only Self-Conscious Principle. We define Spirit as the First Cause or God; the Absolute Essence of all that is. It is also called the great, or the Universal, I AM. When Moses asked God who he should tell the Children of Israel had sent him, the answer was, "Thus shalt thou say, I AM hath sent me unto you." 18 The reason why "I AM" was given is because this is an absolute statement. Spirit is Conscious Mind, and is the Power Which knows Itself; It is conscious of Its own Being. The Spirit is Self-Propelling; it is Absolute and All. It is Self-Existent, and has all life within Itself. It is the Word, and the Word is volition. It has choice because It is Volition; It is will because It chooses; It is Free Spirit because It knows nothing outside Itself, and nothing different from Itself.

Spirit is the Father-Mother God because It is the principle of Unity back of all things. The masculine and feminine principles both come from the One. Spirit is all Life, Truth, Love, Being, Cause and Effect; and is the only Power in the Universe that knows Itself.

SOUL

The Soul of the Universe, not as opposed to the Spirit, but as the principle just beneath It, has always been taught as the receptive medium into which the Spirit lets fall the forms of Its thought. It is subjective to the Spirit; that which is subjective is always impersonal, neutral, plastic, passive and receptive. Wherever you find subjective law you will find something that is compelled to receive and to act upon; consequently the Soul of the Universe has been called a "blind force, not knowing, only doing," and "The servant of the Eternal Spirit throughout the ages." It is the medium of the thought, power and action of the Spirit.

TWO WAYS OF REASONING

There are but two processes of reasoning known to the human mind; one is inductive and the other is deductive. Inductive reasoning is an inquiry into the truth; it is a process of analysis. Deductive reasoning is that process of reasoning which follows an already established premise. It is from the whole to a part. Here is an example of inductive reasoning: I look about and say, "John Smith is good; Mary Jones is good; my neighbors are good;

consequently, God must be good." This is a process of analysis which leads to the conclusion that the Cause back of all things must be Good. Deductive reasoning would operate this way: "God is Good; consequently, Mary Jones, John Smith and my neighbors must be good"; because God is Good they cannot be otherwise.

Since inductive reasoning is an analysis, which is always an inquiry into truth, it follows that God can reason only deductively. That which is Infinite does not have to inquire into the Truth; consequently, there can be no inductive process of reasoning, either in the Spirit or the soul of the Universe. There cannot be any inductive reasoning in the Spirit, because It already knows all things. There cannot be any inductive reasoning in the Soul of the Universe, because It is the Creative Medium, and, if It could reason inductively, It could reject certain thoughts, because It could analyze; and soul or subjectivity can never reject; but is bound by its own nature to accept. It is impersonal, and neither knows nor cares who uses it. It is plastic, because It is immaterial. It is formless, having no mind of Its own. It has been called the Universal Feminine or Holy Womb of Nature, because It is receptive and creative. It is Karmic Law, because It is subjective to the self-knowing mind. It is the medium of all Karmic Law and of all race suggestion.

BODY

The Universe has been called the Great Trinity, or Triune Unity of Spirit, Soul and Body. The body is the result, the effect, the objectification of Spirit. Soul is the Immaterial, plastic and receptive medium; It is primordial or Cosmic Stuff; It is unmanifest form. Body is the result of Spirit working through Soul or Law. There is but one Body of the Universe; It is both visible and invisible; and within this one body are all of the lesser bodies, all of the manifest Universe, including the body of man. "But now are they many members yet but One Body." 19

Spirit is the Absolute Being; and is the only power in the universe which has self-knowingness, volition, choice or will. The soul has no will; It has no purpose to execute other than the purpose that is given It. Soul is the servant of the Spirit, while body is the result of the union of Spirit with Soul. There is the Power, the way that It works and the result of Its operation; the Word, the law, and the effect; Intelligence, substance, and form; the Active Principle, the passive receptivity, and the relative condition. The Spirit of the Universe cannot change; the Soul of the Universe cannot change; the Body of the Universe cannot help changing.

THE CHANGELESS

The Spirit cannot change because there is nothing for It to change into, Spirit being All; this is axiomatic. The Soul of the Universe cannot change; for it is simply Universal Substance and Law; and we know that energy and substance are indestructible and eternal. The Soul of the Universe cannot change; but, as stated above, the body of the universe is forever changing; and this is what constitutes the eternal activity of Spirit within Itself.

Creation does not mean making something out of nothing. If by Creation we mean making something out of nothing, there is no such thing; but if we mean the passing of Spirit into form, then Creation is eternally going on.

It is necessary to understand that the only Active Principle is Spirit—Self-Conscious, Self-Knowing Life, and that all else is subject to Its will. The Spirit is conscious of Its own Thought, Its own Desire and manifestation; and It is conscious that Its desire is satisfied; consequently, It is conscious of that which It manifests; but It is not conscious of any effort or process in Its manifestation.

It is necessary that Soul and Body should exist, because Spirit, without manifestation, would construct only a dream world, never coming into Self-Realization. Since Spirit must be manifested, in order to be Spirit, there must be a way in which It manifests, and there must be a manifestation; hence, Soul and Body.

CAUSE AND EFFECT

If all Cause is existent in Spirit, and if the Law which executes the volition of Spirit is entirely subconscious, or subjective to the Will of the Spirit, and if the body is only an effect, it follows that both cause and effect are spiritual. Involved within the seed, which the Spirit drops into the Creative Medium, is everything necessary to unfold the seed into form. This is why the Spirit never thinks of methods or processes; for that which the Spirit involves must evolve.

UNITY AND MULTIPLICITY

From Unity—which is the One back of all things, through the One Law, which is the medium of the One—multiplicity is manifested, but it never contradicts Unity. When we realize that we are dealing with an Infinite Intelligence, and with an Infinite Law within this Intelligence, we see that there can be no limit placed upon Creation. We think of the world as we see it, but we see it from the viewpoint of only one plane. We see it as matter, which we have divided into eighty or ninety odd elements; but we discover that all of these elements come from one substance. Suppose we should view it from ten different planes, what would happen? We should see ten times as much as we now see. The present hypothesis of science is that the ether is more solid than matter; and this means that there could be a form within the very form that one's body now occupies in space; there might even be a million bodies, each within the other; and each would be just as real as the one that we now think we occupy. The Universe, as we see it, is not even a fractional part of the Universe that actually is. "Eye hath not seen," 20 because it sees only on one plane, i.e., in part.

IMMORTALITY

From the standpoint of immortality, we may have a body within a body to infinity; and when this body is rendered useless, and is no longer a fit instrument through which to function, another one may be already there.

The physical disappearance of Jesus after His resurrection was the result of the spiritualization of His consciousness. This so quickened His mentality that His body disintegrated; and His followers could not see Him because He was on another plane. Planes are not places; they are states of consciousness.

Is it apparent that the Spirit can know nothing outside Itself; that whatever the Spirit knows must be a definite mental image, concept, or idea, in the Consciousness of the Spirit? Is it clear that as the Self-Consciousness of Spirit knows within Itself, It knows upon Itself as Law? Is it clear that the Law can never say, "I will not," but can only act? And is it clear that as the Spirit lets fall the forms of Its thought into the Soul, or Subjectivity of the Universe, these thoughts must manifest as things?

FORMS

Let us take a look at these forms. As we look at the many millions of forms, and see that they are all of different shape and color, and yet we know that they all came from One Stuff, are we not compelled to accept the fact that there is a specific cause, or concrete mental image, back of every idea or thing, a Divine Mental Picture? In the subjective world there must be a correspondent of everything in the objective world; and since the subjective world is a receptive or plastic substance, this correspondence can find its initial starting point only in real Intelligence. Therefore, Intelligence is ultimately all there is in the universe.

ALLNESS OF TRUTH

By a process of axiomatic reasoning, we arrive at the conclusion that Spirit knows nothing outside Itself. The Truth is that which Is; and being that which Is, It must be Infinite and All. Being Infinite or All, the Truth can have nothing outside Itself, other than Itself, or unlike Itself, by which to divide Itself; consequently, the Spirit is Indivisible, Changeless and Complete within Itself. Itself is all that is—both Cause and Effect, the Alpha and the Omega.

VOLITION

There is but one volitional factor in the Universe, and this is Spirit or the Self-Knowing Mind. God did not make God; this is self-evident; hence God is Self-Existent. God did not make Law; Law is coeternal with God. God did not make Substance; this, also is coexistent and coeternal with God. But God did make, and does make, and is making, and will continue to make, from eternity to eternity—forms. We live in a universe of Infinite Substance and numberless forms wherein nothing is moved unless Intelligence moves it.

Mind is dual in its aspect; it is conscious, as the active principle of conscious intelligence, and subconscious, as the passive principle of impersonal receptivity. Body is the result of the knowing of Spirit through Soul. Matter, of itself, has no intelligence, no volition, no power. Since the Law is but a Universal Potential Possibility through which anything might happen, and since it is set in motion by the Word, it follows that every word specializes its own law and carries its own mathematics along with it.

It follows that everything that the Spirit thinks must take form. The Spirit, being Self-Conscious Life, knows and cannot stop knowing. To suppose that it could stop knowing would be to suppose that It could stop being. Since It cannot stop knowing, It must be forever setting in motion the Law of Its own

Being, which Law must be forever projecting the forms of Its thoughts, there by producing things. Creation is always beginning, but never ending. The slightest thought of Intelligence sets in motion a power in the Law to produce a corresponding thing.

When we speak of every thought dropped into the Creative Medium, do we think of God's thought and man's as the same? We think of each as thought; but, whereas man thinks both inductively and deductively, God thinks only deductively. "As he thinketh in his heart, so is he," 21 i.e., as he lets fall the forms of his thought.

God is not conscious of matter, as we are. God is conscious of Himself as form, but not as size. God is conscious of Himself as definite purposefulness, but not as space. God is conscious of Himself as definite outline, but not as limitation. God is conscious of Himself as many, but not as division.

Would there be any difference between a conscious thought, for the purpose of a direct manifestation, and one that might be thought with no idea of the form that would be manifested? There would be a great difference. Trained thought is far more powerful than untrained. If this were not true, the thoughts of the metaphysical practitioner could not neutralize those that caused his patient his patient to be sick. We know a little right thought puts to rout that which is wrong. The day that you say to yourself, "My thought is powerful," you would better be careful. Every thought must manifest according to its intensity.

Ponder over the meaning of the words in Chart No. I. Think what Self-Existent Life is—Life within Itself; get an understanding of the Law which is the Servant of it, and what matter is, until you begin to feel your own self as part of this great scheme of Existence.

ONLY ONE MIND

There is no such thing as your mind, my mind, his mind, her mind and God's Mind; there is just Mind in which we all live, move and have our being. There is Mind and nothing but Mind. We think of Conscious Mind and Spirit as One and the Same.

Things are ideas. What else could they be? There is nothing out of which to make things, except ideas. In the beginning we behold nothing visible; there is only an infinite possibility, a Limitless Imagination, a Consciousness; the only action of this Consciousness being idea.

That which we call our subjective mind is, in reality, our identity in Infinite Mind; in other words, it is the result of our mental attitudes. It is our mental atmosphere or center in universal Subjective Mind, in which are retained all the images, impressions, inherited tendencies and race suggestions as far as we accept them.

We see, then, that this is the Medium through which everything comes to us.

There is One First Cause, having three aspects: Spirit, Soul and Body, i.e., Cause, Medium and Effect; the Father, Son and Holy Ghost; Masculine Activity, Feminine Activity and Result.

We should not think of three Gods, but of the Triune Nature of the One God, the One Cause. We think of Spirit as Absolute, Self-Conscious

Intelligence. We think of Soul as Receptive to Intelligence; and of the Intelligence as always acting upon It. Spirit and Soul intersphere each other; i.e., both have Omnipresence. The Spirit of the Universe permeates the Soul of the Universe, eternally impregnating It with ideas. The Soul of the Universe is the "Holy Womb of Nature," producing the forms which appear in the physical Universe.

The Body of the Universe is the result of the thought of Spirit, operating through the medium of Soul. This Trinity is called the Father, the Son and the Holy Ghost. The Father is Absolute, Positive Intelligence; the Son is the Offspring of the Father; the holy Ghost is "the Servant of The Eternal Spirit throughout the Ages." Spirit is Absolute Intelligence, operating through the Soul of Receptive Intelligence, impregnating It with "The Divine Ideas."

Neither the Spirit nor the Soul of the Universe can change. That which changes is the Body of the Universe. Planets may appear and disappear as do people and things; but the Substance from which things are formed is Changeless.

INDIVIDUALITY

Individuality emerges from the Universal. Psychology teaches the personification of this individuality, which is true as far as it goes; but Metaphysics universalizes individuality by unifying it with the Whole.

There is a Universal Nature of Man, inherent within him, which causes the manifestation of his personality, i.e., The Spirit of God.

The next chart will be about man, and when that is explained you will begin to see the way out of your difficulties if you have any.

Note: Study carefully "The Edinburgh Lectures on Mental Science," by T. Troward; "Creative Mind," by Ernest S. Holmes; "The Axioms of Truth," by Burnell; "Philosophy of Plotinus," by Dean Inge.

FOOTNOTES

18 Exodus 3:14.
19 1 Cor. 12:20.
20 1 Cor. 2:9.
21 Prov. 23:7.

LESSON ONE: RECAPITULATION

The evolution of man brings him automatically to a time when real individuality is produced. From that day any further evolution must be through his conscious coöperation with Life. All nature waits on man's self-recognition and is always ready to obey his will; but he must use nature's forces in accordance with her laws.

Science is the knowledge of certain facts built around some known principle of being. Man never creates; he discovers and uses. In this way all sciences are evolved. We live in a Universe of Law through which runs an element of Self-Knowing Intelligence. "All's Love, yet all's Law."

The Law has done all that it can do for man automatically. It has brought him to the point of individuality, and must now let him alone to make this discovery for himself. Man is potentially perfect, but free will and self-choice cause him to appear imperfect. In reality, all that he can destroy is the embodiment of himself, for the Divine Spark is always intact in Instinctive Man.

Man awakes to self-consciousness, finding himself already equipped with a mentality, a body and an environment. Gradually he discovers one law of nature after another until he conquers his environment through his acquisition of natural forces. Everywhere he finds that nature does his bidding, in so far as he understands her laws and uses them along the lines of their inherent being; for he must first obey nature, then she will obey him.

Man discovers his ability to think, and begins to realize that from within comes a reaction to his thought. He comes to realize that he is threefold in his nature; that he can consciously think; that he has within a mentality which acts upon his thoughts; and that he has a body which is affected by his thinking.

He next discovers that he can think for others, causing a corresponding action in and through their bodies. In this way he discovers that there is a mental medium through which thought operates. He now realizes himself to be a thinking center in a Universal Mind.

Man next discovers that his affairs are also controlled by thought, and that he can likewise think for others and aid in the control of their affairs.

He now realizes that everything in the visible world is an effect; that back of all effects there are ideas which are the real causes of these effects. The Divine Ideas are perfect, but man has the ability to cause them to appear imperfect. Through right thinking he is able to uncover the appearance of imperfection and reveal the Perfect Idea.

Man's idea of the Deity evolves with his other ideas. After a belief in many gods, he comes to realize that there is One Mind and One Spirit back of all manifestation.

There is One Spirit or Self-Conscious Life acting through the Medium of One Mind or Subjective law, producing many manifestations. Multiplicity comes from Unity without breaking up the Unity of the Whole.

Spirit is Self-Knowing, but Law is automatic and obeys the will of Spirit, having no alternative other than to obey.

Like all law, the Law of Mind is an Impersonal Force, and because of Its nature is compelled to act.

Soul and Universal Subjective Mind have the same meaning and are the Creative Medium of all thought and action. Soul is also the Substance of Spirit; i.e., It is the unformed Stuff from which all forms are evolved.

Spirit, acting upon Soul, produces Creation; Spirit, Soul and Substance intersphere each other; each has omnipresence. Creation takes place within Spirit and is the result of the Contemplation of Spirit.

Creation is eternally going on; change is always taking place within that which is changeless; forms appear and disappear in that which is formless.

God thinks or knows within Himself; and as the result of this inner action Creation manifests. Creation is the play of Life upon Itself through Divine Self-Imagination. Spirit must create in order to be expressed.

Spirit, Life, Soul, Substance, Law and Unity are all coexistent and coeternal with each other. The only thing that changes is form.

Life makes things out of Itself by becoming the thing that It makes; there is no effort in the process.

Conscious Mind and Spirit mean the same; they denote that part of the Trinity which is Self-Knowing or God.

Subconscious and Subjective Mind, Soul and Mental Medium, Universal Subjectivity or Law, all have the same meaning; they denote that part of the Trinity which acts as Law.

Body, Creation or the manifest Universe, is simply the result of the Trinity which acts as Law.

Body—Creation or the manifest Universe—is simply the result of the Knowingness of Spirit through Law.

One element alone is really self-conscious and that is Spirit. Both Law and Manifestation are automatic and must react to Spirit.

Soul or Subjective Mind, Substance or unformed matter, and Conscious Spirit permeate all things and all people. There is an Intelligence acting through everything, and everything responds to intelligence.

It cannot be too plainly stated that Spirit, or Conscious Intelligence, is the only Self-Assertive Principle in the universe. "Spirit is the power that knows Itself," and is the only power that is Self-Knowing. Everything else is subject to Spirit. The sole and only operation of Spirit is through Its Word. The Word, acting as Law through Substance, produces Creation.

LESSON TWO: INTRODUCTION

Mental Science, which is the Science of Mind and Spirit, makes a tremendous claim when it states that it can free the individual from the bondage of sickness, poverty and unhappiness; but it makes this statement without hesitation and without qualification; it does not retract from that claim and it never will. It does, however, carefully set forth the conditions under which it operates and the laws governing Life, warning man that, unless he understands these conditions and obeys these laws, he will not receive full benefit from the Science of Mind.

THE WORLD HAS LEARNED ALL IT CAN THROUGH SUFFERING

The world is beginning to realize that it has learned all it can through suffering and pain. Perhaps they were good in their place, but surely there can be no power in the Universe which wishes man to be sick, to suffer pain, to be unhappy and end up in the grave. Surely God could not ordain that man should ultimately be other than a perfect expression of Life.

We should have no intellectual difficulty in realizing that even God Himself could not make an automatic individuality, and this explains why man must suffer on the road to self-discovery. He must suffer, not because pain is a necessity, but because he must have experience in order to become individualized.

WHAT INDIVIDUALITY REALLY MEANS

Perhaps it would be a good idea to elaborate on this and explain just what individuality really means. Individuality means self-choice, volition, conscious mind, personified Spirit, complete freedom and a *power to back up that freedom.*

We cannot imagine a mechanical or unspontaneous individuality. To be real and free, individuality must be created *in the image of perfection and let alone to make the great discovery for itself.*

The answer to the question, "Why did not God make us free and compel that freedom?" is apparent when we realize that even God could not do this. A freedom under compulsion would produce a freedom that would ultimately amount to the very worst kind of bondage. There is no such thing as compulsory freedom; even God Himself could not ordain this; for He could do nothing that would violate His own nature. No; man must be created with the possibility of limitless freedom and then be let alone to discover the fact for himself. On the road to that discovery he must be subject to the Law of all Life, and if in ignorance he violates that Law, he must thereby suffer. This is not, however, because God imposes the suffering or desires it, but simply because it is the necessity of the case.

THE MEANING OF FREEDOM

Freedom of will means the ability to do, say and think as one wishes; to express life as one personally desires. To be able only to think and dream of freedom would not be liberty. To imagine, without the power to manifest that imagination, would be to remain in a sort of dream world which would never come to complete self-realization. This is not the world in which man lives at all, for man's world is one of self-expression, even though that expression appears at times to destroy him.

SIN AND PUNISHMENT. RIGHTEOUSNESS AND REWARD

We do not wish to enter into theological discussions in this course of instruction, but we do wish to make the thought clear to those who care to study it. There is no sin but a mistake and no punishment but an inevitable consequence. Wrong doing must be punished, for the Law of cause and effect must

be eternally operative. Right doing must be rewarded for the same reason.

We do not say that man cannot sin; what we say is, that he does sin or make mistakes and that he is thereby automatically punished, *As long as he continues to make mistakes.* This does not mean that there is an evil power in the Universe; but it does mean that there is an immutable Law of cause and effect running through everything. Sin is its own punishment and righteousness *its own reward.*

The age-long discussion of the problem of evil will never be answered until we realize that it is not a thing of itself but is simply *A misuse of the law of freedom.* The problem of evil will be met only to the degree that we cease doing evil and do good, for evil will disappear when we no longer indulge in it. When the whole world sees the right and does it; then, and not until then, will the problem of evil be solved for the entire race.

THE INCARNATION OF SPIRIT

To return to individuality; it is that which distinguishes man from the mere brute creation; it is the greater Incarnation of God in the human; the Indwelling Spirit of the Most High.

Man is created and left to discover himself, and on the road to this self-discovery he experiences the creations of his own imaginations which ultimately show him the Truth and lead to real freedom.

There is an interesting myth in regard to the creating of man which may serve to point out this fact. It is said that when the gods decided to make man, and make him a Divine Being, they held a long discussion as to where would be the best place to hide his Divinity. Some of the gods suggested that it be hidden in the earth, but others argued that some day man would penetrate the earth and so discover himself; it was then suggested that it be hidden in the depths of the sea, but this idea was rejected, for man would go under the sea and there discover his true nature; it was next suggested that his real nature should be deposited somewhere in the air, but this also was rejected, for he would surely fly through the air and find himself. After a long discussion it was finally agreed that the best place to hide man's Divinity would be *in the innermost nature of man himself*—this being the last place he would look to find it!

This discovery would not be made until he had had all the experience necessary to complete a well-rounded life. "The Word is very nigh unto thee, in thy mouth, and in thy heart, that thou mayest do it." 22

Of course, this is a fable, but how clearly it sets forth the reality of the case! The word is really in our own mouths, and every time we say "*I am*" we are repeating it; for "*I am*" is the secret of nature and the emblem of Eternity.

The story of "The Prodigal Son" is the story of man's return to "His Father's House." How truly the poet puts it when he says that "Trailing clouds of Glory do we come from Heaven which is our home." This is the mystical meaning of that marvelous poem of Robert Browning's, called "Saul." Saul had lost his sense of real life and lay in a stupor in his tent when David came to sing to him, to awaken him to the realization of his true nature. At first David sings of the wonders of Creation and of the delights of life; he tells Saul of his power and glory as a human being; and, as the song expands, he touches the secret spring of Saul's being—"He is Saul ye remember in glory, ere error had bent the broad brow from the daily communion." Then, he plainly tells Saul of the Christ. This revelation finally awakens Saul to "His old motions and attitudes kingly." The healing has taken place and the realization of the Truth has freed Saul from the thraldom of false belief.

DIFFERENT VIEWPOINTS

Some take the viewpoint that man was cast forth to discover himself; and others contend that man decided to do this for himself. It makes no difference what the case may be; man is certainly on the pathway to self-discovery, and everything in his experience points to the truth of this fact. We know that the forces of nature wait on man's discovery of them and obey his will as soon as he understands how to make use of her laws. We certainly have freedom enough when we understand how to use that freedom. The Pilgrim Fathers might have had steam cars if they had understood the nature of steam. It was not pushed into man's experience by any autocratic power, but served him only after he had discovered how to use it. We might say the same of any and all of the laws that we now understand and utilize.

THE LESSON OF NATURE'S LAWS

If we find this to be true of the laws of the mechanical world, why should we not also find it true of those Mental and Spiritual Laws which transcend the mechanical world? No doubt, we shall find latent powers and capacities of which we have never dreamed; powers and abilities waiting to be understood and used. "Behold I stand at the door and knock." It certainly will pay man to spend much time and thought in the study of his own nature; for he will discover things about himself that will cause him to "Arise and shine." 23 Man is to-day, more than ever before, awakening to the real facts of the case, and from now on his evolution will become very rapid. Nothing is impossible; all things are possible to the Great Whole, and man is a part of that Whole.

THE RELATION OF MAN TO THE UNIVERSE OF SPIRIT

As the evidence of design in the Universe proves a Designer, so the evidence of self-choice shows a Power that Knows Itself. The Spirit is Self-Knowing; God knows that God Is. But a Universal Self-Knowingness really means a Universal Personalness; and so we see how God can be Personal to every living soul who believes in Spirit. We could truthfully say—so it seems to me at least—that there is One Infinite Person, in whom we all "live, and move and have our Being"; 24 for we all live in the One.

MAN'S EXPERIENCE

Let us assume that man is on the road to self-discovery. What is he to discover?—That he is really free, but that, in order to be free, he must first go through experiences which will teach him how to use his freedom properly; and, after the lesson is learned, he will be free indeed. Everything seems as if this were true. We have traced man's progress carefully through his journey on this planet from the time when the first face "Was turned from the clod," to now, and what have we discovered? That all nature waits upon man's self-discovery and is ever ready to serve him and do his bidding. Laws and forces undreamed of by our ancestors are now being employed; powers and forces which to prehistoric man would have seemed as gods, are to-day called nature's forces, and we consciously make use of them. Man has gradually merged with nature and her laws, and to-day stands forth as a new being so far as the mechanical world is concerned. It seems as if he had conquered nature and compelled her to serve him.

NATURE WAITS ON MAN

Nowhere on this path has he found nature opposed to him. She has silently waited for his recognition and as silently done his bidding. She will never contradict herself nor operate contrary to her inherent laws; but she will serve whoever comes to understand and use them along the lines of her way of working. Man never created any of these laws but simply uses them, and he can do this only as he first obeys them. "Nature obeys us as we first obey it" is an old saying and a true one. We learn the fundamental principle of a law, obey its mode of operation and then have conscious use of it. It would be absurd to say that nature punished us because we did not make proper use of her laws. She simply will not work harmoniously for us until we harmonize with her; she will obey us only after we have obeyed her. This is, of course, true of any and all law. If we obey, it serves; if we disobey, it seems to punish us.

MENTAL AND SPIRITUAL LAWS

It is the same with those great Mental and Spiritual Laws of our Being. We must come to discover and utilize the inner forces of Mind and Spirit, for they are the highest powers.

Man will be delivered from sin, sickness and trouble in exact proportion to his discovery of himself and his relationship to the Whole.

Law is law wherever we find it, and we shall discover that the Laws of Mind and Spirit must be understood if they are to be consciously used for definite purposes. *The spirit knows and the law obeys.*

Hidden away in the inner nature of the real man is the Law of his life, and some day he will discover it and consciously make use of it. He will heal himself, make himself happy and prosperous, and will live in an entirely different world; for he will have discovered that *life is from within and not from without.*

GOD AND MAN

Man is made out of and from Life; and, as effect must partake of the nature of its cause, so man must partake of the Divine Nature from which he springs.

MAN REENACTS THE NATURE OF GOD

If we realize that God is "Triune" and that man is made in the Image and Likeness of God, we shall see that the whole scheme of Life and the whole nature of the Divine Being is reënacted through man. This, of course, does not mean that man is God; it means that, in his small world of individual expression, his nature is identical with God's. This is what Jesus meant when he said, "As the Father hath Life within Himself so hath He given to the Son to have Life within himself." 25

A single drop of water is not the whole ocean, but it does resemble the ocean and does contain within itself the same qualities and attributes. We might say that man is in God and that God works through man. "I and The Father are One," 26 "The Kingdom of God is within you"; 27 and we might add, "God's in His Heaven, all's right with the world."

THE TWO WAYS TO REASON

There are but two processes of reasoning known to the human mind: inductive and deductive; and from these two ways of reasoning all our knowledge of life has come. Inductive reasoning is the systematic process of reasoning from a part to the whole. Deductive reasoning is the process of accepting certain conclusions as truths and drawing other conclusions from them; it is reasoning from the whole to a part. For instance, in inductive reasoning we would say that everything happens just as if there were what we call electricity and that it is everywhere present. Deductive reasoning says that since electricity is everywhere present, it is always where we are and can always be generated from any center.

Using these two methods of reasoning to deduce the nature of God, we may start with the assumption that God IS, drawing all our conclusions from this premise; or we may carefully study the nature of man and the Universe and so draw the conclusion that a God must exist. Whichever method we use will lead to the same conclusion; namely, that there is a Divine Being and that man is made in His Image and must reënact and portray the same attributes as the Life from which he came.

NOTHING HAPPENS BY CHANCE

Nothing in the Universe happens by chance. All is in accordance with Law, and the Law of God is as Omnipresent as is the Spirit of God. This Law is a Law of Mind, but back of the Law is the Word. "All things were made by Him and without Him was not anything made that was made." 28

Back of our lives is the Law of our Being; and through that Law runs the word which we speak; for "What things soever He (the Son) seeth the Father do, these also doeth the Son likewise." 29

MANY ARE WAKING UP TO THE FACTS

Thousands of people to-day are beginning to realize this and put it into operation, and the results attained would fill more books than one man could read in a lifetime. Thousands to-day are using the silent power of Mind to heal their bodies and bring prosperity into their affairs; and the Law is always working in accordance with the belief of those seeking to use It. As the Universe is run by an Infinite Mind, so man's life is controlled by his thinking; ignorance of this keeps him in bondage; knowledge will free him.

One by one, people will investigate the Truth and put It into operation, and the time will come when disease and poverty will be swept from the face of the earth, for they were never intended to be. They are simply the by-products of ignorance, and enlightenment alone will erase them.

THE TIME HAS COME TO KNOW THE TRUTH

The hour of freedom has struck, the bell of Liberty is ringing, and "Let him that is athirst come." 30 Let us, then, plunge more deeply into our own natures and into the nature of the Universe and see if we shall not find treasures undreamed of, possibilities never imagined and opportunities which the fond thought—yearning for freedom—has often, in our vision of the greater Life, given us.

"Prove me now, herewith, saith the Lord of hosts, if I will not open you the windows of heaven, and pour you out a blessing that there shall not be room enough to receive it." 31

A WONDERFUL EXPERIMENT

It would be a wonderful experiment for any one to make to begin to live as if this promise were true; to talk, think and act as though there were a Limitless Power attending him on his journey through life; as though his every act were directed and guided into expressions of peace, health, happiness and harmony. It is surely worth while, and understanding will make the way so clear before us that we shall some day come to see the logic of it; and then, indeed, shall we really begin to live. Our lives, fortunes and happiness are in our own hands to mold as we will—provided we first obey the Law and learn how to make conscious use of It. "With all thy getting get understanding" 32—an old adage—but to-day as true as ever.

It has been the teaching of all times that man reproduces the Divine Nature; and if he does, we shall expect to find in his nature the same qualities that we suppose must be in the Nature of Life Itself.

WHAT PSYCHOLOGY TEACHES ABOUT MAN'S NATURE

A study of the psychological nature of man verifies the belief in "The Trinity" running through all Life. Man is self-conscious; of this we are sure, for he can say "I AM." This fact alone proves his claim to immortality and greatness. In psychology we learn that man is threefold in his nature; that is, he has a self-conscious mind, a subconscious mind and a body. In metaphysics we learn that the three are but different attributes of the same life. Man's self-conscious mind is the power with which he knows; it is, therefore, one with the Spirit of God; it is, indeed, His only guarantee of conscious being.

THE SELF-KNOWING MIND

It is from this self-knowing mind that man is able to realize his relationship with the Whole; for without it he would be unhuman and most certainly not Divine; but since he has it, he must be Divine.

It is the self-knowing mind alone that constitutes reality, personality and individuality. It is the "Image of God," the essence of Sonship, and the "Personification of the Infinite."

MAN'S UNITY WITH THE WHOLE

We recognize, then, in man's self-knowing mind his Unity with the Whole. For while a drop of water is not the ocean, yet it does contain within itself all the attributes of the limitless deep.

Man's self-knowing mind is the instrument which perceives reality, and cognizes or realizes Truth. All illumination, inspiration, and realization must come through the self-knowing mind in order to manifest in man. Vision, intuition and revelation proclaim themselves through man's self-knowing mind; and the Saints and Sages, the Saviours and Christs, the Prophets and Seers, the Wise and Learned, have all consciously perceived and proclaimed this fact. Every evidence of human experience, all acts of kindness and mercy, have interpreted themselves through man's self-knowing mind. All that we know, say or think, feel or believe, hope or long for, fear or doubt, is some action of the self-knowing mind. Subjective memories we have, and inner, unexpressed emotions we feel; but to the self-knowing mind alone does realization come. Without this capacity to consciously know, man would not exist as an expressed being; and, so far as we are concerned, would not exist at all. The self-knowing mind of man proclaims itself in every thought, deed or act, and is truly the only guarantee of his individuality.

MAN A CENTER OF GOD-CONSCIOUSNESS

With this vast array of facts at our disposal it would be foolish to suppose that man's self-knowing mind is any other than his perception of Reality. It is his Unity with the Whole, or God, on the conscious side of life, and is an absolute guarantee that he is a Center of God-Consciousness in the Vast Whole.

UNITY WITH LAW

We will say, then, that in Spirit man is One with God. But what of the great Law of the Universe? If we are really One with the Whole we must be

One with the Law of the Whole, as well as One with the Spirit. Again psychology has determined the fact to be more than a fancy. The characteristics of the subconscious mind of man determine his Subjective Unity with the Universe of Life, Law and Action.

THE SUBJECTIVE OBEYS THE OBJECTIVE

In the Subjective Mind of man we find a law obeying his word, the servant of his Spirit. Suggestion has proved that the subconscious mind acts upon our thought without question or doubt. It is the mental law of our Being and the creative factor within us. It is unnecessary, at this point, to go into all the details of the Subjective Mind and its mode of action; it is enough to say that within us is a mental law, working out the will and purposes of our conscious thoughts. This can be no other than *our individual use of that greater subjective mind which is the seat of all law and action, and is "the servant of the eternal spirit through all the ages."*

Marvelous as the concept may be, it is none the less true that man has at his disposal, in what he calls his subjective mind, a power which seems to be Limitless. This is because he is One with the Whole, on the subjective side of life.

Man's thought, falling into his subjective mind, merges with the Universal Subjective Mind and becomes the law of his life, through *the one great law of all life.*

There are not two subjective minds. There is but one subjective mind; and what we call our subjective mind is really only *the use that we are making of the one law.*

Each individual maintains his identity in Law through his personal use of It; and each is drawing from Life what *he thinks into it.*

To learn how to think is to learn how to live, for our thoughts go into a Medium that is Infinite in Its ability to do and to be.

Man, by thinking, can bring into his experience whatsoever he desires, if he thinks correctly and becomes a living embodiment of his thoughts. This is not done by holding thoughts but by *Knowing the truth.*

THE BODY

But what about man's body? Is that, too, one with the Body of the Universe? Let us briefly analyze matter and see what it really is. We are told that matter is not a solid, stationary thing; but is a constantly flowing, formless substance which is forever coming and going. Matter is as indestructible as God, as eternal as Timeless Being; nothing can be either added to or taken from it. The very bodies we now have were not with us a short time ago. As Sir Oliver Lodge says, we discard many of them on the path through this life, for the material from which our bodies are composed is in a constant state of flow. Vistas of thought open up along the line of mental healing when we realize this fact; later we will thoroughly discuss and work out a definite technique for the purpose of healing.

Matter is not what we thought it to be; it is simply a flowing stuff taking the form that Mind gives it. How about the matter from which other things than the body are made? It is all the same—*one substance in the universe takes different forms and shapes and becomes different things.*

LAST STAGES OF MATTER

The last analysis of matter resolves it into a universal ether and leaves nothing more than a stuff which may be operated upon.

Matter, in the last analysis, is composed of particles so fine that they are simply supposed to be. In other words, it disappears entirely, and the place where it once was is again "without form and void." 33 Matter, as we know it, is only an aggregation of these particles arranged in such order as to produce definite forms, which are determined by something *which is not material.*

There is no difference between the particles which any one form takes and the particles which all forms take; the difference is not in the minute particles but in their arrangement.

THE UNITY OF ALL BODY

Our bodies are One with the Whole Body of the Universe. Seeds, plants, cabbages and kings are made of the same substance; minerals, solids and liquids are made from *the primordial substance which is forever flowing into form and forever flowing out again into the void.*

THE FORMLESS AND THE FORMED

Nothing could form a formless stuff, which has no mind of its own, except Intelligence operating upon it. Again we come back to the Word as the starting point of all Creation—God's Word in the Great World, man's word in the small world.

One spirit, one mind, and one substance; one law but many thoughts; one power, but many ways of using it; one god in whom we all live, and one law which all operate; one, one, one. No greater unity could be given than that which is already vouchsafed to mankind.

But why is man so limited? Why is he still poor, sick, afraid and unhappy? Because he does not know the Truth—that is the only "Why." But why was he not so made that he would have to know the Truth? The answer is that even God could not make a real man, that is, a real Personified Expression of Himself, without creating him in freedom and leaving him *to discover himself.* This is the meaning of the story of the Prodigal Son and the whole meaning of it.

INDIVIDUALITY MEANS SELF-CHOICE

Individuality means real individualized being and real personified self-choice. We could not imagine an individuality without self-choice; but what would be the use of self-choice unless the ability to choose were backed with the power to externalize that choice? It would remain simply an idle dream, never coming into real self-expression. A little thought will make it clear that, if man is created to express freedom, he must be left to discover himself. Of course, during the process he will have much experience, but in the end he will come out a real being.

The day of man's discovery of himself marked the first day of the record of human history on this planet; and from the day when he first made this discovery he has constantly risen and continuously progressed. All the forces of nature attend him on his way, but he must first discover them in order to make use of them.

THE GREATEST DISCOVERY EVER MADE

The greatest discovery that man ever made was, that his thought has creative power; that is, that it uses creative power. His thought, of itself, would have no power unless it were operative through a creative medium. We do not have to compel Law to operate; all that we have to do is to use It. The Law of Mind is just like any and all other laws of Being. It simply Is.

A COMPLETE UNITY

We have now discovered a Unity with the Whole on all three sides of life or from all three modes of expression. We are One with all matter in the physical world, One with the Creative Law of the Universe in the Mental World, and One with the Spirit of God in the Conscious World.

What more could we ask or hope for? How would it be possible for more to be given? We could ask for no more, and no greater freedom could be given. From now on we will expand, grow and express, only to the degree that we consciously coöperate with the Whole.

FOOTNOTES

22 Deut. 30:14
23 Isa. 60:1.
24 Acts 17:28.
25 John 5:26.
26 John 10:30.
27 Luke 17:21.
28 John 1:3.
29 John 5:19.
30 Rev. 22:17.
31 Mal. 3:10.
32 Prov. 4:7.
33 Gen. 1:2.

LESSON TWO: METAPHYSICAL MEANING OF WORDS USED IN INDIVIDUAL CHART NO. II-B

UPPER SECTION

SPIRIT.—That part of man which enables him to be self-conscious. That which he really is. We do not see the spirit of man any more than we see the Spirit of God. We see what man does; but we do not see the doer.

CHRIST, LOGOS.—The Word of God manifest in and through man. In a liberal sense the Christ means the Entire Manifestation of God and is, therefore, the Second Person of the Trinity. Christ is a Universal Idea, and each one "Puts on The Christ" 34 to the degree that he surrenders a limited sense of Life to the Divine Realization.

SONSHIP.—We are all Sons of God and all partake of the Divine Nature.

MICROCOSM.—The individual world as distinguished from the Universal.

EMMANUEL.-GOD-WITH-US.—Means that Christ is in every one.

PERSONALITY.—The external evidence of individualized being.

INDIVIDUALITY.—Each one is a separate identity in Mind and no two are alike. Each is an Individualized Center of God-Consciousness. Our personality is the use that we make of our Divine Individuality.

CONSCIOUS-STATE.—The conscious-state is the self-knowing mind of man. It is the only thing that distinguishes him from brute creation. Without a conscious-state of mind man would not be at all; or, at least, he would not know that he is. The conscious mind should be carefully guarded, as it is the real man.

MENTAL.—Means that man is mentally conscious.

SPIRITUAL.—Means that man is a Spiritual Being.

REASON: INDUCTIVE AND DEDUCTIVE.—The conscious mind of man can reason both inductively and deductively. It can reason from the Whole to a part or from a part to the Whole.

WILL.—Means conscious ability to determine.

CHOICE.—Ability to differentiate and choose.

VOLITION.—Power to act independently.

INTELLECT.—Mental quality of analysis.

PURPOSE.—Determination with incentive.

DECISION.—Ability to choose.

MIDDLE SECTION

SOUL.—The Subjective Side of Life. Man's place in the One Subjective Mind of the Universe; his identity in Mind. Man's soul life reënacts the Soul Life of the Universe with which it is at One.

SUBJECTIVE.—The Soul is subjective. Read again the meaning of subjectivity as given in the Universal Chart.

SUBCONSCIOUS.—The Soul is subjective to the conscious thought.

UNCONSCIOUS.—Word used in Psycho-analysis to denote soul. It is a poor way of expressing soul-life, for it really is not unconscious. It is subconscious but certainly not unconscious.

CONSCIOUSNESS.—Another way of saying soul. The Bible says, soul; the psycho-analyst says, unconscious; the psychologist says, subjective or subconscious; and the metaphysician says, consciousness. All have the same meaning.

KARMA.—The subjective law of tendency set in motion by the individual. The mental law acting through him. Karmic Law means the use that man makes of his mentality. Karma is not Kismet; for Kismet means "fate," and Karma simply means "the mental tendency." Karma is both individual and Universal.

AURA.—Mental atmosphere or vibration. It extends from a few inches to a few feet around the individual and can be seen by many people.

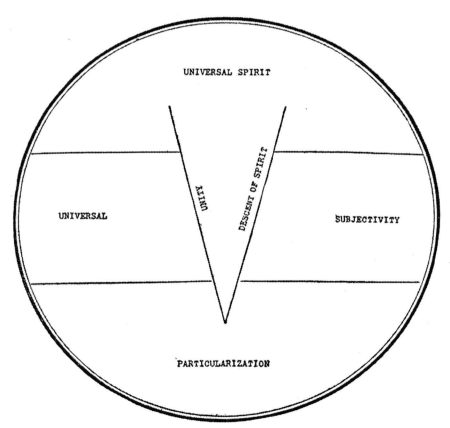

Lesson Two: Metaphysical Chart No. II-A.

This chart shows, first, the Universal Spirit; then the Universal Soul or Subjectivity, which is the medium of all thought, power and action; then particularization or manifestation of Spirit.

The point drawn down through the center symbolizes the descent of Spirit into matter, or form. It is necessary that Spirit be manifested in order to express Itself. The word Unity on the descending line shows that all come from the One. Man reënacts the whole Universal Life, and his nature is identical with Spirit. What is true of the Whole is true of any one of Its undivided parts. Man comes to a point of individualization in the Whole and is subject to the Law of the Whole.

MEMORY.—The soul, or subjective mind, is the seat of memory, and retains within itself everything that the individual has ever said, thought, seen, heard, felt, read or been told; and, indeed, everything that has ever happened to him. It also contains race memory, and may, or may not, contain much of what we call Cosmic Purposes. Cosmic Purposes mean the Ideas of God. The soul of man, being in constant contact with the Soul of the Universe, might contact tremendous powers if it would turn to the One.

CONFLICT.—In the study of Psycho-analysis, which means the analysis of the soul, we learn that the subjective side of thought, being the seat of memory, often retains thoughts and suppressed emotions which more or less tear or bind. This is what is meant by inner conflict.

PSYCHE.—Means soul.

INHERITED TENDENCIES.—The subjective, being the seat of memory, contains the race characteristics and tendencies. We do not inherit diseases, but we do inherit tendencies. This is the way that family and race traits are handed down.

RACE-SUGGESTION.—The tendency to reproduce what the race has thought and experienced.

PRENATAL CONDITIONS.—The tendency to inherit family traits.

IMAGES OF THOUGHT.—The soul, or subjective mind, contains all of our thoughts as mental images or pictures.

AUTO-SUGGESTION.—The soul receives the suggestions of the individual.

REASON DEDUCTIVE ONLY.—That which is subjective can reason deductively only.

LOWEST SECTION

BODY.—The definite outline of flesh, containing all of the ideas which go to make the complete physical instrument.

EFFECT.—That which follows cause. The body is always an effect.

AFFAIRS.—That which happens to the external man.

CONDITIONS.—External things, the result of thought.

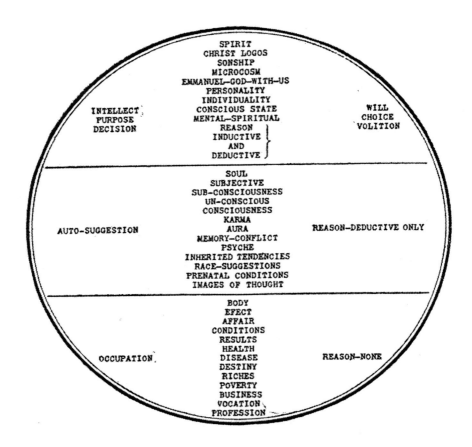

Lesson Two: Metaphysical Chart No. II-B.

This chart shows how man reenacts the Whole and is subject to the law of his own being. If the meaning of this chart is carefully studied it will be made plain that man thinks consciously and that his conscious thought becomes the law of his life. The upper section stands for the Self-Conscious man; the middle section stands for the subconscious man; and the lowest section stands for the man as he appears in the flesh and in the conditions of his life.

RESULTS.—Conditions.

HEALTH.—Result of correct thinking.

DISEASE.—Result of wrong thinking.

DESTINY.—Result of what man thinks.

RICHES.—Result of a consciousness of supply.

POVERTY.—Result of limited thought.

BUSINESS.—Also result of thought.

VOCATION.—The thing that our thought causes us to do.

PROFESSION.—Same as vocation.

OCCUPATION.—Same as vocation.

REASON, NONE.—Everything in the body of man, as well as in his affairs, is the result of what he thinks. Nothing in the external is a cause, and nothing that happens causes itself to happen. Things have no power to reason, but are always the result of some inner cause.

FOOTNOTES

34 Gal. 3:27.

LESSON TWO: THE NATURE OF MAN

In the first lesson we studied the Universal Chart; we are now taking up the individual chart. Whatever is true of the Universe as a Whole must also be true of the individual as some part of this Whole. Man is evolved from the Universe, and is a self-conscious, thinking center of Living Spirit, and, as such, he must, in his nature and being, reproduce the Universe. This is what Jesus meant when He said, "As the Father hath (Inherent) Life in Himself, so hath he given to the Son to have (Inherent) Life in Himself." 35 Inherent Life means real Life. The whole Cosmic Scheme must be reproduced on the plane of the individual, if there is an individual.

We must expect to find in man, therefore, the same inherent attributes that we find in the universe from which he springs.

Chart No. II-A symbolizes, first, the Universal Spirit; next, the Universal Subjectivity, which is called the Soul of the Universe; and third, the particularization or manifestation of Universal Spirit. We have marked Unity on the descending line, because the Spirit emanates, or particularizes Itself, at the point of our personality becoming what we call man. It is essential that we realize the Unity of life, i.e., the Unity of God and man on all three planes.

Let us start with the objective plane: matter or body, devoid of mind or intelligence, has no volition; it may be permeated with intelligence, but it is not intelligent. It is one with the Body of the Universe.

Now, what do we know about the soul? Remember the things that were discussed in connection with the qualities of the Soul of the Universe; and you will find all of them depicted in what is called the psychological, subjective nature of man; for our subjective or subconscious mind reproduces all the attributes belonging to the Universal Mind. When we turn to the spirit of man, we find that it is one with the Spirit of God—that is, man is a self-conscious, thinking, choosing center of individualized intelligence, or God-Consciousness in the great Whole.

So we find man is one with all matter in the material world, one with the Soul of the Universe in the subjective world, and one with the Spirit of God in the conscious world. What we call our objective or conscious mind is as much as we know of God and Life. The objective mind is the spiritual mind for which we have been looking, but it is not fully developed; if this were not so there would be no mind with which to look. The objective mind must be the spiritual mind of man, since it is the only thing about him which knows that it has life and is conscious of itself.

The whole of Spirit is potentially focused in our individual, objective consciousness; but we have not yet evolved to a realization of this, except in a small degree. Back of the objective mind is the subjective mind or soul, which is the medium through which intelligence operates.

There is but One Universal Subjective Mind or Soul; and what we call our subjective mind is simply our use of Universal Subjectivity; for our subjective mind is not a thing apart, but is our place in Universal Subjective Mind; and our place in It is the use that we make of It.

SPIRIT

Turning to the chart of man, Chart No. II-B, we find that the spirit of man is his conscious state of mental and spiritual being; that this mental state is equipped with decision, will, choice, volition, intellect and purpose. We find that it is individuality, personality, and is called Emmanuel or God with us. It is the microcosm within the Macrocosm, which means the little world within the big world; it is also called the Image of God; it is Sonship, the Sonship of the Father; it is the Christ or Logos, which means the Word. It can reason both inductively and deductively, and is the only thing known to us that can reason both ways.

SOUL

We find that on the subjective or soul side man is subconscious; but subconscious does not mean unconscious. Subconscious means subjective to the conscious thought, compelled by reason of its subjectivity to receive what is put into it. The term "unconscious" is used by psycho-analysis. Consciousness is the word that some use in speaking of the soul side of life. It is Karmic Law, because it is the use that we are making of Universal Subjectivity; Karma means the law of cause and effect. Soul contains the memory, because it is the receptacle for the seeds of our thought. It is psyche, soul, psychic; this is where we get the word "psycho-analysis," analysis of the soul. It contains the inherited tendencies, because it is the seat of memory. It also contains race-suggestion; for we are not dealing with a separated and isolated subjective mind, but with the one Subjective Mind. There is a vast difference between thinking of having three or four minds and thinking of having but One which all use. Its reasoning capacity is deductive only, yet it contains an intelligence which is infinite compared with the human concept of intelligence.

BODY

Next we come to the body of man, which is simply the effect of what his thought has been in Mind. Body, effect, affairs, conditions, health, disease, destiny, riches, poverty, business, vocation, profession, results, occupation, any word that stands for the externalization of man's thought and endeavor, we class as a part of the body.

"What a man has, as well as what he is, is the result of the subjective state of his thought." The thinker is conscious mind, but when he thinks, he lets fall the forms of his thought into Subjective Mind, which is the Universal Medium of all thought and action, and as the result of this, the Creative Medium at once sets to work to produce the thing thought of. This is the way that Nature works and it is the way that man works, although he is just waking to this realization.

Plotinus, who was one of the Neo-Platonic philosophers,

personifying Nature, said, "I do not argue; I contemplate; and as I contemplate, I let fall the forms of my thought." This is the way Nature creates; It contemplates through Its Conscious Mind. As the result of Its contemplation, It lets fall the seeds of Its thought into the Universal Subjective, which, being Law, produces the thing thought of. Now we must expect to find, and we do find, the same thing reënacted in man. This means that whatever man thinks (whether it is what he calls good or bad) falls into this Universal Creative Medium, is accepted by It, is at once acted upon, begins to take form, and, unless neutralized, tends to become a thing in the objective world.

LIMITLESS MEDIUM

When we realize that as we deal with our own individuality we are dealing with Self-Conscious Mind, and when we realize that as we deal with subjective mind we are dealing with the Universal Subjectivity, we see at once that we have at our disposal a Power compared to which the united intelligence of the human race is as nothing; because the Universal Subjective Mind, being entirely receptive to our thought, is compelled by reason of Its very being to accept that thought and act upon it, no matter what the thought is. Since we are dealing with an Infinite Power, which knows only Its own ability to do, and since It can objectify any idea impressed upon It, there can be no limit to what It could or would do for us, other than the limit of our mental concept. Limitation could not be in Principle or in Law but only in the individual use that we make of It. Our individual use of It can only equal our individual capacity to understand It, to embody It. We cannot demonstrate beyond our ability to mentally conceive, or to mentally provide, an equivalent. We must have a mental equivalent of the thing we want, in order to demonstrate.

Subjectivity is entirely receptive and neutral, as we have learned, and It can take our thoughts only the way we think them. There is no alternative. If I say, "I am poor," and keep on saying, "I am poor," subconscious mind at once says, "Yes, you are poor." and keeps me poor, as long as I say it. This is all there is to poverty. It comes from impoverished thinking. We deal only with thoughts, for thoughts are things, and if the thought is right the condition will be right. An active thought will produce an active condition. Suppose I have thought poverty year after year, I have created a law, which keeps on perpetuating this condition. If the thought be unerased, the condition will remain. A law has been set in motion which says, "I am poor," and sees to it that it is so. This is, at first, auto-suggestion; then it becomes an unconscious memory, working day and night. This is what decides the law of attraction, because the laws of attraction and repulsion are entirely subjective. They may be conscious to start with, but they are subconscious as soon as they are set in motion. Now suppose I did not say I was poor, but came into the world with an unconscious thought of poverty; so long as that thought operated, I would be poor. I might not have understood the Law, but it would have been working all the time.

There is also a race-suggestion which says that some people are rich and some are poor; so we are all born or come into this world with a subjective tendency toward negative conditions. But we are also dealing with a subjective tendency toward ultimate good; because, in spite of all conditions, the race believes more in the good than in the evil; otherwise, it would not exist. It believes that everything will come out all right, rather than all wrong. This is the eternal hope and sense of all life.

No matter what may be in the soul, or subjective state of our thought, the conscious state can change it. This is what treatment does. How can this be done? Through the most direct method imaginable—by consciously knowing that there is no subjective state of poverty, no inherited tendency toward limitation, no race-suggestion operating through subjectivity; nothing in, around or through it that believes in or accepts limitation in any way, shape, form or manner. The conscious state must now provide a higher form of thought. What does it do? It supplies a spiritual realization, a self-conscious realization, and says, "I partake of the nature and bounty of the All Good and I am now surrounded by everything whichmakes life worth while." What happens then? This Soul side of life, this Universal Medium, at once changes Its thought (because Its thought is deductive only) and says, "Yes, you are all of these things." Whatever is held in consciousness until it becomes a part of the subjective side of thought must take place in the world of affairs. Nothing can stop it. The reason we do not demonstrate more easily is that the objective state of our thought is too often neutralized by the subjective state. There is more fear of poverty than there is belief in riches. As long as that fear remains it is sure to produce a limited condition. Whatever is subjective must objectify. Matter is immaterial, unknowing, unthinking, and plastic in the hands of Law or Mind; and Law or Subjective Mind, which is entirely unvolitional, but not unintelligent, is compelled by its own subjectivity to receive the thought of the conscious mind, which alone can choose and decide. It follows then that whatever the conscious mind holds long enough is bound to be produced in external affairs; nothing can stop it, because we are dealing with Universal Law. This is called Divine Principle. It is the Medium in which we all live, move and have our being on the subjective side of life; our atmosphere in Universal Subjectivity; the medium through which all intercommunication takes place on every plane.

It follows from what we have said that any suggestion held in Creative Mind would produce its logical result, no matter what that suggestion might be. If it were a suggestion of destruction, it would destroy; for this is a neutral field. If it were a suggestion of good, it would construct.

CHRIST AND ANTICHRIST

The Spirit of Christ means that mentality which recognizes the Law and uses It for constructive purposes only. The spirit of Antichrist is the spirit of the individual, or class of individuals who, understanding the Law, use It destructively. The meaning of the Flood or Deluge (which is recorded in every sacred scripture we have read or heard of) is that a race of people were upon the earth who came to understand psychic, or subjective, law as being the servant of the Spirit. They understood themselves to be Spirit, but they did not understand the harmonious Unity of Spirit. They had arrived at an intellectual concept of the Law,—a very clearly defined mental concept; but that knowledge and wisdom were not used for constructive purposes. They used it destructively, and what happened? The confusion which took place in the psychic world (or the psychic atmosphere of this planet) caused its physical correspondence in the form of the Deluge or Flood.

Psyche also means "sea," and it was into this psychic sea that Jonah fell. This is the meaning of the story of Jonah and the whale and is also why, in Revelation, it says: "There was no more sea." 36 It does not mean that Law shall be eliminated, but that the time will come when It will be used for constructive purposes only. The misuse of this Law to-day is called "Malpractice." We have no fear of malpractice, because it can be practiced only upon the person who believes in it. If we say to Mind: "There is no such thing as malpractice," there being only One Ultimate Reality, as far as we are concerned, we are free from it. "Against such there is no law." 37 We recognize Subconscious Mind as the Great Servant of our thought. It is the Medium through which all treatment operates. How do we contact this Universal Subjective Mind, which is the Medium through which healing and demonstration take place? We contact It within ourselves and nowhere else. It is in us, being Omnipresent. Our use of It, we call our subjective mind; but It is Universal Subjectivity.

MAN IS IDENTIFIED IN MIND

Mental treatment recognizes that each individual has his identity in mind and is known in Mind by the name he bears. This Subjective Law knows there is a John Smith and a Mary Jones. Why? Because John Smith and Mary Jones know that there is a John Smith and a Mary Jones. But It only knows about them what they know about themselves. Being subjective to their thought, It could not know anything else; consequently, whatever John Smith and Mary Jones say, It   says, accepts and does. This is a marvelous concept. Unless we have thought it out, it may seem rather startling. But it means this:—that the Law absolutely accepts us at our own valuation. Now this does not mean that it accepts us at an assumption of valuation, but at the actual valuation. It can reflect to us only the actual embodiment of ourselves. It is the deep inner conviction that we carry which decides what is going to happen. So we are each known by the name we bear, and each is daily making some statement about that name. When we say "I am this or that," we are involving in Mind statements which Mind in turn produces as conditions.

TREATMENT

In treatment we turn entirely from the condition, because so long as we look at a condition we cannot overcome it. That is why the mystic said: "Behold my face forevermore." "Look unto me and be ye saved, all the ends of the earth." 38 That is, look up and not down. It is useless to treat one's business, because business is an immaterial thing. It is an unthinking, unknowing thing—a lot of stuff in form, a lot of forms in stuff. That which decides what the business shall be is in Consciousness or Mind. Consequently, we must involve in Mind a correct concept of the business, seeing it as we want it to be; and when we have seen it that way long enough, it will be so.

How long will it take? Until the subjective side of thought accepts the new concept as true, or until we have neutralized the old concept.

Jesus had a great understanding and He gave a clew to that understanding when He said: "The Prince of this world cometh and findeth nothing in me." 39 He meant that race-suggestion found no mental correspondence or equivalent in Him. His consciousness was so clear that it operated directly from the Spirit.

THE AIM OF EVOLUTION

The aim of evolution is to produce a man who, at the point of his objective thought, may completely manifest the whole idea of life—i.e., bring the concept of Unity to the point of particularization, finding nothing in the Law to oppose it. The reason Jesus was able to become the Christ was, that at the objective point of His thought there was a complete realization of the Unity of the Spirit and the Absoluteness of his word. His spiritual and psychical faculties, his objective and subjective mind, were completely poised and perfectly balanced.

It is evident that if this took place in any individual his word would be manifested likewise. It would have to be, because behind the word is Universal Soul, Omnipotent Law. Divine Principle is Limitless, but It can only be to us what we believe It is. Why must we believe It is? Because until we believe It is, we are believing It is not. The reason some people cannot demonstrate the Truth is, they do not realize It. The whole thing is a matter of belief; but belief is scientifically induced into a subjective state through conscious endeavor and effort. Treatment is the science of inducing within Mind concepts, acceptances, and realizations of peace, poise, power, plenty, health, happiness and success, or whatever the particular need may be.

What does a practitioner do? He sets the Law in motion in Universal Mind. Let us suppose that Mary is sick, and that John is a practitioner. She comes to him, saying, "I am sick." He, being a metaphysician, understands that Mind is all; she does not understand this. She feels that she is sick. But he knows that all sickness is mental. He does not try to hold a thought over her, nor does he try to suggest anything to her; for that is not mental treatment. He simply declares the Truth about her; he speaks her name and says: "This word is for her; she is perfect; she is well." In other words, he contradicts what appears to be and declares the Truth about her. What happens? A law is being enacted on the subjective side of life. His word, operative through the Universal Sea of Mind (in which both live) sets in motion a law which objectifies through her body as healing.

Mary thinks a miracle has been performed. She exclaims: "I am healed. I did not have a bit of faith, but john healed me." No miracle has been performed. He used a law which all may use if they will. Suppose Mary were perfectly well, but wanted a position,—what would the treatment be? It would be the same. John would state in Mind what should be done for Mary. There is only One Law, and Mary could demonstrate just as well for herself if she understood It, but she must first see It demonstrated to realize It. This is the state of mind of most people who come for healing. They do not know what ails them; they think their condition is due to some external cause.

Nevertheless, they are healed and exclaim: "This is a marvelous thing, though I do not understand what it is all about." Often they become superstitious about it, as people do about the things they do not understand; once they understand the law, however, healing is no longer a mystery.

The only reason a man has difficulty in throwing off some weakness of character, while believing in Spirit implicitly and having faith that he is going to overcome his limitation, is because he has not induced the necessary mental images in Mind. If he had, he would have overcome his trouble; thinking of his weakness keeps the image of it before him.

In treating, turn entirely away from the condition. Disease and limitation are neither person, place nor thing; they are simply images of thought. Turn entirely from the condition, or the limited situation, to its opposite, that is, to the realization of health, happiness or harmony.

METHODS OF TREATMENT

Although several methods of treatment are used, there are but two distinct methods; one is called argumentative, and the other realization. The argumentative method is a process of mental argument in which the practitioner argues to himself about his patient. He is, consequently, presenting a logical argument to Universal Mind, or Divine Principle; and if that argument carries with it a complete evidence in favor of his patient, it is supposed that the patient will be healed.

The method of realization is one whereby the practitioner realizes within himself the perfect state of his patient; it is purely a spiritual and meditative process of contemplating the Perfect Man; and if the embodiment of the idea is really made, it will at once produce a healing.

Treatment is for the purpose of inducing an inner realization of perfection in the mentality of the practitioner, which inner realization, acting through Mind, operates in the patient.

Between John and Mary there is One Universal Medium which is also in John and Mary; It is not only between them, but in them. As John knows right where John is (since there is only One), he is at the same time knowing right where Mary is, because his work is operative though a field which is not divided but which is a complete Unit or Whole, i.e., Universal Subjectivity. As he knows within or upon himself, he is setting in motion the Law, which operates through the person whom he mentions in his treatment, no matter where the patient may be. There is no such thing as an absent treatment, as opposed to a present treatment.

Mary must have a consciousness of health before the healing can be permanent. It will have to become a part of her subjective thought. If the consciousness did not change she would perpetuate the old thought images and would get sick again; and that is why, in treating, people get well for a while and then become sick again. They are not permanently healed unless the consciousness is healed.

A treatment begins and ends within the thought of the one giving it. The practitioner must do the whole work within himself. He must know the Truth, and as he does that, he sets in motion the Law. A thing which is known by any part of the Universal Mind is known by every part of It, for It is an Undivided

Whole. When you know in one place you know everywhere. When you give a treatment you do not send out a thought, or hold a thought, or give suggestion. A treatment is a positive thing.

If you are treating a certain John Smith, you say (if he is not present), "I am treating John Smith of such and such a place." Then you forget all about him as a personality and give your treatment. It is not necessary to specify the trouble. Once in a great while, you might find yourself mentioning a thing in order to make some statement against it, but probably that is not the best way. Of course there are certain thoughts back of certain things, and a knowledge of the disease might enable you to know better what thought to destroy.

It is like this: Mary Jones comes to John Smith and says, "I have tuberculosis." In answer to this he declares, "This word is for Mary Jones. She is a perfect and complete manifestation of Pure Spirit, and Pure Spirit cannot be diseased; consequently she is not diseased." This is an argument, trying to bring out the evidence in favor of perfection. It is an argument which produces a certain conclusion in the mentality of John Smith, and, consequently, it sets in motion a certain law for Mary Jones. As John does this, day after day, he gradually becomes convinced of her perfection and she is healed. If he could do it in one minute, she would be healed in one minute. There is no process in healing. It is a revelation, an awakening, a realization of Life. Man exists in Divine Mind as a Perfect Image; but he covers himself with the distorted images of his own thought along the pathway of his mental experience.

If using the method of realization, say, "This word or this thought is for Mary Jones." Then begin to realize the Perfect Presence, the Only Perfect Presence. "God is all there is; there is no other Life"; very little argument, but more and more a complete realization. This is very powerful, although it makes no difference which method you use, as they produce the same result. It is a good idea to combine both.

In the case of a child, the treatment should be the same. It would have an effect commensurate with the absolute conviction that the practitioner has. But in the case of an infant, who is subjective to the conscious thought of the people around it, you must teach those people how to think about the child, and see that they do think that way; else you might heal the child and their thought might make it sick again.

In case of failure, it is probable that the trouble is more with John than with Mary, as far as the immediate healing is concerned. However, diseases are the direct results of certain habitual mental attitudes which people entertain, and unless those mental attitudes are changed, there will be no permanent healing. It is the business of the practitioner to discover what those attitudes are and to change them. It is also the business of the practitioner to show people why they are as they are, and to teach them how to overcome undesirable attitudes.

In giving a treatment, you talk to yourself about somebody else.

We must grasp the idea of Universal Subjectivity, the Potentiality of all things, the Divine Creative Medium. This is the Principle through which we are to demonstrate the healing of the body or of the condition; and It acts accurately and mathematically, because It is the Law of cause and effect.

SUBJECTIVE LAW

When we think, we think from conscious intelligence, or Spirit. We will say that the thought becomes subjectified; i.e., it goes into the subconscious mind. But what is man's subconscious mind? It is his atmosphere or mental vibration in Universal Subjectivity. There is no such thing as your subjective mind and my subjective mind, meaning two, for this would be duality. But there is such a thing as the subjective state of your thought and of my thought in Mind. This should be made very clear, for here is where psychology and metaphysics separate; i.e., their understandings are different. When we think, we think into a Universal Creative Medium, a receptive and plastic substance which surrounds us on all sides, which permeates us and flows through us. We do not have to think that we are thinking in It or upon It; for when we think we do think into and upon It; there is no other place that we could think, since It is Omnipresent.

As each subjectifies himself in consciousness he is building around himself a mental atmosphere; and nothing can enter this unless he allows it to, through the avenues of his own thought; but this thought might be conscious or unconscious; in most cases it is unconscious, but the student of Truth is learning to consciously control the stream of thought that he allows to enter his inner and creative mentality.

THOUGHT AND THE CREATIVE MEDIUM

Thought is an inner movement which is the result of one's perception of life and his reaction to it. Every time this movement takes place it takes place within Mind, upon Cause, according to law. We are, without question, dealing with the same Power that molds the planets and all that is upon them; and the limit of our ability to prove this is not in Principle, but is in our understanding of It; in our ability to incorporate within ourselves an embodiment of our ideals.

EACH IS THE LOGICAL RESULT OF HIS OWN THINKING

We are dealing with a neutral, creative power, just as we would be in the case of electricity or any other natural force. It is on a higher plane; for it is the power of intelligence. As we think into this Universal Mind, our thought, in its externalization, will reach its own level, just as water will reach its own level by its own weight and without effort. This is in line with necessity; for the Universe, in order to be at all, must be Self-Existent.

What is meant by the Self-Existence of the Universe? This means a Universe which is Its own reason for being; a Universe which exists by virtue of Itself, being All.

Each one of us is to-day the result of what has gone before, either consciously or unconsciously, no matter what kind of a condition he may be in. As soon as we realize this we shall be better off, because we shall see that since what we now are, or what we now have and experience, is the result of what we have thought; the answer to what we shall be is contained in what we now are; for we can change our thinking.

Man thinks and supposes that he lets go of the thoughts he thinks. But such is not the case; for thought becomes subjectified in Mind, like a seed planted in the soil; it stays there, unless neutralized, and decides the attraction and repulsion in the experience of the one thinking. There is a constant action on the subjective side of life; and it is this unconscious process which decides what is going to happen in the outer expression.

Whatever we think, act, believe in, feel, visualize, vision, image, read, talk about, in fact, all processes which affect or impress us at all, are going into the subjective state of our thought, which is our individualized use of Universal Mind. Whatever goes into the subjective state of thought tends to return again as some condition.

A LAW OF BELIEF

Jesus said, "As thou hast believed so be it done unto thee." 40 Knowing the nature of the law, He did not say, "It is done unto you as you wish." He announced the universality of law when He said, "As thou hast believed so be it done unto thee."

WE ARE DEALING WITH LAW

Some one may say, "I can't imagine God not caring." I cannot either; but we are dealing with law. Does the law of electricity care whether it cooks the dinner or burns the house down? Whether it electrocutes a criminal or warms the feet of a saint? Of course it does not care at all! Does the urge, which impels people to express, care whether a man kneels in ecstasy or lies drunk in the gutter? We are dealing with law. And it follows that, since we are dealing with law, it will ultimately bring back to us the results of the forces which we set in motion through it. Consequently, no person who is enlightened would seek to use this law destructively; for he would know that, sooner or later, the very power set in motion by himself would ultimately destroy him. "All they that take the sword shall perish with the sword." 41 The Spirit of Christ is the spirit which constructively uses the law. The spirit of Antichrist is the destructive use of law. The Spirit of Christ, being in line with the Cosmic Life, will always transcend, neutralize, destroy, and utterly obliterate the spirit of Antichrist; and ultimately only the Spirit of Christ can succeed. "He that hath an ear, let him hear." 42

THE CYCLE OF NECESSITY AND KARMIC LAW

The cycle of necessity means that those things which the individual sets in motion through the law must ultimately swing back to him again. This is the Karmic Law; "The law that binds the ignorant but frees the wise." This law has been announced by every great teacher who has ever lived. Jesus referred to this law when He said, "As thou hast believed so be it done unto thee"; 43 and when He said, "Heaven and earth shall pass away: but my words shall not pass away." 44 It is the law to which Isaiah referred when he said, "So shall my word be that goeth forth out of my mouth; it shall not return unto me void, but it shall accomplish that which I please." 45 This is the law which to-day is called "Divine Principle," or the law of cause and effect; it means that once a tendency is set in motion through law, it is bound to objectify at the level of the subjective concept which entertains it. There is nothing fatalistic about this, for we may consciously change the currents of subjectivity with the conscious thought. Indeed, this is what treatment does.

THE LAW OF ACTION AND REACTION

This is simply the law of cause and effect, and instead of getting too occult or mystical a concept of it we would better think of it simply as something into which we think, and which returns to the thinker what he thinks into it. This law can be applied for concrete purposes, and once it is set in motion the rest works automatically. This is why we may absolutely trust Principle when we understand how it operates. It knows everything and can do anything; but in order to work for us, we must let it work through us. This is the power that Jesus used when He withered the fig tree and when He raised Lazarus from the dead.

WE ARGUE IN MIND

So we argue in Mind; and if we argue toward a belief in health, we will be healed. It isn't a question of suggestion or of the power of thought making us well, for this is but a limited sense of will power. It isn't something over which we must clinch our teeth and will to be; it is something which we have to know. Water doesn't have to will to be wet, it is wet; and if we go into it we will get wet. Life doesn't have to claim to be Life; It simply announces Itself to be what It knows that It Is. So we argue in Mind, not to convince Mind that It is or can accomplish, but to convince ourselves that we are now perfect.

WRONG USE OF MIND

There have been many controversies about the use and the misuse of this power. Some claim that we cannot misuse this power, since there is but One Mind, and It cannot act against Itself. Mind cannot act against Itself; and any person who knows this, and who knows that there is no human mind to destroy, or to be destroyed, is immune from malpractice. But let any one believe in malpractice, and he will open mental avenues of receptivity to it; for we can receive only that to which we vibrate.

Malpractice is the ignorant use of something which of itself is good. It is the wrong use of mental power and will never be indulged in by any one who understands the Truth; neither can one who understands the Truth be affected by it. There could be innocent, ignorant and malicious malpractice. Innocent malpractice, in the form of sympathy with disease and trouble, thereby accentuating these conditions, is often prolific of dire results. Ignorant malpractice would be about the same thing; for instance, when one sees a criminal, thinking of him as such helps to perpetuate the state in which he is manifesting. Malicious malpractice would be an act of centering thought for destructive purposes. When Jesus said, "The prince of this world cometh and hath nothing in me," 46 He meant that he had neutralized all race thought about destruction and so was immune to all false suggestion. This we should all try to do.

SUBJECTIVE BUT NOT UNCONSCIOUS

The subjective mind can deduce only; it cannot, of itself, initiate anything; but this does not mean that it is unintelligent. We must be very careful not to labor under the delusion that because the subjective mind cannot reason it is unintelligent, for it is infinitely more intelligent than our present state of conscious mind, but is, nevertheless, controlled by it.

If our subjective consciousness were always clear, that is, if it never received any false impressions, the Spirit would always flow to the point of objectivity and we would never make mistakes; we would never be sick, poor, or unhappy.

HOW HABITS ARE FORMED

Back in the subjective are the images of thought surrounding us, all acting as living intelligences. It is here that habits are formed; for when one has a habit that he cannot seem to break he is hypnotized by the thought and desire back of that habit; the thought force has grown too strong to be controlled. Habits are healed by neutralizing the thought forces behind them.

LAW IS MIND IN ACTION

There is One Infinite Life acting through Law, and this Law is mental; Law is Mind in action. We are surrounded by an Infinite, Subconscious, Impersonal, Neutral, Plastic, Creative, Ever-Present, Thinking Stuff from which all things come, which, in Its Original State, permeates and penetrates all things. By impressing our thought upon this Substance we can cause It to produce for us that which we think, to the limit of our ability to mentally embody the idea. Impressing our thought upon It is not an external act, for when we impress our thought upon ourselves, we are thinking into It; this is because of the Unity of all Mind. This is one of the great lessons to learn; we do not know anything outside ourselves. This is what Jesus meant when He said, "Ye shall know the Truth and the Truth shall make you free." 47 When we know within ourselves we are knowing at the point of that Individualized Spirit which we are; upon the very Heart of the Infinite, the Ever-Present Substance, which is ever responsive to Itself.

WE ARE BOUND BY OUR OWN FREEDOM

We are all bound, tied hand and foot, by our very freedom; our free will binds us; but, as free will creates the conditions which externally limit us, so it can uncreate or dissolve them. The Universe, being deductive only, cannot refuse man anything.

The very force that makes us sick can heal us; the force that makes us poor can make us rich; and the power that makes us miserable can make us happy. If this were not true there would be duality in the Universe, and this is impossible.

ONENESS WITH ALL LAW

When we know of our Oneness with God and Law, what a great burden will be removed which otherwise would cause us to struggle in making a demonstration! The sense of opposition must forever be removed from the consciousness which perceives Unity.

Instead of saying, "Here is a sick man to heal and I shall have to work hard on this case," we should realize that there is nothing but concept in the Universe and, therefore, say, "I am going to conceive of this man as being absolutely perfect," then the same power which made him sick will heal him. This is the reversal of thought.

That which we call our subjective mind is but a point in Universal Mind where our personality maintains its individualized expression of Spirit. If we think of ourselves as being separated from the Universe we will be limited by this thought; for it is a belief in separation from Good which binds and limits; we are bound by nothing except belief. "They could not enter in because of unbelief," 48 and because they "limited the Holy One of Israel." 49

There is but One Mind. Here is the point: everything we experience, touch, taste, handle and smell; environment, bodies, conditions, money, happiness, friends; all are effects. Is it clear that the infinite and limitless possibilities of that One of which man is a part, depend, in man's expression, upon his own concepts? If he is a point of personality in limitless Mind, which he is, and if all of his life must be drawn from this One Mind, which it must, there cannot be anything else, can there? And if there is nothing else, if there is nothing to move but Mind, and if man is a thinking center in Mind, nothing is going to happen to him that does not happen through him, whether this is the result of his own erroneous conclusions, those of his grandfathers, or the race to which he belongs. It is impossible to conceive of anything ever happening to any one unless the force back of it was set in motion by himself, sometime or somewhere. But this is not fatalistic, for we may change the chain of causation which we have set in motion.

Everything comes from Intelligence; there is nothing but Unity; there is nothing but freedom; there is nothing but completeness; there is nothing but Totality. Begin at the beginning and reason this out time after time till doubt disappears; for you will be neutralizing that subjectivity which rises to slay you. It is necessary that each do this for himself.

DEMONSTRATION

As far as making a demonstration is concerned, when we get the correct consciousness this is the easiest thing in the world; but we cannot demonstrate beyond our ability to mentally embody an idea. The argument is between our experience, what the world believes, and what we are convinced is the Truth.

It should be understood that we can demonstrate in spite of our own selves, in spite of all weakness, in spite of every fear, in spite of all that is in us, because such is the power of the Truth. If we waited to be good before demonstrating, the wheel might turn a million times; but law is neither good nor bad; law is and responds.

The possibility of demonstrating does not depend upon environment, conditions, location, personality or opportunity. It depends upon ourselves and upon nothing else. The Universe will never deny man anything, unless we conceive that it is possible for man to think of something that it is impossible for the universe to produce. Every one who asks receives, according to his belief.

KARMIC LAW

Annie Besant said of Karma, "It is the law that binds the ignorant but frees the wise." That which is called Karma in the Orient, we call cause and effect. The subjective state of consciousness is our Karma; this is the result of the thinking that has gone before, and of the race-suggestion operating through us. Karma is not fate; it is mental law; and it can be changed by right thinking and right action. Karma is not Kismet.

THOUGHT FORCE

Thought force is the movement of consciousness which sets law in operation. The movement of consciousness upon itself creates a motion or vibration in Intelligence and upon Substance, the force of which is equal to the reality of the thought set in motion. For everything that happens in the objective world, there must be something in the subjective world to perfectly balance it. Just suppose for a moment that the Universe is nothing but water, permeated by an Infinite Intelligence. Imagine that every time this Intelligence moves or thinks an icicle is formed in the water, exactly corresponding to the thought. We might have countless numbers of icicles of different forms, colors and sizes; but these icicles would still be water. If we could heat the whole mass, it would melt, and all the forms would again become fluent; nothing would have changed but form. This is all there is to matter; it is Spirit in Form; and as such is perfectly good; to deny matter is poor logic.

First is Intelligence; then the Word, the vision, the image, the concept; then the movement to the thing. Remember, thought is an actual working power; otherwise there would be nothing with which the Universe could be run.

CHOOSING THOUGHT

We have a right to choose what we shall induce in Mind. The way that our thoughts are to become manifested we cannot always see; but we should not be disturbed if we do not see the way, because effect is potential in cause; "I am Alpha and Omega." 50 and all that comes between cause and effect. Cause and effect are really One, and if we have a given cause set in motion the effect will have to equal this cause. One is the inside and the other the outside of a concept or idea.

A practitioner's work begins and ends within himself. If, in doing mental work, the thought should come that the thing cannot be done, you must treat this thought as having no power, but only as an impersonal suggestion trying to gain entrance to your mentality. Realize that there is nothing in you that can hinder you from demonstrating the Truth.

If one says to himself, "I am filled with life, health, strength and vigor," and then goes down the street saying, "I see a poor blind beggar, a criminal and a sick person," he is still treating himself just as much as when he affirmed that he was perfect. We are only as perfect as we perceive others to be. This does not mean that we shut our eyes to those who are in trouble; for we may have sympathy with the one having trouble without having sympathy with his trouble. We must have sympathy with all, for, as one of the great prophets of the new age said, "The Divinity of Christ was made manifest through the Humanity of Jesus."

A certain, specific, intelligent form, or idea in Mind, will produce a certain, specific, concrete manifestation in matter, equal to itself. There is one Infinite Principle, One Infinite Thought-Stuff, One Infinite Creative Power and countless numbers of forms, which appear and disappear as the definite, specific, concrete thought behind them changes.

A practitioner is one who changes the false thought and builds on the Principle of Truth, which executes and manifests the truth that the practitioner embodies. He can demonstrate to the limit of his mental ability and his spiritual capacity to conceive of the Truth.

If one wishes to demonstrate prosperity he must first have a consciousness of prosperity; if he wishes health he must embody the idea of health. A consciousness of health, happiness and prosperity can be induced within through right mental and spiritual practice. By consciousness is meant the inner embodiment of an idea; the subjective image of the idea; the mental and spiritual equivalent of the idea.

INDUCING THOUGHT

While a certain consciousness may be mechanically induced, of course, the more spontaneity put into the mechanical word, the more power the word must have. Since we all must begin right where we are, most of us will be compelled to begin with a mechanical process. This is more than faith, for it is a sure knowledge that we are dealing with Law.

Principle is Changeless Reality. That which we call personality is the instrument through which Principle operates, but It can operate for the individual only by operating through him. It is never bound by the form that It takes, but is forever free. Principle fills all form, and not only fills all forms but surges around them, and is in and through them. Ice is water and water is ice; so God and man exist in an Eternal state of Unity.

When one realizes that he is depending upon Principle, he should educate himself to the point of realization of his ability to use It.

We should always be impersonal in mental work. We do not have to be impersonal in life, for we are brought to the point of personality in order that we might enjoy each other. But in mental work we are dealing with an impersonal Principle. It will operate for one just as quickly as for another, because It is Law. Dare to speak and to know that what you speak is the law unto the thing spoken. One, alone in consciousness with the Infinite, constitutes a complete majority.

Knowing this in your own thought, work in perfect peace and calm; always expect; have enthusiasm; and have a consciousness of love; that is, a radiant feeling flowing through the personality at all times. If one hasn't this he should treat himself until he does have it; for without it, he is diseased in mind. Treat until you feel an inner sense of Unity with the all Good. There is One Mind, and the moving impulse of this Mind is Love.

In choosing words in treatment, say anything that will induce the right mental attitude. Giving formulas is a mistake, for how can any one put a spontaneous thought into the mind of another? Any one can stand in front of a dead man and say, "Arise," but who is going to have the consciousness to make this happen?

PLACE NO LIMIT ON PRINCIPLE

Know your own mind; train yourself to think what you wish to think; be what you wish to be; feel what you wish to feel; and place no limit on Principle. The word which you speak would be just as powerful as the words which Jesus spoke, if you knew it; but know this within and not only without.

After all, all there is, is mental action and reaction. If you have reached the point where the inner consciousness produces all things, then your word is simply an announcement of reality. There will come a time when demonstration will no* longer be necessary.

Know that when you give a treatment, the act takes place in Infinite Mind. Infinite Mind is the Actor and you are the announcer. If you have a vague, subtle, unconscious fear, get still and think, "Who am I? What am I? Who is speaking? What is my life?" Think right back to Principle until your thought becomes perfectly clear again.

Such is the Power of right thinking that It cancels and erases everything unlike Itself. It answers every question, solves all problems, is the solution to every difficulty. It is like the sunlight of Eternal Truth, bursting through the clouds of obscurity and bathing all life in glory. It is the Absolute with which you are dealing and nothing less.

Note: Read carefully "Being and Becoming," F.L. Holmes; "Doré Lectures," T. Troward; "From Existence to Life," James Porter Mills; "Mind's Silent Partner," James Porter Mills; "History and Power of Mind," Richard Ingalese.

FOOTNOTES

35 John 5:26.
36 Rev. 21:1.
37 Rev. 5:23.
38 Isa. 45:22.
39 John 14:30.
40 Matt. 8:13.
41 Matt. 26:52.
42 Rev. 3:6.
43 Matt. 8:13.
44 Luke 21:33.
45 Isa. 55:11.
46 John 14:30.
47 John 8:32.
48 Heb. 3:19.
49 Ps. 78:41.
50 Rev. 1:8.

LESSON TWO: RECAPITULATION

Man reenacts the Divine Nature on all three planes; he is self-knowing in his conscious mind, creative through his subconscious mind, and has a body. He reënacts the Trinity of Being.

Man is in perfect unity with the Whole. His conscious mind is his understanding of God; his subjective mind is the use that he makes of the Universal Creative Medium; and his body is one with the Body of God.

There is but One Mind in the Universe, and man uses It. Man is an identity in the Universe; he is a center of God-Consciousness. At first he is ignorant of this and misuses his power, consequently bringing upon himself misfortune and sickness.

Man's thought operates through the medium of Universal Creative Mind. As he thinks within himself, he thinks upon Creative Mind and sets Law in motion. Since there is but One Mind a person may think for himself, or for some one else, and cause the Law to operate as he directs.

The use of Creative Mind is like the use of the creative soil. Man never creates; he simply uses a Creative Law.

Objective, conscious and self-knowing mind, all have the same meaning; they mean that part of man which knows that it exists.

Subjective, subconscious, unconscious, soul and consciousness have the same meaning; they mean the inner creative medium.

Body, effect and outward conditions all respond to the inner thought.

The Spirit of man, which is his self-knowingness, is the only part of him which has volition or self-choice; all else is automatic law.

Man's conscious thought, acting through law, may change any condition in his experience, provided he can clearly conceive of that condition as being changed. There is no limit to the Law. The limit is not in the Law but in man's ability to embody the Truth and constructively use the Law.

Remember, there is but One Mind and One Law which all people use, consciously or unconsciously, constructively or destructively; One Spirit, One Mind, One Law, One Substance, but many forms. There is only One Ultimate Reality, but within this One there are many experiences. Man is within the One and draws from It any and all experiences in which he believes.

As man thinks he subjectifies thought and sets Law in motion through the Medium of the Universal Mind. This Law works automatically until It is consciously changed.

Man uses a Power which is Infinite as compared with the power of his conscious thought.

Divine Principle means Universal Subjective Law; It is the Medium of all thought and action.

Freedom and bondage, sickness and health, poverty and riches, heaven and hell, good and bad, big and little, happiness and misery, peace and confusion, faith and fear and all conditions that appear as opposites, are not really opposing powers, but are the way that the One Power is used.

Man has within himself the key to every situation, but he must come to realize his relation to the Whole. That relationship is one of Perfect Unity.

LESSON THREE: INTRODUCTION

HEALING

Mental healing means mind healing. The possibility of healing physical diseases through the power of right thinking rests entirely on the theory that we are surrounded by an Infinite Mind which reacts to our thought.

That people have been healed through prayer and by faith in all ages, there is no question. But we live in a Universe of Law and Order, and at no time can that Law or Order be broken; therefore, if people have been healed through prayer and faith, it is because they have somewhere contacted a Law which really exists. To suppose that God would heal one man any more readily than another, would be to suppose that God is human and subject to the changing emotions that we ascribe to the human mind. To believe that the Divine Power would operate for one man simply because he asked It to, but would not operate for all, would be to believe in a God more human than man himself. It is very evident, however, that many times people have been healed through prayer; and either God has especially answered them, while He left others to suffer, or else by the act of prayer they have complied with some law. Again, many people have prayed and their prayers have not been answered; yet they have prayed to the best of their ability. Why have some been heard and others not heard? The only possible answer is that some reached a place in their mentality where they believed, while others fell short of this mental attitude. After all, prayer is a certain mental attitude, a certain way of thinking, a certain way of believing. All prayer is mental; some prayers reach a state of belief, while others fall short of that state. This leads us to suppose that the answer to prayer is in the prayer when it is prayed. True prayer stimulates a belief in Good which nothing else can, and often causes the one who prays to rise to a point in mentality where the healing work may be done according to the Law of the Universe, which is a Law of Mind.

We have no objection to any form of healing. Anything that will help to overcome suffering must be good, whether it takes the form of a pill or of a prayer. We do not oppose doctors nor medical practitioners, but gratefully acknowledge the wonderful work that they have done and are doing. We hold no controversy with any one on the subject of healing. We are glad when any one is healed, or helped, by any method. We believe in any and all methods, and know that each has its place in the whole. We know that man's life is a drama which takes place on three planes;—the physical, the mental and the spiritual. We know that each needs to be taken into account. We believe in proper food, proper exercise, proper clothing, proper sanitation and in everything that is real and sensible. We include all and exclude none.

But, while we do not hold arguments with any one, neither will we allow any one to hold controversies with us. We know that man's life, in reality, is spiritual and mental; and that until the thought is healed, no form of cure will be permanent. We will gladly coöperate with any and all; but we will not accept the judgment of any and all. We know that there is a Law higher than the physical, and we seek to use It. We, perhaps, shall not always succeed, but we shall not become discouraged or confused over the issue, but will continue until we arrive.

We hold no arguments over any form of theology. We believe in any and every church and in all forms of worship. Above all, we certainly believe in God. But we will not allow any one to tell us how to worship God, nor compel us to worship in any way other than the way we choose.

We reject the theory that the Truth has been once and for all time given and that It cannot be added to nor taken from. We know this to be true about the Truth; but we also know that no one, so far, has arrived at a complete understanding of Truth. We expect more light all along the line, and we repudiate any belief that says that all truth has been given.

We know that the authority of man is, in most cases, an assumption and not a reality, and we refuse to be hypnotized into believing in any man-made mandate.

WHAT WE UNDERSTAND ABOUT HEALING

We understand that health is a mental and not a physical state. We seek to heal men's mentalities, knowing that to the degree in which we are successful we shall also be healing their bodies. We know that to the degree in which we are able to see a perfect man he will appear. We feel that man is really perfect, no matter how he appears; and we seek to uncover that perfection which is within every man's life, for this is healing.

We realize that mental healing must also be spiritual healing, for the two cannot be divorced. We know that a belief in duality has made man sick and that the understanding of Unity alone will heal him. We seek to realize that Unity with God in all our healing work. Every treatment must carry with it a realization of God if it is to be a good treatment.

We are not superstitious about this, but understand that it is necessary since all Life is One. God stands to us for the One Life in which we all live.

THOUGHTS ARE THINGS

We know that thoughts are things. We know that thought is intelligent and has power within itself to objectify itself. We know that belief makes thought very powerful. We know that our thought lays hold of Causation and manipulates real Substance. We know that the word of man is the law of his life, under the One Great Law of all Life. We know that thoughts of sickness make man sick, and that thoughts of health and perfection will heal him. We know that a realization of the Presence of God is the most powerful healing agency known to the mind of man. We do not argue over the issue, nor seek to convince any one of its merits. We have passed the stage of doubt and uncertainty; for we *know*. We also know that we can heal only to the degree that we can think from the higher motive; and we know that we should be constantly on the alert, seeking to embody higher thoughts. Meanwhile, we will use the best thought that we have and will expect to heal and help all who ask our aid.

Thought is the conscious activity of the one thinking, and works as he directs; it works through Law, but that Law is consciously set in motion. We know that Law will operate for us to the fullest extent of our belief in, and understanding of, it.

We realize that since our understanding is not yet complete, it is legitimate to use any and all methods that will help humanity; but we do look forward to the day when Truth alone will answer every need. That day will come to the degree that we know it is already here. The mental healer will do all of his work in Mind and will give his whole time and attention to correct knowing; but he will leave his patient free to use any method that will help him. In this way he will get the best results, for everything is good so far as it goes; but a consciousness of Truth alone can really and permanently heal.

LESSON THREE: METAPHYSICAL MEANING OF WORDS USED IN CHART NO. III

UNIVERSAL SPIRIT.—Means the universe of conscious mind and self-determination. The Universal Subjectivity means the Creative Medium of the Spirit, or the Subjective law of the Universe. Particularization means the world of matter and forms. Read again the explanation to Chart Number One. The descent of Spirit means the passing of Spirit into form;—the particularization of Spirit into many things. The point, drawn from the top of the chart to the bottom section, symbolizes the Unity of all Life. Spirit passes through Law into Form. Multiplicity comes from Unity, but never contradicts Oneness. The many are within the One.

Man's life partakes of the Divine Nature, and this chart may be used in the Individual or the Universal sense. Our conscious mind is some part of the One Conscious Mind of the Whole. The Complete Nature of God is reflected in man, and he uses the same law that God uses; for there is but One Law, as there is but One Spirit. Both God and man use the same Creative Medium or the Universal Subjectivity. It is the law of all thought and all action. Things come from One Source through One Common Law and One Common Creative Medium. We think of our lives as One with the Whole on all three planes of expression. We are one with the Conscious Mind, one with the Creative Law, and in our bodies we are one with all matter.

No matter what we are treating or for what purpose, the Medium of all thought is the Universal Law. It particularizes Itself through the power of the word that is spoken into It. The word alone is conscious. The Law is Automatic and the form is without self-determination.

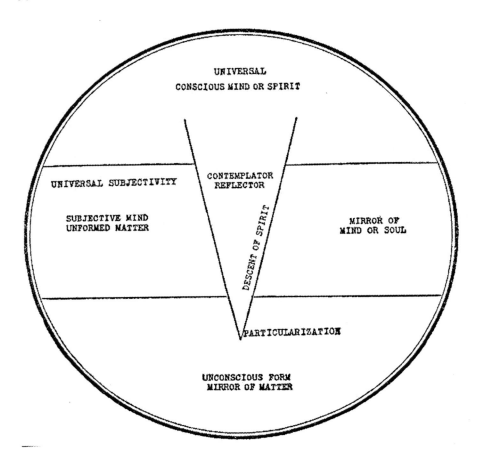

Lesson Three: Metaphysical Chart No. III.

The upper section of this chart shows how the conscious mind, or spirit of man, reflects or contemplates itself, through the medium of soul or subjectivity, into form or matter. The middle section represents the World-Soul or Subjectivity; the Mirror of Mind and unformed matter; the Servant of the Spirit; the lowest section shows the result of self-contemplation as it takes form in the world of matter. Read and carefully study the metaphysical meanings of the words used in the Individual Chart.

CONSCIOUS MIND OR SPIRIT.—Means the Self-Knowing Mind of the Universe. Contemplator, or Reflector, means the conscious thought of the Conscious Mind.

SUBJECTIVE MIND AND UNFORMED MATTER.—Means the substance and the soul of the universe.

MIRROR OF MIND, OR SOUL.—Means that the Subjective side of life acts like a mirror; that is, It reflects the forms of thought that are given It.

UNCONSCIOUS FORM OR MIRROR OF MATTER.—Means that the material world reflects the forms of thought which the Soul holds before it.

This depicts the Creative process and sequence:—first in the chain of Causation is the Word, and this Word is conscious of Itself; next comes the action of Law, reflecting the Word. (This Law is subjective and obeys the Word, reflecting It into form or matter; matter, being at first unformed, or a Universal unformed stuff.) It then takes form, through the power of the word acting upon It, on the subjective side of life.

Soul and Substance are both subjective to the Spirit; and form, or matter in form, has no volition.

In the Trinity of Unity, one attribute alone is really self-conscious, namely, the Spirit, or the Word.

This chart may be used in either the individual or the universal sense, for the individual reënacts the Universal on all three planes.

The manifest Universe is the result of the self-contemplation of Spirit or God. This self-contemplation, through law, reflects its images into the world of form or manifestation.

Man's world of affairs and his body are the result of his inner self-knowingness. He is the result of his self-contemplation.

LESSON THREE: MENTAL HEALING

Whatever exists at all must be the result of a definite image of thought held in the Mind of God or the Absolute, Who is the cause of all. Whether we think of man as a projection of God, an emanation of God, a manifestation or a reflection of God, we must realize that God, or the First Cause, holds man in His Consciousness as a Perfect Being, since the Perfect Mind could not conceive of an imperfect idea. If, on the other hand, we think of man as a part of God, which some schools of thought teach, we should then have to realize that man, as a part of the Divine Being, must inherently be perfect. This is a conclusion which is unavoidable. But man does not appear to be perfect; he certainly appears to have many experiences which are far from ideal. There can be no question but the human man suffers, is sick and has pain and eventually dies. To doubt this would be to doubt the evidence of the only quality we possess whereby we may consider ourselves conscious beings at all. We must, then, reconcile our conclusion of perfection with an experience which is apparently not perfect.

INDIVIDUALITY

While man must be, and is, a Divine Image or a Perfect Idea, yet he suffers and is sick. The answer to this is the same answer which can be given, philosophically, to the whole problem of evil—that man is an individual and does with himself what he wills. The Scriptures say, "God hath made man upright; but they have sought out many inventions." 51 Individuality cannot be automatically produced but must be spontaneous. It could not be real individuality unless it had the ability to think as it chose; and it could not be individuality unless its ability to think as it chose were backed by a power to produce this choice; because, if nothing ever happened as the result of man's choice, he would live in a dream world, and his dreams would never come to objectification. This would be a world of illusion. But man has the ability to choose and is unified with a Law which automatically produces his choice; whereas he does not have the ability to destroy the idea of himself, he does have the ability to deface it, to make it appear discordant; but he cannot destroy the Divine Image.

We live in a Universe of Love as well as in a Universe of Law. One is the complement of the other—the Universe of Love pulsating with feeling, with emotion; and the Universe of Law, the Executor of all feeling and all emotion.

In taking up this lesson on healing, then, let us remember that back of the man which we see is the Divine Image. There is a Perfect Concept, held in the Mind of the Universe as an already accomplished fact, but man is subject to the law of his own individuality.

Let us turn to the Law, and find what It says, in Chart No. III, viz., that man is conscious mind or spirit; this stands for his objective faculty. The objective mind of man is his recognition of life in a conscious state; it is the only attribute of man that is volitional, or self-choosing; consequently, it is the spiritual man. The conscious mind of man is the contemplator, the reflector. The Universe is the result of the Contemplation of the Divine Mind, or the Holy Spirit, which is God. God creates by contemplating His own *I-am-ness*; and this contemplation, through law, becomes the objectification of the Self-Realization of the Infinite Mind.

MAN REËNACTS GOD

The Divine nature is reënacted in man; he is conscious mind and spirit; and, as he contemplates, he reflects his thought into the Universal Subjectivity; it is received and acted upon.

As Mind, or Soul, accepts these images of thought, It operates upon unformed substance and causes it to take definite form as body, which is unconscious form. It becomes definite form, but the form itself is unconscious, because it is made of immaterial substance. Body of itself, without Mind, has no consciousness nor volition. Devoid of mentality, the body neither thinks, sees, hears, feels, touches nor tastes. Take the mentality away from the body and it becomes a corpse. Having no conscious intelligence, it at once begins to disintegrate and to resolve again into the Universal Substance, or unformed matter, from which it came.

Conscious thought or contemplation is a reflector, reflecting through mentality into matter, the forms which consciousness entertains. Although man is inherently a perfect idea, his individuality covers this idea with the forms of thought which he images. Of course, these forms of thought may, or may not, be conscious. Man comes into this life subjective to the race consciousness and with a belief in his own environment; and as he unfolds his own personality he begins to create new subjective thought. He thinks and observes, draws certain conclusions and deductions, and incorporates them within his mentality, until, at last, they also become a part of the relative cause of his objective existence.

Healing is accomplished by uncovering, neutralizing and erasing false images of thought, and letting the perfect idea, or ideal, reflect itself through subjective mind into the body.

When one realizes that everything is Mind and that nothing moves but Mind, and that the only instrument of Mind is thought (which is contemplation in some form or other), he will see that nothing can permanently heal but right thinking. It is the only permanent form of healing that is known, i.e., mental and spiritual healing.

NOT LIMITED BY PRINCIPLE

Realizing that conscious thought operates through a Power which is Infinite, we see that there can be no limit to the power to heal, other than the limit of our ability to conceive that Power as healing. We are limited, not by Principle, but by our ability to conceive perfection. Our thought can bring out a condition as perfect as we can conceive; therefore, the man whose thought is the most God-like will be the best healer. That is why we cannot divorce true mental healing from true spiritual work. The man whose thought is the most God-like, i.e., the truest, the highest, the most noble, the most complete, the most peaceful, will be the best healer because his thought reflects a greater perfection. When thought reaches a higher degree of perfection, it will bring out a still greater development, i.e., as the race consciousness unfolds and evolves.

MENTAL TREATMENT IS REAL

Never forget that the Conscious Mind is the only Actor in the Universe and in man; that the unconscious or subjective mind is compelled, by reason of its nature, to accept; and that it can never reject; that the body is an effect, with no intelligence of its own. We can now see that a mental treatment is a real, tangible, specific operation, working in perfect accord with scientific Law.

When a practitioner treats any one, he does not just hope that his patient will get well; he does not ask that he may be healed; he does not simply desire that he may be healed; he is busy doing a definite piece of mental work, bringing out in his own consciousness (in his own self-contemplative, conscious mind) an understanding that the patient is healed and is perfect.

Treatment is the act, the art and the science of inducing thought within the mentality of the one treating, which thought shall perceive that the body of the patient is a Divine, Spiritual and Perfect Idea. Treatment does not necessarily treat every organ of the body specifically, but it does declare the body to be harmonious and that every specific idea within it is harmonious. It then pays especial attention to what appears to be the physical disorder.

As the result of this treatment which the practitioner gives, Subjective Mind (which is Universal and Omnipresent) accepts the images of his thinking and reflects them in the direction that he specifies.

He is not trying to send out a thought, hold a thought, or suggest a thought. Be sure that you differentiate between suggestion (which is all right, so far as it goes, but is limited) and real metaphysical healing. In metaphysical healing we are conscious that we are dealing with a Universal Principle, or Law, which takes the impress of our thought and acts upon it. Nothing can stop It. Some day we shall know that not even the thought of the patient can stop It, and then that argument will be ended! We are dealing with Something that cannot and does not answer back nor argue. We are directing It for definite purposes, telling It to do certain things which It does. This is what happens when we give a treatment.

Since the Law is Infinite, there is no incurable disease, as opposed to a curable one. The Law knows nothing about disease. It only acts. The practitioner says: "My word is the presence, power and activity of the Truth which is within me, which is Almighty, which is God. There is none other." This word then is the law of the thing whereunto it is spoken and has within itself the ability, the power, and the intelligence to execute itself through the great Law of all Life. This word, being the spontaneous recognition of Living Spirit—Infinite, Ever-Present, and Active—is now completely manifested in and through this person, or thing, about which the practitioner is thinking.

MAN COMES THROUGH SUBJECTIVITY

When man is born, he is born from pure subjectivity into objectivity. He is born from a subjective state of consciousness into an objective state, and he gradually grows into intelligent, self-conscious, objective understanding.

When a baby is born into this world, it is purely subjective; it does not know enough to feed itself; it has no objective faculties, no judgment, no thought processes. But the minute it is born it begins to develop an objectivity through observation; however, it takes a baby longer than it does any other animal, as it is more helpless. A child does not always gain its objective faculties quickly—sometimes it never does during this lifetime. Irresponsible people never become completely objectified on this plane; they are still instinctively subjective.

BORN PERFECT

Since babies are born from subjectivity, they are born, generally speaking, from a perfect condition. You will find that practically everything, when it comes into the world, is perfect; it then takes on objectivity; but it brings with it, subjectively, certain tendencies. Very seldom does it bring disease. Very few diseases are inherited, in spite of all the claims that people make that they inherit heart trouble, tuberculosis, etc. They do not! What they do, however, is to inherit a subjective receptivity toward, and a belief in, those things.

At first, children are happy, free, spontaneous. That is why we like them; they live instinctively. As they grow older and their emotions become more complex and they hear people talk about death, trouble, divorce, love and marriage, and everything else that is good, bad or indifferent, they begin to react to these emotions subjectively.

Everything that opposes harmony and Spontaneous Unity will prove disastrous to the child's health, sooner or later. The inherited part is simply an inherited subjective tendency.

RACE-SUGGESTION

Another prolific source of disease is race-suggestion. *Race-suggestion means the accumulated subjective tendencies of the human race*; these tendencies are operative through any person who is receptive to them.

These, then, are the sources from which most diseases come—conscious observations, suppressed emotions, subjective inherited tendencies, and, perhaps three-fourths of them, from race-suggestion.

DISEASE IS IMPERSONAL

Disease is an impersonal thought force operating through people, which does not belong to them at all. Recognize that it is neither person, place, nor thing; that there is no law to support it; that it is a coward, fleeing before the Truth; that there is nothing but the Truth. There is no limitation imposed upon man anywhere. You must know that the Power you are using is definite, scientific, dynamic, Spiritual, Absolute and complete, and that It will work. Let no fear come into your thought.

Remember that nothing can come through consciousness into objectivity but such thoughts as you claim. The person who has clearly and subjectively realized the Unity of Mind, the Unity of Good, the Presence of God, the Absoluteness of his own Being, the totality of things existing at the point of his own personality, is immune from mental suggestion. He can surround himself with an armor of protection so that false suggestion cannot enter.

As a matter of fact, practically all the world is hypnotized through race concept, and what we need to do is to de-hypnotize it.

HOW TO HEAL

Disease is mentally contagious through suggestion; so we must surround our patients with an aura, or atmosphere, of protection. This is nothing less than the realization of the presence and the power of God, or Spirit, as their Life, as the only Life there Is, as Complete and Perfect in them.

First recognize your own perfection; then build up the same recognition for your patient; then directly attack the thought that binds him, recognizing that your word destroys it, stating that it does, taking into account and specifically mentioning everything that needs to be changed, every so-called broken law or false thought. Then finish your treatment with a great realization of peace, sitting there a few moments in silent recognition that it is done, complete and perfect.

The work must not be thought of as hard; and when we know that there is but One Mind, we shall realize that it could not be hard. Mental treatment is a direct statement in Mind of what we wish to have done and a complete realization that it is done.

MIND IS THE ACTOR

We recognize that everything is in Mind and that nothing moves but Mind; that Intelligence is back of everything, acting through a thought force which is concrete, definite and real. The reason people do not realize that mental healing is possible is that they do not understand the meaning of Causation; they do not realize that Intelligence is back of all things; that there is but One Fundamental Intelligence in the Universe, One Common Mind or One Mind, Common to all people. That which we appear to be is simply the point where this Mind manifests through us. (Man is an Individualized Center of God-Consciousness. Remember, all Law is Mind in Action.)

Every disease that we have must come through Mind in order to operate through us. There is but One Subjective Mind in the Universe. Upon this understanding alone is mental treatment possible (whether it be present or absent); if there were more than One, it would be impossible, for then there would be no Common Medium through which to work, think or act.

There is but One, and we are always thinking into It; so whether a patient is present or absent makes no difference. The only advantage in having him present is that you may talk to him and teach him, and, by analyzing his thought, remove any mental complex or conflict.

The question is often asked: "Is this Subjective Mind, or Law, all that there is to the Divine Nature?" No, of course not. There is the Spirit and the Soul of the Universe, a dual aspect of that which is One; but when you are practicing mental healing, you are dealing with Law, just as definitely as a physicist deals with law.

DISEASE IS NOT ALWAYS DUE TO CONSCIOUS THOUGHT

Any disease, in order to operate through the body, must first be a mental picture in the inner mentality; it must first be subjective, if it is to become objectified. "Disease is an image of thought held in Mind until it appears in the body." This is all there is to it. While every disease is an effect and must first have a subjective cause, the subjective cause, nine times out of ten, is not conscious in the thought of the person who has it; but is, perhaps, largely the result of certain combinations of thinking, which, gathering together around and through the individual who thought and received them, becomes operative through him. Certain combinations of thought, coalescing, produce a definite manifestation.

So, while it is true that every disease has a direct prototype in subjective mind, it is also true that the individual who suffers from the disease, nine times out of ten, never thought he was going to have that particular kind of trouble.

WE DEAL WITH IDEAS

You are dealing with ideas only. Let the physicians deal with bodies, if necessary. There is nothing wrong with medicine or manipulation, provided it relieves suffering, but lest the suffering come again, the mental cause must be removed. Never say to patients: "Don't take medicine, because if you do, the treatments will do you no good"; for this is untrue. Say, instead, "If you feel like taking medicine or going to the doctor, do so." If you follow this method, the time will generally come when your patient will realize that he no longer needs the medicine; he will have unfolded out of the disease, rather than have broken away from it.

Actually speaking, no one needs to be healed; that is, health is an omnipresent reality, and when the obstructions that hinder healing are removed, it will be found that health was there all the time. So, in your work, do not feel that you must heal any one. In fact, assume no responsibility for any one's recovery.

HAVE NO DOUBTS

Suppose, when you treat a patient, you begin to feel a terrible sense of responsibility—what should you do? You should begin at once to treat yourself against that thought, for as long as you have it there is a barrier to healing. Why? Because when you sift that sense of responsibility down to its last analysis, it is a belief that you cannot heal. Do not give in to that belief, because it is nothing but a thought which says that you cannot heal. Nothing but a thought is saying, or could be saying, it. A chair could not say it, and since it is only a thought that says it, it is only a thought that can unsay it. Declare: "My word has the power to heal," and you will find that doubt has gone.

THINKING IN TREATMENT

When you are giving a treatment, you are thinking; you are meeting, opposing, neutralizing, erasing and obliterating all suppression, fear, doubt, failure, morbid emotion and sense of loss—whatever the trouble may be.

Every time your thought hits fairly and squarely, it erases just as definitely as one would erase a chalk line. Such is the mystery of appearance and disappearance.

Why doesn't God heal us? Because we are independent. We have made ourselves sick and we must heal ourselves. In the great world war ten or fifteen million people suffered agony, pain, sorrow and grief—it staggers the imagination to conceive of it. But water was just as wet and the birds sang just as sweetly through it all. Nothing happened, except in man's thought and act; he fought until he tired of fighting; then he stopped. We will be sick until we tire of it; then we will inquire into the cause, eliminate it and be healed.

DO NOT TRY TO GO BEYOND YOUR UNDERSTANDING

Our understanding is not sufficient to enable us to set bones, and, since we cannot walk on the water, we take a boat. We can go only as far as we know. Principle is Infinite, but we can demonstrate only at the level of our own concept.

If a man struggles against a habit, he is building up a mental resistance, but if he does not resist it while you treat him, he will soon find himself liberated.

People say: "I can't take off my glasses." Then wear them; but begin to make the declaration that there is One Perfect Vision seeing through you. This is the Truth. When this statement shall have become a subjective realization, you will be healed and will no longer need glasses.

If a plaster will relieve, use it. If a pill does any good, take it; but gradually lead thought from where it is into the higher realms of consciousness where neither plasters nor pills are needed.

WHAT A PRACTITIONER MUST KNOW

A practitioner knows that disease is mental. He not only knows this; he knows that disease is simply an impersonal thought force, operating through whatever channel it may find. He knows that it is a direct thought force; that there is nothing but Mind in the Universe; nothing to move but Intelligence. He is not dealing with a physical body, nor trying to heal a physical condition.

Right here, let me mention that many people think they must put their hands on their patients to heal them—that there is a certain magnetism, potent in healing. This has nothing to do with the power of which we are talking. Magnetic healing is the transmission of vital energy from one body to another and soon exhausts itself.

We treat man, not as a patient, not as a physical body, not as a diseased condition; neither do we treat the disease as belonging to him, the reason being that if we do, we will fasten the disease to him. We must not think of the disease as being connected with him or as a part of him. The practitioner realizes that man is born of Spirit and not of matter. Spirit is Changeless, Perfect, Complete, and in every respect Pure, Undefiled and Uncontaminated. He realizes this until he sees his patient as a living embodiment of Perfection.

A practitioner, then, is one who, recognizing that there is nothing but Mind to move, definitely, specifically, concretely and consciously speaks from his objective mind into subjectivity and gives direction to Law, which is the Actor.

HEALING IS CLEAR THINKING

Healing is the result of clear thinking and logical reasoning, which presents itself to consciousness and is acted upon by it. It is a systematic process of reasoning which unearths the mental cause or idea underlying disease, and presents the Truth about man's Being, thereby healing him.

For instance, say to yourself: "God is All there is. There is only One Life." When you are treating, if there is any little point that is not clear, stop at once and go back to the last analysis of Ultimate Reality and Absoluteness and build your whole argument upon It, in order to get a clear consciousness.

Repeat: "God is All. There is only One Power, Intelligence and Consciousness in the Universe, only One Presence. Now, that One Presence cannot change. There is nothing for It to change into but Itself. It is Changeless and It is My Life now. It is in me now." Claim that no form of race-suggestion, belief in limitation, subjective idea of limitation, thought of Karma, fatalism, theology or hell, horoscope, or any such beliefs have power. Accept none of them. If you have ever believed in them; if you have ever believed that the stars govern you, or that your environment governs you, or that your opportunities govern you, if you have ever been led to believe by any one that any of these things govern you, recognize that it is a hypnotic condition into which you have fallen, and deny every one of them, until there is no longer anything in you that believes in them.

This is the way to get your consciousness clear. You see what it does; it induces a clear concept of Reality which must reproduce Itself. This process of clear thinking, if carried out every day, would heal any disease, because it would bring a complete recognition of Life.

ONLY ONE LAW

The thing that makes you sick can heal you. You do not need to look for a law of health as opposed to a law of disease; for there is only One Law. This will give a great sense of relief, since it means that there is no power to oppose a correct mental treatment.

People often say to a practitioner: "I want you to hold a strong thought for me." This is a misconception; for there are no strong and weak thoughts in this sense. The most powerful thought is the one that carries the greatest conviction with it. We do not hold thoughts; we simply think them and let Mind operate upon them.

People often say: "It must be a drain to treat so many people; I should think that your will power would become exhausted." This also is a misconception; for will power has nothing whatever to do with real mental healing; its use would imply that the practitioner exercises a personal thought force over his patient. This is false suggestion, which is always some form of hypnotism.

NO SENSATION IN TREATMENTS

It is sometimes thought that in giving or receiving a treatment one must experience some physical sensation. A patient sometimes says, after having received a treatment: "I felt nothing during the treatment." It is not necessary that the patient should feel anything during the treatment, neither is it necessary that the practitioner should feel anything, other than the truth about the words that he speaks.

When we plant a seed in the ground, we do not have a great sensation, and it is not probable that the soil has any sensation. But the seed, planted in the creative soil, will, nevertheless, produce a plant. "What is true on one plane is true on all." Know that you are doing things just as definitely as the gardener. It is the person who knows what he is doing who gets results.

HOW TO REMOVE DOUBT

All thoughts of doubt concerning one's ability to heal come from the belief that it is the personality which does the healing, and not the Law. Never say: "I am not good enough to heal," or "I do not know enough to heal," or "I haven't understanding enough to heal." Know that you are dealing with Law and that It is the Actor. Recognize all such arguments as some form of suggestion and refuse to let them operate through you. You can heal; but you must know that you can.

The day will come when the entire world will believe the Truth, because of the great neutralizing power which It is exercising upon the race consciousness.

THE TRUTH DEMONSTRATES ITSELF

The reason people do not get better results is that they do not understand that principle works independently; the Truth demonstrates Itself. At the root of every one's personality there is One Common Mind. There is but One Subjectivity in the Universe, and all use It. Think of yourself as being in Mind as a sponge is in the water; you are in It and It is in you.

DISEASE IS MENTAL

Every disease that comes up through subjectivity, or appears in the body, must come up through Mind. Bodies, of themselves, do not get sick. For instance, when the Life Principle deserts the body, it is what we call a corpse—a lifeless and inanimate thing; it no longer becomes sick; we understand that it could not get sick unless there were intelligence there to cognize the trouble.

Since the body, of itself, cannot become ill, or hurt, or contract disease, unless there is intelligence there to recognize and feel it, disease is primarily a mental thing. Without mentality it is not; and yet with mentality it appears to be.

For instance, a contagious disease is physically contagious between two living people; but it is not contagious between two dead people. There must be intelligence, even in a contagious disease, for the body to contract it. The dead body cannot catch it from the living because the intelligence has departed.

THE MEDIUM OF HEALING

The thing to remember always is, that there is just One Subjective Mind in the Universe. This is a point that people often do not realize, and because they do not, they cannot see how a person may be treated without touching him; or that a person can be healed at a distance through absent treatment.

If there is but One Subjective Mind in the Universe (and we all remember the meaning of Subjective Mind; It is Deductive, Receptive, Plastic, Neutral, Impersonal and Creative; It is the Stuff from which all things are formed)—you can impress upon It a certain image of thought, or a certain process of realization, and you will get a result; for it is the Actor.

DEPEND ON PRINCIPLE

Through the proper use of this great Subjective Law you can impress upon It a definite idea; and if you, yourself, do not withdraw that idea, or neutralize it by an opposite one, the law will bring it into manifestation.

What we need, then, is to learn the law governing this Principle. When you give a treatment, you are definitely setting in motion a Universal law which must not only accept what you say, but the way in which you say it. If your treatment is given with a sense of struggle, it will manifest that way; if it is given with a sense of peace, then it will manifest in that manner.

Remember that you need assume no personal responsibility for the recovery of your patient. All that you have to do is to make certain statements which Mind is going to carry into effect through him.

One who understands the use of Divine Principle never tries to suggest, hypnotize nor personally influence any one; he is always impersonal in his work; he is stating in Mind directly what he wishes to have done.

When you have occasion to treat yourself, call your own name and then proceed with the treatment, as though you were treating some one else.

Disease will be healed, provided you get at its cause and remove it, and provided the one for whom you are working is willing to surrender that cause. You cannot heal any one of his trouble if it is the result of some mental attitude which he will not surrender. In this case, find out what the mental attitude is and remove it. It is a practitioner's duty to uncover false ideas of Life and replace them with the Truth. If this can be done before the disease destroys the body, a healing will always follow.

DEFINITE WORK IN HEALING

Principle is the Power that made everything; it is Absolute; It will not and cannot be denied. The only thing that can deny God is yourself.

Do not think of disease as an entity, but as an impersonal thought-force. In healing, you are separating the false from the true; the work is definite and dynamic, and is consciously done with a clear purpose always in mind.

If your own thought is clear, and you are able to completely realize the presence of Spirit in your patient, all the power on earth cannot hinder you from healing.

REPEATING TREATMENTS

Always come to a complete conclusion while giving a treatment; always feel that is it is done, complete and perfect. In the intervals between treatments, do not carry the thought of the patient around with you; to do so is to doubt, and this mental attitude must be completely overcome. Each treatment is a complete statement of the Reality of Being. The treatment should be repeated daily until a healing takes place. If it takes five minutes, five hours, five days or five years, the treatment must be kept up until a healing is accomplished. This is the only method that we know. It is not enough to say that everything is all right; this is true in principle, but in fact, it is only as true as we make it. Treat until you get results. A healing takes place when the patient is no longer sick, and until that time mental work must be done.

REMOVE THE COMPLEX

Suppose one is constantly saying: "Everything is all wrong in the world; people are wrong; things are wrong; conditions are wrong; every one is sick; every one is unhappy; nothing is worth while." You, as a practitioner, must remove this complex; for these inner emotions create outer conditions in and through the body and are what cause a great deal of the sickness in the world.

Treatment straightens out consciousness by clear thinking. When the inner consciousness agrees with the Truth, when there is no longer anything within which denies the outer word of Truth, then, and not until then, a demonstration takes place. Specifically go over the thoughts that are wrong and use the power of your word to heal them.

HEALING PAIN

Use the thought of peace and the realization of a Perfect Presence; know that in this Presence there is no tension, there is no struggle, there is no fear, there is no sense of conflict. Know this until there comes to your own consciousness a deep, calm sense of peace and ease, and until every thought of pain is eliminated.

Do the same in the case of fever; treat until it is gone; usually it will go like heat off a stove.

HEADACHE

Suppose that every little while you have a headache. A physician may say that it is caused by some nerve strain; a chiropractor may say that it is something out of joint; the osteopath may say that it is something else; and some other practitioner may say that it is something else; for each has found some twist in the body to fit his theory. All of these twists may be there; but the body could not twist unless you were there to twist it. The metaphysician goes to the twister and untwists his thought, thus freeing the twists in the body. We recognize all the good that doctors are doing, but we insist that the mentality must also be taken into account.

Back of nearly every disorder there is some complex, or mental knot, that needs to be untied; generally, some suppressed emotion which, perhaps, is centered around the affections —the likes and dislikes, the loves and passions, and everything that goes with them. All these knots must be untied and it is the business of the practitioner to untie them.

WHAT RIGHT THOUGHT DOES

Right thought, constantly poured into consciousness, will eventually purify it. Disease is like a bottle of impure water; healing might be likened to the process of dropping pure water into the bottle, a drop at a time, until the whole is clean and pure. Some one might ask why the bottle could not be turned upside down and at once drain out all the impurities. Sometimes this happens, but not often; meanwhile, a drop at a time will finally eliminate the impurities and produce a healing.

In treating, go beyond the disease and supply a spiritual consciousness; never leave a person without the Great Realization of Life and Love, of God and Perfection, of Truth and Wisdom, of Power and Reality. Sense the Divine Presence in and through the patient at all times.

HOW HABITS ARE HEALED

What is a habit? A habit is the form that desire takes; it is a desire for something that will give satisfaction. At the root of all habit is one basic thing, the desire to express life. There is an urge to express in all people, and this urge, operating through the channels of Creative Mind, looses energy into action and compels the individual to do something.

Back of all desire is the impulse of Spirit to express. In man, this impulse must express at the level of his consciousness:

"For each, for the joy of the working and each in his separate star, shall paint the thing as he sees It for the God of things as they are."

Some express constructively and some destructively.

Suppose a man who has the liquor habit comes to you to be healed. You would not pray that he be healed, for you would know that you are dealing with a man who has the desire to express life and who thinks that he must express it in terms of intoxication. He once thought this expressed reality to him; he now knows that it does not, but he has not the will power to stop; for the habit has appeared to take complete possession of him. (It is well to remember that unless we control thought, it will control us.)

In giving the treatment, first recognize who and what he is, saying something like this: "He is the full and complete expression of the Truth, and, as such, he is free from any sense of limitation. He is free from any delusion or fear of delusion. He knows that the Spirit of Truth within him is complete and always satisfied. That thing which calls itself the liquor habit has no power over him and cannot operate through him. By the power of this word, it is now completely destroyed and forever obliterated." Then see him free and satisfied. Wait until you, yourself, are sure of the statements made, realizing that the work is done. This is the treatment.

THE SEED OF THOUGHT

Whether we say our thought goes out, or whether we say it is operated upon by Principle, makes no difference; it is very evident that until a thought is created there is no operation. For instance, a person is sick and he remains sick until some one knows that he is well. It is very evident, then, that as the result of some one's thinking he is healed. We know that the thinking sets in motion some law. Whether the word used heals, or whether it simply sets the Law in motion, really makes no difference. The practitioner is in the same Mind in which his patient lives; consequently, since each is in One Mind, the patient is sick in the same Medium and, in a certain sense, in the same Mind in which the practitioner lives; and because this Mind is Indivisible, the practitioner can, in his own mentality, reach the thought which causes the patient to be sick. Whether we say he sends out a thought, or whether he simply thinks a thought, makes no difference. The simplest way is to say that the practitioner realizes within himself upon the One Mind, through the One Medium, in the One Law.

The practitioner realizes a certain truth for his patient—within himself. Therefore he sets the Law in motion for his patient. (The operation of this Law may be thought of as the same as that of the law whereby water reaches its own level by its own weight.) The practitioner knows within himself; and that self-knowingness rises into the consciousness of his patient. So we do not have to worry about sending out thoughts. It is just like planting a seed in the ground; the practitioner sows the seed and the Creative Mind produces the plant. Does the ground operate on the seed, or does the seed operate upon the soil? We do not know, but we do know that when a seed is put into the ground, something operates upon it and a plant is produced; and that unless a seed is put into the ground, no plant will be produced.

WHAT CAN BE HEALED

What should we try to heal mentally? If we were dealing only with the power of our own thought, our limited concept, we could not heal anything mentally; but if we realize that we are dealing with Universal Principle, how can we set any limit to Its Power?

People are sick because they cover a perfect idea with imperfect thoughts; for sickness is the result of subjectified thinking. Everything which the objective mind has consciously thought has fallen into the subjective. All suggestions received have also fallen into the subjective thought; these suggestions may or may not have been consciously received. This will explain why people may be taken sick with diseases of which they never heard; somewhere, on the subjective side of thought, certain forces have been set in motion which, when objectified, produced certain conditions.

WHY PEOPLE GET TIRED

Let a person say to himself; "I have overworked," and at once there will come up through his consciousness a belief in weariness. People who are constantly complaining of being tired are simply hypnotized into this belief through the law of race-suggestion.

Suppose one had dropped complexes into his subjective thought; suppose desires had torn him, and conflicts had entered into his life; what would have happened? He would have been continually dropping opposing thoughts and concepts into his mentality; and as the mental action took place, they might produce a twisted body; and if over-chaotic, they might produce what is called nervous prostration. It would not, however, be the body that was sick but would be a condition brought about through wrong thought.

Now, if subjective thought were a thing apart from us, if we did not have conscious access to it, we could not change it; but being the result of the way thought has worked, we can consciously change it. If this were not true mental healing would be impossible.

THE IDEA MUST TAKE FORM

Healing, then, takes place to the degree that we send down the right kind of thoughts into subjectivity. This does not mean that we must sit around holding thoughts. We do not hold a seed in our hand when we wish to plant it, and it is the same in healing; we do not hold the thought but seek to realize it and let it work. By thinking consciously and with deep feeling, we implant the right idea in Mind, and Mind reproduces this idea as effect in the body. We must realize that we are using a power compared to which the united intelligence of the human race is as nothing. This should not seem strange; for we know that the united intelligence of the entire race cannot produce a single rosebud, yet any gardener may produce as many roses as he wishes, if he goes about it in the right way. We must remember that what is true on one plane is true on all. Involution and evolution are the law, cause and effect. The practitioner involves an idea in Mind; it is Law and must operate.

If one wishes to treat a patient, he must first treat himself; as he treats himself, that is, as he treats his own mentality, which is simply a point in Mind, he reaches the mentality of his patient. The practitioner cannot erase the thought in the patient's mentality until he has first neutralized the idea in his own thought.

RESOLVE THINGS INTO THOUGHTS

A treatment is a specific thing. If you are treating some one against the belief in scarlet fever, you are making your word operate in such a way as to neutralize a belief in this disease. Each treatment must have, in itself, everything necessary to cover the case. When you treat, resolve things into thoughts; bodies, people, objects and all things. Having resolved everything into thoughts, know that disease is neither person, place nor thing; it has no location, does not belong to any one, cannot operate through any one, is not believed in by any one. Know that it is a false belief, a false image, with no power. Know that the whole thing is mental; then mentally dissolve it.

HEALING INSANITY

In treating some one whose mind appears to be deranged, realize that there is but One Mind, which Mind is God, and is Perfect. This is the only Mind that is; It is the Mind of your patient; It is your own Mind. This Mind, being a Complete, Perfect and Indivisible Whole, cannot labor under a delusion, cannot, for one moment, lose Its Self-Consciousness. After you have realized this Truth about Life, realize that it is also true about the one you are treating; his thought is perfect. If you have this realization in your own mentality, knowing there is just the One Mind, there will be no doubts or confusions; and the mentality of the patient will cease to be deranged.

WHAT A PRACTITIONER DOES

What a practitioner really does is to take his patient, the disease and everything that appears to be wrong right into his own mentality, and here he dissolves all false appearances and all erroneous conclusions. He takes the condition, not as a reality, but as a belief; and right at the center of his own being he neutralizes the whole false thought, thus healing the condition.

The more completely the practitioner is convinced of the power of his own word, the more power his word will have. There must be a complete realization that the power of the word, operating as the Truth and the Reality of Being, can do all things. Therefore, the person whose consciousness is the clearest, who has the most complete idea of Life, will be the best healer.

BACK OF THE APPEARANCE IS THE REALITY

Healing is not creating a perfect body or a perfect idea; it is revealing an idea which is already perfect. Healing is not a process. It is a revelation, through the thought of the practitioner to the thought of the patient. There may be a process in healing but not a process of healing. The process in healing is the mental work and the time it takes the practitioner to convince himself of the perfectness of his patient; and the length of time it takes the patient to realize this perfectness.

It is necessary that the practitioner realize a perfect body; he cannot realize this unless he has already become convinced that the perfect body is there. If he has come to this conclusion, he must not deny it. There is a perfect heart and a perfect idea of heart; there is a perfect head and a perfect idea of head; perfect lungs and a perfect idea of lungs. The practitioner must realize that back of the appearance is the Reality, and it is his business to uncover this Reality. He does this through a process of obliterating false thought; he must deny false conclusions, bring out the evidence of perfection, and produce the healing. Disease is a fact but not a truth; it is an experience but not a reality.

SEEING PERFECTION

When Jesus said to the man, "Stretch forth thine hand," 52 He undoubtedly saw a perfect hand. Did he see the without or the within as being perfect? If everything is mental, and if he saw an imperfect hand instead of a perfect one, no good result could have come through His seeing, according to the law of cause and effect. This is true of all demonstration in healing. A practitioner does not treat a sick man; if he does, he not only will not heal him, but he might become sick himself. The reason for this is simple; he will have entered into the vibration of the patient's thought, and will, himself, experience the results of that vibration. This is an experience that many have when they first begin to practice; they take on the conditions of their patients. So, from what we know, Jesus must have seen only the perfect hand. Even though He might have recognized the false condition, as far as His word of healing was concerned it must have been a recognition of perfection, else it could not have healed.

We must think of the subjective state of our thought as our atmosphere in the Universal Mind; for we cannot separate ourselves from the Universe. There is but One Mind and we are in It; we are in It as intelligence; It accepts our thought and acts upon it. Destructive emotions, desires or ideas, unless they are neutralized, will grow into some bodily condition, and may produce disease. Disease is thought manifested, no matter what the disease may be. We are surrounded by a Receptive Intelligence which receives the impress of our thought and acts upon it.

HEALING LUNG TROUBLE

Suppose a person comes to a practitioner and says: "I am dying of tuberculosis." What is tuberculosis? It is a belief in lung trouble; but lung itself is a universal idea, a perfect idea; and nothing has ever happened to it. It was, is, and will be; but man, through the creative medium of his thought, has caused an appearance of disorder and disease in the lung. Back of all such trouble is a consuming passion, an unexpressed emotion, a strong desire. Healing will take place to the degree that the practitioner neutralizes this belief and perceives the presence of a perfect lung. He realizes that there is a perfect body, perfect lung, perfect being, perfect God, perfect man, perfect expression; he must bring his own thought up to this perception. The word he speaks is law; it is power; it knows itself to be what it is. It is the law unto the case. He is now conscious that the word he speaks will neutralize and entirely destroy the false thought and condition. He says: "There is one body; this body is the Body of God; and it is Perfect; it is never depleted; its vitality is never lowered. There is no wasting away of substance or burning up of substance; for substance is eternal, changeless and perfect." He goes on until he covers what in his own thought appears to be the cause of the false condition. If he does this day after day, the patient begins to get better; though the practitioner never thinks of his patient, other than that his word is being spoken for him; and he never wonders whether his word is taking effect, because he speaks into Intelligence and lets It act. Perhaps, if it is a case that requires a great deal of attention, he treats morning, afternoon, and evening, each time for a few moments; otherwise ten or fifteen minutes each day should be sufficient.

Never think that a sick person is one who simply has a sick body. If you do you will find yourself treating the body. Why shouldn't we treat the body? Because the cause of the disease is not in the body. The body is an effect and not a cause. *Know that bodies and conditions never move; they are always moved upon.* A sick person is one who has a sick thought.

What about accidents? It is part of our belief that as soon as, and to the degree that, our minds become adjusted harmoniously to the Universe, we will be less likely to have accidents.

WE DO NOT SEND OUT THOUGHTS

In practice, we do not try to send thoughts to our patients; for there is but One Mind in the universe. We will say "A" represents a man who is sick; "B" represents a practitioner. "B" thinks into Mind; and whether we say he is thinking within himself or somewhere else does not matter; he is always thinking into Mind, because he is in Mind. "But," one might say, "the patient thinks into his own subjective mind"; yes, but his subjective mind is only his atmosphere in the One Mind. We must get this very clearly, else some day there will be a wall between our thought and its ability to heal some condition, or some person who is at a physical distance.

Both the patient and the practitioner think into One Common Mind; therefore when a patient comes to a practitioner for healing the practitioner does not try to hypnotize him or suggest anything to him; he declares the Truth about him. And to the degree that he brings his own consciousness to a true recognition of perfection—provided there is a receptivity in the thought of the patient—that man will be healed; nothing can hinder it. The practitioner does not try to hold a thought or send out a thought; he simply tries to convince himself of the perfection of his patient. He does not try to make his word operate through his patient but only attempts to know the Truth of what he states. The patient must be receptive to the Truth, and then the Truth will heal him. The practitioner is dealing with Universal Law, backed by Omnipotent Power, which is Divine Principle. This is what Jesus meant when He said: "Ye shall know the Truth and the Truth shall make you free." 53

Every time we think, we are thinking into a receptive, plastic Substance, which receives the impress of our thought. When we stop to realize how subtle thoughts are, how unconsciously we think negation, how easy it is to get down and out, we will see that each is perpetuating his own condition. This is why people go from bad to worse, or from success to a greater success.

VISION

Eye trouble is a belief in limited vision; it is a belief in a separated vision. God sees, and His is the Only Mind there is. It is our Mind; consequently, man sees, whether he knows it or not. Do not fear to claim this; because it is the truth. There is no obstruction to vision; there is no near vision nor far vision; there is no false vision; there is no weak vision nor blurred vision. There is One Perfect Seeing, which is Now seeing through and in me.

HEALING CONSTIPATION

Constipation is due to a belief in limitation or burden and is healed by knowing that there is no restriction, no inaction, no limited action, no bondage, no fear, no congestion. Make the thought realize that there is nothing but freedom; that all action is normal, harmonious and perfect.

Very often the word of healing is spoken and does not appear to operate because some obstruction hinders it. Some people are obstinate, resistant, stubborn; and they must be healed of these beliefs. There is no resistance to Truth, no thought anywhere which can hinder consciousness from perceiving the Truth. Whatever the false condition is, *array mental argument against it in an opposite manner.* Turn the thought over and over, until, either by reason or by chance, you hit upon the thing that is wrong. Any one can heal if he will do this, just as any one, if he goes into the garden and drops seed into the ground, will cause plants to grow. Any one can heal who can get away from the effect long enough to perceive a different cause.

In every treatment the thought of fear must always be handled. One should realize that there is no fear, nothing to be afraid of; and that fear cannot operate through man.

DISEASE NOT AN ENTITY

Man is fundamentally perfect; this is our whole premise; Perfect God, Perfect Man, Perfect Being; this is the whole basis of the argument. Always separate disease from the person suffering with it. Declare very frequently that disease is neither person, place nor thing; that it has no location, no avenue through which to express itself, no expression, no one through whom to express. Never locate disease, because thoughts are things, and if located they will operate. Always separate the belief from the believer, for nothing ails the real man; nothing ever did or ever will.

THROAT TROUBLE

In treating throat trouble the thought to handle is sensitiveness. No one would ever have throat trouble if his feelings were never hurt. You heal a person of sensitiveness by teaching him that no one desires to hurt him, and that no one could if he did so desire. When one becomes really individualized his feelings cannot be hurt; for he will feel complete within himself.

CONGESTION

In colds, congestion and like conditions, the thought to heal is confusion. There should be a consciousness of poise, a recognition of peace; and when this comes into the individual's experience he will no longer have colds.

PARALYSIS

People could be healed of all forms of paralysis through the elimination of the belief in bondage. Use the thought that Life cannot become paralyzed or inactive. As in constipation, there is a thought of restriction back of the thought of paralysis; and often there is a very emotional nature to deal with; and often, though not always, a lot of stubbornness and resistance to heal.

GROWTHS

If the thought of false growths can be erased the manifestation can be healed. Declare, "Every plant which my Heavenly Father hath not planted shall be rooted up." The Heavenly Father is the Reality of Man and is Eternal Presence and Perfection. Dissolve the idea of false growths by knowing that there is nothing for them to feed upon. Erase the belief in your own mentality and you will remove it from the mentality of your patient, and thereby heal his body.

TREATING CHILDREN

In the case of children, remember that the thoughts of the parents influence the child. We will suppose the child's mother is constantly saying: "The poor thing; the poor, little, sick thing!" From the human standpoint this is natural, but it makes the child sick just the same, no matter how loving it may be. This is called unconscious, or innocent, malpractice. It is malpractice, because it is the wrong use of thought; innocent, because it is not intended to harm; unconscious, because she doesn't know what she is doing; ignorant, because she doesn't know the results of such mental action. In such a case the practitioner must realize that there is no mental influence operating through the child, except a belief in perfection.

POWER OF THE WORD

Be specific in treating, be definite and direct in your mental work. You are dealing with Intelligence, so deal with It intelligently. The treatment must realize the patient as perfect; must recognize the word as power; must know that it breaks down every man-made law and casts it out; that it is the law of harmony and the recognition of the Presence of Good; that within itself it is unbounded, and equipped with the power to execute itself; and it must know that it does this. It must know that there is nothing that can change it; that there is no belief which can hinder it; that it cannot be reversed, mislaid, misplaced, neutralized or destroyed by any opposing force; but that it does the thing that it is supposed to do. And it must know that it is continuous and will operate until it does all that it is supposed to do.

Jesus said: "Heaven and earth shall pass away: but my words shall not pass away." 54 Isaiah understood something of this when he said: "So shall my word be that goeth forth out of my mouth: it shall not return unto me void." 55

NO AGE

There are certain thoughts that should always be handled, such as thoughts of race-suggestion, inherited tendencies, prenatal conditions, environment, and mental influences and suggestion. A treatment must be so formulated as to recognize that there is but One Mind; consequently, no thought can flow through It of depression, fear, or suggestion of imperfection. Man is Birthless, Deathless, Ageless Spirit; and this should be the consciousness of our work. This leaves nothing to be born, mature, decay and die. When this thought shall be made clear in the consciousness of the race, people will no longer grow old. Life cannot grow old; It is always the same.

MEMORY

Locke, in "Human Understanding," defines memory as: "The power to revive again in our minds those ideas which, after imprinting, have disappeared, or have been, as it were, laid aside out of sight." Memory is the ability to remember things that have happened; therefore, if something happened two years ago, of which we are not at present thinking, we can remember it, because it is in our subjective thought. We say that we are getting absent-minded, which means that we cannot recall thoughts. A person may be healed of this belief by knowing that the One Mind never forgets Itself. This Mind is our Mind now.

GUIDANCE IN TREATING

If, in treating, it seems impossible to know just what thought to handle, it is well to be still and know that Intelligence within will tell you what to say and how to say it. By doing this some idea will come and you will find that, by using it, you will reach the case.

HOW TO HEAL

Never say: "Here is a patient whom I must heal"; for, if you see him from this angle, how are you going to heal him? If you see a sick man he will remain sick, so far as you are concerned; you cannot heal while you see sickness. Disease is neither person, place nor thing; nobody believes in it; it has no action or reaction; it is neither cause nor effect; it has no law to support it and no one to operate through; there is no one to talk about it or believe in it.

You have nothing to do with the patient's thought as a personality, for as your own thought clears it will heal him. When you give a treatment, first eliminate all doubt and fear from your own thought. Realize that you are a Divine Idea and that your word is the law unto the thing unto which it is spoken. This is what gave Jesus his power; "For he taught them as one having authority, and not as the scribes." 56

REMOVE DOUBT

Suppose a practitioner is not able to convince himself of the Truth of the statements which he makes; how is he going to bring himself to the point of belief? By repeating the affirmation, dwelling on its meaning, meditating upon the spiritual significance of it until the subjective state of his thinking becomes clarified. This is the only reason for repeating treatments; for one treatment would heal anything if there were no doubts. Repeated treatments induce within consciousness a definite concept of an already established fact, even though the fact may not already have become objectified; this is why mental healing is a science. There is no room for doubt in a treatment.

Realize that you treat with your understanding through the Law. Never say: "I am not good enough to treat." There are no good, better and best; this is a delusion; for one is as good as another in the Truth.

Do not allow yourself to become superstitious; for you are dealing with a normal, natural law in the mental and spiritual world. This law is just as real as any other known law. Don't say: "I am not sure that I have enough power to treat"; you cannot heal with this mental attitude. Say, "As I let fall the forms of my thought they are operated upon by Principles I believe. This is the Law of God, the law of man and the Law of the Universe." Never say: "This disease is hard to heal while another is easy." If you find yourself saying this, at once heal yourself. This comes from a belief that we are dealing with a limited power.

NO FEAR

Suppose when you begin to treat, a great surge of fear comes over you and attempts to tell you that you cannot give a good treatment. The thing to do is to treat this fear as a suggestion which has no power and which cannot convince you that you lack the power to heal. Say: "There is nothing in me which can doubt my ability to heal." This will neutralize the fear and free the effort to accomplish.

How do we know when we have treated a patient long enough? When he is well he will need no more treatments; until this time comes treat every day for a realization of perfection.

Does it make any difference whether or not the patient is taking medicine? Not a bit. If this form of healing gives him any relief, let him have it. We all need all the relief we can get. The patient is healed when he no longer needs medicine. Forget the medicine and heal him mentally and he will no longer take pills.

Some think that they dishonor God when they take a pill. God knows nothing about pills; this is superstition, pure and simple; mostly simple. Discard all such thoughts and give your entire attention to realizing perfection for your patient.

Healing is not accomplished through will power but by knowing the Truth; this Truth is that man is already Perfect, no matter what the appearance may be. Holding thoughts has nothing to do with treatment. If you find, when you begin to give treatments, that the process gives you a headache, know that you are doing your work on the mental plane and not through spiritual realization. A treatment should leave the practitioner in a better condition than before he gave it; otherwise it is not a good one.

One might ask: "Is all disease a thought held in the conscious mind of the patient?" No, not necessarily; it may be a subconscious thought; or it may be the result of many thoughts which, gathered together, produce a definite result.

PSYCHO-ANALYSIS

It may be necessary for the practitioner to diagnose the thought of his patient; in fact this is one of the main points in healing. This is psycho-analysis (from psyche or soul). Psycho-analysis is the analysis of the soul or subjective mind. Its teaching is, that within the soul, or subjective mind, all the seeds of our thought fall; and that most of man's physical troubles are caused by some conflict of the emotions and the will. The conscious mind, desiring certain things which it cannot have, sends into the subjective thought opposing desires, which conflict with each other and mentally tear or bind; and as they manifest in the body, they produce disease. It is claimed that seventy percent of all diseases are the results of suppressed emotions; these emotions are not necessarily sex emotions, but may be any suppressed desires. These suppressed emotions cause what are called complexes.

It is probable that when Jesus forgave the man his sins, He realized that the man had a complex of condemnation within himself. The sense of condemnation which the race holds about itself weights it down, and it must be removed. This explains why Jesus said: "Thy sins be forgiven thee." 57 It is feeling that hurts. The thinking man thinks things out, resolves everything into its normal parts and so avoids complexes. It has been said: "Life is a comedy to him who thinks, a tragedy to him who feels."

The practitioner talks to his patient, shows him the Law of Mind, teaches him the way, diagnoses his thought, points out to him that certain mental attitudes produce certain physical results, teaches him how to be harmonious in his thinking, how to be at peace, how to trust and believe in the Good, lifts him up mentally and spiritually and supports his thought until he can stand alone.

A practitioner must be filled with a spirit of Divine Compassion; he must have a deep, underlying sense of unity and sympathy, else he will do but little good; but he must not have sympathy with the disease. The only guarantee of our Divinity is in its expression through our Humanity. Consequently an enlightened soul understands the meaning of sympathy and exercises it, but not morbidly.

DEAL ONLY WITH THOUGHTS

In mental treatment, the practitioner deals with thoughts and does not treat bodies or conditions. He never manipulates, nor need he lay his hands on his patients. He does not hypnotize them; he does not care where they are when he is treating them, or what they are doing; for this would be a limited concept. The practitioner's work begins and ends within his own consciousness.

NERVOUSNESS

The thoughts to cover in nervousness are ones of peace, poise and power. There is no twitching of the nerves; there is no strain or struggle in the universe. Things move harmoniously, quietly and normally; and this action, which is the action of Life, is the truth about the one you are treating. A treatment lasts until the one treating is convinced of the truth which he states; it might last one minute or one hour, or longer.

STAMMERING

The treatment for stammering is one that covers the idea of correct speech. Speech is the Word of God and cannot become impaired, but must be a flow from that One Life which knows Itself to be what it is. Speech is perfect.

ARGUMENT IN TREATMENT

Just a word about argument in treatment; we do not argue to make principle work but to convince our own thought that it already is operating.

To sum up the idea of treating, then:—you are conscious mind: your patient is conscious mind; he has thought, or is thinking, or there has been thought through him, consciously or unconsciously, an idea of imperfection. You, as conscious mind, remove this something which says that he is imperfect. The treatment begins and ends within your own mentality; it must cover the case and leave nothing to be sick, sin or die; then it will be effective. Meditation in treatment; an uplifted receptivity to Spirit will always produce good results. A deep inner sense of the unity of all life enables one to feel that the Great Conscious Mind and Spirit of the Universe, flowing through his mentality, is the Presence and the Power of an Infinite Life, Truth and Love. We should sense that back of the word which we speak is the Power of the Universe surging to express Itself. Then speak the word consciously, knowing that it is Law.

Note: Read and carefully study "Teaching and Addresses," Edward S. Kimball; "The Law of Mind in Action," F. L. Holmes; "The Faith That Heals," F. L. Holmes; "Christian Healing," Fillmore; "Lessons in Truth," Cady; "Primary Lessons," Militz; "Outwitting Our Nerves," Jackson.

FOOTNOTES

51 Eccl. 7:29.

52 Matt. 12:13.
53 John 8:52.
54 Luke 21:33.
55 Isa. 55:11.
56 Matt 7:29.
57 Matt. 9:2.

LESSON THREE: RECAPITULATION

Sickness is an experience but not an Ultimate Reality; it is an effect and not a cause. The body, devoid of mentality, could neither know nor have sensation; it is entirely an effect. The body is made of the same unthinking stuff from which all Creation is formed.

Instinctive Man is Perfect, but his individual use of Life and Law enables him to cover a perfect idea with an apparently imperfect cloak.

Man comes into objectivity with the tendency of the race already subjectified within him, through race-suggestion. The race believes in sickness and limitation, and this suggestion is more or less operative through all people. This suggestion works through the field of the subjective state of the race thought, and will operate through any individual who is receptive to it.

As man becomes individualized, he consciously thinks and continuously pours suggestions into his subjective thought which is the silent builder of the physical body. Through the field of subjectivity thought always works out to a logical conclusion.

Man does not, necessarily, consciously think that he is to have a certain type of physical trouble, but the physical correspondent is a logical outcome of what he thinks.

Disease, of itself, is neither person, place nor thing; it is an image of thought, consciously or unconsciously held somewhere in Mind and will externalize wherever it finds an avenue of operation.

Disease is entirely mental in its origin, since no person could be sick unless he had intelligence; it is the result of thinking about, and believing in duality, or a power apart from God.

Disease can be healed through reversing the thought and turning to the Spiritual Realization of Life. It is impossible to divorce real mental healing from true Spiritual Realization, since God is ALL.

The use of mental argument in healing rests upon the theory that we are surrounded by a Universal Mind which reacts to our thought.

Right mental practice is the constructive use of Mind, i.e., a mental argument given for the purpose of presenting the Spiritual Truth about man. Wrong mental practice is the destructive use of Mind, i.e., a mental argument given for the purpose of presenting a false claim about man.

Right mental practice is called the Spirit of Christ. Wrong mental practice is called the spirit of Antichrist; it is malpractice and may or may not be consciously used. To think of any one in a negative way is some form of malpractice and is harmful. Malpractice may be ignorant, innocent or malicious. It is always some form of suggestion.

Man is known in Mind by the name he bears, and any statement made in Mind about his name will cause some action to take place through Law towards him. This is the basis of all mental healing.

A practitioner is one who recognizes Man as a spiritual reality. Since there is but One Mind, the practitioner does this within himself. Through the medium of the One Mind these statements rise to objective conditions in his patient, according to the practitioner's belief and according to the ability of his patient to receive the Truth. Healing is accomplished through the act of setting Subjective Law in motion. The more Spiritual or Godlike the mentality of the practitioner, the more powerful the treatment.

A mental treatment begins and ends within the thought of the practitioner because he is in the same Mind in which his patient lives. Treatment is inducing right concepts within the subjective side of life.

Absent and present treatments are the same; for there is no absence in the One Presence.

One disease would be as easily healed as another if the thought were as sure of itself in one case as another.

There is no personal responsibility in healing; the practitioner directs the Power and lets It work. One does not hold thoughts in mental healing; he looses thought. A practitioner does not try to suggest, hypnotize or mentally influence; he simply knows that man is now a spiritual being and holds to that belief,—no matter what the appearance may be. Right mental treatment does not tire the one giving it.

Personal magnetism has nothing to do with mental healing. The whole basis of the possibility of mental healing rests upon the premise that we all live in One Creative Mind which reacts to our belief. It is as though there were a Universal Ear listening to, and hearing, everything that we say, feel or think, and reacting to it.

Healing is not a process, but a revelation; for the revealing of the perfect man always heals. The process is the time and thought that it takes to arrive at the correct understanding of man's perfect state in Spirit.

Any one can heal who believes that he can, and who will take the time to put that belief in motion through the Law.

To daily see the perfect man and to daily declare for his objective appearance is correct mental practice and will heal.

A treatment recognizes that all is Mind and that everything is mental; it resolves all disease into thought; neutralizes the false thought and recognizes the true. Nothing can stop it from operating except a lack of faith in the reality of the Truth and man's ability to use It.

In giving mental treatment the practitioner first realizes his own being as spiritual; he then recognizes the perfect state of his patient's being; then he attacks the false claim and brings the evidence of Truth to bear against it, thinking in such a manner as to completely destroy the false claim and to realize the Truth.

LESSON FOUR: INTRODUCTION

Mental Science is not a "get-rich-quick scheme," neither does it promise something for nothing. It does, however, promise the one who will comply with its teaching that he shall be able to bring into his life and experience greater possibilities and happier conditions.

The Science of Mind is based entirely upon the supposition that we are surrounded by a Universal Mind into which we think; this Mind, in Its original state, fills all space with Its Presence. Since It fills all space, It fills the space that man uses in the Universe. It is in man as well as outside of him. As he thinks into this Universal Mind he sets in motion a Law which is creative, and which contains within Itself a limitless possibility.

THE LAW IS INFINITE

The Law through which man operates is Infinite, but man appears to be finite; that is, he has not yet evolved to a complete understanding of It. He is unfolding from a limitless potential but can bring into his experience only that which he can conceive. There is no limit to the Law, but there appears to be a limit to man's understanding of It. As his understanding unfolds, his possibilities of attainment will increase.

It is a great mistake to say: "Take what you wish; for you can have anything you like." We do not take what we wish, but we do attract to ourselves that which is like our thought. *Man must become more if he wishes to draw a greater good into his life.* We need not labor under the delusion that all we have to do is to say everything is ours. This is true in reality; but in fact, it is only as true as we make it. We provide the mold for the Creative Law, and unless the mold which we provide is increased, the substance cannot increase in our experience; for Mental Science cannot hold forth a promise that will do away with the necessity of complying with law.

The Law is a law of liberty, but not a law of license. It is exact and exacting, and unless we are willing to comply with Its nature and work with It, along the lines of Its inherent being, we will receive no great benefit. Every man must pay the price for that which he receives, and that price is paid in mental and spiritual coin. An avenue must be provided through which the Law may work as a law of liberty, if It is to free us. This does not mean that we must please the Law; for It is impersonal and neither knows nor cares who uses It, nor for what purpose; but, because It is impersonal, It is compelled, by Its very nature, to return to the thinker exactly what he thinks into It. The Law of mental equivalents must never be overlooked; for "Whatsoever a man soweth, that shall he also reap." 58

THE POSSIBILITIES OF THE LAW

The possibilities of the Law are infinite; and our possibilities of using It are limitless. We may, and should, receive full benefit, and we will to the degree that we understand and properly use It.

There is a law of unfoldment in man which says that he can advance only by going from where he is to the place where he would like to be. This is not because the Law is limited but because It is law. As man unfolds in his mentality, the law automatically reacts to him. The way to work is to begin right where we are, and, through constantly applying ourselves to the Truth, to gradually increase in wisdom and understanding; for in this way alone will good results be obtained. If, day by day, we have a greater understanding and a clearer concept; if daily, we are realizing more of Truth and applying it in our actions, then we are on the right path, and eventually we will be made free.

SPIRIT AND MENTAL LAW

It is impossible to divorce spiritual understanding from the proper use of mental law. The Spirit within man is God, and only to the degree that we listen to, and seek to obey that Spirit, shall we really succeed. The Law is a blind force, and lest we misuse It, we should be very careful to *follow only a constructive course.* But the Law is Absolute, and we should trust Its impersonal action implicitly. It can do anything for us that we can conceive of Its doing. It is the law of freedom to all who believe in and obey It.

The highest realization that we can have is a recognition of the Omnipresence of Spirit. This will set in motion greater possibilities and will, automatically, provide a larger concept of life. We should daily train our thought to recognize the Spirit in everything we do, say, or think. There is no other way, and to try any other way would be to make a complete failure. "Render to Cæsar the things that are Cæsar's; and to God the things that are God's." 59

A constant realization of the Presence of Spirit will provide a sense of Divine Companionship that no other attitude could produce. Why should we not take the highest and best? God Is,—and we should realize this fact and make use of it; as soon as we recognize that God Is, we can turn to the Law and tell It what to do.

We have no record of Jesus ever asking God to do things for Him; He gave thanks, and then commanded the Law to work. This is the correct manner of approach to the Spirit and the Law. This is not superstition but the fact in the case, and we would better realize it.

The Law is subject to the Spirit and is Its servant. Man is Spirit, but until he knows this he will be only half using the Law; for he will not have a clear understanding to fall back upon.

DEMONSTRATION, OR BRINGING THINGS TO PASS

We hold no argument with any one over the possibility of demonstrating the Law. There is such a thing as Universal Law and Mind, and we can use It if we comply with Its nature and work as It works. We do not argue, ask, deny, nor affirm; *we know*. Thousands are to-day proving this Law, and in time, all will come to realize the Truth.

We can demonstrate to the level of our ability to know; beyond this we cannot go. But we will constantly expand and increase in knowledge and understanding, thereby continuously growing in our ability to make use of the Law; in time we will be made free through It.

It is a wonderful experiment and a great adventure to make conscious use of the Law, to feel that we can plant an idea in Mind and see it gradually take form.

The student should take time every day to see his life as he wishes it to be, to make a mental picture of his ideal. He should pass this picture over to the Law and go about his business with the inner assurance that on the invisible side of life something is taking place. There should never be any sense of hurry nor worry about this; just a calm, peaceful sense of reality. Let the Law work through, and express Itself in, the experience. There should be no idea of compulsion; we do not have to make the Law work; it is Its nature to work, and all that we need to do is to make use of It. In gladness, then, we should make known our desires, and in confidence we should wait upon the Perfect Law to manifest through us.

OUR PART

Our part is to be ready and willing to be guided into truth and liberty. If, in the making of a demonstration, it becomes necessary to change our mode of living, then the Law will point the way and we will follow. Our correct choice will be part of the working out of the Law. All doubt and fear must go, and in their place must come faith and confidence; for we shall be led by the Spirit into all good.

TREATMENT

Treatment is not for the purpose of making things happen; it is to provide, within ourselves, an avenue through which they may happen. Treatment opens up the avenues of thought, expands the consciousness, and lets Reality through; it clarifies the mentality, removes the obstructions of thought and lets in the Light. We already live in a Perfect Universe, but It needs to be mentally seen before It can become a part of our experience. Treatment removes doubt and fear; lets in the realization of the Presence of Spirit; and is necessary while we are confronted by obstruction or obstacles. Every problem is primarily mental, and the answer to all problems will be found in Spiritual Realizations.

MEDIUM BETWEEN MAN AND HIS MANIFESTATION

The subjective state of man's thought decides what is to happen to him. The subjective state of his thought is the sum-total of his thinking and knowing; It is the medium between the relative and the Absolute, between the Limitless and the conditioned. Whatever is involved in it will evolve; therefore, treatment is the act, the art and the science of systematically and consciously inducing such thoughts as we wish to see expressed. When there is no longer anything within our mentality that denies our word, a demonstration will be made; nothing can stop it, for the Law is Absolute. The question might be asked: "If this is true, why not affirm that we have what we desire and let it go at that?" This is true in Principle, but in practice and in fact, it is only as true as we make it; that is, we cannot demonstrate beyond our ability to know the Truth. We should begin, then, with the things that we do know, and from that basis evolve a greater knowledge.

We should approach the Law normally and naturally and with a sense of ease. There is nothing peculiar or weird about this; it is a natural Law, working in a normal way, and must be thought of in this light.

We should come to consider the Law and the Spirit as friends and think of them as such; in this way we will gradually go from good to more good and from peace to a greater peace. This is the natural unfoldment of Reality through man. We should expect the best and so live that the best may become a part of our experience.

FOOTNOTES

58 Gal. 6:7.
59 Mark 12:17.

LESSON FOUR: THE CONTROL OF CONDITIONS

In taking up this subject, let us very clearly understand that we do not differentiate between Conscious Mind and Spirit; there is no difference, for they are One.

The Spirit of Intelligence, which is God, in order to do something for us must do that thing through us, and what It is to do must first become a part of our mentality before it can become an individual experience. *Our mentalities are but the spirit working through us as individuals.*

In the new schools of thought there are those who claim to demonstrate only by the Spirit; also those who claim to demonstrate only by the Mind. This is a distinction which is suppositional rather than real and is impossible, because, if there were two powers, we would at once have duality and our philosophy of Unity would be contradicted. There is but One Active Intelligence, whether it be the Universal Intelligence or Universal Spirit individualized in us.

We do, however, distinguish between the phase of mind which we call conscious and the phase which we call unconscious or subjective, as has already been explained.

In demonstrating conditions, the only inquiries we need to make are: do the things that we want lend themselves to a constructive program? Do they express a more abundant life, rob none, create no delusion, but instead, do they express a greater degree of livingness? If they do, then all the power in the universe must be behind them. If it is money, automobiles, houses, lands, stocks, bonds, dresses, shirts or shoestrings, cabbages or kings,—all of which come from the same source,—there can be nothing, either in the Law or in the Spirit back of the Law, to deny us the right to the greatest possible expression of life.

So we need not hesitate to use the Law for personal motives, for we have a perfect right to do so. It is good for every one to express himself, provided that in so doing, he does not destroy the independence of others.

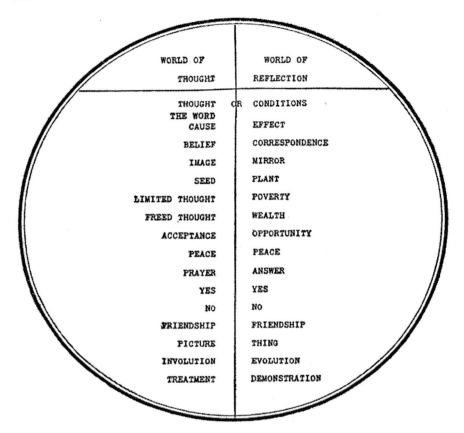

WORLD OF THOUGHT	WORLD OF REFLECTION
THOUGHT OR THE WORD	CONDITIONS
CAUSE	EFFECT
BELIEF	CORRESPONDENCE
IMAGE	MIRROR
SEED	PLANT
LIMITED THOUGHT	POVERTY
FREED THOUGHT	WEALTH
ACCEPTANCE	OPPORTUNITY
PEACE	PEACE
PRAYER	ANSWER
YES	YES
NO	NO
FRIENDSHIP	FRIENDSHIP
PICTURE	THING
INVOLUTION	EVOLUTION
TREATMENT	DEMONSTRATION

Lesson Four: Metaphysical Chart No. IV.

HOW IDEAS MANIFEST AS THINGS.

This chart is divided into two sides, representing the world of thought and the world of reflections. It represents the law of cause and effect. The world of thought is the world of ideas, while the world of reflections means the results of thought. The world of reflections is entirely a world of effects and is, of itself, unconscious and unknowing. Consider everything on the left side of this chart to be thoughts or ideas; and consider everything on the right side to be the automatic results of the law as it works out into effects. By using this chart in conjunction with the explanations already given, it will be plain just how the law of cause and effect works from the idea to the thing.

LAW OF REFLECTION

In turning to the Law, then, realize that It is a Law of reflection. "Life is the mirror of king and slave." Chart No. IV is divided into two parts with a suppositional line in the center; on one side is depicted the world of thought and on the other, the world of the reflections of thought. The world of thought is the world of our individuality; it is the part of us that knows. The other is the world of soul or receptivity and of reflections. In the thought is the cause that reflects the effect; the belief that reflects the correspondence. Here is the image; and here is a form. Here is the limited thought, the result of which reflects poverty. Here is the freed thought, the result of which reflects wealth. Here is a thought of peace which reflects peace. Here is a prayer and here is its answer; the answer to prayer is in the prayer when it is prayed, and the answer is identical with the prayer. Here is Yes and here is Yes; and here is No and here is No. Why is this? Because the Law takes us at our own valuation; if we say "Yes," It says "Yes"; and if we say "No," It says "No"; for It can only reflect; It cannot initiate anything. So here is friendship and over here is friendship. Emerson said: "If you want a friend, be a friend"; and so, as the idea of friendship dawns upon the consciousness, the law of attraction produces friends; for one is the picture and the other is the thing. This is the great teaching of Involution and Evolution, the thought involved and the result evolved; one is the treatment and the other is the demonstration.

We mean by demonstration, bringing into our experience something which we had not experienced before; bringing it in as the result of conscious thought; and unless it is possible to do this the whole science is a mistake and a delusion.

Unless there is a Divine Principle, Universal Soul or Subjectivity, or Medium, which, of Itself, without any help or assistance, can produce things, and will, then there is nothing in this teaching. But there is Divine Principle; and what It does for us, It must do through us. Our part in the demonstration is to set the word in motion, thus compelling, through the law of subjectivity, the result or manifestation.

ATTRACTING FRIENDS

When we are dealing with Causation, we are dealing with that which has involved within Itself all effect, as it unfolds. We may leave it to the Law to compel right action. With this in mind, let us go on to treatment.

Suppose we wish to attract friends. We must begin to image ideal relationships, be they social or otherwise; to sense and feel the presence of friends; to enjoy them in our own mentalities, not as an illusion, but as a reality; not as a dream, but as an experience; to declare that their presence is now here; that they know it and that we know it. But we must never look to see if they are here, because this would imply doubt and would neutralize our word. We can attract the kind of friends we wish if we specifically designate the kind; but we must never think of certain people, or that a particular individual must be one of them, for this would be hypnotic; just thinking the idea will bring the right kind of friends.

In order to have this friendship enduring, true, really worth while and a thing of beauty, we should cultivate an attitude of friendship toward everybody and everything.

THE PRINCIPLE OF PROSPERITY

We are surrounded by a Universal Subjectivity, a Subjective, Creative Consciousness, which is receptive, neutral, impersonal, always receiving the impress of our thought, and which has no alternative other than to operate directly upon it, thus creating the things which we think.

Each one should realize that there is nothing in him that denies that which he desires. Our unity with our good is not established while there is anything in us that denies it.

People often say: "How shall I know when I know?" If you knew you would not ask this question; the very fact that you can ask it proves you do not know; for when you know that you know you can prove it by doing.

Thought sets definite force in motion in Mind, relative to the individual who thinks. For instance, I am known in Consciousness as Ernest Holmes, for that is my name; and every claim made for me, which I accept, operates through avenues of mind-activity and returns to me as some condition.

In practice, always forget the limitations of individuality. Each treatment should embody a recognition of the Whole, because It is Omnipresent.

WE DEAL WITH ABSOLUTENESS

We deal with Absoluteness; this is the attitude that we should have. What we need is to know the Truth. This does not mean that we need not be active; of course we shall be active; but we need not compel things to happen. A good demonstration is made when the Truth, gathering Its own power, lifts one out of his environment; and until that time comes he should stay where he is, in order that he may know when he has made a demonstration.

It is not a good demonstration if, when we give our treatments, we have to struggle just as before. Principle is Absolute, and in so far as any individual can actually induce, within consciousness, upon Principle, a definite, concrete acceptance of his desire, it will manifest, even if every thought on earth had to change to compel it. If it were a bit of information that only one person on earth knew, and he was in the center of Africa, it would be produced.

PRAYER IS ITS OWN ANSWER

Cause and effect are but two sides of thought; and Spirit is both Cause and Effect. Prayer is its own answer. Now, if the one who prays only partly believes, then there is a tendency to set an idea in motion; if the next day he wholly doubts, this idea must be wiped out. In dealing with Mind, we are dealing with a Force which we cannot fool. We can fool ourselves; we can fool others; but we cannot cheat Principle out of the slightest shadow of our most subtle concept; for this is impossible. The hand writes and passes on, but the writing is left there, nevertheless; and the only thing that can erase it is a writing of a different character. We must either transcend all that has gone before, by walking above it, neutralize it by an opposite state of consciousness, or endure it.

Get a sense of self-mastery, of being equal to every occasion. There is nothing too great; there is no obstacle that you cannot surmount; no obstruction that you cannot dissipate by the power of Truth, if your concept of Truth is dynamic enough and clear enough, and if the embodiment is complete.

IF YOU KNOW

If you know that the Power with which you are dealing is Principle and not personality; if you know and believe that Mind is the only Actor, Cause, Effect, Substance, Intelligence, Truth and Power that there is; and if you have a real embodiment of your desires, then you can demonstrate.

If you lack, if you are poor, if you are without friends, if you are without opportunity, don't fight anything; but be sure to erase from your consciousness any sense of that lack.

You erase thought from consciousness by pouring in an opposite thought; this opposite thought meets the other and neutralizes it; that is, it rubs it out, just as we rub a chalk mark off a board. Take a consistent, positive, aggressive mental attitude in the Truth.

We walk by falling forward; water falls by its own weight; the planets are eternally falling through space; for everything sustains itself in nature. The only reason that man is limited is that he has not allowed the Instinctive Life to come out through him, and the reason why this is possible, is that his own Divine Individuality, as soon as it was evolved, compelled Infinity to appear in his experience as duality, because he believed in duality.

Take no personal responsibility for making anything happen. Throw your word into Mind, and know that Mind receives it; Mind believes it; Mind accepts it; Mind acts upon it; and Mind produces it.

NO PERSONAL RESPONSIBILITY

No matter how great a responsibility may rest in that which must be done, never let one minute's responsibility rest in your own thought about it, because that to which the mind gives birth is, and *every idea is bound to produce an effect exactly like its cause.*

When we make a demonstration we must take what goes with it. Therefore, all demonstrations should be made in peace, confidence and joy and in the realization of Divine Love and Perfection as permeating everything. The reason for this is evident, for we are dealing with the law of cause and effect. We are not depending upon chance, but upon Law.

We must know that we are dealing with the substance from which all things are made—people, brains, monkeys—everything that is. Nothing moves but Mind, and we are dealing with the Mind that is the Mover, the Creator, the Cause of all that is or is to be.

HELPING AN INVENTOR

Suppose an inventor came to you and said: "I am trying to perfect a piece of machinery and have not been able to work out the right plan." You sit with him for treatment; that is, you concentrate in Mind, in order to produce the desired idea through him. You know that all ideas come from Mind and that Mind is always unfolding Its Ideas through man. You say: "John Smith is an inventor; a certain idea is trying to operate through him and there is nothing in him that can obstruct this idea." Then state that this idea is known in Mind, and is now flowing through him. If you do this, thinking clearly, new ideas will begin to operate through him and he will discover the thing he needs.

LOOK ONLY AT WHAT YOU WANT

Never look at that which you do not wish to experience. No matter what the false condition may be, it must be refuted. The proper kind of a denial is based upon the recognition that, in reality, there is no limitation; for mind can as easily make a planet as anything else. The Infinite knows no difference between a million dollars and a penny. It only knows that IT IS. It would be just as easy to demonstrate a million dollars as it would be to demonstrate ten cents, if the mental concept embodied the idea of a million dollars.

It is the consciousness back of the word that forms the word. Consciousness means the inner embodiment of an idea through the recognition of Truth and a direct relationship to the Divine. The greatest Teacher Who ever lived was the most spiritual man; for the more universal and comprehensive the thought, the more Godlike it must become.

A good treatment is always filled with the recognition of the Presence of God or Good. Even in Spiritual Things we are still dealing with the law of cause and effect, for God is Law. The more exalted the thought, the more heavenly, the more boundless, the more Godlike or Christlike the thought, the more power it will have. This is why the greatest Teacher should become the Saviour; He couldn't help it. A great teacher would have to be a Saviour.

DEFINITE PLAN

We will say that there are four men, "A," "B," "C," and "D." "A" receives 15 a week, "B" receives 50, "C," 75, and "D," 100. Now these four are all without positions and they come to a practitioner for mental treatment. The practitioner takes the thought that there is nothing but activity; he neutralizes, in his own thought, any belief in inactivity and declares that each of these four men is divinely active and occupied. Without question he has set in motion a law which will respond and will reproduce something for each of these four. We will suppose that his treatment is a good and an effective one; they receive it, and consequently each one of them receives a position. You will find that each does not receive the same compensation, for in all probability "A" will receive 15 per week; "B," 50; "C," 75, and "D," 100. "But," one might say, "he spoke the same word for each; why did they not all receive 100 per week?" Because, while his word was used for each in a like manner, each could receive only his fill, his mental capacity to comprehend. Each was full, and no doubt running over; but the molds which their perceptions of life provided were limited to the subjective remembrance already set in motion by themselves. Each attracted to himself, out of the Universal Good, that which he could comprehend. It is the old statement that water will reach its own level by its own weight, and without effort. So a treatment will only level itself in the objective world at the level of the subjective thought and realization.

This does not mean that each of the above-stated men will always have to receive the same compensation; for with an enlarged consciousness he would receive more.

ATTRACTION

Every one automatically attracts to himself just what he is, and you may set it down that wherever you are, however intolerable the situation may be, it is just where you belong. There is no power in the Universe but yourself that can get you out of it. Some one may help you on the road to realization, but substantiality and permanence can come only through the consciousness of your own life and thought. Man must bring himself to a point where there is no misfortune, no calamity, no accident, no trouble, no confusion; where there is nothing but plenty, peace, power, Life and Truth. He should definitely, daily, using his own name, declare the Truth about himself, realizing that he is reflecting his statements into Consciousness, and that they will be operated upon by It.

This is called, in mysticism, High Invocation; invoking the Divine Mind; implanting within It seeds of thought relative to one's self. And this is why some of the teachers of older times used to teach their pupils to cross their hands over their chests and say: "Wonderful, wonderful, wonderful me!" definitely teaching them that, as they held themselves, so they would be held. "Act as though I Am and I will Be."

One of the ancient sayings is that, "To the man who can perfectly practice inaction, all things are possible." This sounds like a contradiction until one gets down to the inner teachings; for it is only when one completely practices inaction that he arrives at the point of the true actor. For he then realizes that the act and the actor are one and the same, that cause and effect are the same; which is simply a different way of saying: "Know the Truth and the Truth shall make you free." To reduce the whole thing to its simplest form, whatever one reflects into Mind will be done.

HOW TO DEMONSTRATE A HOME

Suppose you wish to demonstrate a home; daily, looking into Mind, visualize it just as you wish it to be, making the picture as clear as possible; for it is a lack of clearness of thought that hinders demonstration. Then sit there about ten minutes, saying, "It is, it is, it is." Perhaps thoughts will come in which say "that it is not." Pay no attention to such thoughts but return to your meditation, and seeing the picture anew, say again, "It is, it is, it is." Use no effort, but simply see the picture very clearly and declare for its presence.

Never look for results from treatment; for if you do you will not find them. This is in accordance with law, for what you look for you know that you do not have and are only trying to fool yourself into thinking that you do have. Treatment is not a process of hypnotism; it is a process of self-knowing; and if you really know you will be sure to demonstrate.

Treatment is the art, the science and process of systematically inducing within consciousness concepts of definite desires as already accomplished facts and experiences in life.

RESIST NOT

When Jesus said "Resist not evil," 60 He meant that non-recognition of evil is the only way to avoid it. This is true according to the law of cause and effect; for what we persist in recognizing, we persist in holding in place. That which we non-recognize, we neutralize, and it is no longer there, so far as we are concerned. In making a demonstration, don't try to demonstrate; for demonstrations are not made through effort, because this would contradict one of the fundamental principles of the universe, which is the Self-Existence of Causation. In other words, nothing can come before that which is, consequently everything must come out of that which is; and within that which is, is the inherent possibility of that which is to be. All things exist as a potentiality, as a possibility, now. "I Am Alpha and Omega." 61 Try to get a recognition of your desire and pass the whole thing over to Mind, and let It operate. Just know that the desire is already a fact, and quietly say to yourself, as often as the thought comes into mind: "It is done." The lighter the thought is, the less care or worry over it, the better. The best work is done when the element of struggle is entirely left out.

HEALING A MISUNDERSTANDING
Suppose one says: "I have had a terrible misunderstanding with a friend of mine and it has come to a point where we do not even speak to each other." What is the fundamental error which has brought about this condition? A lack of the realization of the Unity of all life, a belief in duality. Destroy this belief in duality; recognize that there is but One Mind; see God in each, and the trouble will be healed. We all live in the One Mind of God.

FATE
If one believes in fate he must be healed of this thought, for there is no such thing as fate. If one believes that planetary forces have anything to do with life he must be healed of this thought. Break down everything except the recognition of the One Perfect Power, which is not contingent upon any place, person, condition, time of year, or anything but Itself. A demonstration is made when it comes through straight from the Truth.

The one who wishes to make a demonstration must first clear up his own subjective atmosphere; the reason being that he may be objectively making statements which his subjective thought may be denying. In this way we often neutralize our word as fast as it is spoken.

A treatment is scientific in that it is the act of inducing into Subjectivity ideas which neutralize false images of thought and which let the Truth come through into expression. The reason that we need such a science is that we do not have a perfect faith; for if we had a perfect faith we would have washed clean the subjective thought and no doubts would be there. Until the time comes when one can say to the sick, "Get up and walk," and have them do so; or say, "There is money," and have it appear, he must take the process of inducing thought for the purpose of accumulating a subjective belief in the things which he desires; this belief, as soon as it is complete, *is the demonstration*. The demonstration takes place within and not without.

ATTRACTION OF PERSONALITY
One might say, "I have no personality with which to attract people." There is but One Person; this Person is manifested through every living soul. It is radiant, vibrant, dynamic; It is The Personality; It is Complete; It is, It is.

The ones to whom we are the most strongly attracted are not necessarily the ones who are the most beautiful physically; but are the ones from which we receive that subtle emanation, "that something." What is "that something"? It is not that which shows, but that which floats through from within. It is the inner recognition of Reality.

SEE LIFE EXPRESSED

One should analyze himself, saying, "Do I look at myself from a standpoint of restriction? Do I see life as limited to the eternal round of getting up in the morning, eating, going to work, coming home, going to bed, sleeping, getting up again?" and so on. Break the bonds of necessity and see life as one continuous expression of the Infinite Self; and as this conception gradually dawns upon the inner thought, something will happen in the outer conditions to let up on the greater demands of the law of necessity. If one were doing the work he should be doing, he would never become tired, because the energy which holds the universe in place is tireless. The reason why we become tired is that we have cross currents of thought over our work. This arises from a belief in duality.

A treatment is the scientific act of inducing concepts in Mind, which operates upon them and manifests them in external affairs, just as the picture is held subjectively. During the process we meet, contact, neutralize and erase any and all opposing mental forces or conditions which deny our greater good.

Never limit your view of life by what you or any one else has ever accomplished. The possibility of life is inherent within the capacity to imagine what life is, backed by the power to produce this imagery or Divine Imagination. It is not a question of failing or of succeeding; it is simply a question of sticking to an idea until it becomes a tangible reality.

The illusion is in the way that we look at things. We have looked at some things and they have looked evil to us; we must look at them until they look good. We have looked at some one and he has looked sick to us; we must look at him until he looks well. We have seen discord; we must see harmony.

Look at harmony and people will become harmonious. We have looked at poverty, degradation and misery until they have assumed a gigantic form. Now we must look at harmony, happiness, plenty, prosperity, peace and right action until it appears.

LOOK TO THE ULTIMATE

In treating, we conceive of the ultimate of the idea, but never of the process. Never treat a process; never look for one. We plant a seed, and there is in that seed, operating through the creative soil, everything that is going to happen until it comes up, unfolds, and produces a plant. The ultimate of effect is already potential in cause. This is the mystical meaning of those words, "I am Alpha and Omega." 62 Our word should be the alpha and the omega, the beginning and the end of the thing thought of. All cause and effect are in Spirit. Cause and effect are bound together into one complete whole. One is the inside and the other is the outside of the same thing.

Once you have driven the peg into the ground, stick to it. Never let anything cause you to doubt your ability to demonstrate the Truth. Conceive of your word as being the thing. See the desire as an already accomplished fact and rest in perfect confidence, peace and certainty, never looking for results, never wondering, never becoming anxious, never being hurried nor worried. Those who do not understand this attitude will think that you are inactive, but remember, "To him who can perfectly practice inaction, all things are possible."

NO MISTAKES

In mental work, we must realize that there is One Infinite Mind, which is consciously directing our destiny. Declare every day that "no mistakes have been made, none are being made, and none can be made"; declare, "There is One Supreme Intelligence which governs, guides and guards, tells me what to do, when to act, and how to act"; then act with perfect assurance. Declare, "everything necessary to the full and complete expression of the most boundless experience, joy and life, everything is now"; know this, see it, feel it and be it. Do this every day for a few minutes; we should all do this until the time comes when it will no longer be necessary. When that time comes, we will know it, because our demonstrations will have been made.

Suppose one says: "I have made a lot of mistakes in my life. I had opportunities which I did not grasp." This is a direct belief that there is but one opportunity which comes to man, and if he does not take it he will have no more. This is a belief in limited opportunities, and it must be denied completely and specifically. We exist in Limitless Opportunities, which are forever seeking expression through us, and are expressed in and through us.

Know that there is no condemnation; for nothing can condemn unless we believe in condemnation. Destroy the thought that would lay limitation or bondage upon any situation or condition. "Loose him, and let him go." 63

Talk to yourself, not to the world. There is no one to talk to but yourself, for all experiences take place within. Conditions are the reflections of our own meditations, and nothing else. There is but One Mind to think, but one thing that It can think; that Mind is our Mind now. It never thinks confusion; It knows what it wishes, and how to accomplish what it desires. It is what It desires.

CAUSES AND CONDITIONS

Pay no attention to what happens in the objective world when you are making a demonstration. We interpret causes by conditions only as we realize that a condition must partake of the nature of its cause. If there appears to be confusion in the condition, then there must have been confusion in the thought back of it. Pay no attention to the objective expression so long as you know you are getting the right subjective recognition. The way to work out a problem scientifically is to take it up in thought daily and conceive of it as already being an accomplished fact in experience. Get the idea of the desire as already embodied in the Absolute. Unless one believes that there is an Absolute, how can he do this? We must believe that we are dealing with Reality and with nothing less than the Absolute.

If we are radiating thought into Divine Mind, what is there that can hinder It from operating on this thought? Nothing, for It knows no hindrances. Be sure that there is nothing destructive in the reaction; for there must be no element of destructiveness in our work. Daily hold your desire as an already accomplished fact and go about your business with joy and gladness, with peace and quiet confidence; the Law is then sure to act. During the process many things may happen that will appear to be destructive. You may pass through good fortune and bad; but if you can come to the point where you are not disturbed by what happens on the outside, you have found the secret. If, as Jesus said, we "Judge not according to the appearance, but judge righteous judgment," 64 remembering that "things which are seen were not made of things which do appear"; 65 out of any chaos we can produce harmony, provided we keep our thought steady. The answer to prayer is already in the prayer when it is prayed.

PERFECT ACTION

Assume a case of treatment for prosperity. Suppose one comes to you and says: "Business is bad; there is no activity." How are you going to treat him? Are you going to treat activity or business, customers, conditions or what? There is but one thing to treat, as far as the practitioner is concerned, and that is *himself*. The practitioner treats himself, the reason being that his patient's and his own mind are in the One Mind.

There is but one activity, which is perfect. Nothing has happened to it; nothing can cut it off; it is always operating. There is no belief in inactivity. What is this statement for? To neutralize the belief in inactivity. A word spoken in Mind will reach its own level, in the objective world, by its own weight; just as in physical science we know that water reaches its own level by its own weight. You must destroy the thoughts of inactivity. Man cannot become either discouraged or afraid if he realizes that there is but One Mind which he may consciously use. The real man knows no discouragement, cannot be afraid and has no unbelief.

"Who plants a seed beneath the sod
And waits to see it turn away the clod,
Has faith in God."

And he who knows of the power with which he is dealing, and who plants a seed of thought in Subjectivity, knows that it will come up and bear fruit.

Bring out the idea of Substance. Make consciousness perceive that Substance is Spirit, Spirit is God, and God is all that there is. Once you acquaint the consciousness with this idea, it is implanted in the Creative Power which is externalizing in your life.

MENTAL EQUIVALENTS

The Law is Infinite and Perfect; but in order to make a demonstration we must first have a mental equivalent of the thing we *desire*. Consequently, the range of our possibilities at the present time does not extend far beyond the range of our present concepts. As we bring ourselves to a greater vision, we can then induce a still greater concept and thereby demonstrate more in our experience. In this way there is a continuous growth and unfoldment taking place. We do not expect to give a treatment to-day and have a million dollars to-morrow. But, little by little, we can unfold our consciousness through the acquisition of greater and still greater mental equivalents, until at last we shall be made free. The way to proceed is to begin right where we are. It is not scientific to attempt to begin somewhere else. This would be chaotic. One who understands the systematic use of the Law will realize that he is where he is because of what he is; but he will not say, "I must be where I am because of what I am." Instead, he will begin to disclaim what he appears to be. As his statements loosen wrong subjective tendencies and false mentality, providing in their place a correct concept of life and Reality, he will automatically be lifted out of his conditions; and impelling forces, which will sweep everything before them, will set him free, if he trusts in Spirit and in nothing else.

Stay with the One and never deviate from It; never leave It for a moment. Nothing else can equal this attitude. To desert the Truth in the hour of need is to prove that we do not know the Truth. When things look the worst is the supreme moment to demonstrate to yourself that there are no obstructions. When things look worst is the best time to work, the most satisfying time. The person who can throw himself, with a complete abandon, into that Limitless Sea of Receptivity, having cut loose from all apparent moorings, is the one who will always receive the greatest reward.

TREATING FOR ACTIVITY

Suppose you have a store and wish to attract customers, which means activity in this kind of business. Every day see the place filled with people. Make a mental picture of this. You are dealing with Intelligence, so work intelligently. Ask for what you wish and take it. If you were treating for activity in a store in Boston you would not be treating some one in Kalamazoo for the mumps. Remember that you are dealing with Intelligence; *it is going to evolve your concept exactly as you involve it.* If one could take a picture of his objective circumstances and his subjective mentality, he would find that they would be identical; for one is the cause of the other; one is the image and the other is the reflection of that image.

RECEIVING INFORMATION

Suppose that we wish a special piece of information; we should say, "I wish to know this thing and I do know it. Whatever instrument is necessary to present it to me is now in full operation." This is a direct declaration that we have the desired knowledge, that that which we wish to know we do know. Say, "The Spirit of Intelligence within me tells me what I should know," or, "Everything that I should know I do know." It does not matter how we get this knowledge; we would not care if we read it on a sign, or in the dictionary, or if it were told us, or if it were sent to us; but we should consider the demonstration complete provided we received it. Say, "Everything necessary for the complete fulfillment of this idea is now in full operation, and I accept it."

NO FAILURES

If one appears to have failed he should realize that there are no failures in the universe. We should completely erase the idea of failure by stating that there are no failures. If one believes that he failed last year he will be likely to fail again this year, unless the false thought should be erased.

Now here is a place where it looks as though one were lying to himself, but he is not; for he is declaring the truth about the Spirit that indwells him; this Spirit never fails. Affirm, "This word blots from the book of my remembrance any sense of lack, limitation, want or fear of failure. There is no failure, no person to fail; failure is neither person, place nor thing; it is a false thought and has no truth in it; it is a belief in lack and there is no lack; it is a belief in a limitation which does not exist."

Thought is very subtle, and sometimes you may find, when you are making such a statement, that arguments will rise against it. Stop right here and meet those arguments; refuse to accept them.

OPPORTUNITY

Suppose you are treating your business and something from within says, "There are too many people in this business"; handle the thought of competition at once; say, "There is no competition or monopoly." You must do something to free the endeavor to express itself. Treatment is a thing of itself; it is an entity of Infinite Intelligence, Life and Action, and nothing can hinder its operation except unbelief or a lack of adequate mental equivalents. "They could not enter in because of unbelief," 66 and they "tempted God and limited the Holy One of Israel." 67

Never depend upon people, or say that things must come from this or that source. It makes no difference where things come from. Say that they are and let them come from where they will; and then, if something appears to happen which points to a place for them to come from, it is correct to say, "If this is the place, then there is nothing which can hinder." This is not hypnotic, for you are simply guarding against the possibility of some false thought coming in and hindering your demonstration.

Nothing moves but Mind. God makes things through the direct act of becoming the things which He creates. This is what we do, for our thought becomes the thing thought of. The thought and the thing are one, in reality. *"What a man has as well as what he is, is the result of the subjective state of his thought."* Keep on subjectifying thought until the balance of your consciousness is on the affirmative side, and nothing can hinder it from demonstrating. This is inevitable, for this is the way that the Law operates.

NO MISTAKES

Regarding mistakes,—declare that there are none, that there never were and never will be any. Say, "I represent the Truth, the whole Truth and nothing but the Truth; It is unerring, It never mistakes; there are no mistakes in the Divine Plan for me; there is no fear; there is no limitation, poverty, want nor lack; I stand in the midst of eternal opportunity, which is forever presenting me with the evidence of its full expression. I am joy, peace and happiness; I am the spirit of joy within me; I am the spirit of peace within me, of poise and power; I am the spirit of happiness within me; I radiate life; I am Life. There is One Life; that Life is my Life now." It is not enough to say, "There is One Life and that Life is God." We must complete this statement by saying, "That Life is my Life now," because we must couple this Life with ours in order to express It. We are not becoming This Life, but are now, in, and of, This Life. There is no other Life.

God is not becoming; God Is. God is not growing; God is Complete. God is not trying to find out something; God already knows. Evolution is not the expression of a becoming God, but is simply one of the ways that a God Who already Is, expresses Himself; and as such, it is the logical result of involution and is eternally going on.

DEMONSTRATION BY PROOF

If one is in a position which is distasteful, subject to circumstances over which he apparently has no control at the time, how should he act? He should not leave the place where he is until his thought has drawn him to a better one. In making a demonstration, we should not shove anything before us, carry anything with us nor drag anything after us. We should stay where we are until our word takes us somewhere else; for this is the only proof that we have demonstrated.

HANDLING A SCHOOLROOM

A teacher, in dealing with the thought of pupils, should treat their thought as a unit. The individuality of the room, of which each pupil is a part, is a perfect idea. There is One Mind operating in, around and through all these pupils, controlling them, directing them and inspiring them; there are peace, calm, satisfaction and enlightenment here. Realize the Active Presence of the One Mind, working in, around and through all, and you will find that this will harmonize the most discordant state, provided the teacher, the one who is thinking, really knows the Truth.

THE LAW OF CORRESPONDENCE

The limit of our ability to demonstrate depends on our ability to provide a mental equivalent of our desire; for the law of correspondences works from the belief to the thing. But we can provide a greater mental equivalent through the unfolding of consciousness; and this growth from within will finally lead to freedom.

What we demonstrate to-day, to-morrow and the next day is not as important as *the tendency which our thought is taking.* If, every day, things are a little better, a little happier, a little more harmonious, a little more health-giving and joyous; if, each day, we are expressing more life, we are going in the right direction.

And so we meditate daily upon the Universe of the All Good, that Infinite Indwelling Spirit which we call God, the Father, Incarnate in man; trying to sense and to feel this Indwelling Good as the Active Principle of our lives. This is what the mystics call "The Man of the Heart," or "The Angel of God's Presence." This is why they taught that there are always Two; for there is what we seem to be and what we really are; and as we contact this Higher Principle of our own lives—Which is Perfect and Complete, needing nothing, wanting nothing, knowing everything, being happy and satisfied,—and as we daily meditate upon this Indwelling God, we shall acquire a greater mental equivalent.

For those who have thought small thoughts all of their lives a very good practice is to dwell upon the bigness of the universe. Think how many stars there are; think of how many fish there are in the seas, and how many grains of sand on the beach. Think of how big the ocean is; of the immensity of space, the bigness of everything, the grandeur of everything, Mechanically, if necessary, compel the mentality to cognize Reality. Compel the consciousness to recognize the Truth through pure reason, if no other conviction comes.

Think, see and feel activity. Radiate Life. Feel that there is that within which is the center and circumference of the universe. The universe is the result of the Self-Contemplation of the Lord. Our lives are the results of our self-contemplations, and are peopled with the personifications of our thoughts and ideas. Accept this without question, for it is true.

Nothing is real to us unless we make it real. Nothing can touch us unless we let it touch us. Refuse to have the feelings hurt. Refuse to receive any one's condemnation. In the independence of your own mentality, believe and feel that you are wonderful. This is not conceit; it is the truth. What can be more wonderful than the manifestation of the Infinite Mind?

"Awake thou that sleepest, and arise from the dead, and Christ shall give thee light." 68 "Prove Me, now herewith, saith the Lord of Hosts, if I will not open you the windows of heaven, and pour you out a blessing, that there shall not be room enough to receive it." 69 "Be firm and ye shall be made firm." "Act as though I am and I will be." "Onlook thou the Deity and the Deity will onlook thee." "As thou hast believed so be it done." 70 "Ask and it shall be given unto you." 71 "So shall my word be that goeth forth out of my mouth—it shall prosper." 72

Note: Read and study "That Something"; "The Edinburgh Lectures," T. Troward; "The Law and the Word," T. Troward; "Creative Mind and Success," E. S. Holmes; "How to Visualize," Behrend; "Financial Success Through Creative Thought," Wattles.

Footnotes

60 Matt. 5:39.
61 Rev. 1:8.
62 Rev. 1:8.
63 John 11:44.
64 John 7:24.
65 Heb. 11:3.
66 Heb. 3:19.
67 Ps. 78:41.
68 Eph. 5:14.
69 Mal. 3:10.
70 Matt. 8:13.
71 Matt. 7:7.
72 Isa. 55:11.

LESSON FOUR: RECAPITULATION

Limitation and poverty are not things but are the results of restricted ways of thinking. We are surrounded by a Subjective Intelligence which receives the impress of our thought and acts upon it. This Intelligence is a natural Law in the Mental World, and consequently It is neither good nor bad. It can only be said of It, that It Is, and that we may consciously use It.

The Law is a Law of Reflection; for life is a mirror, reflecting to us, as conditions, the images of our thinking. Whatever one thinks tends to take form and to become a part of his experience.

The Medium of all thought is the Universal Mind, acting as Law. Law is always impersonal, neutral, receptive and reactive.

A sense of separation from good causes us to feel restricted; and a sense of our Unity with Good changes the currents of Causation and brings a happier condition into the experience.

Everything in the so-called material universe is an effect and exists only by virtue of some mental image behind it.

Man's individuality enables him to make such use of the Law as he desires; he is bound, not by limitation, but by a limited thought. The same power which binds him will free him when he understands the Law to be one of Liberty and not one of bondage. The power within man can free him from all distasteful conditions, if the Law governing this power is properly understood and utilized.

The Law of Mind, which is the Medium of all action, is a Law of perfect balance; the Objective World perfectly balances the images within the Subjective World. Water will reach its own level by its own weight; and, according to the same law, consciousness will externalize at its own level by its own weight. Cause and effect are but two sides of the same thing, one being the image in Mind and the other the objective condition.

The manifest universe is the result of the Self-Contemplation of the Lord. Man's world of affairs is the result of his self-contemplation. He is, at first, ignorant of this, and so binds himself through wrong ideation and action; reversing this thought will reverse the condition.

There is neither effort nor strain in knowing the Truth. Right action will be compelled through right knowing; therefore, when we know the Truth, It will compel us to act in the correct manner.

Attraction and repulsion are mental qualities, and may be consciously utilized for definite purposes. Man, automatically and according to Law, attracts from without the correspondences of his inner mental attitudes. Inner mental attitudes may be induced through right thinking and correct knowing. The subjective state of thought is the power always at work; it is the result of the sum total of all beliefs, consciously or unconsciously held. The subjective state of thought may be consciously changed through right mental action. The conscious thought controls the subconscious, and in its turn, the subconscious controls conditions.

Visualizing, or mentally seeing right action, tends to produce the picture in external affairs.

Since the Law is mental, one must believe in It, in order to have It work affirmatively for him; but It is always working according to our belief, whether we are conscious of this fact or not.

Demonstration takes place through the field of the One Universal Mind; we set the Power in motion; the Law produces the effect. We plant the seed and the Law produces the plant.

One should never allow himself to think of, or talk about, limitation or poverty. Life is a mirror and will reflect back to the thinker what he thinks into it.

God's plan for man is a perfect one, and when we harmonize with it we will become free from all bondage. The more spiritual the thought, the higher the manifestation. Spiritual thought means an absolute belief in, and reliance upon, Truth; this is both natural and normal.

All is Love yet all is Law; Love is the impelling force and Law executes the will of Love. Man is a center of God-Consciousness in the great Whole; he cannot deface his real being, but may hinder the Whole from coming into a complete expression through his life. Turning to the One with a complete abandonment and in absolute trust, he will find that he already is saved, helped and prospered.

There is One Infinite Mind from which all things come; this Mind is through, in and around man; It is the Only Mind that there is, and every time man thinks he uses It. There is One Infinite Spirit, and every time man says, "I am," he proclaims It. There is One Infinite Substance; and every time man moves, he moves in It. There is One Infinite Law, and every time man thinks he sets It in motion. There is One Infinite God, and every time man speaks to This God, he receives a direct answer. One! One! One! "I Am God and there is none else." 73 There is One Limitless Life which returns to the thinker what he thinks into It. One! One! One! "In all, over all and through all."

Talk, live, act, believe and know that you are a center in the One. All the Power there is; all the Presence there is; all the Love there is; all the Peace there is; all the Good there is and the Only God that is, is Omnipresent; consequently, the Infinite is in and through man and is in and through everything. "Act as though I am and I will Be."

Footnotes

73 Isa. 45:22.

LESSON FIVE: INTRODUCTION

A mystic is not a mysterious person; but is one who has a deep, inner sense of Life and Unity with the Whole; mysticism and mystery are entirely different things; one is real while the other may, or may not, be an illusion. There is nothing mysterious in the Truth, so far as It is understood; but all things, of course, are mysteries until we understand them.

A mystic is one who intuitively perceives Truth and who, without mental process, arrives at Spiritual Realizations. It is from the teachings of the great mystics that the best in the philosophy of the world has come.

The civilization of to-day is built around the teachings of a few people who have intuitively perceived Spiritual Truth. Our great code of law was given by Moses, a man who through the mystic sense perceived that we live in a Universe of Law. Our greatest code of ethics was given through the perception of the prophets, culminating in such teachings as those of Jesus and Buddha. Who was there who could have taught such men as these? By what process of mentality did they arrive at their profound conclusions? We are compelled to recognize that Spirit Alone was their Teacher; they were, indeed, taught of God.

The mystic intuitively senses Reality and instinctively knows The Truth; and in this way all of the best in literature, music and art have come.

Our great religions have been given by a few who climbed the heights of spiritual vision and caught a fleeting glimpse of Ultimate Reality. No living soul could have taught them what they knew, and it is doubtful if even they themselves knew why they knew.

The great poets have been true mystics and have revealed, through their poems, the Presence of God. Men like Robert Browning, Tennyson, Wordsworth, Homer, Walt Whitman, Edward Rowland Sill, and others of like nature, have given us poetry which is immortal, because they had a mystic sense of life: the perception of a Living Presence. All true philosophers are mystics; the old prophets were mystics; David, Solomon, Jesus, Plato, Buddha, Plotinus, Emerson, and a score of others, all had the same experience: the sense of a Living Presence.

The greatest music ever composed was written by the hand of a mystic; and the highest and best in art has come from the same source.

Man has compelled nature to do his bidding; he has harnessed electric energy, caught the wind, trapped steam and made them all obey his will. He has invented machines to do the work of thousands; he has belted the globe with his traffic and built up a wonderful civilization; but in few cases has he conquered his own soul.

The highest and best that we have in civilization is the result of the mystic sense which has been perceived by a few in each age. All that modern appliances and inventions give us in the way of comfort and luxury, good and necessary as they are, may be counted as nothing compared to the teachings of Jesus. By this, we do not mean to decry modern civilization, education or anything that goes with it; for we are firm believers in anything and everything that makes life interesting and worth living. We believe in science, art, religion, education, commerce, government, industry, agriculture, and all that goes to make up a well-rounded experience in life; but we repeat, what would they amount to, if thought of in any other light than as passing things?

The mystic has revealed things that do not pass as ships in the night; he has revealed Eternal Verities and has plainly taught us that there is a Living Presence indwelling All.

TRUE MYSTICISM AND THE PSYCHIC SENSE

There is a vast difference between mysticism and psychism, between a mystic and an ordinary psychic. The psychic capacity will be thoroughly discussed in Lesson Six, and the reader will remember that it is the power to read subjectively; it may be dealing with a reality or with an illusion. The average psychic must become more or less subjective in order to do good work. At best, and even though in a normal state of mind, he can only read subjective pictures and tendencies; at best, he is generally dealing with human thought. Should he penetrate that thought, he would then become a mystic.

A mystic does not read human thought but senses the Thought of God. The question might be asked, "How do you know that he senses the Thought of God?" Because the mystics of every age have seen, sensed and taught *the same truth*. Psychic experiences more or less contradict each other, because each psychic sees a different kind of mental picture; but the mystic experiences of the ages have revealed *one and the same truth.*

WHAT THE MYSTICS HAVE TAUGHT

Without exception, all of the mystics have taught that there is but One Ultimate Reality; and that this Ultimate Reality is *here now, if we could but see it.*

Strange as it may seem, the great mystics have all believed in a Personal God; that is, a God who is Personal to all who believe in Him. They have not, of course, believed in an *anthropomorphic god*; but they have believed in a God who consciously works in and through man; and they have adored and worshiped this God.

The great mystics have been illumined, that is, they have, at times, seen through the veil of matter and perceived the Spiritual Universe. They have taught that the Kingdom of God is *now present and needs but to be realized*; and they have, apparently, sensed that this Kingdom is within.

A psychic sees only through his own subjective mentality; consequently, everything that he looks at is more or less colored by the vibration of his own thought; he is subject to hallucinations and false impressions of every description. This is why, generally speaking, no two psychics ever see the same thing.

Mystics have all seen the same thing, and their testimony is in no way confusing; this is because the Spirit within them has borne witness to the Truth.

NO ULTIMATE EVIL

One of the most illuminating things that mysticism has revealed, is that evil is not an ultimate reality. Evil is simply and experience of the soul on its journey toward Reality; it is not an entity but an experience necessary to self-unfoldment; it is not a thing of itself but simply a misuse of power. It will disappear when we stop looking at, or believing in, it. We cannot stop believing in it as long as we indulge in it; so the mystic has always taught the race to turn from evil and do good.

ULTIMATE SALVATION OF ALL

The mystics have taught the ultimate salvation of all people and the immortality of every soul. Indeed, they have taught that immortality *is here and now, if we would but wake to the fact.* "Beloved, now are we the Sons of God." 74 Since each soul is some part of the Whole, it is impossible that any soul can be lost. "God is not the God of the dead, but of the living." 75 Damnation has been as foreign to the thought of the mystic as any belief in evil must be to the Mind of God.

FREEDOM FROM BURDEN

The great mystics have taught that man should have no burdens, and would have none, if he turned to "The One." "Come unto Me all ye that labor and are heavy laden and I will give you rest." 76 As Jesus must have known that it would be impossible for all men to come unto Him as a Personality, He must have meant that we should come into His understanding of Life and Reality; that is, to come unto the Great God. Some day we will learn to lay our burdens on the Altar of Love, that they may be consumed by the fire of faith in the Living Spirit. Man would have no burdens if he kept his "High watch" toward "The One"; that is, if he always turned to God.

UNITY OF ALL

Jesus prayed that all might come to see the Unity of Life. "That they may be One, even as we are One," 77 was His prayer as He neared the completion of His great work on this planet. All mystics have sensed that we live in One Life. "For in Him we live, and move, and have our being." 78 The Unity of Good is a revelation of the greatest importance; for it teaches us that we are One with the Whole, and One with each other. This realization alone will settle the question of human inequality. The real Fatherhood of God and the Actual Brotherhood of Man will be made apparent on earth to the degree that men realize True Unity.

REALIZATION OF INDIVIDUALITY

No great mystic ever lived who denied the reality of individuality. The higher the sense of Truth, the greater will be the realization of the uniqueness of individual character and personality. The Real Self is God-given and cannot be denied; it is the place where God comes to a point of Individualized and Personified Expression, and should be thought of in this light. "I am the Light of the world." 79

NORMALCY

All mystics have been normal people, that is, they have lived just as other people have lived. The only difference has been that they have sensed a greater Reality; namely, the Presence of the Living Spirit. The true mystic in every age has come into the world of affairs and lived among men, sometimes as a teacher, and sometimes in the ordinary walks of life, but always in a perfectly natural way. There is nothing peculiar or strange about a mystic. People who shroud themselves in a cloak of mystery are not true mystics but are laboring under mental delusions and subjective hallucinations. They may be sincere in their beliefs, but they are none the less wrong in their methods. It is a question if a real mystic would even realize that he is a mystic. He would be more liable to think of himself simply as one who understands that he is One with the Whole.

THE GREAT LIGHT

It is impossible, perhaps, to put into words or into print what a mystic sometimes sees, and it is as hard to believe it as it is to put it into words. But there is a certain inner sense which, at times, sees Reality in a flash which illuminates the whole being with a great flood of light. This, too, might seem an illusion unless the testimony were complete; for every mystic has had this experience; but some have had it to a greater degree than others. Jesus was the greatest of all the mystics; and once, at least, after a period of illumination, His face was so bright that His followers could not look upon it.

In moments of deepest realization the great mystics have sensed that One Life flows through *all*; and that all are some part of that Life. They have also seen Substance, a fine, white, brilliant stuff, forever falling into everything; a Substance, indestructible and eternal. At times, the realization has been so complete that they have been actually blinded by the light. There are instances where for several days after such an experience, the one having it could not see on the physical plane; for he had seen the Inner Light. Remember, all this takes place when in a perfectly normal state of mind and has nothing whatever to do with the psychic state. It is not an illusion but a reality; and it is during these periods that real revelation comes. Perhaps a good illustration would be to suppose a large group of people in a room together, but unaware of each other's presence; each is busy with his own personal affairs. We will suppose the place to be dark and that some one comes in and takes a flash-light picture of the room and its occupants. Should this picture be shown to anyone who was in the room before it was taken, it might be hard for him to believe that all of the objects in the picture were actually in the room. This is, of course, a poor analogy, but it does serve to elucidate a point. In flashes of illumination, the inspired have seen *Into the very center of reality*, and have brought back with them a picture of what they have seen and felt. Again, we know that this has not been an illusion or simply a subjective hallucination, for each age has had its mystics, and every age has produced the same results. *All have seen the same thing.* The testimony is complete and the evidence is certain.

WHAT THE MYSTICS HAVE TAUGHT ABOUT THE INDIVIDUAL

All of the great mystics have taught practically the same thing. They have all agreed that the soul is on the pathway of experience, that is, of self-discovery; that it is on its way back to its Father's House; and that every soul will ultimately reach its Heavenly Home. They have taught the Divinity to Man. "I have said, Ye are gods; and all of you are children of the most High." 80 They have told us that man's destiny is Divine and sure; and that Creation is Complete and Perfect NOW. The great mystics have all agreed that man's life is his to do with as he chooses; but that when he turns to "The One," he will always receive inspiration form On High.

They have told us of the marvelous relationship which exists between God and man, of a close Union that cannot be broken; and the greatest of the mystics have consciously walked with God and talked with Him, just as we talk to each other. It is difficult to realize how this could be; it is hard to understand how a Being, so Universal as God must be, can talk with man; here, alone, the mystic sense reveals the greater truth and knows that, Infinite as is the Divine Being, It is still Personal to all who believe in Its Presence. It is entirely possible for a man to talk with the Spirit; for the Spirit is within men, and "He who made the ears" can hear.

INSTINCT AND INTUITION

That quality in an animal which directs its action and tells it where to go to find food and shelter, we call instinct. It is, really, Omniscience in the animal. The same quality, more highly developed, makes its appearance in man; and is what we call intuition. Intuition is God in man, revealing to him the Realities of Being; and just as instinct guides the animal, so would intuition guide man, if he would allow it to operate through him. Here again, we must be careful not to mistake a psychic impression for an intuitive one. Psychic impressions seek to control man; intuition always remains in the background and waits for his recognition. "Behold, I stand at the door." 81

All arbitrary control of man stopped as soon as he was brought to a point of self-knowingness. From this point he must discover himself; but intuition, which is nothing less than God in man, silently awaits his recognition and cooperation. The Spirit is always there if we could but sense Its Presence. Mystics have felt this wonderful power working from within, and have responded to it; and, as a sure evidence that they were not laboring under delusions, they have all sensed the same thing; had the impressions been psychic only, each would have seen and sensed a different thing; for each would have seen through the darkness of his own subjective mentality.

ILLUMINATION AND COSMIC CONSCIOUSNESS

There is such an experience as Illumination and Cosmic Consciousness; It is not a mystery, however, but is the Self-Knowingness of God through man. The more complete the operation of that Power, the more complete has been man's conscious mentality; for the illumined do not become less, but more themselves. The greater the consciousness of God, the more complete must be the realization of the True Self,—The Divine Reality.

Illumination will come as man more and more realizes his Unity with the Whole; and as he constantly endeavors to let the Truth operate through him. But since the Whole is at the point of the Inner Mentality, it will be here alone that he will contact It. "Speak to Him, thou, for He hears."

The only God man knows is the God of his own Inner Life; indeed, he can know no other. To assume that man can know a God outside himself is to assume that he can know something of which he is not conscious. This does not mean that man is God; it means that the only God man knows is within. The only place that man contacts God is within; and the only life man has is from within. God is not external, but is Indwelling, at the very center of man's life. This is why Jesus said that the Kingdom of Heaven is within, and why He prayed, "Our Father Which art in Heaven." 82

THE HIGHEST PRACTICE

The highest mental practice is to listen to this Inner Voice and to declare for Its Presence. The greater a man's consciousness of this Indwelling I AM is, the more power he will have. This will never lead to illusion but will always lead to Reality. All great souls have known this and have constantly striven to let the Mind of God come out through their mentalities. "The Father that dwelleth in Me, He doeth the works." 83 This was the declaration of the great Master, and it should be ours also; not a limited sense of life but a limitless one.

THE POWER OF JESUS

The occult significance of the power of Jesus is easily understood when we study His method of procedure. Consider His raising of Lazarus from the dead. He stood at the tomb and gave thanks; this was recognition. He next said, "I Knew that Thou hearest me always"; 84 this was unification; then He said, "Lazarus, come forth"; 85 this was command. The method is perfect and we will do well to study and follow it. This method can be used in all treatment. First, realize that Divine Power Is; then unify with It, and then speak the word as "one having authority," for the Law is "the servant of the Eternal Spirit throughout all the ages."

TURNING WITHIN

We should turn within, then, as have all of those great souls who have blessed the world with their presence; we should turn within and *find god*. It should seem natural to turn to the Great Power back of everything; it should seem normal to believe in this Power; and we should have a sense of a Real Presence when we do turn toward the One and Only Power in the entire Universe. This method is by far the most effective. It gives a sense of power that nothing else can, and, in this way, proves that it is a Reality. It would be a wonderful experiment if the world would try to solve all of its problems through the power of Spirit. Indeed the time will come when every one will, "From the highest...to the lowest."

A sense of real completion can come only to that soul which realizes its Unity with the Great Whole. Man will never be satisfied until his whole being responds to this thought, and then, indeed, "Will God go forth anew into Creation."

"To as many as believed gave He the Power."

Footnotes

74 1 John 3:2.
75 Matt. 22:32.
76 Matt. 11:28.
77 John 17:22.
78 Acts. 17:28.
79 John 8:12.
80 Ps. 82:6.
81 Rev. 3:20.
82 Luke 11:2.
83 John 14:10.
84 John 11:42.
85 John 11:43.

LESSON FIVE: THE PERFECT WHOLE

Chart No. V represents the Triune Unity. The other charts were divided into Spirit, Soul and Body, symbolizing the Conscious part of Existence; the Law through which It operates; and the result of the operation. But those lines were entirely arbitrary. No such lines could exist, for the threefold Universe, with all of Its attributes, interspheres Itself. We find the Spirit, or Conscious Mind, the Soul or Subconscious Mind, and the Body, which is the manifestation of the union of Spirit and Soul, simultaneously present at every point. This chart represents the Indivisible Whole, within which are all of Its parts; the Absolute, within which is the relative; the Uncreated, within which is all Creation.

Creation is the giving of form to the Substance of Spirit. Spirit, being All and Only, there is nothing for It to change into but Itself; therefore, It is the Changeless, within which must take place all change or manifestation of Itself. Change is simply motion within Life.

The Infinite, of Itself, is Formless, but within It are contained all of the forms which are the expressions or the outlines of Its experiences.

Spirit is the Limitless, within which is all space; Spirit is Timeless, within which is all time. "Time is the sequence of events in a Unitary Whole." Creation and experience are eternally going on, but a particular experience is measured by time and has a beginning and an end.

The big circle represents the Universal, within which is the individual; the One Person within Whom are all people. There is really but One Person in the Universe; but within this One Person all people live, "for in Him we live, and move, and have our being." 86 It is the Source and center of all Life, Power, Action, Truth, Love, Mind, Spirit, the Ever and the All. It is, of course, God.

THE TRIUNE UNITY

THE INDIVISIBLE WHOLE —

WITHIN WHICH IS ALL OF ITS PARTS

THE ABSOLUTE WITHIN WHICH IS THE RELATIVE

THE UNCREATED WITHIN WHICH IS THE CREATED

THE CHANGELESS WITHIN WHICH IS ALL CHANGE

THE FORMLESS WITHIN WHICH IS ALL FORM

THE LIMITLESS WITHIN WHICH IS ALL SPACE

THE TIMELESS WITHIN WHICH IS ALL TIME

THE UNIVERSAL WITHIN WHICH IS THE INDIVIDUAL

THE ONE PERSON WITHIN WHOM ARE ALL PEOPLE

SOURCE AND CENTER OF ALL LIFE POWER AND ACTION

TRUTH,LOVE,MIND,SPIRIT,THE EVER,AND THE ALL

<u>GOD</u>

Our Father
which art
in
Heaven

THE
SON

PERSONALITY....INDIVIDUALITY

<u>M A N</u>

Lesson Five: Metaphysical Chart No. V.

This is the Mystic's chart and shows how the Universal becomes the Particularization of Itself through man. Man comes to a point in the Universal, or God, and is the Idea of God as man. The Father is represented as the Whole just back of, or above, or within, man. This is the Indwelling God to Whom we pray and with Whom we talk. The mystic has the ability to consciously talk to God and to consciously receive a direct answer from the Spirit. In this chart it is shown that the Absolute contains the relative, within Itself, but is not limited by the relative. We must remember that the relative does not limit, but expresses, the Absolute. All change takes place within the Changeless. All form subsists within the Formless. All conditions obtain within that which is Limitless; and Creation is eternally going on within that which is Uncreated. All are activities of the One Mind and Spirit of God. All people come to a point of individuality within that which is universal.

INDIVIDUALITY

The point within the big circle represents the personality and individuality of man, indicating that he is a center in the Divine Mind or God.

Man is the Personification of the Infinite Life; and so we place, just above this point and on the inside of it, "The Son"; and just above this (with no line to divide them) are written the words, "Our Father which art in Heaven," 87 taken from the Lord's Prayer. There is no difference between God, the Absolute, which is Our Father in Heaven, and the Son, so far as actual Being is concerned. The Son is simply a point where God recognizes Himself as Personality or Individualized Being. It is within that we find the Unity of God and man; there is no separation.

Man, having his existence in the Unitary Whole, which is Indivisible, is compelled to accept the fact that his life is God or Spirit; but to say that man is God, which is equivalent to saying that any part equals the whole, is to contradict logic and reason, and limit the Limitless Idea. It is enough to say that we are at one with the Whole. It is both within and without. In perhaps a more liberal sense we could say man is in God; immersed in God; saturated with God. God permeates all life, and in man we find that this Infinite Mind or Intelligence comes to a point of Individualized Self-Consciousness.

Theoretically, we believe that the personality which we possess is on the pathway of self-discovery; for everything bears witness to this belief; as fast as we discover any truth, it is there to use. We never create Truth—we discover and use It. We believe, then, that as man continuously unfolds his personality, he will find latent capacities of which he has never dreamed.

FURTHER EVOLUTION

Since his whole life is the unfoldment of intelligence, according to law, man can only evolve as he recognizes greater possibilities—there could be no other way. The arbitrary process of evolution ceased when man became an individual; and any further evolution will be through self-recognition; but back of him is the whole of Life surging to express Itself. This is what is known as the Divine Urge. It is that Instinctive, Omniscient "I am" in man, always pushing him on and up; but It can only express for him as It flows through him. That person has the greatest power who the most completely recognizes himself to be one with this Infinite Mind. That is why Jesus said: "I speak not of myself" (it is not this individualized point); "but the Father that dwelleth in Me" (that is, God, our Father, Which is in Heaven); "He doeth the works." 88

The evolution of man, which is the unfoldment of Spirit through his personality, will be more complete when his objective and subjective faculties are more perfectly balanced; that is, when he has conscious control of the spiritual forces which surge for expression. The psychological nature has to change somewhat, and the subjective tendencies that hinder the Whole from coming to a point of conscious contact must be neutralized. This would produce illumination or the consciousness of his Unity with the Whole.

In treatment, we work until we penetrate the false thought within and break through to Reality. There is no limitation, either in Infinite Intelligence or in Infinite Law. The whole limitation which we experience is not, of itself, a reality or an entity, but is simply one of the forms within the formless which we are outlining.

THE TRUTH IS KNOWN

Our conscious intelligence is as much of Life as we understand. We have stopped looking for the Spirit, because we have found It; It is what you are and It is what I am; we could not be anything else if we tried. The thing that we look with is the thing that we have been looking for. That is why it is written: "I have said, Ye are gods; and all of you are children of the most High." 89 We have stopped looking for the Law. We have found It. In the Universe we call It the Universal Subjectivity or Soul; in our own experience we call It the subjective state of our thought, which is our individual use of Universal Law. We have found the Law and demonstrated It. We find that both the Law and the Spirit are Limitless. What is it that we need for a greater freedom? Nothing but a greater realization of what we already know.

We should never hesitate to say that we know the Truth, because we do; for the realization of the Unity of God and man is the Truth. We simply need a greater realization of this. How are we to get it? Only by penetrating deeper and yet deeper into our own Divine Nature; pushing farther and farther back into the Infinite. Where are we to do that? There is no place except within that we can do it. Who is to do it for us? No one. No one can. People can heal us; they can set the Law in motion for us and help us to become prosperous;—that is good and helpful; but the evolution of the individual, the unfoldment of personality, the enlightenment of the Soul, the illumination of Spirit, can come only to the degree that the individual himself purposes to let Life operate through him. "Let this Mind be in you which was also in Christ Jesus." 90 This is the Mind of God,—the only Mind,—the Supreme Intelligence of the Universe.

THE ANSWER IS IN MAN

The answer to every question is within man, because man is within Spirit and Spirit is an Indivisible Whole. The solution to every problem is within man; the healing of all disease is within man; the forgiveness of all sin is within man; the raising of the dead is within man; Heaven is within man. That is why Jesus prayed to this indwelling "I am" and said: "Our Father Which art in Heaven." 91 He also said: "The Kingdom of God is within you."92

Each of us, then, represents the Whole. How should we feel toward the Whole? In the old order, we thought of the Whole as a sort of mandatory power, an autocratic government, an arbitrary God, sending some to Heaven and some to hell; and "all for His glory." Now we are much more enlightened and we realize that there can be no such a Divine Being. We have meditated upon the vastness of the Universe of Law, and we have said: "God is Law; there is a Divine Principle Which is God." In the new order, we are liable to fall into as great an error as the old thought fell into, unless we go much deeper than thinking of God simply as Principle. God is more than Law or Principle. God is the Infinite Spirit, the Limitless, Conscious Life of the Universe; the One Infinite Person within Whom all people live. The Law is simply a Force.

GOD—INFINITE PERSONALITY

God or Spirit is Supreme, Infinite, Limitless Personality. And we should think of the Divine Being as such—as completely responsive to everything we do. There should come to us a sense of communion, a spontaneous sense of Irresistible Union. If we had that, we would demonstrate instantaneously.

An evolved soul is always a worshiper of God. He worships God in everything; for God is in everything. God not only is in everything, but He is more than everything He is in. "Ye are the light of the world"; 93—that is, God in us. All that we are is God; yet God is more than all we are.

The nearer consciousness gets to the Truth, the more Cosmic sweep it has, the more power it has. Angels wait upon individuals who perceive Cosmic Purposes and Powers, because the Whole is crowding forth into expression. Let a man recognize a Cosmic Purpose, which is the expression of Life, Truth and Love; let his thought vibrate to the higher and grander realization of life, and see how—automatically—he becomes more powerful.

The process of healing and demonstration is, at first, mechanical and scientific; then the fire of Spirit is added to make it real. One is technique—the other is the pulsating life and glow. We need the recognition of love, coupled with a scientific understanding of what we are doing. Thoughts are things, and diseases are the direct result of specific thoughts somewhere in consciousness. Poverty is the direct result of a subjective state of thought which binds.

UNITY

All Manifestation of Life is from and invisible to a visible plane; and it is a silent, effortless process of spiritual realization. We must unify, in our own mentalities, with Pure Spirit. To each of us, individually, God, or Spirit, is the Supreme Personality of the Universe; the Supreme Personality of that which we, ourselves, are. It is only as the relationship of the individual to this Deity becomes enlarged that he has a consciousness of power.

There should always be a recognition in treatment of the Absolute Unity of God and man; the Oneness, Inseparability, Indivisibility, Changelessness; God as the Big Circle, and man as the little circle. Man is in God and God is in man; just as a drop of water is in the ocean, while the ocean is in the drop of water. This is the recognition Jesus had when He said: "I and my Father are One." 94 There is a Perfect Union; and to the degree that we are conscious of this Union we incorporate this consciousness in our word, and our word has just as much power as we put in it, no more and no less.

Within this Infinite Mind each individual exists, not as a separated, but as a separate, entity. We are a point in Universal Consciousness, which is God, and God is our Life, Spirit, Mind and Intelligence. We are not separated from Life, neither is It separated from us; but we are separate entities in It, Individualized Centers of God's Consciousness.

We came from Life and are in Life, so we are One with Life; and we know that Instinctive Life within, which has brought us to the point of self-recognition, still knows in us the reason for all things, the purpose underlying all things; and we know that there is nothing in us of fear, doubt or confusion which can hinder the flow of Reality to the point of our recognition. We are guided, daily, by Divine Intelligence into paths of peace wherein the soul recognizes its Source and meets It in joyful Union, in complete At-one-ment.

HOLD TO THE GOOD

Such is the power of clear thought that it penetrates things; it removes obstructions, the reason being that there is nothing but consciousness, nothing but Mind. The only instrument of Mind is idea. See with perfect clearness and never become discouraged nor overcome by a sense of limitation. Know this:—that the Truth with which you are dealing is absolute. All of God, all of Truth, all there is, is at the point of man's recognition; and every time you give a treatment, and all the way through it, keep bringing this back to your remembrance.

Never struggle; say, "There is nothing to struggle over; everything is mine by Divine Right; Infinite Intelligence is my Intelligence; Divine Love is my Love; Limitless Freedom is my Freedom; Perfect Joy is my Gladness; Limitless Life is my Energy."

Let us *blind ourselves to negation*, as far as we are mentally able to. *Let us not talk, think, or read about anything destructive*, whether it be war, pestilence, famine, poverty, sickness, or limitation of any kind. Looking at this from a practical standpoint, there is all to win and nothing to lose. The rapid progress we would make if we should do this would be wonderful.

We are always dealing with First Cause. Nothing else can equal the satisfaction that comes to one when he perceives himself, from the silence of his own soul and the activity of his own thought, actually bringing about a condition without the aid of visible instrumentalities. There is nothing else as satisfying as to heal some disease purely by the power of thought; this shows that we are dealing with First Cause.

We must definitely neutralize confusion and doubt. We should take time, daily, to conceive of ourselves as being tranquil, poised, powerful,—always in control of every situation; as being always the highest concept of the Divine which we can imagine. We should never hesitate to think of ourselves in this way. The Ancients used to teach their pupils to say to themselves—"Wonderful, wonderful, wonderful me!"—until they lost sight of themselves as Mary Smith or John Jones, and perceived themselves as Divine Realities. Then, when they came back to the objectivity of Mary Smith and John Jones, they brought with them that subtle power which distinguishes Spiritual Growth,—the Atmosphere of Reality.

THE INFINITE IS PERSONAL TO ALL

Undoubtedly the power of Jesus lay in His recognition of the Infinite Person as a Responsive, Conscious, Living Reality; while, on the other hand, He recognized the Law as an arbitrary force, which was compelled to obey His will. He combined the personal and the impersonal attributes of Life into a perfect whole. The Infinite is Personal to every soul who believes in the Infinite. It is a mistake to so abstract the Principle that we forget the Living Presence; it is the combination of the two that makes work effective.

THE CHRIST

Who is man? He is the Christ. Who is the Christ? The Son, begotten of the only Father;—not the only begotten Son of God. Christ means the Universal Idea of Sonship, of which each is a Member. That is why we are spoken of as Members of that One Body; and why we are told to have that Mind in us "which was also in Christ Jesus." 95 Each partakes of the Christ Nature to the degree that the Christ is revealed through him, and to that degree he becomes the Christ. We should turn to that Living Presence within, Which is the Father in Heaven, recognize It as the One and Only Power in the Universe, unify with It, declare our word to be the presence, power and activity of that One, and speak the word as if we believed it; because the Law is the servant of the Spirit.

If we could stand aside and let the One Perfect Life flow through us, we could not help healing people. This is the highest form of healing.

We have gone through all of our abstract processes of reasoning and have found out what the Law is and how It works; now we can forget all about It, and know that there is nothing but the Word; the Law will be working automatically. We must forget everything else, and let our word be spoken with a deep inner realization of love, beauty, peace, poise, power, and of the great Presence of Life at the point of our own consciousness.

REALIZATION

We do not dare to throw ourselves with abandonment into a seeming void; but if we did, we would find our feet planted firmly on a rock, for there is a place in the mentality, in the heights of its greatest realizations, where it throws itself with complete abandonment into the very center of the Universe. There is a point in the supreme moment of realization where the individual merges with the Universe, but not to the loss of his individuality; where a sense of the Oneness of all Life so enters his being that there is no sense of otherness; it is here that the mentality performs seeming miracles, because there is nothing to hinder the Whole from coming through. We can do this only by providing the great mental equivalents of Life, by dwelling and meditating upon the immensity of Life; and yet as vast, as immense, as limitless as It is, the whole of It is brought to the point of our own consciousness.

We comprehend the Infinite only to the degree that It expresses Itself through us, becoming to us that which we believe It to be. And so we daily practice in our meditations the realizations of Life:—"Infinite, indwelling Spirit within me, Almighty God within me, Perfect Peace within me, Complete Satisfaction within me, Real Substance within me; that which is the Truth within me." "I am the Truth," Jesus said. He said: "I am the way; I am the Life; no man cometh unto the Father but by Me." 96 How true it is! We cannot come unto the Father Which art in Heaven except through our own nature.

Right here, through our own nature, is the gateway and the path that gradually leads to illumination, to realization, to inspiration, to the intuitive perception of everything.

The highest faculty in man is intuition, and it comes to a point sometimes where, with no process of reasoning at all, he realizes the Truth intuitively. So we should daily meditate, particularly if we are practicing right along.

MEDITATION

Any practitioner should take a certain time every day to meditate within himself, to realize that the words which he speaks are the words of Truth. Being the words of Truth, they cannot fail to be fulfilled; they are a law unto themselves within the Great Law. They know themselves to be what they are. They are immutable, irresistible, unassailable; they are eternal and complete, having intelligence, knowledge and understanding within themselves.

Every treatment must be a complete thing within itself. It is an unqualified statement of Being and pays no attention to appearances. If it did, it would not be efficacious. It rises above all appearance and may contradict every experience the human race has ever had; but it is real just the same. The treatment begins and ends within the mentality of the one giving it; and the demonstration takes place within the mentality of the one giving it; and, to the degree that it does take place there, it is a good treatment and will be a good demonstration.

If you have a patient who says: "I am sick," and you are able to neutralize your belief of that man as being sick, or any man as being sick, and can see him perfect, he will come to you and say: "I am healed." The practitioner must know within himself. He never thinks of projecting his thought, sending it out or holding it. He simply takes the whole condition and brings it into the great realization of Life.

Declare:—"Perfect Life within me, God within me, Spirit within me, Good within me, Almightiness within me, Loving Intelligence within me, Peace, Poise, Power, Happiness and Joy within me, Life, Truth and Love within me, Omniscient Instinctive I am within me, Almighty God within me." It is not enough to say that God is. The concept must be brought home to the mentality of the individual and unified with it, in order to have it expressed through him.

If we need financial healing, we should say: "Infinite Substance within me, Infinite Activity within me, flowing through me into everything I do, say or think, quickening into action all those things that my mentality touches; Infinite Activity within me, unerring, never mistaking, always doing the right thing at the right time, always knowing what to do, knowing how to do it and doing it; Infinite Executive Power within me, the Great Executive, the great I am, the All-Knowing and All-Seeing, the All-Wise within me; Infinite Substance within me, forever expressing Itself through me; Infinite Supply flowing through me and flowing to me;—irresistible supply, unassailable supply, limitless." As you say this, stop and think of the things you want—seeing them as realities—much as one would look at pictures on the wall.

Repeat:—"Infinite Substance within me, Infinite Supply flowing through me and to me, Infinite Activity around me and within me, Infinite Intelligence within me, directing me, guarding me, governing me, controlling me; the One and Only within me and through me, that is, Almighty God within me. There is no other, or beside which there is none other. Infinite love within me, seeing all, knowing all, loving all, One in and through all." Carry this concept out until you see that you live in everybody and everybody lives in you. Then continue: "Infinite One, comprehending, seeing, knowing, understanding, living in and including the All, within me." Realize what this means. "I am One with all people. There are no enemies. There is only the One, in all and through all."

If we would spend half the time making such affirmations that we spend complaining, finding fault, fussing, being sad and sorry for ourselves, we would soon be healed. "Infinite Wisdom within me"; stop and think what this means,—the Intelligence that operates through everything, visible and invisible. "Infinite Wisdom within me; Infinite Intelligence within me; Infinite Power within me";—feel what this means: The Power that holds the planets in place; a power to which the united force of the human race is as nothing. "Infinite Intelligence and Infinite Power within me, the great Executor; Infinite Energy and Wisdom within me,—the All-Knowing, the Unerring Mind of the Universe;—Infinite Peace within me, Infinite Peace, undisturbed and unalterable; Infinite Life, Infinite Peace within me"; that means there is no disturbance, no commotion, no trouble. There is only Infinite Peace; the power that stilled the waves and told the winds to be calm is the Power with which we deal. "Infinite Peace within me, Infinite Joy within me, the Joy that causes the leaves of the trees to clap their hands." It is the Joy that sings in the brook, the music of the spheres, the Joy of the sense of completion. "Infinite Joy within me, not somewhere else, but within me"; It is the Good which is urging Itself forth through every act which we call human or humane. We see it in the hand that gives and in every human act. That is the "Infinite Good that is within me,"—Infinite everything, whatever the need may be. Meditate upon the abstract essence of the thing; then bring it to a concrete point within your own mentality and see what it means as it manifests, declaring that it is.

This great teaching plainly shows the way to liberty and freedom. It is a pathway continuously unfolding from a Limitless Source to a Limitless Source. "Arise, shine, for thy light is come." 97 "I am that I am." 98

Note: Read and study "Cosmic Consciousness," Bucke; "Twelve Lessons in Mysticism," Hopkins; "The Impersonal Life" and "Creative Process in the Individual," T. Troward; "Bible Mystery and Meaning," T. Troward; "Sayings of Jesus," Red Letter Testament.

Footnotes

86 Acts. 17:28.
87 Luke 11:2.
88 John 14:10.
89 Ps. 82:6.
90 Phil. 2:5.
91 Luke 11:2.
92 Luke 17:21.

93 Matt. 5:14.
94 John 10:30.
95 Phil 2:5.
96 John 14:6.
97 Isa. 60:1.
98 Exodus 3:14.

LESSON SIX: THE LAW OF PSYCHIC PHENOMENA: INTRODUCTION

It is taken for granted that the average person of to-day is more or less acquainted with the facts concerning psychic phenomena. It would be useless, in a course such as this, to attempt any exhaustive research work; this has already been done by those eminently able to furnish the data.

There is within man a power that can communicate without the tongue, hear without the ear, see without the eye, talk without the mouth, move ponderable objects and grasp things without the hand; and perform many other feats that are usually connected only with the physical instrument. All these facts have been completely proved, and it is no longer necessary to produce evidence to substantiate these facts.

While the above stated facts have all been proved, the reason for their being has not been so thoroughly or logically discussed, and it is the purpose of this article to explain the fundamental reasons behind the law of mental action which is called psychic; for if a thing happens, there must be a reason for its happening and a law through which it operates.

The only excuse for taking up this topic in a course of lessons in Mental Science is that, being the phenomena of Mind, it should come under the category of known mental actions.

PSYCHIC PHENOMENA AND IMMORTALITY

Psychic phenomena are closely associated with immortality in people's minds for the reason that they deal with those unseen powers which we think of as being attributes of the soul; and also because many people have attributed the phenomena largely to the agency of discarnate spirits.

NO APOLOGIES

While no apologies are made for the ensuing pages, yet, in justice to the Truth, it must be said that many of the world's eminent scientists have investigated the subjects to be discussed, and so far, to the author's knowledge, none of them have ever refuted the ensuing facts.

The powers which are exhibited through the psychic life do really exist in man, and someday he will make conscious use of them and will, thereby, be greatly benefited. Meanwhile, every one is urged to be most careful in his approach to the subject. A little knowledge is a very dangerous thing, and it is to be regretted that very few people exhibiting psychic powers appear to know what the law is that underlies the phenomena. Many are led astray through ignorance, and one should be most careful in handling the topic. But, as stated above, this subject, coming under the known laws of mental action, must be dealt with.

God has given us a mind with which to know, and a power with which to discern, the Truth, and it is a terrible mistake to misuse that power. The whole end and aim of evolution is to produce a man who, in his self-conscious state, may depict the Divine Nature. We can do this only to the degree that we remain ourselves at all times.

We will take up the study of this subject just as we would approach the study of any other law, with an open mind, without any superstition and free from any sense of the unnatural. Nature is always natural, and only those things are mysteries which we do not understand.

LESSON SIX: METAPHYSICAL MEANINGS OF WORDS USED IN CHART NO. VI

The upper section represents the Conscious Mind, the Self-Knowing Mind, which we call Spirit. The middle section represents the Psychic Sea, that is, the Subjective World; this is the world of thought forms and mental pictures. This has been called "The illusion of Mind," because it contains many pictures, which are pictures only, and have no real form behind them. As a picture that is hung on the wall is not really a person—but is simply a picture—so the Psychic Sea may contain pictures which, while they are real as pictures, are not real from any other sense. It does not follow that everything in the psychic world is an illusion, for it contains much that is true. We should be very careful to distinguish the false from the true.

The lower section of the chart represents the objective world. This world also reflects many false forms, such as disease and limitation. They are not things of themselves, but are the results of wrong mental pictures in the Subjective World.

Neither the psychic pictures nor the world of forms are self-creative; both are effects.

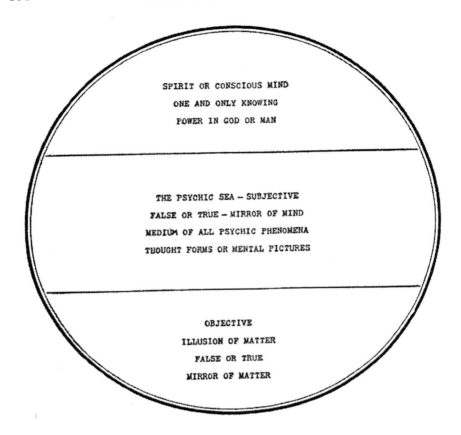

SPIRIT OR CONSCIOUS MIND
ONE AND ONLY KNOWING
POWER IN GOD OR MAN

THE PSYCHIC SEA -- SUBJECTIVE
FALSE OR TRUE -- MIRROR OF MIND
MEDIUM OF ALL PSYCHIC PHENOMENA
THOUGHT FORMS OR MENTAL PICTURES

OBJECTIVE
ILLUSION OF MATTER
FALSE OR TRUE
MIRROR OF MATTER

Lesson Six: Metaphysical Chart No. VI.

This is the psychic's chart and should be carefully considered, as it shows that the Spirit, or Conscious Mind, operates through a mental field, or law, which is a world of reflections. Thought is first reflected into Mind and then into matter. Read again the meaning of the conscious and the subconscious aspects of being. The world of Subjectivity is the Psychic Sea and the Medium of all subjective action. From the standpoint of man's thoughts it may be false or true, according to the way in which he thinks. It is the picture gallery of the soul, both from the universal and the individual sense. The illusion of matter means that the false mental pictures will produce a false form in the world of objectivity. Mind is not an illusion, but might contain false pictures which would be illusions; matter is not an illusion but may take on false conditions. We must learn to separate the false from the true.

LESSON SIX: PSYCHIC PHENOMENA

Psyche means soul; psychic phenomena are the phenomena of the soul. We have already seen that what we call the soul is, really, the subjective part of us. We do not have two minds, but we do have a dual aspect of mentality in what we call the objective and subjective phases of mind. The objective mind is that part of the mentality which functions consciously; it is the part of us which really knows itself; and without it we would not be real of conscious entities.

THE SUBJECTIVE MIND

Our subjective mind is our mental emanation in Universal Subjectivity; it is our individual use of mental law. It is also the avenue through which Instinctive Man works, carrying on the functions of the body; for it is the silent builder of the body. The subjective mind of the individual is the working of Instinctive Man within him, plus all of his conscious and subconscious experiences.

SEAT OF MEMORY

The subjective mind is the seat of memory and of instinctive emotion. Being the seat of memory, it contains a remembrance of everything that has ever happened to the outer man. This memory is perfect and retains every experience of the individual life. The subjective mind also contains many of the family and race characteristics which have been experienced by individualized man. It retains these memories, partly, at least, as mental pictures or impressions. This is proven by the fact that pictures have been taken of the subjective thought and definite outlines developed. This does not necessarily mean that every impression is retained as a mental picture, but that, in all probability, anything that the outer eye has definitely seen is retained as a more or less distinct picture.

The subjective mind is a picture gallery, upon whose walls are hung the pictures of all the people whom the individual has ever known and all the incidents which he has ever experienced.

SUGGESTION AND SUBJECTIVITY

The subjective mind being deductive only in its reasoning powers is compelled by its nature to retain all the mental impressions that it has ever received. It, therefore, contains much that the objective mind has never consciously known. When we realize that the individual's subjectivity is his use of the One Subjective Mind, we shall see that a subjective unity is maintained between all people, and that individual mentalities which are in sympathetic vibration with each other must, more of less, mingle, and receive suggestions from each other. This is the meaning of mental influence, which is, indeed, a very real thing. This also means that the subjective mind receives suggestions from the race and is, more or less, influenced by its environment; all this takes place on the silent side of life and is mostly unknown to the receiver.

Race-suggestion is a very real thing, and each individual carries around with him, and has written into his mentality, many impressions that he never consciously thought of or experienced; for there is a silent influence going on at all times between people under this law.

SUBJECTIVE COMMUNICATION

It is almost certain that between friends there is, at all times, a silent communication, a sort of unconscious mental conversation going on subjectively. When this rises to the surface of conscious intelligence, it is called mental telepathy. This communication with others is going on at all times, whether the conscious mind is aware of the fact or not. We are always receiving impressions that are more or less vague, and it is seldom that they come to the surface; but they are there nevertheless and are gradually building into our mentalities impressions and forms of thought that are unconsciously and silently perceived.

SUBJECTIVE MIND AND INSPIRATION

Since the subjective mind is the storehouse of memory, it retains all that the eye has seen, the ear heard or the mentality conceived. Since it contains much that the outer man never consciously knew, and is the receptacle of much of the race-knowledge, through unconscious communication, it must, and does, have knowledge that far surpasses the objective faculties.

Realizing that the subjective draws to itself everything that it is in sympathy with, or vibrates to, we see that any one who is sympathetically inclined toward the race, or vibrates to the race-thought, might pick up the entire race-emotion and experience, and, if he were able to bring it to the surface, he could consciously depict it. Many of the world's orators, actors, and writers have been able to do this; which explains the reason why many of them have been so erratic; for they have been more or less controlled by the emotions which they have contacted.

Our greatest speakers are able to contact the subjective mentality of their audiences and in this way, not only to tell the audience what it wishes to be told, but also to send out a strong vibration that will make an equally strong subjective impression on those who are listening. It is a well-known fact that many speakers are able to connect with the mentality of an audience in such a manner as to be able to completely control it. Napoleon seemed to be able to do this, which was one of the reasons why he had such tremendous influence over his followers.

Singers and poets generally enter into more or less of a subjective state while singing or writing. In the case of a singer or actor, this enables him to respond to the emotion of his listeners and to be able to reflect back to them an equally strong emotion. It might work the other way; that is, he might, himself, awaken the emotion in his hearers. This we call temperament, and no singer, speaker or actor can be a great success without it.

In the case of a writer, this enables him to enter into the race-thought and perfectly depict race-emotion and race-endeavor. Poets are an especially good example of this ability; for poetry, like song, is the language of the soul, and none can write good poems unless he allows the soul to come to the surface. We could not imagine a great poem written mechanically. Artists lose themselves in their work and musicians often do the same; this we call inspiration.

In preaching, it is probable that the orator of the pulpit often so enters into the longings of men's hearts that he reveals them to themselves. He is able to depict their thoughts and emotions, and coupling his own with theirs, give birth to a great discourse; we say that he is inspired.

Any one contacting the subjective side of the race-mentality with the ability to permit it to come to the surface, will have at his disposal a knowledge that many lifetimes of hard study could not possibly accumulate. But, if one had to surrender his individuality in the process, he would be better off to remain ignorant.

Enough has been said on this subject to show the source of human inspiration. There is, of course, a much deeper seat of knowledge than the subjective mind; that is, the Spirit. But direct contact with Spirit is Illumination, and is a quality which has been developed in but few people; the few who have developed this quality have given the world its greatest literature, religion and law.

MENTAL ATMOSPHERES

Each person has a mental atmosphere which is the result of all that he has thought, said, done, and consciously or unconsciously perceived. This mental atmosphere is very real and is that subtle influence which constitutes the power of personal attraction; for personal attraction has but little to do with looks; it goes much deeper and is almost entirely subjective. This will explain the likes and dislikes for those with whom we come in daily contact. We meet some, only to turn away without a word, while others we are at once drawn toward, and without any apparent reason; this is the result of their mental atmosphere or thought vibration. No matter what the lips may be saying, the inner thought outspeaks them and the unspoken word often carries more weight than the spoken. As Emerson said: "What you are speaks so loudly that I cannot hear what you say."

In contacting people, we are instantly attracted or repelled, according to the vibrations which we feel. A person whose atmosphere is one of love and sunshine, whose nature is to be happy, who lives a clean, wholesome life in a free atmosphere, will always attract friends.

Children feel mental atmosphere very keenly and are drawn to those who are inwardly right, shunning those who are inwardly wrong. It has been truly said that people whom children and dogs do not like are dangerous. Animals are almost entirely subjective and feel mental atmospheres more keenly than do most people. A dog instinctively knows one's attitude toward him and, acting accordingly, is immediately a friend or foe. Personal atmospheres vary in their intensity, there being as many varieties as there are people; for each creates his own atmosphere in Mind.

HOW TO CREATE PERSONAL CHARM

Personal charm may be easily created by learning to love all and hate none. Truly did the great Emerson say: "If you want a friend, be one." If one wishes to have friends, he should become friendly; if he wishes love, he should learn to love. There is no excuse for any one being without a power of attraction, since it is a mental quality and may be consciously induced through right practice.

THE ATMOSPHERE OF PLACES

As all people have a mental atmosphere, so do all places; and as the atmosphere of people is the result of their thoughts, so the atmosphere of places is the result of the thoughts that have been created in them. Places are permeated with the thoughts of the people who inhabit them; in this way, mental atmospheres are created and may be easily felt by those contacting them.

How often we have had the experience of going into a place, only to feel that we were not wanted, and became so disturbed that we wished immediately to leave. How often, on the other hand, we have gone into places where we felt such a warmth and inner glow that we wished to remain. This is the result of the mental atmosphere surrounding the place or room. This is why we love our homes; they are filled with love and affection and we feel at peace within their walls. This is why one likes to return home after his day's work; for he knows that here is a place where he will be away from the world with all of its cares and worries. It is a wise wife who understands this law and who keeps the atmosphere of the home pleasant. Such a one will seldom lose her mate, but will hold him through the strong ties of love and affection with which she floods his abode. Many an unhappy home could be harmonized if this law were better understood and practiced.

The atmosphere of the home should never be clouded with the uncertainties of the outside world. Here, in the palace of human love, all else should be forgotten and an atmosphere maintained which will be a shelter from the world. Here love should be the ruling passion and harmony should reign supreme. Here, above all other places, should the Kingdom of God be established and families should dwell together in peace and joy.

Too often, jealousy and deceit rob the home of its joy, while mistrust and doubting make it so unpleasant that it becomes an impossible place in which to live. But all this can be changed by reversing the wrong thoughts and in their place creating thoughts of love and tenderness toward one another.

There is nothing more unfortunate for a child's mind than to be compelled to live in an unhappy home. The home should stand for heaven on earth, and unless it does, it will not stand long, but will be buried in the ashes of dead hopes.

The atmosphere of the desert is wonderful, for it is free from the thoughts of men's confusion and fear, and so is a place of great peace. Here, indeed, away from the haunts of men's terrible struggles, quiet may be found and peach regained. It is the same with the mountains, the lakes and the trackless deep. This is what we love about Nature; her marvelous calm and deep peace; for she speaks to us and tells of a life undisturbed by the strife of man. She does, indeed, bear a message from On High, and happy is the one who can talk to her and learn from her, for she is wonderful and filled with light.

Even the slightest things seem to be possessed of a soul, or subjective atmosphere. How often we see a familiar coat or hat hanging on a peg, while in it we seem to see the person who wears it; it seems to look like him, and so it does, for it retains the emanation of his atmosphere, and really is permeated with his personality. Everything has an atmosphere which we sense and to which we react accordingly; if it is pleasant we like it, and if unpleasant we dislike it.

THE RACE-MIND

Just as each person, place or thing has a subjective atmosphere or remembrance, so each town, city, or nation has it individual atmosphere. Some towns are bustling with life and action while others seem dead; some are filled with a spirit of culture, while others seem filled with a spirit of commercial strife. This is the result of the mentalities of those who live in these places. A city given over to the pursuit of the higher endeavors will react with an atmosphere of culture and refinement, while one whose dominant thought is to acquire wealth will react to an atmosphere of grasp and grab. This is very definite and is felt by all who enter such places.

Just as a city as its atmosphere, so does a whole nation; for a nation is made up of the individuals who inhabit it; and the combined atmospheres of all the people who inhabit a nation creates a national mentality which we speak of as the psychology of that people.

THE MIND OF HISTORY

When we remember that Subjective Mind is Universal, we will come to the conclusion that the history of the race is written in the mental atmosphere of the globe on which we live. That is, everything that has ever happened on this planet has left its imprint on the walls of time; and could we walk down their corridors and read the writings, we should be reading the race history. This should seem simple when we realize that the vibrations of the human voice can be preserved in the receptive phonographic disc, and reproduced at will. If we were to impress one of these discs with the vibration of some one's voice and lay it away for a million years, it would still reproduce those vibrations.

It is not hard then to understand how the walls of time may be hung with the pictures of human events and how one who sees these pictures may read the race history.

TELEPATHY

Telepathy, or thought-transference, is such a commonly known fact that it is useless to do other than to discuss it briefly. However, there are some facts which might be overlooked unless we give them careful attention. The main fact to emphasize is that mental telepathy would not be possible unless there were a medium through which it could operate. This medium is Universal Mind; and it is through this medium that all thought-transference or mental telepathy takes place. Forms in matter and solid bodies may begin and end in space, but thought is more fluent.

Telepathy is the act of reading subjective thought, or of receiving conscious thought without audible words being spoken. But there must be a mental tuning in, so to speak, just as there must be in radio. We are surrounded by all sorts of vibrations, and if we wish to catch any of them distinctly, we must tune in; but there is a great deal of interference, and we do not always get the messages clearly. We often get the wrong ones, and sometimes many of the vibrations come together and seem to be nothing but a lot of noises, without any particular reason for being. It is only when the instrument is properly adjusted to some individual vibration that a clear message may be received.

This is true of mental telepathy, which is the transmission of thought. The receiver must tune in with the sender. It does not follow, however, that the sender knows that he is being tuned in on; in other words, one might pick up thoughts just as he picks up radio messages; and just as the one broadcasting may not know who is listening in, so the one sending out thought may not know who is listening in. Happily, but few people can listen in mentally, and these few only with more or less certainty of success. It would be terrible to be compelled to listen in on all the thoughts that are floating around. But, fortunately, we can only receive those messages to which we vibrate; and so the whole thing is a matter of our own choice. We are individuals in the mental world just as in the physical; and a wise person will protect himself mentally just as he would physically.

TUNING IN ON THOUGHT

Some seem to have the ability to tune in on thought and to read it, much as one would read a book. These people we call psychics; but all people really are psychic, since all have a soul or subjective mind. What we really mean is, that a psychic or medium is one who has the ability to objectify that which is subjective; to bring to the surface of conscious thought that which lies below the threshold of the outer mind. The medium reads from the book of remembrance; and it is marvelous how far-reaching this book of remembrance is.

MENTAL PICTURES

As everything must exist in the subjective world before it can in the objective, and as it must exist there as a mental picture, it follows that whatever may have happened at any time on this planet is today within its subjective atmosphere; i.e., the experiences of those who have lived here. These pictures are hung upon the walls of time, and may be clearly discerned by those who can read them.

Accordingly, since the Universal Subjectivity is a Unit and is Indivisible, all these pictures really exist at any, and every, point within It simultaneously; and we may contact anything that is within It at any point, because the whole of It is at every point. Consequently we may contact at the point of our own subjective mind (which is a point in Universal Subjective Mind) every incident that ever transpired on this planet. We may even see a picture that was enacted two thousand years ago in some Roman arena; for the atmosphere is filled with such pictures. This has been called "The Illusion of Mind" (the psychic sea). This does not mean that Mind is an illusion, but that it might present us with an illusion unless we are very careful and are quite sure that what we are looking at is a real form and not simply a picture.

It is very important that we understand this; for each person in his objective state is a distinct and individualized center in Universal Mind; but in his subjective state every one, in his stream of consciousness, or at his rate of vibration, is universal, because of the Indivisibility of Mind. Wherever and whenever any individual contacts another upon the subjective side of life, if he is psychic, i.e., if he objectifies subjectivity, he may see a thought form of that person, but it does not necessarily follow that he would be really seeing the person.

CONDITIONS NECESSARY FOR THE BEST RESULTS

The conditions necessary for the best results in psychic work are faith and expectancy; for the subjective responds to faith and seems clouded by doubts. Doubt appears to throw dust in its eyes, while sympathetic faith and willing belief render the veil much thinner and the consequent messages much clearer. This explains why many unbelieving investigators fail to receive the desired results, and go away saying that the whole thing is a fraud. Whatever the nature of the subjective may be, we did not make and we cannot change it; we shall be compelled to use this force, like all other forces in nature, according to its own laws, and not according to the way we think it should act.

It has been completely proved that the subjective mentality responds more completely when fully believed in; and any one wishing to investigate the psychic life would much better accept this fact and act upon it, rather than dispute it and receive no results. If the law is complied with the results will be certain.

Some psychics go into a trance while giving subjective readings, while some can do this in a normal state. The trance state varies from a slight subjectivity to a completely submerged mentality, i.e., from simply getting in tune with thought while in a conscious state of mind, to becoming completely submerged in an unconscious state in order to get in tune with thought. It is never good to lose one's self-control, but many people do this and, in so doing, have brought to light remarkable evidence of the ability of the inner mind to perform wonderful tasks.

DEEP TELEPATHIC MESSAGES

It is possible at times for a psychic to tell one most of the incidents that have happened in his life, and also to tell of his friends and many of the incidents that have happened to them. This is done by entering the subjective realm of the individual and reading the thoughts and mental pictures that are hung on the wall of his memory. When a psychic tells one something about his friends, he is entering their thought through the sympathetic vibration of the one whose thought he is reading. We are always in mental contact with our friends on the subjective side of life; and a psychic, tuning in on these vibrations, reads the thoughts that come over the mental wireless.

READING THE HISTORY OF THE INDIVIDUAL

Often a psychic will enter a person's mentality and give him a fairly complete history of his past and of the family from which he came, going back, perhaps, for several generations, naming ancestors and the things that engaged their attention while on earth. He is reading the records of what has already happened and is a subjective remembrance of his family.

For instance, people have often said to me: "I saw Emerson standing behind you this morning." Of course they did not see Emerson; what they saw was a mental picture of him; the reason being that I am a student of Emerson, and each is surrounded by the forms of the people he knows and the forms of those whose thought he studies.

PERSONAL READINGS

One is surprised when he goes to a medium and is told his own, and perhaps his mother's name, and is told by the medium that his mother stands beside him. The psychic often tells just how she looked while in the flesh. Now it might or might not be, that what the medium says is true; for, while this personality might be consciously near, the chances are more than even that she is not, but that the medium is simply looking at a picture of her as she once was while in the flesh.

A medium might, by reading one's subjectivity, be able to tell something about people who were not present at the time; because each, through a sympathetic vibration of thought, is connected with the subjective emanations of those whom he likes, of those with whom he is associated and of those to whom he vibrates. These people might be in the flesh or out of it.

The personal reading appears to be limited either to the immediate individual or to some one with whom he is in contact. The value of subjective mind reading is more or less uncertain. Generally all that a psychic can tell is about something that has already happened or something that might happen as the result of a subjective tendency already set in motion. There are, however, deeper messages than these.

STREAMS OF CONSCIOUSNESS

Each, being an individual identity in Mind, is known by the name he bears, and by the vibration which he emanates. For, while we are all One in Mind and Spirit, we each have a separate and an individualized personality. This is the only way that Spirit can individualize, making it possible for many to live in the One.

Each, then, is represented by his stream of consciousness; and each, continuously functioning in Mind, builds around himself an aura or mental atmosphere, which, in its turn, is constantly flowing out as a stream of consciousness.

Because of the Unity of Mind, each is one with the All; and at the point where he contacts the All, he universalizes himself. This will be easily understood when we realize that man always uses the One Mind. He is in It and thinks into It; and because It is Universal, his thought may be picked up by any one who is able to tune in on that thought, just as we pick up radio messages. A radio message, broadcast from New York City, is immediately present all around the world. Hard as this concept may be to grasp, we know it to be the truth.

Let us shift the basis to mentality and we shall see that the same thing happens when we think. We think into the One Mind, and this thought is immediately present everywhere. It is in this sense that each one is universal. According to the Unity of Mind, thought is everywhere present, and so long as it persists it will be. What is known in one place may be known in all places.

NO OBSTRUCTIONS TO THOUGHT

Time, space and obstructions are unknown to Mind and thought. It follows, then, that any one tuning in on our thought will enter into our stream of consciousness, no matter where we are or where he may be. And if we still persist after the body shall have suffered the shock of physical death, this law must still hold good; for past and present are one and the same in Mind. Time is only the measure of an experience, and space, of itself, is not apart from, but is in, Mind.

ENTERING THE STREAM OF THOUGHT

A psychic can enter the stream of thought of any one whose vibration he can mentally contact, be that person in the flesh or out of it; and since we are all psychic, all having a soul element, we are all, doubtless, communicating with each other to the degree that we sympathetically vibrate toward each other. (This explains the medium through which absent treatment takes place.)

We do not all have the ability to objectify psychic impressions, and ordinarily they never come to the surface; however, they are there just the same. This is the reason why we often feel so uneasy when in the presence of certain people, or when we mentally contact some condition, having an uneasy inner feeling but without any apparent reason.

THE VIBRATION OF A BOOK

As we read and study people's thought, we gradually enter into the current of their consciousness and begin to read between the lines; we are unconsciously reading their inner mentalities. This is why we enjoy reading the thoughts of the great mentalities of all ages. More that is unwritten comes to us than mere words could possibly convey.

WHY SAINTS HAVE SEEN JESUS

Many of the saints have seen Jesus in this way. That is, through studying His words and works, they have so completely entered His thought that they have seen a picture of Him; for the pictures of everything and everybody are hung on the walls of time and any one who can enter may read. It does not follow that these saints have seen Jesus, but that they have, without doubt, seen His likeness, or what the world believes to be His likeness, hung on the walls of time. When we look at a picture of a person we are not looking at the person, but at a likeness of him.

MANY MENTAL PICTURES

We are all surrounded by mental pictures, and a good psychic sees these pictures clairvoyantly and reads our thoughts telepathically. A good medium has the ability, more or less clearly, to bring these pictures and thoughts to the surface and objectify them; but it does not follow that he is really communicating with the people whose pictures he sees.

THE HUMAN AURA

Every one constantly radiates some kind of a vibration, and consequently is always surrounded by some kind of a mental atmosphere. This is called the aura; it extends from a few inches to a few feet from the body and sometimes even farther. It varies in color and density with the varying degrees of consciousness. In moments of spiritual realization the aura is bright yellow, merging into almost a pure white; and in moments of rage it is dark and murky in appearance. There are as many colors in the aura as there are varying degrees of thought-activity in the mentality.

HALO

The halo which artists have portrayed around the heads of the saints is real, and not an idea of the artists. There is a more pronounced emanation from the head than from any other part of the body, because thought operates through the brain more than through any other part of the human instrument.

It is said that the face of Jesus shone so brightly, at times, that His disciples could not look upon it without becoming blinded by its brilliancy.

UNPLEASANT ATMOSPHERES

In a combat of wills the atmosphere sometimes appears to strike sparks as though a battle were being waged on the subjective side of life. Unpleasant people always have a disagreeable atmosphere and morbid people always depress. A radiant aura emanates from the one who lives a normal, happy life, and who is always at peace within himself.

HABIT

Habits are formed by first consciously thinking, and then unconsciously acting. But few realize that when one consciously thinks, something must happen to his thoughts. What one thinks to-day will to-morrow be a part of his memory; and since memory is active, what he thinks to-day as a conscious thought will to-morrow be submerged but active thought.

This is how a habit is formed; first it is a desire, then comes the expression of this desire, then the desire becomes subjective and the subconscious action of thought causes it to be performed automatically. First we control thought, then thought controls us.

"First the man takes a drink,
Then the drinks takes a drink,
Then the drink takes the man."

Constant repetition gradually forms such a thought force on the subjective side of life that the very force created, in its turn, controls the one who created it. How careful we should be about what we let down into the deeper currents of mentality! All habits are formed in much the same way; they are at first conscious; then they become unconscious or subconscious. A person may create such a strong desire that it will compel him to put it into execution; this is called mania.

MANIA

Literally speaking, mania is a desire too strong to be controlled. We speak of one having a mania for certain things; that is, he has subjectified so much desire along some particular line that he becomes controlled by the very power which he has set in motion. Morbid people are more liable to do this than normally minded ones. For instance, let a sensitive person become despondent and he may think of committing suicide. This thought, at first, may be put aside as unworthy, but as it returns it receives a little more attention, until at last it may become so strong that it is irresistible.

Most murders are committed from this mental attitude; and most murderers are people who are mentally sick. Some day this will be better understood; such people will be considered sick and will be healed mentally. This shows how very careful we should be to control our thinking, never allowing the mentality to conceive ideas which we do not wish to see manifest. After all, these things are mental attitudes, and the best way to heal them is through mental treatment.

OBSESSION

Obsession is another form of mental control and may or may not be conscious at its inception. People may become obsessed with desires, thoughts, ambitions, habits, suggestions or other mental influences; and if the spirits of undeveloped entities surround us, it seems entirely possible that people may become obsessed by them.

The obsession of desire produces a mania to express that desire; for thought demands an outlet. Some are so obsessed by their ambitions that they are constantly driven to the accomplishment of them. Some are obsessed by the suggestion of their environment, for the mental atmosphere of places often obsesses people, compelling them to do certain things and without any apparent reason. In studying a case of obsession we should take all the facts into consideration and reason from effect back to cause.

PERSONAL INFLUENCE AND OBSESSION

People often become mildly obsessed by the mentalities of those surrounding them; this is called personal contagion. Many take on the color of their environment, and this should be guarded against, for it is a mild form of hypnotism. It is, of course, brought about through the suggestive power of unconscious mental action, and may or may not be malicious. We should never allow ourselves to become controlled by anything that we do not consciously allow to enter the thought. If one feels an influence silently demanding attention, he should at once declare that there is no power, in the flesh or out of it, that can control him except, of course, the One Perfect Mind.

OBSESSION OF DISCARNATE SPIRITS

If we are surrounded by discarnate spirits, they, also, might control us through suggestion; that is, if we allowed them to do so. By thinking toward us with a strong desire, they might so implant this desire on the subjective side of our thought that it would come up from within, causing us to do certain things which we never consciously thought of doing. This, of course, is hypnotic influence; but all mental influence is hypnotic, varying only in degree. If it is true that discarnate spirits are around us (and it appears to be true), we should carefully guard against the possibility of any mental influence from them. The statement that *only the one mind controls* will protect us from any and all wrong mental influences of whatever nature, whether emanating from those in the flesh or out of it.

GENERAL THEORY OF OBSESSION AND MENTAL INFLUENCE

All obsession, of whatever character, is some form of mental influence, and can easily be destroyed by making the above stated affirmation. We should never for one instant allow the suggestions of other mentalities to control us. The day will come when people will choose the thoughts that they allow to enter the mind as carefully as they now choose the food they eat. Staying close to the thought of the One Mind is a safe and sure protection from any and all wrong mental influence.

INSANITY

Insanity is the complete control of the conscious mind by the unconscious or subjective mind. Dwelling too long on one idea, or some sudden shock, seems to produce this state. It is easily healed by knowing that there is but *one mind, and that it cannot forget itself. There is one mind in god, and this mind our mind now.*

THE PSYCHIC POWER MUST BE CONTROLLED

The psychic power should always be under full control of the conscious mind; otherwise, all sorts of influences may be picked up, which, operating under the guise of seemingly real individualities, control the one who admits them. When the psychic power is under full control of the conscious mind, it furnishes a wonderful storehouse of knowledge; for, being the seat of memory of both the individual and the race, it contains much that we do not consciously know.

NORMAL STATE

A normal condition would be a complete balance between the objective and subjective mentalities. This would give an immediate access to all the wisdom of the human race, and might even extend much farther, for it could give access to a higher state, which is now more or less clogged by contrary suggestions.

The subjective side of thought is the sole and only medium between the relative and the Absolute. If one were in full control of his inner mentality he could, at once, enter the Absolute, and his every word would bear fruit. Jesus was such an One.

In attempting to accomplish this we do not have to come under control of any power other than that of our inner selves and our higher selves; anything less than this is dangerous. Many seem to think that simply because they are under control they must be dealing with spiritual power. *No greater mistake was ever made.* Jesus, Who was fully illumined, always kept His full state of conscious thought and personal volition.

THE AIM OF EVOLUTION

The aim of evolution is to produce a man who, at the objective point of his own self-determination, may completely manifest the inner life of the Spirit. Even the Spirit does not seek to control us, for It lets us alone to discover ourselves.

The most precious thing that man possesses is his own individuality; indeed, this is the only thing that he really has, or is; and for one instant to allow any outside influence to enter or control this individuality is a crime against man's real self.

THE STATE OF TRANCE

The trance state is any state of mentality that allows itself to become submerged. It varies in degree from simply allowing the mind to become receptive, which is harmless, to a complete self-denial of the objective consciousness, i.e., allowing any and all influences to be picked up. This is very dangerous.

There are many normal psychics who can, while in a perfectly objective state, read people's thoughts and perform many other wonderful feats of the mind. This is normal and no harm can come from it. It is, indeed, one of nature's ways of working and is most interesting.

NORMAL PSYCHIC CAPACITIES

Any psychic power that can be used while in a normal state of mind is harmless and helpful; that is, any psychic power which can be used while one is in a perfectly conscious state of mentality. Many have this power and find that it is helpful as well as interesting. This power can be developed by knowing that the *Within and the without are really one.*

ABNORMAL PSYCHIC POWERS

Abnormal psychic powers are developed in the full trance state; that is, when the medium becomes controlled by surrounding influences. In this state some wonderful and hidden powers of mind are revealed.

In certain psychic states people can see, hear and read others' thoughts; travel abroad and perform many other marvelous feats, which in the conscious state seem impossible. No doubt the time will come when all these powers will be under the control of the conscious mind; man will then be much less limited.

CLAIRVOYANCE

Clairvoyance is a state of mentality wherein the medium is able to see things that the objective eye cannot see under normal conditions. It is the physical eye reproduced on the mental side of life, only with a greatly extended vision. Time, space and obstructions are swept away, and the operator can as easily look through a closed door as, in a normal state, he looks through a window.

PSYCHOMETRY

Psychometry is a clairvoyant state wherein the operator is able to psychometrize, or read from the soul or subjective side of things. Mention has already been made of the fact that everything has its mental atmosphere which is the result of the thoughts surrounding it. To psychometrize anything means to read from this mental atmosphere and to tell what it radiates. Sometimes the operator seems able to take a piece of ore or metal and give a perfect description of the location from which it was taken. This will explain why some mediums wish to hold an object which has been used by the sitter; for through this avenue the medium is able to enter the inner thought of the person sitting.

CLAIRAUDIENCE

Clairaudience may be called the ear of the soul; it is the ability to hear the inner voice speak, and is a most remarkable mental attribute. Some hear these voices silently, while to some they come as independent voices.

It appears as though the instinctive man tries to tell the outer man of certain things or to give him warnings. Sometimes these warnings come as visions and sometimes in dreams. This power is uncertain and should be carefully watched, as we are not always able to tell whether the impression is real or simply some suggestion of a surrounding mental influence. A good way to test this is to know that all impressions must come from the Perfect Mind.

INDEPENDENT VOICES

Sometimes independent voices speak forth, apparently from the air, and may be conversed with by the hour. I have talked with these voices, but, so far, have not been able to determine whether or not they ever told anything beyond the subjective knowledge of those present. I have been unable to satisfy myself as to whether they were caused by those present in the flesh or whether they were caused by some form of spirit life. The fact remains that such voices do speak and that they are real. I have held animated and interesting conversations with such voices hours at a sitting, and it has been a most wonderful experience; but, so far, it seems impossible to determine their exact nature. Time and a more complete investigation alone can give the real proof.

APPARITIONS

Apparitions, or thought forms, often appear during mental stress. For instance, people often see some friend just before he passes from this life. Sometimes the apparition appears before the incident takes place; an explanation of this will be made later in this chapter. This type of phenomenon is not at all uncommon; nearly every one has some record of such experiences. When one is asleep he is entirely subjective, and this will explain why so many of the above referred to incidents take place during sleep. But impressions received while in the sleeping state do not always come to the surface.

GHOSTS AND PHANTASMS OF THE DEAD

People often see the forms of those who have passed from this life. Many have been alarmed over seeing such forms, as though there might be danger from them; but whether or not we believe them to be the forms of the dead or the living, they certainly can do no harm.

It is claimed by some that ghosts are always the result of some form of violent death, and that those who pass out in a state of peace never leave a ghost behind. Of the truth of this statement I am NOT absolutely sure, since all must leave behind the forms used while in the flesh, and each must leave behind him a thought form of himself.

GHOSTS SOMETIMES CAN SPEAK

It is a well-known fact that ghosts sometimes have the ability to speak or convey some kind of a message to the living. And it is also generally conceded by those who have investigated such matters, that once a ghost has had the opportunity to speak, it is seldom ever seen again.

If we suppose a ghost to be a real entity, we can easily see how it could speak or telepathically convey a message. If, on the other hand, we assume that a ghost is only a form of thought, we can imagine that it might be equipped with the power to convey a message, after which it would gradually fade away. For thought has some power to express itself. I hold no brief for either case, since I have been unable to make up my own mind as to just what a ghost really is.

In such a case as this it is a mistake to assume anything, other than the fact that such appearances do make themselves known to people under certain conditions. The matter will have to rest at this point until further investigation proves what a ghost is.

PROJECTING THE MENTALITY

Under certain states of mentality it is possible to project the mentality and travel far from the body. Just what it is that projects is difficult to say; and we are not so much concerned about what it is that projects as we are interested in the fact that there is something about the mentality which can project itself. Since there is but One Mind, perhaps nothing has to project; perhaps we simply see through the One Mind, which must have and hold, within Itself, all that is.

CRYSTAL GAZING

Crystal gazing is a form of concentrating the mentality in such a manner as to make it possible for the subjective to come to the surface. The operator, looking steadily at a bright object, gradually becomes subjective and consequently able to read thought.

BLACK MAGIC

Black Magic has been taught and practiced from time immemorial. It is the act of thinking toward some one for the purpose of doing him an injury.

THE MODERN CURSE

To-day, black magic is called by another name, but "a rose by any other name would smell as sweet." To-day it is called malpractice. Malpractice takes several different forms; namely, malicious, ignorant and unconscious. Malicious malpractice is the act of arguing in Mind that some certain person is something that he ought not to be. In some cases it is supposed to even take the form of saying that he is not present in the flesh. If this were persisted in, and the one being damned should receive the condemnation, he might begin to feel sick; and if this were carried to a final conclusion, he would, perhaps, "pass from this vale of tears."

Mention is made of this, not as being something to fear, but as one of those things which to-day is being more or less discussed and believed in by many. So far as we are concerned, we believe only in the One Mind, *And we know that it cannot be divided against itself.* This will settle the question of malicious malpractice for all time.

We hear of people who live in constant terror of malpractice, and it seems certain that some do try to use this force to do injury to others; but no one with real understanding of the Truth will be affected by it, nor seek to use it; for this would be playing with fire; and we are the servants to the things which we obey.

If our thought is still operating on a level where such things are possible, we had better find it out, straighten up our thought and be healed; for, after all, malpractice is only wrong thought suggestion, and we do not believe in wrong thought suggestion.

Innocent and ignorant malpractice causes much disease and discomfort, through sympathy with sickness and fear for people's safety. We should sympathize with the one suffering, but never with that from which he suffers; for this would make him worse instead of better.

AUTOMATIC WRITING

Automatic writing is an interesting phenomenon of the mind. It is a mental control which uses the arm and hand for the purpose of writing messages.

There are several forms of automatic writing; one, the Ouija board, which is small smooth board, upon which is written the alphabet. Upon this board is placed a small, pear-shaped, three-legged instrument, which points to the letters and spells out words. Another form is to put a pencil through the board; and still another form, and one even more interesting, is when the pen is held in the hand which is controlled by some force not known, but supposed to be the subjective thought of either the operator or of some one present.

Some believe that the arm is under control of a discarnate spirit. Many and long have been the discussions on this point, and I do not care to enter into them; but one thing is certain, the phenomenon transpires, and many wonderful messages come through in this manner.

INDEPENDENT WRITING

The most interesting writing of all is what is called independent writing; that is, where the pencil simply tips up and writes without any one touching it. I have seen this done and can vouch for its reality. Here, indeed, is ample cause for speculation, and we are compelled to admit that either some unconscious force of those present grasps the pencil, or that some spirit force does.

HUDSON'S THEORY

I am well aware of the theory which Hudson worked out along these lines, but I have not been able to explain everything on his basis; and I fear that he overworked his theory.

His idea was that we have no right to assume the presence of an unknown agency when there is a known one present. In other words, he said that the phenomenon is caused by some form of mental action which he called subjective; and that we have no right to assume a spirit to be the cause when we know that there are people present in the flesh; and that, since people in the flesh, as well as those out of it, have a mind, we must assume that the phenomena are caused by those present in the flesh. By the same token, and with the same logic, it could be proved either way. That psychic phenomena are caused by some form of mental power, there can be no question; and the student of the workings of mind will rest content here, knowing that mental power can operate in independence of the physical instrument; for this is the great lesson to learn.

SMELLING WHERE THERE IS NOTHING TO SMELL

A most peculiar and interesting phenomenon takes place in the act of smelling where there is, apparently, nothing to smell. The mentality, in connecting with the vibrations of a rose, can produce its odor independently of the presence of the flower.

I have seen a case where the vibrations of a certain man were brought into the room when he was in an intoxicated condition. The smell of whiskey was so strong that the influence was asked to remove its presence. Perhaps this is what is meant by occult perfume.

GRASPING OBJECTS WITHOUT THE HAND

It is a commonly known fact, to those who have spent time investigating these thing, that objects are grasped and held independently of the physical touch. This is shown in independent writing and in telekinetic energy.

TELEKINETIC ENERGY

Telekinetic energy is defined as "the ability to move ponderable objects without physical contact." This form of energy is displayed in that class of mental phenomena which cause objects to move without any physical agency, and is, therefore, caused by some form of mental energy, or by some agency other than physical.

TABLE TIPPING

Table tipping is so common as to cause but little comment, but it does help to prove a principle of mind, namely, that an object can be moved about from place to place without the aid of any physical contact.

RAPPINGS

Rappings on the walls and floor are also too common to mention, but should be classed in the category of telekinetic energy.

THEORY OF ECTOPLASM

One of the investigators has advanced the theory of ectoplasm, which is a formless stuff emanating from the body of the medium. I have no doubt but this theory is correct as far as it goes; but am not willing to advance it as being sufficient to explain all the phenomena. For instance, according to this theory, if any one stands in front of the medium the emanation is blocked and no results will follow. I have sat in a room and had a glass of water brought from another room and held to my lips while I drank it. It was a real glass and real water and I was really there, and in a perfectly normal state of mind. I could not possibly account for the above-stated incident on the theory of ectoplasm; but I could account for it through the theory of mental power.

LEVITATION

The theory of ectoplasm certainly will not account for levitation, where the body of the medium is lifted from a chair and carried to some other place in the room. This can be accounted for only on the theory that there is a power that transcends the better-known physical laws. Experience has taught that there are many things in life that cannot be accounted for on any other basis than that of a mind power which operates independent of any, and of all, physical agencies.

INTERESTING THOUGHTS

It is interesting to realize that we have such marvelous powers; and no doubt the time will come when we shall make common use of them. They are for some purpose and, as we live in a Timeless Universe, this purpose will be made known just as soon as we are ready for it.

WHAT IS THE CAUSE?

Whether psychic phenomena are caused by the agency of spirits or by some inner power of our own mentality makes no difference. That they are caused by mind power is apparent; for they are not caused by what we call physical force at all, but by some finer power than we, at present, well understand.

CAUSE FOR THOUGHT

It gives reason for thought when we realize that such inner powers exist. Some power, independent of the body, can see, hear, feel, smell, touch and taste without the aid of the physical instrument. Some power of intelligence within us can travel, communicate, project itself, recognize and be recognized, without the aid of the physical instrument. That there is a reason for this is certain; that this reason is natural and normal, no one can doubt, for nature is always natural, and only that is a mystery which is not understood.

TIME WILL PROVE ALL THINGS

Time and experience, alone, will unravel the mysteries of the human mind, with its many and varied activities. So far we have but touched the outskirts of its garments. To deny these inner attributes is not only intolerant, but is downright ignorance. It is all right to say that we do not understand them; but to openly deny them is to place us, not among the unbelievers, but among those who do not know the facts.

THE SPIRIT OF PROPHECY

Subjective mind can deduce only; it has no power of initiative or self-choice, and is compelled, because of its very nature, to retain any and all suggestions that it receives. The best illustration of this is in the creative soil, in which the gardener puts his seed. The soil does not argue nor deny, but goes to work on the seed and begins to create a plant which will represent the type of manifestation inherent, as an idea, in the seed. That is, from a cucumber seed we get cucumbers; and from a cabbage seed we get cabbages. Always the law maintains the individuality of the seed as it creates the plant; never does it contradict the right of the seed to be what it really is. Involved within the seed is the idea of the plant, as are also those lesser ideas which are to act as a medium between the seed and the plant. Involved within the seed are both cause and effect; but the seed must first be placed within the creative soil if we wish to receive a plant. In the creative soil, or in the seed, the full and perfect ideas of the plant must exist as a completed thing, else it could never be brought forth into manifestation.

The idea of the full-grown plant must exist somewhere in the seed and soil if it is ever going to materialize.

A LESSON IN SUBJECTIVITY

This teaches us a lesson in subjectivity. Thoughts going into the subjective are like seeds; they are concepts of ideas, and acting through the creative medium of Mind, have within themselves the full power to develop and to express themselves. But how could they express unless they were already known to Mind? They could not, and so Mind must view the thought as already completed in the thing; and Mind must also contain the avenue through which the idea is to be expressed. Every thought sets in motion in Mind the fulfillment of its purpose, and Mind sees the thing as already done.

Mental tendencies set in motion cast their shadows before them; and a psychic often sees the complete manifestation of an idea before it has had the time to materialize in the objective world.

This is what constitutes the average spirit of prophecy; for prophecy is the reading of subjective tendencies, and seeing them as already accomplished facts. The subjective mind can deduce only, but its power of logic and sequence appears to be perfect.

EXPLANATION

For illustration, suppose that there is a window one mile away; I am throwing a ball at this window, and the ball is halfway to it, going at the rate of one mile a minute. Now you come in, measure the distance, compute the speed with which the ball is passing through the air and say, "The ball is halfway to the window; it is traveling at the rate of one mile a minute; in just one half a minute the window is going to be broken by the ball passing through it." Let us suppose that you are the only one who sees the ball, for the rest are looking at the window; and in half a minute it is broken. How did you prophesy that the window was to be broken? By drawing a logical conclusion of an already established premise.

This is much like what happens when a psychic exercises a spirit of prophecy. They are generally unconscious as to why they do what they do, because they are getting their own subjective contact with the condition and simply interpreting what comes to them. But this is the logical, deductive, conclusive power of their subjective thought, seeing a thing completed, by first seeing a tendency set in motion, and computing the time that it will take to complete it. There are but few, however, who have any reliable spirit of prophecy.

Let us carry this thought further; the race has its subjectivity, from an individual to a nation. This is its karma, its subjective law set in motion. Each nation has its subjective causation, and the prophet of a nation could, and would, read its subjective tendency; and this is what the old prophets did, for they were psychics, every one of them, from Moses down. They were able to interpret the subjective causation of their race and so predict that certain things must follow.

There is, however, a still higher spirit of prophecy which but few have perceived, and those who have perceived it have been illumined. Within the subjective mirror of Mind there must also exist the Divine and Cosmic Purposes,—the very Thoughts of God. An illumined person, who is also psychic, might read these great Cosmic Purposes; and in this manner some of the great prophets have read the destiny of the race. They have told us that the destiny of man is divine, that he is immortal now, that he need not die to become immortal, but that *he is immortal.* It was in contact with this great Law, and from It, that Moses received the Ten Commandments, the Mosaic Law. It is through the avenue of subjectivity, which is the medium between Spirit and man, between the Absolute and the intellect, that all of the prophets have prophesied and all of the sages have taught; for it contains Infinite Wisdom, Knowledge and Law.

The subjective mind is the source of much inspiration; for it contains all the thoughts which the race has ever created, and at times one contacts these thoughts and becomes inspired by them. The subjective mind is the source of much revelation because it contains the Purposes of God, and if the soul were to turn to the One, it surely would reflect into the outer mind the Light of the Eternal.

SUMMARY

We have shown that mind, independent of the body, can, and at times does, perform each and every function which we usually associate with the physical being. While most people may have to go into a trance state to perform these acts, there are a few who can produce the same results while in a perfectly normal state, that is, while in a self-conscious state. I wish to make this very plain, for there is a belief that an abnormal state must be entered into before these phenomena can be produced. I not only challenge such a statement, but entirely refute it as being altogether wrong. I have myself, while in a perfectly normal state, seen or experienced nearly everything that has been discussed under this heading.

I am willing to admit that ordinarily a trance state is developed before the best results can be obtained; but to say that it MUST be developed is to contradict my own experience and refute my own observations. I have never, at any time, gone into a trance state, and would no more consider doing so than I would consider jumping from the roof of a ten-story building. If, then, I were to refute my sanity during these experiences, by what manner of judgement could I consider myself to be sane at all? It is useless for those who know nothing at all about psychic phenomena to deny its reality. I can understand any one saying that he does not understand it, but I cannot grasp the position of an individual who denies something of which he is entirely ignorant.

We will say then *that every act of the human instrument which we call the body can be reproduced through some agency which is not physical, or through some agency that physics cannot explain.* We will call this agency some power of mind with which we are not yet well familiar. It is all simple enough, anyway, for our bodies could not move unless we were here to move them, and so every act is mental, even though we use the body as an instrument.

I can find no explanation for the above-stated facts, unless we suppose that we have a mental body which reproduces the physical one; and which can function without its counterpart, and is entirely independent of it.

It makes no difference whether we attribute the phenomena to spirits or whether we say that we are unconsciously producing it ourselves, *the fact will still remain that the phenomena are produced* and can be accounted for only on the basis that we either have a mental body, which acts independent of the physical one, or that the power of thought alone, and without any physical instrument, can operate upon matter. Personally, I prefer to accept the theory that we have a mental body, since this appeals to me as being more reasonable and certainly much more human.

If we assume that spirits have the ability to move ponderable objects without physical contact, we are assuming that they have a mental body, or that they operate their thought to produce the phenomena. For, once granted that the phenomena are really produced, it is self-evident that some kind of an explanation must be forthcoming.

There are but two possible answers from what is to-day known: either the minds of departed souls or the minds of those present in the flesh produce the phenomena. This eliminates any other possible agency, for the theory of ectoplasm cannot answer all of the facts.

Lesson Six: Psychic Phenomena and Immortality

THE MEANING OF IMMORTALITY

Immortality means to the average person that man shall persist after the experience of physical death, retaining a full recollection of himself and the ability to recognize others. If his full capacities go with him beyond the grave, he must be able to think consciously, to reason, will, affirm, declare, accept, reject, know and be known, communicate and be communicated with; he must be able to travel about, see and be seen, understand and be understood; he must be able to touch, taste, smell, hear, cognize and realize. In fact, if he is really to continue as a self-conscious personality, he can do so only to the degree that he maintains a continuous stream of consciousness and self-knowingness.

This means he must carry with him a complete remembrance; for it is to the remembrance alone that we must look for the link that binds one event to another, making life a constant stream of self-conscious expression. To suppose that man can forget and still remain himself is to suppose that he could cut off the entire past and at this moment be the same personality that he was a moment ago. Remembrance alone guarantees personality. Individuality might remain without remembrance, but not so with personality; for what we are is the result of what we have been, the result of what has gone before.

Man, then, if he is to have an immortality worthy of the name, must continue, as he now is, beyond the grave. *Death cannot rob him of anything if he be immortal.*

WHERE DID MAN COME FROM AND WHY?

It is useless to ask why man is. It can only be said of man that he is; for if we were to push his history back to some beginning, we should still be compelled to say that he is. If man's life is of God, then it comes from a source which had no beginning; and so the question as to why he is must forever remain unanswered.

God could not tell why God is; to suppose that Life could give an excuse or reason for being would be to suppose an absurdity. Life Is, and right at this point all inquiry into Truth starts, and from this point alone must this inquiry continue.

We are not so much interested in why we are, as we are interested in what we are. That we are some part of Life, no one can deny and keep faith with reason. Let us not bother about questions that can never be answered, but pay attention to those which have an answer.

MAN AWAKES WITH A BODY

When man first woke to self-consciousness, he had a body and a definite form, showing that Instinctive Life, which is God, had already clothed Itself with the form of flesh. Body, or form, is the necessary outcome of self-knowingness. In order to know, there must be something that may be known; in order to be conscious there must be something of which to be conscious. Some kind of a body or expression there always was and always will be, if consciousness is to remain true to its own nature.

WHAT IS THE BODY?

Body is a concrete idea, existing in time and space, for the purpose of furnishing a vehicle through which Life may express Itself. The physical universe is the Body of God; it is a manifestation of the Mind of God, in form. It is that Creation which, while It may have beginnings and ends, of Itself neither begins nor ends. The Manifestation of Spirit is necessary if Spirit is to come into Self-Realization; hence, Body.

MATTER

We say that body is composed of matter, but what is matter? Science tells us that matter is an aggregation of small particles arranged in some kind of form; we are also told that matter is in a continuous state of flow. Strange as it may seem, we do not have the same physical bodies that we had a few months ago; they have completely changed; new particles have taken the place of the old; and the only reason why they have taken the same form is, that Instinctive Man has provided the same mold. Our bodies are like a river, forever flowing; the Indwelling Spirit alone maintains the identity.

If we assume that immortality simply means persisting in the physical body, then we already have immortalized ourselves many times right here on earth.

THE ETHER OF SCIENCE

We are now being taught that the ether is more solid than matter. We know that the ether penetrates everything; it is in our bodies, at the center of the earth, and throughout all space. This means that within our present bodies there is a substance more solid than the body which we see. This idea is very far-reaching; for it shows that we might have a body right within the physical one, which could be as real as the one of which we are accustomed to think. If Instinctive Man has molded the outer body in form, why should It not also mold the inner one into definite form? There is every reason to suppose that It does and no reason to suppose the opposite. In all probability, there is a body within a body to infinity. "In my Father's house are many mansions." 99

We do not depart from reason when we assume this; for, while we used to say that two bodies could not occupy the same space at the same time, we must remember that we were talking about only one plane of expression. The new idea of matter and ether has *proved that more than one body may occupy the same space at the same time*; for it has been proved that there is a substance which can occupy the same space that our body does. No doubt, as time goes on, it will also be proved that there is something still finer than the ether; this may go on to infinity. There is every reason to suppose that we have a body within a body to infinity, and it is our belief that we do have.

THE RESURRECTION BODY

The resurrection body, then, will not have to be snatched from some Cosmic shelf as the soul soars aloft, but will be found to exist already *within;* *everything is from within, for life is within.* The resurrection body of Jesus shone so that it could not be looked upon, because it was a more spiritual one than the physical eye is used to beholding.

CONCLUSIVE FACTS

The facts are conclusive that we have a spiritual body now, and do not have to die to receive one. We now remember the past, and have already outlived the physical body many times during life. It looks as though we were already immortal and would not have to die to take on immortality.

If there are many planes of Life and consciousness, perhaps we only die from one plane to another. This thought makes a strong appeal and seems to answer the question completely.

IN WHAT MENTAL STATE DO WE GO OUT?

Some think that death robs us of the objective faculties, and that we pass out in a purely subjective state; but we are unable to follow the logic of such an assumption. To suppose that the objective faculties die with the brain, is to suppose that the brain thinks and reasons. This is proved to be false through the experience of death itself; for, if the brain could think, it would think on and on forever. No; the brain does not think; the thinker thinks through the brain, perhaps; but of itself, the brain has no power to think or feel. Detach the brain and it will not formulate ideas, nor work out plans. *The thinker alone can think.*

It is logical to suppose that we pass from this life to the next in full and complete retention of all our faculties. Jesus revealed Himself to His followers after His resurrection, to show them that death is but a passing to a higher sphere of life and action. To know that we maintain an identity independent of the physical body, is proof enough of immortality. This, together with the fact that remembrance maintains a constant stream of recollection, and the realization that mentality can operate independently of the body, performing all of its normal functions without its aid; and that the new theory of matter and ether furnishes proof of the possibility of a body within a body to infinity; and that the Instinctive Man is constantly forming matter into the shape of a body, should prove to anyone that we are not going *to attain immortality; but that we now are immortal.*

WHAT CAUSES PSYCHIC MANIFESTATIONS?

It would be interesting to know whether the spirits of the supposed dead cause the manifestations which we see in the séance chamber. One thing is certain: these manifestations are either caused by those who are supposed to be dead, or else they are caused by those now in the flesh; for, since they happen, something must make them happen. Whether the manifestations are caused by the dead or the living, the agency used is either a mental body or the direct power of thought operating upon objects. Of course, in the conveyance of mental messages, telepathy explains the agency; but in physical manifestations, some kind of contact either takes place or else thought directly works on objects.

Hudson, in his "Law of Psychic Phenomena," carefully goes through an elaborate process of reasoning, the result of years of painstaking investigation, and completely proves that all of the manifestations do take place. He then goes through an extensive argument to show that they are not caused by spirits, saying that we have no reason to suppose the presence of an unknown agency, when we know that there is one present who could be producing the phenomena. Now, if our reasoning power is correct, and it is proved that physical manifestations take place through some power that is mental, and if it is proved that those who have passed on might still be near us, then we cannot see where the argument against spirit agencies could be considered perfect. We are inclined to feel that the very facts in the case prove that these manifestations could be produced by either the living or the dead; and such, we believe, to be the case.

TELEPATHY DOES NOT EXPLAIN EVERYTHING

Telepathy does not explain everything. It may explain much, but certainly not all. Telepathy could not explain certain visions which people sometimes have when passing out. We once knew a woman who practically passed out and was, indeed, thought dead for nearly a day and night; but was finally restored to consciousness to continue here for another year. She plainly saw and talked to several members of her family who had gone on some years earlier. It is not strange that those who have gone before are interested in us and wish to see us when we go over. If we had friends in London and were to send word that we were coming over, they would certainly wish to meet us. Our friends on the other side must be just as interested in us as they ever were.

Telepathy cannot explain how Jesus could take some of His more advanced disciples aside and let them talk with the departed. It clearly states that this incident took place; and, if we cannot believe this, how can we believe any of the other events in the life and experience of this most remarkable Person?

SPIRIT COMMUNICATION

There are thousands of cases on record where people have penetrated the veil of flesh and seen into the beyond. If we cannot believe the experience of so many, how can we believe in any experience at all? Of course, there is a large field for deception, and it is not probable that all communications are real; but, to state positively that they are all illusions, is to throw the lie into the face of human thought and say that is never sees clearly. There is certainly more argument and evidence in favor of the theory of spirit communication that against it, and, so far as we are concerned, we are entirely convinced of the reality of this evidence.

If spirits really exist, and if we all live in One Mind, and if mentality can communicate with mentality without the aid of the physical instrument, then spirit communication must be possible; and since we know that the above-stated facts are true, we have no alternative other than to accept the conclusive evidence and realize that while it may be difficult to communicate with the departed, yet it is possible.

COMMUNICATION MUST BE MENTAL

It is evident that any such communication must be mental; it would be thought transference or mental telepathy, at best. Now if the supposed entity knows that we wish to communicate with it, and if it is consciously present trying to communicate with us, then it must, by the power of its thought, cause its message to come up through our subjectivity to an objective state of recognition; consequently how very difficult to receive a coherent message! For instance, suppose that one tries to think a lecture to an audience, how much would they receive? Yet this is exactly what would happen under the very best condition if the departed were trying to impress our thought. I believe that they do seek to communicate with us and that they often succeed, perhaps more often than we realize; but I repeat, "How difficult it must be!"

Whether or not the spirits are present is uncertain. Just because a psychic sees the picture of a person around us, does not mean that he is really there; for the pictures of all our friends are always in our mental atmospheres. It is quite absurd to suppose that at any time we wish we can call any one we ever knew and make him talk to us. We are unable to do so here; and psychological and metaphysical laws are the same on every plane.

WE DO NOT CONTROL SPIRITS

To suppose that we can compel the attention of one out of the flesh, any more than of one in it, is an absurdity. And if we could, what would we hope to gain? People out of the flesh know no more than they did when in the body. I believe that we do communicate with the subjectivity of those who are departed, whether they know that we are doing so or not; but the messages that come, in our present state of evolution, are very incoherent. I believe that an unconscious communication goes on, more or less, all the time, and that those people whom we have greatly loved are still conscious of us; and are, without doubt, seeking to influence us; but it could only be a mental influence. We might feel a vague sense, much as the niece of Oom Peter did in "The Return of Peter Grimm." She felt a vague sense of her uncle; that he was trying to impress her with his thought and desire. She felt a blind groping, and that is probably the best that we would get.

THE PSYCHIC POWER SHOULD NOT BE FORCED

We all have psychic capacities, but they should never be forced; for it is only when the subjective comes to the surface while in a normal state that a normal psychic power is produced. The average psychic must go into a semitrance to let the subjective come through; this is never good nor right, but is always destructive. The psychic capacity is normal only to the extent that it can be used while in a self-conscious state. Don't misunderstand what I am saying. It is known as the "power of darkness," but is all right if understood. Many people are bothered by their psychic powers, constantly seeing things, continually getting impressions; they are very near the surface of subjectivity, and it bothers them. This can easily be healed and should be.

There is a normal psychic capacity, and some are able to discern mental causes with perfect ease. Jesus was such an One; He was able to tell the woman that she had been married five times, and that the man with whom she was living was not her husband. He read that out of her thought; but He did it while in an objective state; for He was able to consciously and objectively exercise His subjective faculties. This is perfectly normal; but to let go of the volitional and choosing faculties, which alone constitute individuality, and become immersed in subjectivity, is very dangerous. One might become obsessed by discarnate spirits, earth-bound entities, elementals, thought forms, desires or other forces floating around; for we cannot close our eyes to the fact that all of these things do exist.

It is a crime against individuality to allow the conscious faculties to become submerged. We should control the subjective and not let it control us. The teaching of the illusion of mind sprang up because men of wisdom perceived that people might mistake the shade for the reality, the form for real substance, the hollow voice for revelation, and thereby be misled. That is why they warned against these things and against having familiar spirits; and they were absolutely right. Never let any voices speak to you unless you are in perfect control of the situation. Never admit any mental impressions or images that you do not wish to receive or that you cannot receive consciously. Say: "There is no power in the flesh or out of it but the One, which can enter my consciousness. Any thing that obeys the One, conforms to the One, believes only in the One and comes only through the consciousness of the One, is perfectly welcome, but anything other than that cannot come."

The only value that an understanding of psychic phenomena can have, is that without it we do not understand the complete workings of mind. We do not understand experiences people often have; and in a consistent philosophy which deals with mind, the lack of an understanding of psychic phenomena would be inexcusable. For any one in this day to say that powers of clairvoyance, telepathy, thought transference, clairaudience or telekinetic energy are not exercised, is to admit his own ignorance.

These things do happen and are continuously happening in more and more instances. The thing to do is not to deny what happens, but to find a logical and scientific explanation of it. It is our business to explain all mental action, in so far as it is explainable; and so we must find and answer which will cover the law of psychic phenomena. Mind, with the laws governing It, is the whole answer, for each plane reproduces the one next to it; and psychic phenomena are reproductions of man's physical capacities on the mental plane. "What is true on one plane is true on all."

NOTE: Read and carefully study "Law of Psychic Phenomena," Hudson; "Life After Death," Hyslop; "The Unknown Guest," Maeterlinck; "Science and Immortality," Lodge; "The Hidden Power," Troward; "From the Unconscious to the Conscious," Geley.

Footnotes
99 John 14:2.

LESSON SIX: RECAPITULATION

Psychic phenomena are the phenomena of the soul, or subjective mind. The subjective mentality is man's atmosphere in Universal Mind; it is the seat of his memory and the avenue through which Instinctive Life works.

The subjective mentality, being deductive only in its reasoning power, is compelled to retain all of the impressions that it receives, but, of course, these impressions can be erased, consciously.

Man is Universal on the subjective side of life, and in this way is connected with the subjectivity of all with whom he is in harmonious vibration.

Mental suggestion operates through the subjective mind, and a silent influence is always going on through this avenue in the form of race-suggestion. A silent communication takes place at all times between friends on the subjective side of life; when it comes to the surface, it is called mental telepathy.

The subjective mind, being in contact with the race-thought, has a much greater knowledge than the conscious mind. It is through this avenue that human inspiration comes. Orators and actors contact the subjective side of their audiences and, in this way, wield a tremendous influence. Singers, poets and writers enter the subjective race-thought and interpret it; this enables them to depict the race-emotions.

Each person has a subjective mental emanation or atmosphere which is the result of all that has ever been consciously or unconsciously said, thought or done by that person. The mental atmosphere of a person is his power of attraction. It is the result of his inner thoughts. The mental atmosphere of a place is the result of all that has been thought, said or done in that place. The mental atmosphere of a place is its power of attraction. We love those places whose mental atmosphere is one of love and peace; this is why we like our homes. The home should always be kept sacred and its atmosphere should always be one of love.

Things are possessed of a soul element and continuously emanate this atmosphere.

Each city or town has a special atmosphere which is the result of the mental emanations of those who inhabit it. The same may be said of nations; each has its national mentality.

The history of the whole race is subjectively written on the unseen walls of time, and may be reproduced by one who can read the race-mentality.

Telepathy, which is the act of reading subjective thought takes place through the medium of Universal Subjectivity. In order to mentally receive a message, and bring it to the surface, one must be in tune with the vibration of that message.

Since the whole field of subjectivity is Universal, it follows that everything that has ever been thought, said or done, is retained in the race-thought; and since this field is a unit, all of the vibrations are ever present, and may be contacted at the point of any one's mentality.

In his objective state, man is separate and distinct, but on the subjective side of life he is universal.

The conditions necessary for the best results in psychic work are faith and expectancy; this is because the subjective mentality is the seat of the instinctive emotions and responds to feeling.

A psychic, going into more or less of a subjective state, is able to enter the vibration of an individual's thought and read from the book of his remembrance. The personal reading seems to be limited to the subjective remembrance, although this is often very far-reaching.

Each maintains a stream of consciousness in the One Mind, and any one contacting this stream may objectify it. Because of the Universality of the Medium, the individual stream of consciousness is always omnipresent, whether the one from whom it emanated be in the flesh or out of it.

Time and space are unknown in Mind, the past and the present are one. In reading the thought of people set down in books, we enter their vibration, and in studying their thoughts we enter their stream of consciousness.

Every one who ever lived on earth has left behind a mental picture of himself; these pictures are often seen when one is in a subjective state. This does not mean that we really see the person; what we see generally is the picture.

The human aura is the mental vibration or emanation of the individual. The idea of the halo surrounding the heads of the saints is explained in this way. The personal atmosphere varies with the changing thought and emotion, and is sometimes pleasant and at other times unpleasant.

Habits are formed through conscious thought becoming subjective, and in its turn, controlling the one through whom it operates. Mania is a strong desire, subjectified, which becomes an obsession.

People may become obsessed with their own ideas or with those that operate through them from some foreign source, whether this source is from some one in the flesh or out of it. Obsession is always some form of mental suggestion. Insanity is the loss of the objective faculty.

The psychic power must always be controlled. A normal state is a perfect balance between the objective and the subjective faculties. This is the aim of evolution: to produce a man who, at the point of his objective faculty, may perfectly control the subjective. A trance state is abnormal, and only that psychic faculty is normal which is under full control of the self-discerning mind.

Clairvoyance is the ability to see without the physical eye. Psychometry is a clairvoyant state wherein the medium is able to enter the subjective side of things and read the atmospheres surrounding them; this is why mediums often wish to hold some familiar object in their hands while giving readings.

Clairaudience is the ear of the soul. Independent voices sometimes come from the air, proving that some inner power is able to express itself audibly. Apparitions are thought forms, and may come from the living or from the dead; at times they come as a warning.

Crystal gazing is for the purpose of concentrating the mind, in order that it may become subjective.

Black magic, the curse of malpractice, all mean the use of thought power for destructive purposes.

Automatic writing takes place when the arm is under control of the subjective mind of the operator or by the subconscious mind of some one else, either in the flesh or out of it; it is a form of suggestion, either conscious or unconscious. Independent writing is where the pencil writes without physical contact. This shows that some inner power has the ability to grasp solid objects without physical contact. Table tipping and rappings are from the same source. It is thought by some that these manifestations come from the agency of what is called "ectoplasm," or a subtle emanation of the body; this theory, however, does not explain all of the facts. Mind alone can do this. Levitation or the ability to move the body is another fact well known to investigators.

The power of prophecy is limited to some subjective tendency already set in motion; for mental tendencies cast their shadows before them. There is a higher power of prophecy which contacts the Cosmic Purposes and reads the thought of God.

Man reproduces, on the mental plane, all of the physical faculties.

IMMORTALITY

Immortality means that the individual shall persist after the experience of physical death, carrying with him a complete remembrance and an unbroken stream of consciousness; for if man be immortal, death cannot rob him of anything.

Man cannot conceive of himself, either as being born or as dying; he lives, and cannot think of himself from any other standpoint. Even though a person should conceive of himself as dying and imagine his own funeral, he would still have to conceive of himself as consciously being there, and so prove that he did not die at all. It is the same with birth; we can imagine being born into this world, but we cannot imagine the self as being non-existent; for, while thinking of the self as being born, we are still consciously thinking; thus proving that we were before we were physically born.

All inquiry into the Truth starts with the self-evident proposition that Life Is.

When man first woke to self-consciousness on this plane he already had a body. Consciousness always clothes itself in some kind of form.

Matter, from which the body is made, is a fluent substance, forever taking the form that intelligence gives it; it flows in and out like a river; we yearly immortalize ourselves, so far as the body is concerned.

The ether, being more solid than matter, proves that we could have a body within the one that we now occupy. Since matter in form is only a certain rate of vibration, it follows that, in dealing with Infinite Life, we are dealing with an infinite number of vibrations; consequently, we might have a body within a body to Infinity.

In reality, the body is a spiritual idea; the flesh simply covers it for the purpose of providing a physical instrument through which Spirit may function on this plane.

Man departs this body only to find himself already equipped with another one. He carries with him every attribute that he now possesses, and goes forth in complete retention of his individuality.

Since there is but One Mind, it follows that it is possible to communicate with the departed; but, as the communication must come through the subjective, it is difficult to receive clear messages; and it is impossible to know whether or not the ones with whom we think we are communicating are consciously present.

It is never safe to go into a trance state in order to communicate with the departed, as in so doing, one might subject himself to the mental influences of lesser mentalities. Individuality is sacred and must never be tampered with nor controlled, except by the conscious mind.

The value of an understanding of psychic phenomena lies in the fact that they are the phenomena of Mind and must be accounted for.

Every plane reproduces the one just below or just above it; psychic phenomena are the reproductions, on the mental plane, of the principle just below the mental, which is the physical.

PART III: SPECIAL ARTICLES

Note: It is well for the student to carefully read and study the following articles, as they have a distinct bearing on the preceding lessons.

ABSOLUTENESS AND RELATIVITY

Absolute is defined as, "Free from restrictions, unlimited, unconditioned." "The Unlimited and Perfect Being, God."

Relativity is defined as, "Existence only as an object of, or in relation to, a thinking mind." "A condition of dependence."

The Absolute, being Unconditioned, is Infinite and All; It is that Which Is, or the Truth. It is axiomatic that the Truth, being All, cannot be separated, limited nor divided; It must be Changeless, Complete, Perfect and Uncreated.

Relativity is that which depends upon something else; and if there be such a thing as relativity, it is not a thing of itself, but only that which functions within the Absolute and depends on It.

We wish to affirm relativity without destroying Absoluteness. This can be done only by realizing that the relative is not a thing apart from, but is an experience in, the All-Comprehending Mind. The relative does not contradict the Absolute, but affirms It; and the relative alone guarantees that there is an Absolute.

The Absolute is Cause, the relative is effect; the Absolute depends upon Itself, being Self-Existent; the relative must depend upon the Absolute.

We should be careful not to deny the relative, simply because it is not absolute. To suppose that there could be an Absolute without a relative, would be to suppose that there could be an unexpressed God or First Cause; this is unthinkable and impossible. The Consciousness of God must be expressed, hence the relative. The relative is not apart from, but is in the Absolute; and, as such, it is perfectly good and necessary. Time, space, outline, form, change, movement, action and reaction, manifestation and creation, all are relative; but all are real.

Relativity subsists within existence and inherent Life is potential and latent with limitless possibilities.

The relative and the Absolute do not contradict each other.

THE PROBLEM OF EVIL

Evil will remain a problem as long as any one believes in it. This may sound rather startling until one has taken the time to think the matter through to a conclusion. Evil, of itself, is neither person, place nor thing, but is only a certain use that we make of life. We call that evil which we feel is the wrong thing to do; but our ideas of good and evil change with the unfoldment of our thought about, and belief in, life; for what was thought to be good yesterday, is to-day considered evil; and what, yesterday, was considered to be evil, is to-day called good.

Generally speaking, we may consider evil to be that which is destructive in its nature, and good to be that which is constructive

Evil, then, will disappear in the exact proportion that we cease using destructive methods; and good will appear to the degree that we embody constructive methods. To turn from evil and do good is the desire of every soul who is consecrated to the Truth; this we can do only as we cease talking about, believing in, or doing evil.

The problem of evil will continue to be a problem just as long as we believe in it. Good will appear only as we embody it. Each soul has within a sure test, a something which directs and guides it. This Something is the Spirit of God and It knows no evil.

As there is no sin but a mistake, so there is no punishment but an inevitable consequence. As long as we make mistakes we shall be sinning; and just so long, we shall automatically be punished; for the law is certain and sure. As we turn to the Good, we will stop doing evil and, therefore, stop sinning.

The problem is solved as we turn from all that hurts, all that is destructive, all that denies the Good, and turn with our whole being into the light and toward the Truth. Evil is swallowed up in the Good as we learn to live daily in the Presence of God. "I will forgive their iniquity and I will remember their sin no more." 100 That is, it will be completely blotted out; it will cease to be.

With our whole heart, with our whole being, in sincerity and honesty, with a complete trust in the Good, yearning toward It with a soul-desire that will be satisfied, we should turn to God, as the Supreme Presence, as the Complete Life, forsaking any belief in evil; we should turn so completely to the Spirit that our souls will become illumined by the Light Eternal.

Evil will cease to be when we stop looking at it; it never really was and is but a supposition. Let us, then, turn to the Path of Light and look to the God Within. Let us say, "Thou Infinite, Indwelling God, within me, knowing no evil, teach me of Thy ways, and in Thy wisdom make me wise. Almighty God within me, direct me into the way of the All Good." Let us turn completely from any and every belief in evil and do good. The problem will thus be solved and we shall realize that only the Good remains.

FOOTNOTES

100 Jer. 31:34.

THE MEANING OF THE FALL

The story of the fall typifies race-experience as brought about through its belief in duality. Man is created perfect; that is, he starts on his journey as a perfect being, but he also starts as an individual; and this, of course, means that he starts with self-choice. Self-choice would have no real meaning unless it were backed by the power to externalize this choice and experience the effect of it. Man has the ability to choose and to externalize his choice; for he is a real individuality.

THE GARDEN OF EDEN

The Garden of Eden typifies man's original state of perfection before he began to have experience. The Tree of Knowledge means the Life Principle which can be used both ways. It bore the fruit of the knowledge of both kinds of experience, good and evil, freedom and limitation. Man must choose which kind of fruit he will eat. "Choose ye this day whom ye will serve." 101 Man makes his choice consciously but generally in ignorance. The serpent typifies the Life Principle viewed from the materialistic viewpoint; it casts man from his perfect state through his belief in duality and separation. Man chose to depart from Good, and man alone must choose to return to It. God lets him alone; for he is a free agent and may do as he wills with himself. When man decides to return to his Father's House, he will find that his Father is still there. "Act as though I am and I will be." "Onlook the Deity and the Deity will onlook thee." "Be firm and ye shall be made firm." "As though hast believed so be it done unto thee." 102 "Ask and it shall be given unto you; seek and ye shall find; knock and it shall be opened unto you." 103 God's Creation is Perfect and we must wake to the fact and know that we are now in the Kingdom of Heaven.

FOOTNOTES
101 Josh. 24:15.
102 Matt. 8:12.
103 Matt 7:7.

SALVATION AND GRACE

As the fall of man was brought about through his own act, so the rise of man will be accomplished through his own act. God already Is. Salvation is not a thing but a Way; the way of salvation is through the realization of man's unity with the Whole. Grace is the givingness of the Spirit to Its Creation and is not a special law, but is a specialized one. In other words, Grace Is, but we need to recognize It. It is not something that God imposed upon us, but is the logical result of the correct acceptance of life and of a correct relationship to the Spirit.

We are saved by Grace to the extent that we believe in, accept and seek to embody, the Law of Good; for the Law of Good is ever a Law of Liberty and never one of limitation. Limitation is not a thing, but is a belief. Freedom is a Divine Reality, while limitation is an illusion, a false belief.

Salvation is an act of man and not an act of God. Man damned himself and man must save himself, if he ever is saved. He will save himself to the exact degree that he stops damning himself. He will live in Heaven when he stops living in hell. He will be healed when he stops being sick. He will become rich just as soon as he stops being poor. He will become as God when he stops masquerading as the devil. He will be happy when he stops being miserable. He will be at peace when he stops becoming confused. He will be filled with joy when he stops thinking sadness. He will live when he stops dying. He will be perfect when he stops looking upon imperfection; and he will be saved when he stops damning himself. *He will be one when he stops being two. Man, man, man, man, man, man, man;* "The great Thou—I—and the great I—Thou."

THE PERFECT UNIVERSE

We must realize the Perfect Universe if we wish to embody the greatest good. If the Universe were not Perfect It could not exist for a single moment. It is self-evident that we live in a Perfect Universe; and, if so, then everything in It must also be perfect.

The Truth is Indivisible and Whole. God is Complete and Perfect. A Perfect Cause must produce a Perfect Effect. Disregarding all evidence to the contrary, the student of Truth will maintain that he lives in a Perfect Universe and among perfect people; he will regulate his thinking to meet this necessity and will refuse to believe in its opposite. At first he may appear to be weak; but as time goes on, he will prove to Itself that his position is a correct one; for that which appears imperfect will begin to slip from his experience.

To daily meditate on the Perfect Life and to daily embody the Great Ideal is the way to sure salvation; this is a royal road to freedom and is happiness to the soul of man. We cannot afford to believe in imperfection for a single instant. Let us learn to look as God must look, with a Perfect Vision; let us seek the Good and the True and believe in them with our whole heart; let us say daily to our inner selves: "Perfect God within me; Perfect Life within me, Which is God; Perfect Being within me, Which is God, come forth into expression through me and become that which I am; lead me into the paths of perfection and cause me to see only the Good."

By this practice, the soul will become illumined and will acquaint itself with God and be at peace. "Be ye therefore perfect, even as your Father Which is in heaven is Perfect." 104

FOOTNOTES

104 Matt 5:48.

IMAGINATION AND WILL

Coué announced a great truth when he said that imagination is superior to the will; but he did not explain the philosophy behind this truth. It is a fact that what he said is true, but we wish to analyze the fact and discover the reason back of it; for if anything is true there is always a reason for its being true.

Will is an assumption, pure and simple. We do not will to live; we live because we have life and cannot help living. The use of the will could not make us anything that we are not; for it is not possible to get out of a bag anything that the bag does not contain. We live because life is within us. Perhaps this is what Jesus meant when He said, "Which of you, by taking thought, can add one cubit to his stature?" 105

We did not make Life and we cannot change It, but we can use It; and the use of Life is through the imagination; because this faculty has, at its roots, the very well-spring of life and action. Imagination carries with it feeling and conviction, which mean life and action; it awakens within us all the finer forces of nature and stirs into action latent powers which otherwise would never come to the surface.

At the very root of the whole matter we find that the Creative Power of the universe does not create through will, but through imagination, imaging, feeling, and knowing. To suppose that God must will things to happen would be to suppose that God had some opposing force to contend with.

Will power may be necessary in its place, but as a creative agency it is non-existent; it is not creative but directive; and used from this standpoint it is a wonderful force; whereas, used from any other angle, it becomes destructive and will mentally weary the one using it. To feel that we have to will things to happen casts doubt into the face of Creation and presupposes that Life is not Self-Existent and Self-Propelling.

Imagination taps the very roots of Being and utilizes the same Power that brought the worlds forth from Chaos. "The worlds were framed by the word of God." 105 Imagination is the power of the word, while will is the directive agency, denoting the purpose for which the word is spoken.

Man reproduces the power to create and, in his own life, controls his destiny through the activity of his word. This word cannot be willed; but it can be imagined, or imaged forth, into expression.

FOOTNOTES

105 Matt 6:27.
105 Heb. 11:3.

HOW TO VISUALIZE

Visualizing means mentally seeing the things that you wish to have or to do. When you mentally see the things you desire, and see them very clearly, you are presenting Universal Mind with images of thought; and, like the creative soil of the ground, It at once tends to project them into form. If the thought image is clear it provides a good mold; if it is imperfect the mold is a poor one. This does not mean that one must set his mind or hold thought; it simply means that he must think clearly. There is no power in holding thoughts; indeed, the real secret of successful mental work is to loose thought and let Mind operate upon it.

The first thing to do is to decide what you wish to image into Mind. After having become composed in thought, begin to see the complete outcome of your desires, in mental pictures. Suppose that you wish to demonstrate a home; you should know just what kind of home you wish. Of course, if you simply thought of house you would get something, but the more definite the picture the better the results will be. In order to make the picture complete, decide just what kind of a home you wish to live in; then, in the silence of your thought, mentally look at this house; go from room to room, stopping here and there to look at some piece of furniture or at some picture on the wall. Make the whole thing real, as far as possible; enter the house, sit down and feel that you are actually living there, saying, "I am now living in this house." You have set a word in motion through the Law which will bring a realization of your desire, unless you, yourself, neutralize the picture by doubting it. Do this every day until the house appears. Use the same process in visualizing anything.

In order that you may fully understand just what I mean, I will illustrate by drawing a mental picture which I will ask you to follow as you read these lines. Imagine that you are with me; we will suppose that I am a man about six feet tall, with light hair and complexion. We are sitting on the front porch of a house that is painted green; it is a two-story house and sits quite far back from the road; there are tall trees standing in front of the house through which the sun is shining. We can see the little shadows as they play upon the porch through the open spaces between the trees. The breeze is gently blowing and the leaves are waving back and forth. I am talking to you, saying, "Let us take a walk together." We immediately rise from our seats, which are made of wicker, and walk down three stone steps to a gravel walk, leading to the street. As we go out through a stone gate we are suddenly met by a dog which is running along the street; he is a large, yellow dog, and is running rapidly. We watch him as he runs, barking, down the street, till he turns a corner,—and our picture is at an end. Now, if you have carefully imaged each step in the above picture, you will understand what visualizing means.

THE SEQUENCE OF THE CREATIVE ORDER

In the creation of any form it is necessary for its image to exist in Mind before it can come into realization in the external. The Law, being only a neutral force, cannot initiate anything, and cannot, of Itself, choose to create anything. It is a Doer only, not a Knower. The Word alone knows; so we may assume that each word is a law unto itself, through the One great Law of all Life.

MAN'S CREATIVE POWER MARVELOUS

Man's creative power in his world is marvelous; for every time he thinks he sets the Law in motion. As his thought sets the Law in motion it is specializing It for some definite purpose; and in this way his word becomes the law unto the thing which he speaks. Of course man never really creates, but his use of Creative Power makes his word creative through the Medium of Mind. This should give to all a sense of freedom and a realization that there is neither competition nor monopoly. It leaves each to work out his own salvation, not with fear or even trembling, but with a calm sense of peace and assurance.

CONCENTRATION

To concentrate means to bring to a point. To concentrate the mentality means to bring the thinking to bear on one point of interest and to hold it there. Concentration has little to do with will power. Indeed, the misuse of will often renders concentration impossible.

The simplest practice for concentration is always the best. Nature always works along the lines of least resistance; and mental power is only a force of nature and should always be thought of in a natural way.

If you wish to concentrate on some particular idea or thought, bring the attention to it; then hold it there, but without effort. At first you may find that the thought wavers; do not oppose this, but mentally brush the wrong thought aside, much as you would brush a fly from the face with the hand. Be sure that you make no great mental effort, feel at ease and at peace, gently bringing the thought back to the point of attention.

Let us illustrate this by supposing that one is going to concentrate on the thought of happiness. Taking the word "happy" into the mentality, say, "I am happy"; without effort or mentally trying, just think the words, "I am happy." In a few minutes you may find that your thought has begun to wander. Right here be sure and not bring the attention back with a bang; just say again, "I am happy," making no effort to destroy the other thought, but returning to the starting point, "I am happy." Make the whole thing easy and natural, and soon you will find that you can hold the attention as long as you desire.

It is always a mistake to oppose thoughts that interfere; when one begins to do this he will at once find that he is resisting something, thereby disrupting his whole meditation.

It is unnecessary to concentrate on an external object; for *Concentration is always from within and never from without.* The only place that the mind can know is within itself.

In concentrating, lay aside all will power and resistance, letting the thought realize the words upon which you wish to concentrate. This will be found a simple but most effective method, and by far the most prolific of results.

In teaching a child to concentrate, it is well to have him take something in which he is particularly interested. As a child's mind wanders more or less aimlessly about, it is well to have him write some thought on paper; and, looking at it, see how long he can center his interest on the mental picture that the words suggest.

THE MIRROR OF THE SUBJECTIVE

It has truly been said that Mind is a mirror. If we could realize how completely this law works, no doubt we would greatly alter our manner of thinking. It is impossible to create even the slightest thought without causing some reflex action in Mind; and the deeper the emotion the deeper will be the penetration of thought and the more complete will be the reaction.

Thought is the most subtle of all the forces which we know anything about, and but few understand what a tremendous power it has, either for good or for ill. To learn how to control one's thought means knowing how to control one's body and destiny.

Subjective mind can reason only deductively; consequently, it is compelled, by reason of its nature, to accept whatever thought gains entrance to it. So the mirror of Mind is, in reality, the working of the law of cause and effect through the mentality. The subjective mind, being the seat of memory, must contain all the thoughts which have ever gone into it, whether these thoughts have been conscious or not. But when a person is told that he has thoughts which he never consciously created it is a little hard to understand. He must realize, however, that constant contact with life opens the door to many impressions which were never consciously created. This fact, together with the realization that whatever falls into the subjective mind must be acted upon, answers the question.

Of course, we do not imagine that certain things are going to happen to us; but we do think certain kinds of thoughts which, brought to their logical conclusions, would produce definite effects. Remember that the subjective mind reasons deductively only; and all this becomes quite evident.

The subjective side of thought, being the creative agency within, must at once set to work to produce anything which is given it, no matter what the emotion may be. How wonderful! But this shows how very careful one should be in choosing the kind and type of emotion to be made into form; for something must happen to all the thoughts which submerge.

The subjective mind never argues nor contradicts what is put into it; the thought is at once accepted and acted upon. If one says that he is sick, it at once begins to create a sick condition; for, like a mirror, it reflects; and being creative, what it reflects it tends to create and to cast forth as a condition.

Like any other natural force, subjective mind was not created by man and he cannot change its mode of operation; but, while he may not change a natural force, he may change his manner of approach to it. Man cannot change his own inherent nature; but he can, and should, learn to make the best use of all his forces. Subjective mind will never change its own nature, but will always reflect to the thinker what he thinks into it. Man did not make this law nor can he change it; but, like any other law, once understood, it becomes an obedient servant.

The use of this law is entirely mental and is within the grasp of every one; it is so simple that all can understand; it is the law of mind in action, and this law is set in motion by correct thinking and knowing.

But how few know why they think or what they think! How few control even the slightest emotion or allow the emotions to express in a constructive manner! No doubt the time will come when a complete control of the subjective will be gained and man will then be much less limited.

But the race is made up of individuals, and the place to begin is right at home. We, who have affirmed these great laws of mind to be realities in the human experience, must so prove them in our expressions of life that the rest, looking on, may read the sign and follow the signal. It is possible to do this, and the reward is great.

At first the road may be hard and beset with many difficulties; there may be failures and discouragements; but the end is certain. We fall, only to rise again into a greater realization of life and action; and, like the pilgrim of old, to renew the journey. We shall need a backbone instead of a wishbone here as in all other places. It is not in wishing but in knowing and in doing that we shall find the reward of true merit. It behooves each one to make the effort to consciously control the processes of his thought.

This does not mean sitting around in some dark corner with the hand at the brow, impersonating Socrates or Plato; it means out in the world, in the midst of affairs, at home and abroad, wherever our work takes us. We need not leave the world; for we may engage in all of its activities without being controlled by them; we may be in the world of affairs as masters and not as slaves.

Surely this hope, held before the waiting thought, will so stimulate our endeavors that we shall go forth into life and the great game of living with a new song upon our lips and a new joy within, springing forth into the dawn of a new day.

PERSONALITY

Personality is the result of man's experience; it is the sum total of all that he has said, done, felt, thought, hoped for and believed in; it is the result of his reactions to the events of life as they come and go. Factors to be considered in the development of personality are heredity, race-suggestion, environment, child training, education, auto-suggestion and, indeed, anything and everything that impinges upon consciousness. Therefore, we are what we are and where we are because of the nature of our accumulated consciousness.

FACTORS NECESSARY FOR A DYNAMIC PERSONALITY

It goes without saying that all people desire a dynamic, radiant personality; and it is self-evident that certain palates are essential to produce this result. The external personality really reflects the soul, and its building may be likened to a mental garden where the harvest depends upon the kind of seed that is sown. Each one chooses for himself just what kind of materials he will use and each builds according to the pattern of his own desires. "Whatsoever a man soweth, that shall he also reap." Just as a fine architect uses only the best materials and plans most carefully how to construct his building, so should we, in the building of personality, choose most carefully the kind of materials we wish to use.

HIGH CHARACTER.—First of all, it should be founded upon the rock of high character, high ideals, and built for Eternity as well as for to-day.

SINCERITY.—Sincerity in every human relationship is essential.

ABILITY.—To be a master of one thing and to daily improve.

ENTHUSIASM.—A keen interest in people and things at home and abroad; it has been called "The Fortune-Teller of Life." Enthusiasm is compelling and sweeps everything before it.

SERVICE.—Service is the keynote to success and implies constructive work; also, loyalty to your work and to all concerned in it.

WHOLESOMENESS.—A clean-minded man with high ideals is always sought after. The reading of fine books, listening to good music and becoming acquainted with the best in art and literature will soon implant in the mentality a quality of wholesomeness that is most desirable.

SUCCESS.—A consciousness of success must be developed; this can be done by creating clear pictures of success and working toward them daily. Decision and assertion are aids to this end and must not be overlooked.

SELF-CONFIDENCE.—Implies peace and poise and knowing what to do in every situation.

POWER AND STRENGTH.—Are also born of peace and poise.

SENSE OF HUMOR.—This is most necessary to have, as it lightens the burdens of life and makes one's self and others happy. Without it things seem dull and drear. This has no barb or sting and implies the ability to laugh at one's own expense.

GOOD MANNERS.—Not servile but courteous.

TACT.—Saying or doing the right thing at the right time.

THOROUGHNESS.—Implies system and the ability to carry things out to a definite conclusion. This quality is essential to success.

CHARM.—Personal charm is that indefinable something which makes every one a friend. It is the result of genuine friendliness, sympathy, kindliness and unselfish interest in others.

MAGNETISM.—The result of an abundant vitality on the physical plane; of intellect and temperament on the mental plane; and of atmosphere or consciousness on the Spiritual plane.

TENDERNESS.—Sympathetic union with people; real compassion.

LOVE.—The Universal Urge to express, the Self-givingness of Spirit.

ORIGINALITY.—Try to create; do not imitate; think for yourself. Read Emerson's Essay on "Self-Reliance."

INCENTIVE.—Have wholesome ambitions and definite objectives which are constructive in their nature. Any ambition is wholesome which brings only good results to one's self and all concerned.

SUITABLE HUMILITY, SIMPLICITY AND GENUINENESS.—These attributes keep one from being over-ambitious and from being too aggressive.

EMOTIONAL CONTROL.—Presupposes poise and self-mastery.

SPIRITUALITY.—Looking for the good in all and having faith, belief, and trust.

HEALTH.—Is a great factor in creating a dynamic, vibrant personality.

VOICE.—A clear, resonant, well-modulated tone at all times.

DRESS.—Clothes reflect one's idea of "The Eternal fitness of things." Colors particularly have a peculiarly subtle effect on the wearer and upon those with whom he comes in contact.

Strictly speaking, personality is the use that we make of our individuality. Individuality means that which we really are; it means the point in Life where we exist and can say, *I am.* Perhaps it could be defined as a point in Mind where Life recognizes Itself as some Person. Each person is an Individualized Center of God-Consciousness, a self-knowing center of Life and Action.

It follows, then, that personality is much greater than it seems to be; for it is the use of Divine Individuality and has, back of it, a limitless possibility. It is the coming forth of God, or Life, into Self-Expression.

Man's personality is not a thing to be lightly spoken of or decried as human or ineffective. Within and behind it are boundless possibilities, and few, indeed, realize what a tremendous power it wields, either for good or for ill.

To-day we are hearing much about this power and the way to develop it; for as yet we express only in part, being unaware of the Whole. Latent forces surge to express through man; Divine impulse seek expression through him; a Cosmic Urge forever beats against the threshold of his consciousness, demanding expression; hence, all his subtle longings and unspoken thoughts.

To develop or express the self is the great need of the human race; but though feeling, sensing, inwardly knowing and realizing a greater good, man stumbles blindly along the pathway of life, expressing only in part.

Like all the other faculties of the Great Within, personality may be consciously unfolded and expressed, if we let it come through.

We all desire a powerful personality, and all may have one if they pay attention to a few fundamental facts of Being; for personality is the expression of something that already exists and simply needs to be allowed to come forth.

Any one wishing to develop a pleasing personality must first become pleasant. He must think pleasing thoughts. All animosity and vindictiveness must be swept aside if the soul is to express itself in terms of greatness.

There is no place for smallness in the full life and no place for meanness in the liberal mind. A broad-minded, tolerant attitude must be maintained toward all. This is not a goody-goody idea but a plain statement of fact.

A sense of calm and peace is essential to a well-rounded personality. The din and roar of the outer struggle for existence must not find entrance to the soul if Reality is to be expressed.

Poise and balance are the mainsprings of reality and cannot be overlooked. We are not attracted to people who are always fussed up and fretful, who are never satisfied and are always unhappy. Misery and unhappiness are unknown to the Spirit of man, and we should make them unknown to the outer man.

Sensitiveness and morbidity must be swept side as unworthy of the great Ideal. Refuse to have the feelings hurt. Friends do not wish to hurt the feelings of those whom they love, and none but friends need be admitted.

Personality is but half expressed until we realize that within we are complete. Wholeness is the keynote to perfection and self-esteem is not egotism but is self-realization. Completion is from within and not from without; and no one can add to, or take from, that which is already complete. The Soul and Spirit are already perfect and whole.

Love is the great loadstone of Life; and without this quality of Spirit, shining through Life's action, everything becomes dull and drear. Goodness and human kindness are the handmaids of Love and Life, and cannot be separated from Reality.

Irritation, vexation and confusion go hand in hand to rob man of his birthright to peace, comfort and harmony. As children of the dust they must be brushed aside as unfit companions of the soul.

Anger and malice, revenge and animosity cannot breathe the same atmosphere as goodness and purity, and they will fall away as we climb to those heights where the Indwelling Spirit lives.

Self-confidence and courage go hand in hand with real worth and are but the declarations of man's Wholeness. There is nothing petty or little about greatness.

Mental alertness and animation but signify that man lives in a life of everlasting interests and activities.

Honesty and sincerity show forth the fundamental principles of Being, and without them man expresses only a make-shift of himself, a false and deluded sense of Reality. No real person can be dishonest or insincere. Truth alone shines to Eternal Day.

The complete, well-rounded, dynamic personality contains all of these qualities and attributes; and they will come forth into expression to the exact degree that we allow them to flow through us.

Personality is not false but real; it is the shining through of the Real Self,—the man God made.

Physical appearance has but little to do with those inner, subtle powers of attraction which decide what the Indwelling Ego is to attract to Itself. The Inner Man transcends all that is external and compels attention without effort. To be conscious of this Inner Self is to know the Real Man, to know the truth about personality and the power of attraction. As a rose unfolds, so the personality of man unfolds and blossoms forth into complete expression.

A few simple practices will soon develop such a powerful personality that it will become a magnet, drawing to its center with a force that cannot be denied. *These practices begin and end within man; for he is the center of his own universe, and nothing happens to him unless he lets it.*

Know that Life flows through you and cannot be hindered in Its expression. Know that the All Good is yours now. Act, think, believe, speak as though you were now all that you have ever dreamed. *And be sure that you believe the same thing about all people, for none of us lives unto himself alone, but each lives unto all, within the one life.*

Live constantly from this inner conviction, never stooping to anything less than the All Good; and you will soon discover that something is taking place that never took place before in your experience. *Do not try to make things happen; simply know that they are happening.*

Daily realize your Unity with the Whole and the Unity of the Whole with you. *You will soon develop such a powerful personality that all who come in contact with you will wish to remain in your presence.*

REPRESSION AND SUBLIMATION

THE SPIRIT OF SEX

We have discovered, from the preceding chapters, that the Universe is threefold in Its nature. It is Spirit, Soul and Body; Spirit as the active, projective, masculine factor; Soul as the receptive, creative, feminine factor; and Body, which is the result of the union of Spirit with Soul. The Spirit impregnates the Soul with Its Ideas, and the Soul gives form to these Ideas and clothes them with flesh. But this is the Trinity of Unity, a Triune Oneness; for the Three are really one.

Life is Androgynous, i.e., It contains within Itself both the masculine and the feminine factors. The male and the female of Creation come from One Principle; all come from the One and all will return to the One; all are now in the One and will forever remain in the One.

DESIRE

Back of all manifestation must be the desire to create, the urge to express; this is called the "Divine Urge." But this Urge, operating as Law produces energy. Desire gathers energy for creative purposes and utilizes power to express itself. So dynamic is this Urge that it will cause a little seed to break open the most solid earth, in order that it may express itself in the form of a plant. It is the coming forth of Spirit into expression, the loosing of energy into action, and is apparent in all Creation.

THE SPIRIT IS EXPRESSED

The Spirit, being Absolute, is always expressed; It has no unfulfilled desires. *It is always satisfied and happy because it is always expressed.* Creation is the result of the desire of Spirit to express Itself; It is the unfoldment of the Divine Ideas, Evolution is the time and process of this unfoldment. Involution is the idea in Mind, and evolution is the coming forth of the idea into expression. Involution precedes evolution, and evolution follows involution with a mathematical precision, propelled by an Immutable Law.

That which is involved must evolve, else the Spirit would remain unexpressed. As this is unthinkable, we may set it down that evolution, or the manifestation of desire and energy, is bound to take place whenever desire sets power and energy in motion. From this law we cannot hope to escape, and it would be useless to make the attempt.

MAN REËNACTS THE DIVINE NATURE

Man, as we have discussed, reënacts the Divine Nature and makes use of the same Laws that God uses. We find in man the same androgynous nature that we find in God. This nature we call his objective and subjective faculties.

His objective mentality impregnates his subjective with ideas; and in its turn, the subjective, gathering force and energy, projects these ideas into forms.

Back of every act of man is some form of desire to express. This desire, of course, is purely mental in its nature. All that man is, is his mentality, both conscious and subconscious, plus what he expresses.

The Divine Urge is strong in man and constantly causes him to seek some form of self-expression. It is Divine because It is the desire of Spirit to express Itself through him; and like all the other forces of Nature, this energy can work through man only at his bidding; consciously or unconsciously, for he is an individual and has self-choice.

This Urge or Energy is called "Libido," which means "The emotional craving, or wish, behind all human activities, the repression of which leads to psycho-neuroses."

CONGESTED EMOTIONS

The energy set in motion through this urge is the dynamic power of Mind, and unless it becomes expressed, it will congest and cause a conflict within the mentality.

Inhibited action produces conflicts and complexes which mentally tear and bind; and as they manifest their physical correspondents, they produce nervous disorders. It is claimed that a large percentage of diseases is caused by the suppression of some form of emotion. This does not necessarily mean the suppression of the sex emotion, but might mean any desire that remains unexpressed. Some form of desire is back of every impulse that the mind can conceive, some impulse to express life. Any unexpressed desire will eventually cause a complex. Things will stand just so much pressure and no more; when the limit is reached an explosion will follow, unless some avenue for expression is provided.

IRRITATION, AGITATION AND FEAR

People who are constantly being irritated have suppressed some desire to speak their minds. It may not appear as though this were the cause, but thought is very subtle, and only a careful study of its workings reveals the real facts. All irritation and agitation are mental in their cause, and a sense of calm and peace alone can heal them.

Fear is an intense emotion, and if bottled up, secretes poison in the system. Fear must be removed from the mentality if one is to be healed and is to function normally.

Anger, malice, vindictiveness and kindred emotions are but subtle forms of fear arising from a sense of inferiority. All of these emotions must be swept off the board if one is to gain peace, calm and poise. The union of peace, with calm and poise, alone can give birth to power; for without these attributes of reality, power is dissipated and lost in the shuffle.

IF WE WERE EXPRESSED

If we were completely expressed we would never become sick or unhappy. The average person goes through life expressed only in part and always with a sense of incompletion and dissatisfaction. Something must be done to make the individual complete if he is to remain normal and happy and really live.

EMOTION AND INTELLECT

Emotion is strong in man, and in the well-balanced person it is controlled by the intellect; but in many people there is a conflict between the emotions and the intellect; and in too many cases the emotion gains the ascendancy.

Our strongest emotions center around the ideas of fear, hate, love, sex and worship, with all of their many ramifications and meanings.

Emotion, uncontrolled, produces chaos; unexpressed it produces confusion, conflict and complex; for energy will have an outlet. Bottled up, it creates a pressure that is the cause of much damage to the physical man, and produces most of our nervous disorders. Expression is normal when the intellect decides how the emotion is going to manifest. "He that is slow to anger is better than the mighty; and he that ruleth his spirit than he that taketh a city." 108

THE CONFLICT OF DESIRE

When an emotion conflicts with the will and becomes suppressed it returns to its subjective state, but remains active; it will come up in some other form; it will not be put down. It may remain in a subjective state for years; but eventually, unless neutralized, it will manifest. Let one go for years with some unexpressed longing and he will have created such a desire that it will have become irresistible in its inclination toward expression.

People often become seething caldrons within because of inhibited action. Energy must find an outlet.

THE EMOTION OF SEX

Human love and the affections often go hand in hand with sex desire, even when not recognized as such. An affectionate nature is generally a passionate one. Love is the most wonderful thing in the world and creates the highest form of energy known to the mind of man. It will be expressed at the level of the passions or else become transmuted into Spiritual Coin of real and lasting value. But the ideas on sex are likely to become over-emphasized in modern literature along these lines. Sex is normal in its proper sphere; if it were not, it would not be; for nature does nothing without some good and ample reason.

THE TRUE MEANING OF LOVE

The true meaning of love is a wonderful thing; for it is the desire of the soul to express itself in terms of creation. Creation is brought about only through the self-givingness of the lover to the object of his love. This is why, when we love people, we will go to the limit to help or serve them; nothing is too great, no sacrifice is enough. The true lover gives all and is unhappy in not having still more of himself to give to the object of his adoration.

Because of our emotional nature, love is generally expressed through the sex desire. But too great an expression of this desire is destructive, for it depletes the vitality and demagnetizes the one who overindulges. This is the meaning, and the whole meaning, of the story of Samson and Delilah. "He that hath an ear, let him hear." 109 All people look, and occasionally someone sees.

SEX NOT NECESSARY TO THE EXPRESSION OF LOVE

The sex relationship is not necessary to the expression of real love. Love is the givingness of the self, and if this givingness is complete sex will take care of itself. But energy must have some outlet. It is only when the unexpressed desire remains in the subjective that destruction follows in its wake and strews the shores of time with human derelicts. Liberty and license, freedom and bondage, heaven and hell, happiness and misery, good and bad, all, all, are tied up in human desires. Energy is energy and will be expressed or blow the top off, just as a pipe will stand only so much pressure before bursting. Millions are daily being blown up, mentally and physically, through the suppression of desires. Desire is a dynamic force and must be taken into account.

WHEN SEX BECOMES DESTRUCTIVE

Sex desire becomes destructive only when it remains an unexpressed longing. This theory is not put forth to encourage free love nor to advocate indiscriminate relationships; for neither the one nor the other is believed in by the writer. It is stated as a fact patent to any thinking person. "Libido," may be expressed through more than one avenue; through transmutation, freeing life's energies and lifting them into an avenue of constructive expression; or through sublimation, transfusing the essence of energy into high action and producing a magnetism that is irresistible and wonderful in its scope. The atmosphere of one thus charged is complete; for the energy then takes the form of real Love and is the highest and most powerful vibration on the physical plane.

MALE AND FEMALE

Man, coming from Unity, is both male and female, and has, within himself, both attributes of reality. In some the male predominates; in others the female. We have two distinct types in man and woman; but they are types of one fundamental principle. There is also an intermediate sex; that is, one in which the two attributes seem to be almost equally balanced. The greatest men and women of the ages have belonged to this type, for it is a more complete balance between the two which are really one. But this is too great a topic to discuss in this course of lessons.

THE SOLUTION

The solution to the problem of desire is to transmute any destructive tendency into some form of action that is constructive. However, an intellectual form of expression alone will not do this, for only those things to which we may give the complete self will solve the problem. Love is the givingness of the self to the object of its adoration. We should all have something that we love to do, something that will completely express the self, something that will loose the energies of Life into action and transmute the power into creative work. We should learn to love all people and not just some people.

It is very disastrous to feel that we cannot live unless we possess some one individual, body and soul. This is not love but is an idea of possession, which often becomes an obsession. No soul is really complete until he feels compete within himself.

This does not exclude the great human relationships which mean so much to all of us; but it does take the sting out of life and does free the individual to love all, adore some, and find happiness everywhere.

To feel that love is unrequited creates a longing so intense that it tears the very heart out of life, and throws the one so feeling into a fit of despondency from which it is, indeed, hard to recover. This feeling is met in the Truth by knowing that Love is Eternal and Real and cannot be added to nor taken from.

This may seem like a hard teaching; but the problems of humanity deal largely with the human relationships and until they are harmonized, there can be no lasting happiness.

Happiness is from within, like all the other qualities of the Spirit. Within, Man is already complete and perfect; but he needs to realize this truth.

I can imagine some one saying: "This is too impersonal a teaching." It is not impersonal at all; this does not mean that we care less for people; indeed, we shall find that for the first time in life we shall really care; but the sting will have gone.

Refuse to have the feelings hurt. Refuse yourself the pleasure and morbidity of sensitiveness. Come out of the emotional intoxication and be *yourself*. Never allow the thought to become depressed nor morbid. Engage in some form of activity that will express the better self. Do not attempt to draw life from others; live the life that God gave you; it is ample and complete. "But," people will say, "I believe in affinities." If by this one means that each is only one-half of a real person and must find the other half in order to be expressed, he is mistaken. Such persons usually find a second affinity as soon as the first disappears. We all have a natural affinity for each other, since we all live in One Common Mind and in One Unified Spirit. It is all right if we wish to specialize on some particular love; but the hurt will remain unless love has a broader scope than when narrowed down to one single person.

Live, love and laugh! Let the heart be glad and free; rejoice in the thought of life and be happy. Realize God, in and through all, and unify with the Whole. Why take fragments when the Whole is here for the asking?

PSYCHO-ANALYSIS

Psycho-analysis is a system of analyzing the soul, or the subjective mentality. It is a mental process of diagnosis which seems to be technically perfect when used by those who understand it. It goes into the past and unearths the objectively forgotten emotions, brings them to light and causes them to be self-seen and so dissipated. It is based upon the theory that Nature is Perfect and when let alone will flow through man in a perfect state of health. The purpose of the analysis is to uncover the complex and heal the conflict, through removing it. It takes into account every experience that the individual has ever had, paying much attention to his early training, and more especially to his mental reactions to life.

It is a wonderful system, and in the hands of the right people, is prolific of much good. But, in the thought of the writer, it is a thing without a soul, a skeleton without flesh. It lacks the warmth, the fire and the reality of spiritual realization. It is useless to remove a mental complex, unless at the same time we place in its stead a real realization of what life means. It is useless to tear down unless, at the same time, we build up. The proper analysis of the soul, coupled with real spiritual recognition, will do wonders, however, and is well worth while.

SELF-ANALYSIS

Go through a process of self-analysis; look into your own past and carefully remove every complex. This is easily done by the one who is not afraid to look himself in the face. Find out what you are afraid of and convince the mentality that there is nothing to fear. Look the world squarely in the face; sift the mentality to its depths, removing every obstruction that inhibits the free flow of those great spiritual realizations, such as will be found in the meditations that follow these lessons.

METAPHYSICS

The right kind of mental work will go beneath the surface and destroy the subjective cause of the complex, thereby easing the conflict. It will then supply a Spiritual Realization that will open the avenues of thought to the great Whole. This alone is real and lasting.

FOOTNOTES
108 Prov. 16:32
109 Rev. 2:7.

THE ATONEMENT

Atonement is defined as reconciliation: "To make an expiation for sin or a sinner," and "To be at one." The definition for sin is, "To commit sin, transgress, neglect or disregard the Divine Law; to do wrong or offend." Literally speaking, sin means missing the mark or making a mistake. "There is no sin but a mistake and no punishment but a consequence." To assume that man could sin against God would be to suppose that a Divine Law could be broken. To suppose that Divine Law could be broken would be to assume that man has the power to destroy Divine Harmony and wreck the universe with his actions.

Man may have power to go contrary to Law, but certainly he has no power to break it. Man cannot break a law, but the law can break him if he goes contrary to it.

There is no doubt but that all of man's troubles come from his disregard of law, through ignorance. There can be no doubt that much of his trouble will be over when he comes to understand the law, and to consciously coöperate with it.

We live in a Universe of Law and a Universe of Love. The Law of God is Perfect, and the Love of God is also Perfect. The Law of God is the way in which the Spirit works; the Love of God is the Self-Givingness of the Spirit to Its Creation. The unity of Love and Law produce a harmonious Universe and a Perfect Creation.

Man, because of his individuality and the use that he makes of it, may go contrary to both Love and Law; but so long as he does this he will suffer. This is the real meaning of sin and punishment.

Man has gone contrary to the Law of Harmony and Love, and no doubt this is the reason for all his troubles. He will be saved to the degree that he returns to a state of harmony and unity with God and with Life. He can do this only as he first comes to realize that God is Love and that he lives in a Universe of Law.

The greater lesson that can be taught to the race is the lesson of Love and of Law. The lesson of Love teaches us that Life gives and that God is Good; while the lesson of Law teaches that there is a way to freedom through real Love.

If Love is the Self-Givingness of Spirit, then that man who most completely loves, will most completely give of himself to Life. The man who loves his work gives himself to it; the one who loves his art gives himself to it. We give ourselves to our friends and to our families and to the causes which we really love. Love is always the giving of the self to something; but the idea of self-givingness is not a morbid one and should never be thought of in this light.

We have always thought of the Atonement of Jesus as the act of His giving Himself, through suffering on the cross, as a sacrifice for the sins of the world. But God surely does not need that any man shall suffer for Him, nor sacrifice himself to please Him. This would, indeed, be a limited idea of the Divine Being. God does not need an At-one-ment, since He is already at one with himself and with all Creation. It is man, not God, who needs an At-one-ment. The act of atonement must be on the part of man and not of God. Man may need salvation, but God is already conscious of Complete Life and Being.

MAN'S WHOLE TROUBLE

Man's whole trouble lies in the fact that he believes himself to be separated from the Source of Life. He believes in duality. The At-one-ment is made to the degree that he realizes the Unity of Good. Man needs, and always has needed, to know the Truth about himself and God; and anything that helps to fill this need would be an act of atonement.

Now a man who had reached the understanding at which Jesus must have arrived would find the ordinary channels of expression inadequate to portray His concept of Life. Jesus could have had no desire to become rich; neither did He wish to be made a king, nor to receive the plaudits of the world. He wished to show to the world what the Love of God could really mean in the lives of men; He wished to show that the Self-Givingness of Spirit is complete; to prove that Life completely gives of Itself to Its Creation. This he could do only to the degree that He let God become Man through His own Individuality.

CAREFUL PREPARATION

The whole thought and attention of Jesus was given to the accomplishment of one supreme purpose: to show that God is a Living Reality in the lives of all men. He must show the Nature of the Divine Being; he must take the place of God and reveal the Love and tender care of the Creator for Its Creation. No more complete plan was ever organized in the mentality of an individual than the plan of Jesus to prove the reality of Spirit.

His thought, being psychic, that is, being able to read mental causes, told Him just what would happen if He did this. (See chapter on Prophecy in lesson on Psychic Phenomena.) He knew that he would have to suffer physical agony, and for a time, at least, be misunderstood and abused. He also knew that the lesson would prove for all time that God is Love. He knew that in the end the lesson which He was to teach would be accepted by all; and in this way He would become a Living Witness to the reality of Divine Love and Goodness.

Carefully He worked out His plan and patiently He waited for the right time to come to complete His life work; and when this time came, He unflinchingly gave of Himself to the necessity of the case. Man must come to understand God if he is ever to realize his own nature; he must come to know Spirit as a Living Reality and not as a myth.

THE VICARIOUS ATONEMENT

The Vicarious Atonement was the conscious giving of the Self to the needs of the human race—an example for all time that God is Love. Jesus perfectly understood the Law of Life and consciously chose to make an example of Himself that would cause all people to see what a real At-one-ment could mean. In order to do this, He had to take on the sins of the world; that is, He had to enter into men's mistakes in order to rectify them; not because God demanded this, but because man needed the example.

The suffering of Jesus, as He contacted the disorders of men's minds, was His vicarious atonement for the race. It was a wonderful example of what one man could do in proving the Unity of Good.

Any person who contacts the race-mind with the desire to lift it above its own level, will, thereby, go through a vicarious atonement. But the thought of morbidity that theology had given to the message of atonement is entirely erroneous. It is not a morbid thing but a glorious one. Atonement could not be morbid, but must always produce a realization of Unity and of Good. The life of Jesus is not a sad story, but is the account of a Man Who so completely realized His own At-one-ment that He had realization to spare and to give to all who believe in His teaching. His life was a triumphant march from the cradle into Eternity, and not from the cradle to the grave. He swallowed the grave in victory, because of His At-one-ment. Jesus left no grave and no dead man behind Him.

The At-one-ment, then, is a glorious recognition of fulfillment and completion. The vicarious part is lost in the greater realization of Unity and of Good. Jesus is the most Triumphant Figure of all history and the only Man, of Whom we have record, Who completely knew His own Nature. All thought of sin, shame, iniquity, poverty, sickness, obscurity and death are swept away with the empty tomb. No wonder that this lesson still remains and His teachings still hold good, for Reality never changes.

THE GIVINGNESS OF SPIRIT

As the human side of Jesus gave way, more and more, to the Divine Realization, He more and more completely became Divine; that is, He more completely became God, Incarnated in and through Man. In this mystic way He took the place of God, and we may, perhaps, say that through Him God proved the Love of God. Of course this is a crude way of putting it, but it does serve to point a moral and is, perhaps, the best way that we can conceive of the greatest lesson of all history.

THE WORLD HAS LEARNED ALL THAT IT SHOULD THROUGH SUFFERING

The world has learned all that it should through suffering. God does not demand that man suffer; and man suffers simply because he is ignorant of his own nature and because he misuses his power. Jesus proved the Truth and departed this life in joy, having fulfilled His Divine Mission. The lesson has been taught and the evidence is complete. The grave has been swallowed up in the Victory of Life and Love; and the tomb is empty for all time. "Why seek ye the living among the dead?" 110 The time has come for rejoicing and not for sorrowing; for the fulfillment of that peace which was promised. "Peace I leave with you." 111 There need be no more sorrowing nor crying; for Reality is now known. Life is Triumphant and Love reigns Supreme.

OUR PART IN THE ATONEMENT

The Vicarious Atonement is over, but the real At-one-ment has only begun. We are just beginning to realize what Love and Life mean. Every time we give of ourselves to others, helping them to overcome their troubles, we are performing an At-one-ment; we are proving the Unity of Good.

FOOTNOTES

110 Luke 24:5.
111 John 14:27.

THE PERSONALITY OF GOD

In our metaphysical abstractions we have come to the conclusion that God, or First Cause, must be Infinite; and it is difficult to perceive how a power which is Infinite can, at the same time, be personal. Yet the soul longs for a responsive universe; and the heart yearns for a God Who responds to the human desire.

To take from the individual his idea of God as a personally responsive Intelligence, and leave him only a cold, unresponsive Law, is to rob the individual of his greatest birthright and to throw him, naked and bare, into the midst of an Eternity which holds no attraction.

To think of the Universe in terms of Law only, is to make of God only an Infinite It, a cold an bitter Principle, lacking that warmth and color which the soul craves.

This difficulty is removed when we realize that the Law of Mind is like any other law; it is a natural force, and, like all law, should be thought of from this angle. But back of, and working in and through the Law, there is a responsive Intelligence and a knowing Spirit, Which is God, the Father of all; and Who responds to all.

We will think of Mind, then, as Law, and of God as Love; we will use the Law and love the Spirit back of, and through, the Law. In this way, we will be robbed of nothing, but will see that the way to freedom is through Love and by Law.

JESUS AS A SAVIOUR

Jesus stands forth from the pages of human history as the greatest Figure of all time. His teachings contain the greatest lesson ever given to the human race; and His life and works, while on earth, provide the grandest example that was ever given to man.

In the Higher Thought no attempt is made to rob Jesus of His greatness or to refute His teachings; indeed, the Higher Thought Movement is based upon the words and the works of this, the most remarkable Personality that ever graced our planet with His presence; and, until a greater figure appears, Jesus will still remain the great Wayshower to mankind, the great Saviour of the race.

Let us not waste time, then, in theological discussions which lead nowhere; but, following the example set before us, let us also do the works which He did. "The works that I do, shall he do also; and greater works than these shall he do; because I go unto my Father." 112

FOOTNOTES
313:112 John 14:12.

SELF-EXISTENT LIFE

The most important thing that any student of the Truth can understand is the real meaning of self-existence. Whatever the nature of First Cause is, It must be Self-Existent, or else It could not be at all. It is, perhaps, hard to comprehend that there must be, and is, a Power which exists simply because It is what It Is; and yet this is the mainspring of all right metaphysical work and endeavor.

We must come to believe in, and trust, that Power of Life and Intelligence which is God, or First Cause. We must understand that we deal with First Cause whenever we think, at any, and at all, times. If we had to gather energy with which to energize the Creative Principle of Life, where should we go to get the energy with which to energize It?

We are constantly thrown back upon the fundamental proposition that Life already Is; and that we use a Power which already Is. Let us then, without doubt or fear, throw our word into that Great Receptivity and trust It to do the work.

THE SUPREME AFFIRMATION

Strange as it may seem, the human thought can affirm only; it can never deny; for, even at the moment of denial, it really affirms the presence of that which it denies.

We speak of denials and affirmations as though they were opposed to each other, but such is not the case. Fear and faith are but different ways of expressing positive beliefs about something. Fear is a positive belief that we will experience something that we do not wish to have happen, while faith is a positive belief that we will experience something that we do wish to have happen.

The nature of Being is such that real denial is impossible; for there is but One Mind in the Universe, and It is always "yea and amen."

We are constantly affirming our way through life; and since affirmation is the only mental action possible, it behooves us to find the greatest affirmation and use it.

The Supreme Affirmation is, "I AM"; and, as such, It was given to Moses. This affirmation is constantly with us, and every time we speak we use it in some form. We must be careful to use it only as an upbuilding force.

CHRIST AND ANTICHRIST

The Spirit of Christ is the spirit of one who understands the Law and who uses It for constructive purposes only.

The spirit of Antichrist is the spirit of one who, understanding the Law, uses It for destructive purposes.

The Law, of Itself, is neither good nor bad, but is a Neutral Force, obeying all, and may be used for any purpose. But those truly instructed in the Law will never attempt to use It destructively; for they will understand that, by so doing, they would subject themselves to the very power which they have set in motion.

There is a power surrounding us which can be used either way, that is, constructively or destructively; but one instructed in the Truth will use this power only for the good of all. A most solemn warning is given to any one who would be so rash as to misuse his power.

If the thought is kept close to Good, to Love and to the Spirit, and if there is never any desire to do other than that which is constructive, there is no danger.

The Law is there to use and It is a Law of Liberty to all who constructively contact It. Anything which makes for a greater expression of life, either for the individual or for the race, and which has no element of destruction in it, is good.

We should not hesitate to use the Law for the benefit of our personal affairs or those of our friends or for any who ask our help; but we should be very careful to use It constructively.

EVOLUTION

All emerge from that One Whose Being is ever present and Whose Life, robed in numberless forms, is manifest throughout all Creation.

Creation is the logical result of the outpush of Life into self-expression. It is the coming forth of Spirit into manifestation, the externalization of an internal idea, through the objectification of a subjective image.

The One encompasses and flows through the All, spilling Itself into numberless forms and shapes. These forms and shapes, propelled by a Divine Urge which brings them into being, seek still further expression because of the dynamic power with which they are equipped.

This is the real meaning of evolution; for evolution is the result of intelligence and not its cause.

Each evolving thing has, within itself, an impulse implanted by the Divine; and since the Divine is Limitless and Perfect, It must and will, ultimately, bring all Creation to a state of perfect manifestation.

That which, to the human eye, appears as imperfect, is imperfect only because the human eye sees imperfectly or in part; i.e., the human does not see the real idea back of the external image.

There is a philosophy which states that there is a "Becoming God," and which attempts to prove this assertion through evolution; but this philosophy is inconsistent with the ultimate nature of Reality; for, if ultimate Reality were in a state of "becoming,' from what source would It gather Its impulse to become, and from whence would It draw Its power to express Itself?

A "becoming" or evolving God, or First Cause, is not consistent with true philosophy; while, on the other hand, an unfolding God, or First Cause, is consistent with Reality.

It is one thing to say that God is unfolding through His Idea of Himself but quite another thing to say that He is gradually becoming conscious of Himself. One is true while the other is false.

A "becoming" God implies a state of imperfection, or a state of being which does not recognize its perfection, at the very root of all being. An unfolding God implies a forever-out-pouring Spirit and a forever-manifesting Deity, or First Cause.

The unfoldment of this First Cause is what we call evolution. Since this unfoldment is not yet complete, i.e., since the idea is still in an unfolding state, it appears as though we lived in an imperfect universe.

To a few, who have been able to see behind the veil of matter, the perfect idea has been apparent; and these few have given to the world its greatest code of law, morals and ethics. These few have been the great mystics of the race, and to them the world owes a debt which can be paid only to the degree that the world comes to understand their teachings.

Evolution is the time and the process through which an idea unfolds to a higher state of manifestation; and since ideas are Divine Realities, evolution will forever go on.

PART IV: DAILY MEDITATIONS FOR SELF-HELP AND HEALING

In these short meditations I have tried to set forth some ideas which my experiences in mental healing have given me. I have found that a few brief statements, mentally affirmed, followed by a silent meditation, have been most effective in the healing work.

Most of the meditations have been written in the first person in order that those using them may be able to do so just as they are written.

It is not claimed that there is any occult power in these words, but that words similar to these are effective in inducing a greater realization of life. They contain thoughts which I have found to be most helpful.

Try them, my good reader, and see if they will not bring to life a deeper meaning and a greater joy. Whatever brings to the mentality a greater realization of life has, within itself, a healing power. I believe that these meditations will help all who take the time to use them.

First, decide which meditation you wish to use; then become quiet and composed. The body should be relaxed but the mentality should be active. Then, carefully read the meditation several times, phrase by phrase, endeavoring to realize the meaning of the words and trying to enter into the atmosphere of the thought. After having done this, meditate upon the words, following that meditation until you feel a sense of realization.

BODILY PERFECTION

COME, AND LET ME HEAL YOU

Come to me and I will heal you.

The inner power of Life within me is God, and it can heal anything.

I will to heal and help all who come to me.

I know that the realization of Life and Love within me heals all who come into Its presence.

I love the thought that I silently bless all who enter my atmosphere.

It is not I, but The Father Who dwelleth in me; He doeth the works.

I heal all who come near me.

HE IS MIGHTY WITHIN ME TO HEAL

God within me is mighty to heal.

He healeth me of all my diseases and cures me of all.

God within is now healing me of all my infirmities, sickness and pain and is bringing comfort to my soul.

God is my life; I cannot be sick.

I hear the voice of Truth telling me to arise and walk, for I am healed.

I am healed.

I DO NOT INHERIT DISEASE

There is no inherited tendency to disease, nor ill health.

I am born of Pure Spirit and am free from the belief in material existence.

False ideas cannot be transmitted from one to another, and I am free from all race-suggestion.

My Life is from Above, and I remember that I was always Perfect and Complete.

An Inner Light shines forth and frees me from the bonds of all false belief.

I came from the Spirit.

NO CONGESTION

There is no congestion nor stoppage of action.

Life, flowing through me, is Perfect and Clear;

It cannot be stopped, retarded nor hindered.

I feel the One Life flowing through me now.

It eliminates all impure secretions and washes me clean from all suggestion of false deposits in the flesh.

I am Clean, Pure and Perfect, and my Word eliminates all else.

There is no congestion.

NO FALSE GROWTH

"Every plant which my Heavenly Father hath not planted, shall be rooted up."
There is no false growth and nothing for one to feed on. I am free from all thought of, or belief in, anything false or fearsome.
I cast out all fear and with it all manifestation of Fear.
A false idea is neither person, place nor thing, and has no one to believe in it nor experience it.
I am now One with The Perfect Life of Complete Wholeness.
My Word casts out all fear.

NO WEARINESS

There is no weariness.
Mind and Spirit do not become tired nor weary, and I am Mind and Spirit.
The flesh cannot become weary, since it has no mind of its own.
I am free from all illusions of weariness.
My whole being responds to the thought of Life.
I am alive with the Great Vitality of the Spirit.
I am alive with spirit.

PERFECT HEALING

My hearing is perfect.
It is God in me hearing His own voice.
I hear That Voice, and no belief in inaction can hinder that hearing.
There are no impaired organs.
Every idea of the body is now complete and perfect and functions according to the Divine Law.
I open my ears to hear.
I am receptive to Truth and can understand it.
Open my ears that I may hear.

PERFECT VISION

There is One Vision and One ability to see, One perfect seeing.
My eyes are open and I see and behold one Perfect Life.
No suggestion of imperfect vision can enter my thought.
I perceive that all people can see, and that the One, looking through all, sees and cannot be limited in vision.
I am one with that complete ability to see, to know and understand the Truth.
I do open my eyes and do see.
Nothing in me can hinder this Word from operating through me and manifesting through my eyes.
Open my eyes that I may see.

THE ALL-SEEING EYE

The Eye of the Spirit cannot be dimmed, neither can it be impaired in Its ability to see.
My eyes are the Vision of my Indwelling Lord; they are the Windows of my Inner Spirit and are always open to the Vision of Truth.

I see with the Vision of the Spirit, and that ability cannot be weakened nor lost; it is forever effective.

My word which I now speak is the Law of Perfect Sight and my eyes are open and I see.

Spirit sees through me.

THE HEALING OF THE FLESH

My flesh is the Manifestation of the Spirit in my body.

It is kept perfect through the Law of God.

"In my flesh shall I see God."

The mantle of flesh is perfect and complete here and now.

It is one with the Body of God, and cannot be sick, nor suffer.

My flesh is perfect.

THERE IS NO PAIN

There is no pain nor inflammation.

All fear is swept away in the realization of Truth.

I am free from every belief in pain.

The Spirit cannot pain, and I am Pure Spirit and cannot be hurt nor harmed.

I am free from all pain.

COMPLETENESS

HAPPINESS AND COMPLETION
I am happy and complete to-day and forever.
Within me is that which is Perfect and Complete.
It is The Spirit of all Life, Truth, and Action.
I am happy in the sure knowledge of the Inner Light.
I cannot be sad nor sorry, but must radiate Joy and Life,
For Life is within me now.
I am happy and complete.

HERE AND NOW
Perfection is already accomplished.
I do not have to wait for the Perfect Life.
I am that Perfect Life here and now.
To-day I express the Limitless Life of the All Good.
To-day I manifest my Completion in every part of me.
To-day I am saved.
Here and now I am healed.

MAJESTIC CALM
The Inner Mind is still.
The Soul reflects the Most High.
The Spirit of man is God.
In the great calm of the All Good,
I rest in peace and security.
My life is now reflecting the Perfect Whole.
I am Peace; I am Calm.
I am security and complete satisfaction.
I am One with God.
I am filled with peace.

NO LOSS
There is no loss.
Nothing can be lost, misplaced nor forgotten.
There was never any loss nor confusion.
Creation is Perfect and Complete, and within the One are all things, and are all known to the One.
I am now in complete harmony with the Whole and I cannot lose nor misplace anything.
I am constantly finding more and more Good.
I know that there is no loss.

OH, FOR A TONGUE TO EXPRESS

Oh, for a tongue to express the Wonders which the Thought reveals!

Oh, for some Word to comprehend the boundless idea!

Would that some Voice were sweet enough to sound the harmony of Life.

But Within, in that vast realm of thought where the Soul meets God, the Spirit knows.

I will listen for that Voice and It will tell me of Life, of Love and Unity.

Speak to me, Spirit.

O SOUL OF MINE, LOOK OUT AND SEE

O Soul of mine, look out and see; look up and know Thy freedom.

Be not cast down nor dismayed; be uplifted within me and exult, for Thy Salvation has come.

Behold the wonders of the Great Whole and the marvels of the Universe.

Look out and see Thy good. It is not afar off, but is at hand.

Prepare Thyself to accept and believe; to know and live.

Let Life enter and live through Thee, Soul of mine, and rejoice that Thou hast vision so fair and so complete.

Rejoice that the Perfect Whole is so completely reflected through Thee.

My light has come.

SEEING THE PERFECT

My eyes behold the complete and perfect in all Creation,

"In all, over all and through all."

I see the perfect; there is nothing else to see, and no suggestion of otherness can enter my thought.

I know only the perfect and the complete.

I am perfect and whole, now.

I see the Good.

THE CIRCLE IS COMPLETE

The Circle of Love is complete.

It comprehends all, includes all, and binds all together with cords of Everlasting Unity.

I cannot depart from Its Presence nor wander from Its care.

My Love is complete within me.

The Love of God binds me to Itself, and will not let me go.

I shall make a home for you, O my wonderful Love, and we shall journey through life hand in hand.

I shall sit in your Presence and learn the wondrous things You will tell me;

For You are God.

Love sits within me.

THE THINGS THAT ARE

The things that are, were and evermore shall be.

Time, Chance and change begone from my thought!

The Changeless is here to stay, and the Timeless cannot cease from Being.

The things that are shall remain, though heaven and earth should pass away.
I rest secure and safe within the Life of Endless Perfection and Completion.
My whole Being responds to the Realization of the Complete Whole.
I am that which Is.

DIVINE COMPANIONSHIP

A SONG OF HOPE

My Life is in Thee, O Inner Presence.
I look upon Thee and hope springs forth into realization.
O Hope within me, undying evidence of Good,
Thou dost completely hold me in Thy loving embrace,
And from this fond caress assurance shall be born, and confidence and love.
My hope is in Thee.

BE STILL AND KNOW

"Be still and know that I am God."
I am still in Thy Presence.
I am quiet and peaceful, for I put my trust in Thee.
A great stillness steals over me and a great calm quiets my whole being, as I realize Thy Presence.
The heart knows of Thee, O Most High within.
It is still in Thy Presence, and it puts its whole confidence in Thee alone.
In Thy Presence I am still.

CAST ASIDE ALL DOUBT

Cast aside all doubt, O Soul of mine, and be unafraid, for Thy power is from On High.
He Who sitteth in the heavens shall be Thy champion;
Thou need not fear; Come forth, O Spirit, from within and express Thyself through me and let not my doubts hinder Thy approach.
My faith shall go forth to meet Thee, and my confidence shall embrace Thee.
My waiting thought shall bid Thee welcome to my house of Love,
And Joy shall accompany us through the ages yet to come.
I lay aside all fear and doubt.

DIVINE COMPANIONSHIP

I have an Inner Friend who walks and talks with me daily.
He is not afar off, but is within me, a constant companion.
I shall never become lonely, for my Friend is always near.
I have but to speak and He answers.
Before ever my lips spoke He told me of His love.
O my kind Friend, how dear to me is Thy presence.
The Spirit within me is my Friend.

HIS EYE IS ON THE SPARROW

"His eye is on the sparrow and I know He watches me."

This is a blessed thought, for it means that we cannot wander from His Presence, nor depart from His care.

Always He will watch over us and comfort us.

Forever we shall sit in His house and ceaselessly He will care for us.

The All-Seeing Eye cannot overlook any one, and all, all shall be kept in His care.

All are kept in His care.

HOPE CANNOT DIE

Hope cannot die. Eternal Hope is forever warm and fresh within me; the deathless Hope built upon the rock of sure knowledge.

O Hope Sublime, O Life Supreme, behold I come to Thee as a tired child, and Thou dost rekindle within me the fires of Faith.

Strong, swift and sure, Faith springs forth into action and my entire Being rises to meet the Dawn.

Hope, Faith and Love are in me.

I AM NOT ALONE

I am not alone, for a Presence goes with me and daily accompanies me on my travels.

Always I shall find this Divine Companion with me.

He will not desert nor allow me to go alone.

He will always be with me and near me, and will always provide for every want.

My life is hid with Christ in God.

I WENT TO THE MOUNTAIN

I have discovered a Secret Place within, where the thought goes into a mountain high above the din of the world.

I have found in this mountain a Place of Peace and rest,

A Place of joy and comfort to the heart.

I have found that the Secret Place of God is within my own Soul.

I will listen for Thy Voice.

THE JOY OF THE SOUL

My Soul within me rejoices at the realization of Life.

I am made glad as I behold my inner Light;

I cannot be sad nor depressed, for the All Good has claimed me as Its own.

O Soul within me, rejoice and become glad, for Thy Light has come and Thy Day of Salvation is at hand.

Be still within me and behold Him Who sitteth On High.

Reflect to me Thy revelation and flood me with Thy marvelous Light.

I rejoice in my Life within me.

FREEDOM

FREEDOM

Yes, I know that the Truth has freed me from the bonds of fear.

I am not afraid. I adore thee, Most High within me; I trust in Thee and abide in that hope that knows no fear; I am Free Spirit and cannot be bound.

The One Life flowing through me is Perfect and Complete. I am not apart from It. I am One with It in Marvelous Unity and Freedom; One with the Complete Whole.

I was born free and must always remain free. The realization of freedom permeates my whole being and sinks into the innermost parts of me.

I love it, adore it, I accept it.

I am free.

FREEDOM FROM SIN

I am free from belief in sin; there is neither sin nor sinner.

There is no judgment against any one.

God does not condemn, and man cannot.

All fear of sin is removed from me; all theological belief in punishment is gone from me.

I do not allow myself to receive such suggestions, for I perceive that they are lies.

I am free from all lies and from all liars.

I live by the One Power, and no thought can enter to disturb me.

There is neither sin nor sinner.

FREE FROM SENSITIVENESS

My feelings cannot be hurt.

No one wishes to harm me, and there is nothing in me that can believe in any separation from the All Good.

I perceive that I am free from all people, and I cannot be harmed nor mistreated.

I have such a sense of unity with all that the circle is complete and perfect.

I love my friends and they love me, and that love is in, and of, God, and cannot be marred nor hindered.

I am filled with joy and love, forever.

I KEEP THE PROMISE

I shall keep the promise that I have made to myself.

I shall never again tell myself that I am poor, sick, weak, nor unhappy.

I shall not lie to myself any more, but shall daily speak the truth to my inner Soul, telling It that It is wonderful and marvelous; that It is One with the Great Cause of all Life, Truth, Power and Action.

I shall whisper these things into my Soul until it breaks forth into songs of joy with the realization of Its Limitless possibilities.
I shall assure my Soul.

LOVE GLEAMS THROUGH THE MIST
Through the mist of human fear love gleams and points the way to freedom.
I now decree and declare that I am free from all sense of bondage.
I am made perfect and whole through knowledge of the Real Life within me.
No illusions can enter my thought.
I know that there is One Power, and I know that this Power now protects me from all harm.
As Perfect Love casts out all fear, so my fear flees before the knowledge of Truth.
I am not afraid.

NO BONDAGE
There is no bondage nor limitation.
Every part of me moves in perfect harmony and freedom.
I cannot be tied, bound nor made inactive, for
I am Free Spirit, and the Power of my Life is from on High.
There is no inaction nor false action,
And I am now completely Free.
I am free.

NO CONDEMNATION
There is no condemnation in me nor operating through me.
I am free from the belief or thought of men.
I walk my own way, immune to all suggestion of condemnation.
Only those thoughts can enter my mentality which I allow to enter.
I do not, and cannot, receive adverse thoughts.
Only those thoughts which are helpful and life-giving can find entrance to my house.
There is no condemnation.

NO FALSE HABIT
There are no vicious nor false habits.
Ever desire of my thought and heart is satisfied in the Truth.
I do not long for anything nor feel the lack of anything.
I am complete within myself; I am perfect within myself; I am happy and satisfied within myself.
I am One with All Life within me.
I am free.

NO HYPNOTISM NOR FALSE SUGGESTION
There is no hypnotism nor false suggestion.
I represent the One Mind which cannot act against Itself nor can It act against me.

I am immune to all suggestion and cannot receive false thoughts, nor harbor them.
I am surrounded with a circle of Love and Protection.
Asleep or awake, I am free from false thoughts.
I see the nothingness of all belief in, or fear of, otherness; and I know that The One and Only Mind, alone, can act.
Only the Good can enter.

NO MISTAKES

There are no mistakes; none have ever been made and none ever will be made.
Nothing ever happened in the past to hinder or hurt.
There is no past, and I know, and can see, that there is no belief in any past to rise against me.
I live in the Now, free from any yesterdays or to-morrows.
Now, I am Happy, Free and Complete.
My Word erases any and all beliefs in mistakes and sets me free.
I Am Free!
I am free from any beliefs in the past.

THERE ARE NO RESPONSIBILITIES

The Spirit has no responsibilities.
Its work is already accomplished and Its purposes are already fulfilled.
The Spirit knows no want nor fear.
It is complete within Itself and lives by virtue of Its own Being.
I am Spirit and cannot take on the fears of the world.
My work is accomplished and my ways are made straight before me.
The pathway of Life is an endless road of Eternal Satisfaction and Perfect Joy.
My Life within me is Complete and Perfect, and has no cares nor burdens.
It is Free Spirit and cannot be bound.
I rejoice in that Freedom.
I rejoice in freedom.

THE TIME HAS COME

The time has come, the hour has struck.
The power from within has come forth and is expressing through my word.
I do not have to wait; to-day is the time.
To-day I enter into all Truth; to-day I am completely saved and healed and made happy.
To-day I enter into my inheritance.
To-day the Truth has made me free.

WITHIN THY LAW IS FREEDOM

Within Thy Law is freedom to all who will believe.
I believe in Thy Law and I love Thy precepts.
I know that Thy Law is perfect and It is a delight to my Soul, for It is illumined with Thy Words of Power.
Thy Law is complete freedom to me, and to all for whom it shall be spoken.
I speak the Word of freedom to all, and all shall receive it.
I am free in Thy Law.

HARMONY OF LIFE

BEAUTY

I behold the Beautiful and the Pleasant.
My eyes see only that which is beautiful to look upon.
I will not see anything else nor believe in anything else.
I know that beauty has entered into my life, and will always remain there.
I see only the beautiful.

FRIENDSHIP OF THE SPIRIT AND OF MAN

The Friendship of the Spirit and of man is mine now and forever.
Even now I see the countless numbers of friends coming and going around me.
I enter into this friendship and this companionship with gladness and rejoicing.
I receive my friends.

HE WILLS ME TO BE

It was God Himself who willed that I should be.
I have no cares nor burdens to bear.
I am reminded of the great command:
"Come unto Me all ye who labor and are heavy laden and I will give you rest."
I do come into the Light and I do know that all cares
And responsibilities fall from me as I let the
Light of Wisdom direct my ways.
He wills me to be; therefore, I am.

I SERVE

I serve the world.
I wait upon the Lord within all men;
I call forth glory from On High through the minds of all people.
I obey the will of Him Who inhabits Eternity.
I do the works of Him Who dwelleth among the heavens.
My Lord within commands and I obey.
I do good to all people.

I SHALL NOT DOUBT NOR FEAR

I shall not doubt nor fear, for my salvation is from On High, and the day of its appearing is now at hand.
I shall not doubt nor fear, for my whole being responds to the realization of Life within and around me.
I shall not fear, for the Hosts of Heaven are waiting upon me and the Law of the Universe is my Salvation.
I shall not fear.

I WAS TOLD TO LIVE

I was told to live and to love, to laugh and to be glad.
I was told to be still and know of the One Almighty Power, in and through all.
I was told to let that Power work through and in me.
I believed that voice and I received my Good.
I am healed—The joy of Life.

LAW

I meditate upon the Law of God.
It is a Perfect Law and is now working for me and in and through me.
"The Law of the Lord is perfect."
I speak into that Law and it is done unto me.
Thy Law is in my heart.

LOVE

The Love of the All Good is within me and through me.
That Love goes out to meet all who come into my atmosphere.
It radiates to all and flowing through all.
My Love within me is Perfect.
Thy Love within me is Perfect.

LOVE DISSOLVES ALL FEAR

Greater than fear is Love.
Love dissolves all fear, casts out all doubt and sets the captive free.
Love, like the River of Life, flows through me and refreshes me with its eternal blessings.
Love cannot be afraid; it is fearless and strong, and is mighty in its works.
It can accomplish all things through the Inner Light of that faith in the All Good,
Which fills my very Being with a Powerful Presence.
Love casts out all fear.

MY AFFAIRS

My affairs are in the hands of Him
Who guides the planets in their course,
And Who causes the Sun to shine.
Divine Understanding attends me on the Way,
And I shall not be hindered in my work.
My affairs are controlled by Perfect Intelligence,
And cannot be hindered from expression.
I know that all that I do is done from the One Motive:
To express Life; and Life will be expressed
In and through me. I cannot hinder it.
I am controlled by Intelligence.

MY BUSINESS

My business is directed by Divine Intelligence.
The All-Knowing Mind knows what to do and how to do it.

I do not hinder, but let It operate in my affairs.
It prospers and directs me and controls my life.
My affairs are managed by Love, and directed by
Wisdom, and they cannot fail to prosper and expand.
My affairs are in His hands.

MY PROFESSION

My profession is the Activity of the Great Mind working through me.
As such It is a Divine Activity and is constantly in touch with Reality.
I am inspired in my work from On High with lofty ideals,
And my thought is illumined by the All-Knowing One.
I am inspired.

NO DELAYS

There are no delays in the Divine Plan for me.
Nothing can hinder the operation of this Law unto my Life and Action.
Obstructions are removed from my path, and
I now enter into the realization and manifestation of complete fulfillment of
right desires.
I do not have to wait, for the Law waits upon me at every turn in Life's road.
Now it is done unto me.

NO MISREPRESENTATIONS

No one can lie to me; none can mislead me.
I am free from the belief in all lies and untruths;
I know and speak only the Truth, and the Truth alone can be spoken to me.
I know the false and can understand the Real.
I cannot be fooled nor misled; I am guided by Truth alone.
There is no lie nor liar.

NO OBSTRUCTIONS

There are no obstructions to Life's Path; no hinderance to man's endeavors.
Let my Word be the Law of elimination to all thought of hinderance or delay.
And let the thing that I speak come forth into manifestation at once.
I behold it and see that it is even now done, complete and perfect.
I receive now.

NO OVER-ACTION NOR INACTION

There is no over-action nor inaction in Divine Law, for everything moves
according to perfect harmony.
Every idea of my body functions in accordance with this Law of Perfect Life.
I now perceive that the action within me is perfect, complete and harmonious.
Peace be unto every part of me, and perfect Life to every member of my body.
I act in accordance with Divine Law.
I am Perfect Life throughout my whole Being.

ONE WITH PERFECT ACTION

I am One with Perfect Action. Everything that I do, say or think is quickened into action through this right understanding and this correct knowing.

The harmonious action of the Great Whole operates through me now and at all times.

I am carried along by this Right Action and am compelled to do the right thing at the right time.

There is nothing in me that can hinder this action from flowing through me.

The action of God is the only action.

PEACE, POISE AND POWER

Peace, Poise and Power are within me, for they are the witnesses of the Inner Spirit of all Truth, Love and Wisdom.

I am at peace within me, and all about responds to that Great Calm of the Inner Soul which knows its rightful place in the All Good.

Power is born from within me and passes into my experience without effort or labor.

I rest in Security and Peace, for the Inner Light shines forth and illumines the way.

I rest in Thee.

STILLNESS AND RECEPTIVITY

I am still and receptive to Life.

I let Life flow through me into all that I do, say or think.

I shall let my Life be what it is, and shall not worry nor complain.

I am now entered into the Secret Place of the Soul where complete quiet reigns supreme and where God talks to me.

I receive.

THANKSGIVING AND PRAISE

I will give thanks to my Inner Life for all Its Marvelous Wonders, and for all Its Wonderful Works.

I will sing and be glad, for I know that I am hid with Truth in a Perfect Life.

The fulness of Joy is mine.

THE DIVINE PROMISES ARE KEPT

The Divine Promises are all kept; not one is changed.

God has told me that my Life is Perfect;

He will never desert or leave me to travel alone.

I know that from this day on and forevermore

I shall live under Divine Protection and Love.

I live under Divine Protection and Love.

THE INNER LIGHT

The Light of Heaven shines through me and illumines my Path.

The Light Eternal is my guide and my protection.

In that Light there is no darkness at all.

It is a Perfect Light shining from the altar of a perfect Love.

O Light and Love within me, Thou art welcome.
Light shines through me and illumines the Way.

THE NIGHT IS FILLED WITH PEACE

I wrap myself in the mantle of Love and fall asleep, filled with Peace.
Through the long night Peace remains with me, and at the breaking of the new day I shall still be filled with Life and Love.
I shall go forth into the new day confident and happy.
I rest in Thee.

THE SEAL OF APPROVAL

The Seal of Approval is upon me, and I am not condemned by the thought or act of man.
I will fear no evil, for I know that the Great Judge of all controls my every act.
Let every fear of man be removed from and let the Silence of my soul bear witness to the Truth.
God approves of me.

THE SECRET WAY

There is a Secret Way of the Soul which all may know.
It is the Way of Peace and Love.
This Secret Way leads into places of joy
And into the house of good.
It is the Way of the Spirit, and all may enter who will.
I tread the Secret Way of good, the Path of Peace,
And I enter into "The Secret Place of The Most High."
The Secret Place of The Most High is within me.

THE SHINING PATH

The Pathway of Life shines before me unto the Perfect Day.
I walk the pathway of the Soul to the Gate of Good.
I enter into the fulfillment of my desires.
Nothing need be added and nothing can be taken from the All Good which is forever expressing Itself in me.
Daily shall I receive Its great blessings and my Soul shall rejoice forevermore.
I am now entered into my good.

THE THINGS I NEED COME TO ME

Whatever I need comes to me from the All Good.
Divine Intelligence working through me always knows just what I need and always supplies it when I need it.
This Law is unfailing and sure, and cannot be broken.
I receive my Good daily as I go along the pathway of Life, and I cannot be robbed of my birthright to freedom and happiness.
I receive my Good.

THE WAY IS MADE CLEAR BEFORE ME

The Way is made clear before me; I do not falter nor fall.

The Way of the Spirit is my Way, and I am compelled to walk in it.

My feet are kept on the Path of Perfect Life.

The Way is prepared before me, and that Way is a Path of Peace, of Fulfillment and Joy.

The Way is bright with the light of Love and Kindness.

The Way I tread is a pleasant and a happy one.

I see the Way and I walk in It.

IMMANENT POWER

AS LOVE ENTERS, FEAR DEPARTS
As Love enters, fear vanishes.

I am so filled with Love that no fear can enter my thought.

I am not afraid, for I know that a Perfect Intelligence guards and governs my every act.

Perfect Love casteth out all fear.

I am unafraid and strong in my faith in Him Who keeps me from all harm.

Perfect Love casteth out all fear.

HE WILL KEEP THEE
The Inner Spirit of man is God, and my Inner Spirit is the Realization of my Life.

I know that my Inner Spirit will keep me from all harm, and will not let destruction come near me.

I am unafraid in the midst of confusion, and unmoved in the face of calamity.

I am confident in the presence of seeming danger, and fearless before any sense of trouble.

He will keep me.

INFINITE LIFE WITHIN
Infinite Life within me, which is God, guard Thou my feet and keep Thou my way.

Let me not stray from Thee, but compel me to do Thy will.

I am guarded and governed by an Infinite Intelligence and an Omnipotent Power.

No mistakes can be made and none ever have been made.

An unerring judgement operates through me and I am lead by the Spirit of Truth into all Good and into all Peace and Happiness.

Infinite Life within me.

MY FEET SHALL NOT FALTER
My feet shall not falter, for they are kept upon the path of Life through the Power of the Eternal Spirit.

Guide Thou my feet; compel my way; direct my paths and keep me in Thy Presence.

My feet are guarded, and I am guided into the All Good.

He guides my feet.

NO HARM SHALL BEFALL THEE
No harm shall befall you, my friend, for a Divine Presence attends your way and guards you into The All Good.

Loving kindness awaits you at every turn of Life's road.

Guidance is yours along the pathway of experience,
And an Infallible Power protects you.
God, Himself, and no other is your Keeper.
I proclaim this for you.

POWER TO LIVE

I have the power to live the life of good.
My power is from On High; it cannot be taken from me.
It will not leave me desolate.
Power flows through me and is in me, and
I can now feel and sense it.
The Power to live is in me and I cannot desert me.
It is my power and is continually present.
I am the power to live.

THE CIRCLE OF LOVE

A circle of love is drawn around me and mine, and all.
No harm can enter that Sacred Circle, for it is the Love of God.
It is a complete protection from all evil.
"I will fear no evil, for Thou art with me."
There is no evil and no harm.
I am free from all sense of fear.
Love surrounds and protects me.

THE CIRCLE OF PROTECTION

I draw around me a circle of love and protection.
No harm can enter nor find place within that charmed circle of life and love,
for it represents God's Loving Care and Eternal Watchfulness.
I will rest within me now, and I will speak comfort to my Soul and tell It of all
the wonders of its life, safe from the din of strife and fear.
I am protected from On High.

THE POWER WITHIN BLESSES ALL

The Power within me is blessing all mankind, and is forever healing all with
whom I come in contact.
The Power within me is God, and It must bless and help and heal all who
come near It.
Silently the work goes on, and silently all are being helped by this Inner
Power which is operating through me.
I will give thanks that my Power within is silently blessing and helping
everyone to whom my thought reaches.
The Life within me blesses all mankind.

THE QUICK ANSWER

My answer comes quickly and surely back to me from On High.
My answer will not fail me, for the Law of the Universe is the Power through
which it comes.
I shall not doubt nor fear, for the answer is swift and certain.
My answer comes.

INSPIRATION

A SONG OF JOY

There is a Song upon my lips to-day; it sings of the glad heart and the happy ways of Life.

I will listen to my song, for it carols to me the glad tidings of Great Joy, of Love and Life.

It tells me of the Wondrous Journey of the Soul and the Boundless Life in which my life is hid.

I am filled with joy.

BORN OF ETERNAL DAY

Child of All Good, you are born of Eternal Day.

There is no evening of the Soul, for it shall live forever.

It is Deathless and Perfect, Complete and One with the Everlasting.

No thought of to-morrow can disturb the calm of him who knows that Life is one Eternal Day.

No fear can enter where Love reigns, and Reason keeps faith with Hope.

The thoughts of the to-morrows and the yesterdays are swallowed up in the great realization of the Perfect Here and the Complete Now.

To-day I completely accept my wholeness.

I ARISE AND GO FORTH

I arise and go forth into the Dawn of the New Day, filled with faith and assurance in the All Good.

I arise, I arise, I sing with joy!

I proclaim the One Life: "In all and through all."

I arise, I arise, I shout with gladness that is within me.

I declare this day to be Complete, Perfect and Eternal.

I respond to Life.

INSPIRATION

Come, Thou Great and Infinite Mind and inspire me to do great deeds.

Acquaint me with Thy knowledge and in Thy wisdom make me wise.

I would be taught of Thee, Inner Light, and inspired by Thy presence.

I will listen for Thy Voice and it will tell me of great things to be done.

I will walk in Thy Paths and they will lead me into All Good.

I will be inspired from On High.

O Wonderful Presence, flooding me, filling me with Thy Light,

Thou dost inspire me!

I feel the inspiration of Spirit.

THE DAWN HAS COME

Out of the darkness of the long night the Dawn has come.
I rise to meet the new day, filled with confidence and strength.
I arise and go forth into the dawn, inspired and refreshed by the Living Spirit within me.
O Day, you shall never die; the sun shall never set upon your perfect glory.
For the Lamp of the Soul has been re-kindled with the oil of Faith,
And Love has cleansed the windows of Life with the spirit of gladness.
They shall nevermore grow dim with fear, for Perfect Love casteth out all fear.
I am renewed in strength through knowing Good.
My light has come.

I AM COMPLETE IN THEE

Almighty God, Everlasting Good, Eternal Spirit, Maker of all things and Keeper of my Life, Thou art All.
Infinite Presence within, in Whom all live; Joy Supreme, flooding all with gladness, I adore Thee.
Eternal Peace, undisturbed and quiet, I feel Thy calm.
O Thou Who dost inhabit Eternity and dost dwell within all Creation, Who Dost live through all things and in all people, hear Thou my prayer.
I would enter Thy gates with joy and live at peace in Thy House.
I would find a resting place in Thee, and in Thy presence live.
Make me to do Thy will and from Thy wisdom teach me the ways of Truth.
Compel me to follow Thee and let me not pursue the paths of my own counsel.
O Eternal and Blessed Presence, illumine my mind and command my will that my Soul may be refreshed and that my live may be renewed.
As deep cries unto deep, so my thought cries unto Thee and Thou dost answer.
I am renewed and refreshed; my whole being responds to Thy love, and I am complete in Thee.
All my ways are guarded and guided, and I shall live with Thee eternally.
O Lover of my Soul and Keeper of my Spirit, none can separate us, for we are One.
So shall Thy Wisdom guide me, Thy Presence dwell within me, Thy Love keep me and Thy life envelop me now and forevermore.
I rest in Thee.

PRESENCE OF THE ALL GOOD

A MARVELOUS SENSE

A marvelous sense steals over him who waits on Good, and in patience bides his time.

A feeling of some Unseen Presence silently creeps over the waiting thought, and the Voice of God speaks through the mist and says: "Be not afraid."

It is all for a purpose; and when you cannot trace, you must trust. This is not an illusion, but a reality; for time proves all things, and he who will wait for his time to come shall be rewarded; and Good shall come to him, for God Himself shall be his Companion and Champion.

I wait on Thee.

COMPLETE CONFIDENCE

My confidence in The All Good is complete.

My faith in the Power of Spirit is supreme.

I have no doubts nor uncertainties.

I know that my Good is at hand, and

I realize that no fear can hinder

That Good from making Its appearance in my life and affairs.

I know that my Life and Good are complete.

Evil cannot touch nor hinder my work.

I rest in security, for

THE ONE MIND IS MY COMPLETE REFUGE AND STRENGTH.

I am serene and confident.

DRAWING THE GOOD

I draw my Good to me as I travel along the Way of Life, and nothing can keep It from me.

My Good will always follow me.

I accept the Good and rejoice that it is with me.

I accept the Good.

I FEAR NO EVIL

"I will fear no evil, for Thou art with me."

I will not be afraid, for the All Good is constantly with me and is always near at hand to guide and comfort.

There is no evil in the Truth, and no power of darkness to hinder the Light from shining.

I will not be afraid, for there is One within Who protects and keeps me from all harm.

I fear no evil.

I HAVE KNOWN, ALWAYS

I have always known the Truth, and no fear can keep my inner knowledge from me.

My wisdom from within comes forth into daily expression.

Knowledge from On High is given to me, and I shall always be led of the Spirit.

I know the Truth.

I MEET MY GOOD

To-day I meet my Good; it knows me and will not let me depart from it.

My Good is at hand, and I cannot be robbed of it.

Good is forever expressing itself to me and mine.

I can even now see and hear and feel the All Good in and around me.

It presses itself against me, and fills me with a great surge of Life.

My Good is at hand.

MY ATMOSPHERE

My atmosphere is attracting the Good; it is constantly on the alert to see and know the Good, and to bring it into my experience.

There is that within me that calls forth abundance and happiness from Life.

I am surrounded with an atmosphere of Peace, Poise and Power.

All who come in contact with that great Calm of my Life are made strong and confident, are healed and blessed.

"Bless the Lord, O my Soul, and all that is within me, bless His Holy Name."

I am hid with Christ in God.

MY GOOD IS COMPLETE

My Good is complete; it is finished; it is now here and is conscious of me and of mine.

I do not have to wait for my Good; it is at hand and ever ready to spring forth and express itself to me.

I accept my Good and gladly acknowledge it to be my daily companion.

My Good is mine now, and I can see it and feel it and know it.

To-day I claim my Good.

MY OWN SHALL COME TO ME

From far and near my own shall come to me. Even now it is coming to me, and I receive it.

My own is now manifesting itself to me, and I see and know its presence. My own shall know and respond to me.

The drawing power of that inner Spirit within me is now attracting and drawing into my experience all that is good and perfect. There is nothing within me to hinder nor to delay it.

My own cannot be kept from me, neither can I keep my good away from me. I receive it now.

I now receive my good.

MY OWN SHALL FIND ME

My Own shall find me; no matter where I go, It will follow and claim me.
I cannot hide myself from my Own.
My Own shall come to me, even though I deny it; for there is nothing in me
that can hinder it from entering and taking possession of my Soul.
My own is now expressed.

MY SOUL REFLECTS THY LIFE

My Soul reflects Thy Life and rejoices in the happy thought that it looks on
Thee alone.
O Soul of mine, look out and up and on; and reflect to me the wondrous Life
of the All Good.
Look thou upon The One, and be saved.
Behold thou His Face forevermore.
My Soul reflects Thy Life.

OUT OF THE DEPTHS OF LIFE

Out of the deep places of life my Soul has cried unto Thee and Thou hast
made answer.
Out of the turmoil and struggle and strife I have come unto Thee, and Thou
hast heard me and understood.
I shall nevermore be sad, for I have found what the Soul craves—the Inner
Life and Love of the All Good.
Thou hast heard.

SORROW FLEES FROM ME

As the Great Joy of Life comes into my Soul, flooding me with its wondrous
light, all sorrow and sadness flee from me.
I shall not grieve, for nothing is lost nor gone from me.
My own cannot be kept from me.
My own knows me and will follow me wherever I go.
I am filled with the Joy of living and the Great Peace that comes to all who
believe.
I am made glad forevermore.

SUBSTANCE AND SUPPLY

The Substance of the Spirit is my Daily Supply.
I cannot be without my Good.
I can see that the constant stream of Life flowing to me brings
into my experience all that makes Life happy and worthwhile.
I rest in security, knowing that Infinite Good is within and is expressing
through me.
I receive my good.

THE EVER AND THE ALL

Life always was and evermore shall be, "World without end."
All the Power there is, is mine now.
All the Life, Truth and Love of the Universe is now and forever

Flowing through my Soul.
The All Good cannot change.
I shall always have access to my Eternal God within me.
I am Changeless Life within me.

THE HOUSE OF LOVE

I dwell in the house of Love;
"A house not made with hands, eternal in the heavens."
My dwelling place is filled with peace and eternal calm.
Love attends me in my home of the Soul, and
Joy awaits upon me in the "Secret Place of the Most High."
My house is built for me by the hand of Love, and
I shall never leave this Home of the Spirit, for it is always present.
I shall abide in this home forevermore.
My house is a house of love.

SPIRIT OF GOD WITHIN

ARISE, MY SPIRIT
Arise, my Spirit, arise and shine.
Let Thy light illumine my path, and let Thy wisdom direct my way.
Compel my will to do Thy bidding, and command my Soul to look to Thee.
I will follow Thee, my Spirit, and will learn of Thee all that I need to know.
I will sit in the Silence and listen and watch, and
I will see Thy light and hear Thy voice.
II will follow Thee and will not depart from Thee,
for in Thee alone is Peace.
Arise and shine.

BIRTHLESS AND DEATHLESS
The Spirit within me is Birthless and deathless;
It was not born and It cannot die.
I have no fear of death, for I perceive that
Death is an illusion and not the Truth.
I was born of the Spirit, and I live in the Spirit,
And shall continue to live in and by the Spirit.
The Spirit within me lives forever.

COMMAND MY SOUL
Spirit within me, command my Soul to do Thy bidding;
Compel me to follow the course of Truth and Wisdom.
Control my inward thoughts and my outward ways,
And make me to understand Thy Laws.
Command my Soul to turn to Thee for guidance and light;
To turn to Thee for wisdom and knowledge.
Let the paths of my Life be made straight and sure;
Let the Journey of my Soul find its completion in Thee.
Command my Soul to do Thy bidding.

DESPAIR GIVES WAY TO JOY
Despair gives way to joy at the thought of Thee, Indwelling Good.
I cannot be sad when I think of Thee.
My sorrow is turned to gladness and my shame to rejoicing.
My tears are wiped away and the sunlight of the Spirit shines through the
clouds of depression and lights the way to Heaven.
Thy Joy has made me glad.

FREE SPIRIT WITHIN ME

Free Spirit within me, Unbound and Perfect, teach me Thy ways and make known to me Thy Limitless Completion.

O Spirit of Life, control my every action and thought.

Compel me to follow Thy light that I too may be free and complete.

I will follow Thy footsteps and learn of Thee all the wondrous secrets of Life.

I will follow Thy light into the Perfect Day.

Free spirit within me.

FULLNESS OF LIGHT

The Light of Life is full within me and around me.

It shines forth into the Perfect Day.

O Light within, lighting my path to peace,

I adore and love You and I let You shine.

Go forth and bless all who come to You, Light within.

My Light radiates to all and through all.

My light has come.

HE WHO INHABITS ETERNITY

He Who inhabits Eternity keeps watch over me and mine.

"He Who neither slumbers nor sleeps" forever keeps watch over all.

I will rest in the assurance of Love and Protection.

O Thou Great Overshadowing Presence,

I am conscious of Thy care; I am aware of Thy loving kindness. I rest in Thee.

Be still and know.

I LISTEN

I will listen for Thy voice, Inner Presence.

It will guide me and acquaint me with all knowledge.

Thy voice is sweet and tender; it is always kind and gentle.

O Lover of my Soul, how I adore Thee! How I love Thee!

How I love Thy voice; it thrills me with gladness and joy.

It fills me with peace and calm, and it soothes me.

It quiets me and gives me wonderful rest.

I listen, O Divine Speaker, I listen to Thee alone.

I listen for Thy voice.

JOY HAS COME TO LIVE WITH ME

Joy has come to live with me. How can I be sad?

I do so love Thy presence, which is Joy within me.

It makes me glad, and I sing, for I am so filled with Thy Spirit that I cannot be depressed nor unhappy.

I am filled with the joy of the Spirit, and I overflow with the gladness of life.

Thou art a Happy Companion to travel with me through Life, wonderful Joy, Thou art so radiant and beaming.

It is impossible to be sad in Thy presence.

I shall give myself to Thee and remain with Thee, for Thou art complete and satisfying.

I find fulfillment in Thee and joy forevermore.
I am filled with the Spirit of Joy.

KNOWLEDGE AND WISDOM

All Wisdom and Knowledge is from within.
And my God, Who is All-Knowing, is also within.
I am guided and guarded along Life's road into the All Good.
My Mind is instructed from On High,
And my Wisdom cometh from afar.
The Spirit within me is All Wisdom.

MY THOUGHT IS IN THEE

My thought is in Thee, Inner Light.
My words are from Thee, Inner Wisdom.
My understanding is of Thee, Inner God.
I cannot be hid from Thee, my Inspiration and my Life.
My thought is in Thee.

O LOVE DIVINE

O Love Divine within me, I am overpowered by Thy Presence.
I am speechless, for words cannot utter the things that Thou hast revealed to me.
Why dost Thou love me so, and why clasp me so close to Thy Eternal Heart?
O Blessed Presence, I know, for Thou hast claimed me as Thine own.
I shall nevermore walk apart from Thee.
The love of God is within me.

PEACE STEALS THROUGH THE SOUL

Peace steals through the waiting Soul, and the comfort of the Spirit comes into the stillness of the heart.
Peace, like an ocean of Infinite Life, reflects itself through me and calms every turbulent feeling.
I am at peace and rest in the knowledge of the All Good which is at hand.
I rest in peace.

STAND FORTH AND SPEAK

Stand forth and speak, Spirit within me.
Proclaim Thy presence, announce Thy course.
Declare through me Thy wondrous works and
Let the children of men hear Thy voice.
Behold, He maketh all things new.
The Spirit within speaks words of Truth and Life to all.
The Spirit within me is God.
I speak the Truth.

SUBTLE ESSENCE OF SPIRIT WITHIN ME

Subtle Essence of Spirit within me, flowing through me;
Elixir of Life in my veins purifying me with Thy marvelous Life,

I let Thy Spirit cleanse me from all false thought and ideas;
I let Thy Life flow through me in a complete and Perfect Whole.
I feel the presence of Spirit within me.

THE CHRIST WITHIN

My Life is "hid with Christ in God";
The Inner Man is the image and likeness of the Spirit of God.
I let that Inner Man come forth into expression in my life;
He will guide my feet into all Truth and Wisdom.
The Christ within me is free from all worry, and cannot be hindered by any opposing force.
My Christ within me is now perfect.
My Christ is within me.

THE EVERLASTING ARMS

His Arms enfold me, His Strength upholds me,
His Presence fills me with Life and Joy.
I shall nevermore be sad nor depressed, for I know that I do not walk Life's path alone.
There is One Who goes with me and tells me all the things that I should know.
There is a Presence with me guiding me into the Perfect Way.
I rejoice in knowing that I am not alone.

THE MANTLE OF LOVE

Like a cloak His Love is wrapped around me. Like a warm garment It shelters me from the storms of life.
I feel and know that an Almighty Love envelops me in Its close embrace.
O Love Divine, My Love, how wonderful Thou art. I am open to receive Thy great blessing.
Love envelops me.

THE VOICE OF TRUTH

The Voice of Truth speaks to me and through me.
The Voice of Truth guides me and keeps me on the Path of the Perfect Day.
I will listen to the Inner Voice and It will tell me what to do in the hour of need.
I shall be told everything that I ought to know when the time of need arrives, and I shall not be misled.
The Voice of Truth cannot lie, but always speaks to me from On High.
Nothing enters but This Voice, for it is the Voice of God.
God speaks to me.

THE WITNESS OF TRUTH

There is a Witness within me who knows the Truth and who will not let me enter into falsehood.
My Inner Guide keeps me on the Pathway of Life and directs me at all times to that which is right and best.

I shall never be without this witness of the Spirit, for I believe in It and accept It as the Great Companion of the Soul.
The Spirit within me is perfect now.

THROUGH THE LONG NIGHT WATCHES

Through the long night watches Thou hast been with me.
In the dark places of human ignorance Thy hand hath guided me,
Thy light hath lighted the pathway of desolation to a land of plenty.
I have perceived Thee from afar, and my soul hath yearned to Thee, O Thou Mighty One!
The Spirit within me hath urged me on to the goal, and I have not been misled.
I have been guided and guarded through the long journey, and Thy Presence hath been made known to me.
I awake from the dream and reenter the house of my Lord clothed with Peace and robed in colors of Light.
The Spirit of Truth watches over me.

THY STRENGTH IS SUFFICIENT

O Spirit of man and God within me, Thy Power is great, and Thy Knowledge goes beyond the range of human experience.
Thy Wisdom excels that of all else, and beside Thee there is none other.
In Thy Strength do I daily walk and live;
In Thy Presence do I always rest in peace and joy.
Spirit within me and without, Powerful Thou art, and Great;
Wonderful is Thy Might, and Complete is Thy Understanding.
I let Thy Mighty Strength flow through me,
And out into all the paths of my human endeavors.
Life from within expresses through me.

WAITING ON THEE

In waiting on Thee there is fulness of Life.
I wait on Thee, my Inner Lord; I listen for Thy voice.
I hear Thy word; I do Thy will; again I wait on Thee.
And listening, I hear Thee say: "Be perfect, be complete; live, love, be glad."
Sit thou in the stillness and let thy Lord speak.

WHOSE RIGHT IT IS TO COME

He has come Whose right it is.
He has made His home within me, and will nevermore depart from me.
I shall walk no more alone, for One walks with me
Who knows the path of Life, and Whose feet will never falter nor fail.
My Inner Light shines through the mist of human beliefs
And frees me from the bondage of fear and limitation.
I shall walk with You, my Friend, and shall learn of You the ways of Life and Freedom.
We shall travel together from this day, and none can part us,
For we are united in the perfect bonds of an everlasting unity.
I walk with Thee.

THE POWER OF THE WORD

I CONTROL MY MENTAL HOUSEHOLD AND CONQUER ALL FEAR AND DOUBT

I conquer my mental household and cast out all fear and doubt.
Let my Word cast out all sense of fear and doubt and let my thoughts be lifted unto Him Who lives Within.
My Word has dissolved all fear within me, and has cast out all doubt.
My Word shall guard my thought and make me receive only that which is Good and Perfect.
I control my life.

MY WORD COMES BACK TO ME

My word comes back to me laden with the fruits of its own speech.
My Word is the Law unto my Life, and the Law unto everything that I speak.
O Word, go forth and heal and bless all humanity.
Tell them of their Divine Birthright.
Tell the stranger that he is not alone, but that One goes with him Who knows and cares.
Tell the sick that they are healed and the poor that they cannot want.
Tell the unhappy of the joy of the Soul, and break the bonds of those who are in prison.
My Word shall come back to me blessed of God and man.

MY WORD SHALL BEAR FRUIT

The Word of my mouth shall bear fruit.
It shall accomplish and prosper, and shall not return unto me void.
My Word is the law unto the thing whereunto it is sent, and it cannot come back empty-handed.
I send out my Word, and it is law unto my life.
My Word is Power.

NOTHING CAN HINDER

Nothing can hinder my Word from working;
It will work, and nothing can stop it.
My word is the Law unto that thing whereunto it is spoken, and will become fulfilled in the right way and at the right time.
My Word is complete and perfect, and is the presence and the
Power of the One Mind that is in and through all.
I speak that Word and know that it will accomplish.
I wait in perfect confidence for the Word to fulfill itself in my life.
My Word is law.

O MAN, SPEAK FORTH THY WORD

O man, speak forth thy word and be not afraid.
Did you not know; have you not heard?
His Divinity is planted within thee, and thy word is one with all power.
The Spirit of the Most High is thy Spirit, and the word of God is thy word.
Thy freedom is hid within thee, and thy inner light shall illumine they way.
Speak, man, and be free! Announce and proclaim thy works!
Let thy word go forth with power, and thy Spirit shall conquer all.
Spirit within me, speak.

THE POWER OF THE WORD

The Word is a might Power, and that Word is in me and through me now.
My Word is one with the All Good and cannot fail to accomplish the desired ends.
My Word goes forth with Power unto everything that I do, say or think.
The Word is my Power by day and by night.
I will speak the Word and trust in the great Law of Life to fulfill it.
I speak the word in full confidence.

THE WORD OF POWER

My Word is a Word of Power, for I know that it is the Word of the Great God within me.
My Word shall accomplish and prosper, and shall do good unto all who call upon my name.
My Word is a tower of strength and cannot be denied.
It is complete and perfect here and now.
My Word is the Word of God.
My word is the word of God.

THE UNASSAILABLE TRUTH AND THE IRRESISTIBLE WORD

The Truth within me is unassailable, and the Power of the Word is irresistible.
I can even now feel that my Word has gone forth with Power and Reality, and that it will accomplish that purpose for which it was created.
Limitless is its Power and wonderful are its works.
It can be nothing less than the Almighty working in and through me.
I will let this Word of the Spirit go forth from my mouth, and heal and bless the world.
It shall be as a strong tower unto all who call upon it.
The Truth is Complete and Perfect, and is within me now.
My Word is complete and perfect, now.

I BEHOLD IN THEE HIS IMAGE

I behold in thee His Image.
In thee, my friend, I see God and through you I feel His presence.
I see in the hand that gives, His hand;
And in the voice that speaks of Love, I hear Him speak.
For His lines have gone out into all places,
And from the highest to the lowest, all, all partake of His nature.
"For He is all in all, over all and through all."
I perceive that God is in all people.

UNITY

I SEE NO EVIL

I see no evil; I behold only the good.
I have seen the drunkard lying in the gutter, and the saint kneeling in ecstasy before the high altar of his faith; but I have found no difference.
I have perceived that each, in his own tongue, is seeking to express the One Life.
I will not separate and divide; I cannot condemn nor censure, for I know that there is but One in All.
I know that all came from the One, and all will return to the One.
I know that all are now in the One, and that each is seeking to express the One.
I know and love all.

I SHALL NEVER DIE

I shall never die, for the Spirit within me is God and cannot change.
My life is hid within the Universe of Love and Light, and that Light shall live forever.
Go, fear of death and change; begone from my thought, fear of death and uncertainty.
That which is cannot become that which is not; and that which I am can never change.
The Spirit of Eternity is enthroned within me, and the Life of Endless Ages flows through my being.
From Eternity to Eternity my Life flows along its way of peace and harmony.
Time brings but more glory to crown me with its pleasures.
My life is forever.

LOVE TO THE WORLD

My Love goes out to everyone in the world;
I do not exclude anything, for I love all Nature and everything that is.
My Love warms and lightens everything that it touches, and it goes out into all places.
The Love flowing through me is a Power to all who come into contact with it, and all feel and know that I love.
Love within me is Complete and Perfect.
Love within me is Complete.

MY LIFE IS ONE WITH GOD

My life is in God; it cannot be hurt nor hindered in its expression.
God lives and expresses through me; His work is complete and perfect in me now.

I know His life to be my life, and I know that my life is complete and perfect. *My Life is in God.*

NO MISUNDERSTANDINGS

There are no misunderstandings.

All is made clear between the ideas of Good.

No false sense of separation can come between people, nor disturb the realization of the Unity of All Life.

I perceive that I am one with all people, and all are One with me.

There is no separation.

There is no separation.

THE DIVINE PLAN FOR ME

The Divine Plan for me is Perfect. I am held in the Mind of God as a Complete and Perfect Expression of Life and Truth.

No power can hinder nor mar this Inner Image of Reality, for It is God-given and God-kept.

God gave and God will keep.

THE PERSONALITY OF GOD

The Great Personality of God is my Personality; the Limitless Knowingness of The Spirit is my Knowingness, and the One Mind is my mind.

All, All live in One Infinite Person, and each manifests the One Who is formed through and in all.

Man is the Personality of God in manifestation and cannot be left without the Inner Witness of the Spirit.

I now realize that the Infinite Personalness of the Spirit is my Personality, and I rejoice to know the Truth about myself.

God is my Personality.

THE RADIATION OF LIFE

The life of God within me radiates and shines forth from me in a constant stream of Light to all.

The One Life flowing through me is Life to all who come near.

The One Power operating through me is flowing into everything that I contact.

Life radiates from me.

UNITY

To-day I realize that I am One with the All Good; my God and I are One.

I cannot be hid from His face.

I behold Thee, O Most High, enthroned in my temple of flesh.

Thy secret place is within me. I feel Thy presence,

I hear Thy voice, I rejoice in Thy Light.

To-day my body responds to the Divine Behest: "Be perfect."

I know of my perfection and wholeness; I am complete and perfect now.

Let every thought of disease flee from me, and let Thy Light shine.

O Light Eternal, O Light of my Life, I come into Thy presence with joy and thanksgiving.
So be it.

WITHIN THEE IS FULNESS OF LIFE

Within Thee is fulness of Life.
Within Thee is complete Joy and everlasting Peace.
Within Thee is all.
Thou art in me as I am in Thee, and we are all in all.
My Life is full and complete within me, and that Life I give to all men freely;
And from all I receive again that which I have given,
For it is One in All.
I am One with the fulness of All Life.

GLOSSARY

This glossary gives the Metaphysical meaning of the words as used in these lessons. It is not claimed that the definition of the words used in this glossary will, in every case, keep faith with the regular dictionary definition. The words are defined in such a say as to bring out the meaning with which they are used in this course of instruction.

It will be necessary for the student to carefully study the meaning of these words, together with the explanation of the words used in the different charts; in this way, the desired objective will be obtained, and there will be no confusion.

(The glossary in the original book is not in alphabetical order. The original order has been retained.—JBH)

ALPHA.—That which is first.

AXIOM.—A self-evident truth.

ABSOLUTE.—"Free from restriction." See Chart No. I.

AFFIRMATION.—To state positively and maintain as being true.

AURA.—The mental atmosphere surrounding a person.

APPARITION.—"A specter of phantom. The act of appearing."

ATTRIBUTE.—The being, essence, nature and substance of.

ALL-GOOD.—God or Spirit.

ANALYSIS.—Resolving things into their first elements.

ANDROGYNOUS.—Having the characteristics of both sexes.

ACCUMULATED CONSCIOUSNESS.—The sum total of all that one has ever said, thought, done or seen, consciously or un-consciously.

ACTIVE PRINCIPLE OF LIFE.—The Self-Conscious Spirit.

AXIOMATIC REASONING.—The deductions drawn from self-evident truths.

BODY.—The outward form.

BODY OF THE UNIVERSE.—The manifest Creation, the Body of God, both visible and invisible.

BEING.—That which has existence.

BLESSING.—Constructive thought directed toward any one.

BIBLE.—"The sacred books of any race or people."

CONSCIOUSNESS.—The perception of existence.

COSMIC CONSCIOUSNESS.—Perception of The Whole.

COSMIC MIND.—The Mind of God.

COSMIC CONCEPTION.—The Divine Mind giving birth to Its Ideas.

CONCEPT.—An idea in mind.

CONSCIOUS MIND.—The self-knowing mind in God or man.

CREATION.—Passing of Spirit into form.

COSMOS.—The Universal World, visible and invisible.

CAUSATION.—That which stands back of things as the Intelligent Cause.

CREATIVE MIND.—The Universal Soul or Subjectivity. The Feminine Principle of the Universal Life.

CREATIVE MEDIUM.—From the Universal Sense, it is the World-Soul; and from the individual sense, it is the subjective state of man's thought.

COSMIC STUFF.—The stuff from which all forms are made.

COSMIC URGE.—The desire of Spirit to express Itself.

COSMIC PURPOSE.—The ideas of Spirit propelling themselves into outer expression. The desire of Spirit executing itself.

CREATIVE SERIES.—Any particular and concrete manifestation of Spirit.

COEXISTENT.—That which exists with.

COETERNAL.—Always existing. Uncreated.

CONDITIONS.—That which follows cause; the effect of law.

CORRESPONDENT.—The mental picture of cause of anything.

CONCENTRATION.—Bringing the attention to a focus.

CHANGE.—The appearance and disappearance of forms.

CHRIST.—The total manifestation of God, from the plant to an angel; from a peanut to the entire Universe of expression. Christ in Man means the idea of Sonship, the Perfect Man as He must be held in the Mind of God.

CONCRETE CAUSE.—Definite idea.

CONCEIVE.—To give birth to an idea.

COMPENSATION.—The law of balance in the mental world. Cause and effect.

CONTEMPLATE.—To know within the self.

CLAIRAUDIENCE.—The ability to perceive sounds without the ear.

CLAIRVOYANCE.—The ability to see mentally. See without the eye.

CURSE.—Mentally used to destroy.

CONFLICT.—Inner mental struggle, conscious or unconscious.

COMPLEX.—The result of mental struggle, conscious or unconscious.

DIVINE PRINCIPLE.—Spiritual Causation operating through Universal Law.

DIVINE SCIENCE.—The facts known about mental and spiritual law.

DIVINE URGE.—The inner desire to express life.

DIVINE IDEAS.—The Ideas of God.

DIVINE NATURE.—The true nature of all things.

DEITY.—God.

DESIRE.—Life wishing to express Itself.

DISCARNATE SPIRITS.—Entities out of the flesh.

DIAGNOSIS.—Unearthing mental causes.

DEDUCTIVE REASONING.—Reasoning from the whole to a part.

DREAM WORLD.—World of thoughts that are Unexpressed.

DISEASE.—The result of inhibited mental and spiritual action.

DEVIL.—The personification of evil.

DENIAL.—The mental act of denying the false appearance.

EFFECT.—That which follows cause. The result of some inner action.

EGO.—The real self. The inner man.

ESOTERIC.—Inner.

EXOTERIC.—Outer.

EVOLUTION.—The passing of Spirit into form.

EVIL.—That which seems destructive.

EMANATE.—To flow forth from.

ETHER.—A universal medium which is supposed to be the last known analysis of matter; it interspheres all things and all space. The fine particles of matter, or electrons, are supposed to be cemented together by the ether. Ether seems to be, to the material world, what mind is to the mental world; i.e., a universal medium.

ETERNAL.—Everlasting, without beginning or end.

EMMANUEL.—"God with us."

EQUIVALENT.—The mental likeness of a thing. The mental cause back of anything. The idea of the thing in the Subjective World.

EXISTENCE.—Having real being within itself. The cause of its own being, depending upon nothing but itself. Different from subsistence.

EMOTION.—Mental energy, set in motion through feeling.

ELEMENTALS.—Unevolved entities in the invisible world.

ENTITIES.—Anything that exists, visible or invisible.

EARTH-BOUND.—An entity unable to leave this plane.

FORM.—Any definite outline in time and space. Forms may be visible or invisible. In all probability, all space is filled with many kinds of forms.

FACULTY.—Any mode of bodily of mental behavior regarded as implying a natural endowment or acquired power—the faculties of seeing, hearing, feeling, etc."

FUNCTION.—"The normal action of any organ."

FAMILIAR SPIRITS.—Refers to the control of consciousness through the instrument of some invisible agency.

FATHER-MOTHER GOD.—The Masculine and Feminine Principles of Being as included in the Androgynous One, or First Cause.

FIRST CAUSE.—That which is the cause of all things. The Uncreated, from which all Creation springs. The First Cause is both Masculine and Feminine in Its Nature, and includes the Intermediate Principle of Creative Activity.

FORMLESS SUBSTANCE.—The ultimate stuff from which all forms are created, universally present, in an unformed state, and acted upon by conscious and subconscious intelligence. It is the nature of the Soul to give form to the ideas with which It is impregnated; hence, Soul contains Substance within Itself.

FEMININE PRINCIPLE.—The Universal Soul. In man, the subjective or subconscious intelligence.

GOD.—The First Cause, the Great I Am, The Unborn One, The Uncreated, The Absolute or Unconditioned, The One and Only. Man comprehends God only to the degree that he embodies the Divine Nature.

GHOST.—The mental form of any person in the flesh or out of it.

HABIT.—Any act that has become a part of the subconscious mentality.

HALO.—The emanation that appears around the head.

HUMANITY.—The multiplied expression of God as people. The many who live in the One.

HELL.—A discordant state of being.

HEAVEN.—A harmonious state of being.

HYPNOTISM.—The mental control of another.

HOLY GHOST.—The third Person of the Trinity. The Servant of the Spirit. Used in the sense of the World,—Soul or Universal Subjectivity.

INDWELLING EGO.—The Spirit of man as differentiated from his soul or subjective mentality. The Real Man which is the conscious part of him.

INDWELLING GOD.—The Real Man is as much of God as he is able to embody. The Divine Spark, Birthless and Deathless.

INDWELLING CHRIST.—Generic man, manifesting through the individual. The idea of Divine Sonship. The Real Man. As much of this reality appears as we allow to express through us.

IMMACULATE CONCEPTION.—All things are immaculately conceived, as all things come from the One.

IMMORTALITY.—The Deathless Principle of Being in all people.

INTUITION.—The ability to know without any process of reasoning. God knows only intuitively.

IMAGE.—The mental likeness of anything.

INSPIRATION.—From the human side, means contact with the subconscious of the individual or the race. From the Divine, means contact with the Universal Spirit.

ILLUMINATION.—Inspiration reaching Cosmic state. A direct contact with Reality or God. A complete intuitive perception.

INSTINCTIVE LIFE.—The One in everything.

INSTINCTIVE MAN.—The Spiritual Man.

INHERENT LIFE.—Real life as distinguished from latent life.

INNER SIGHT.—The spiritual capacity of knowing the Truth. It is a mental quality which brings the mentality to a comprehension of Reality.

INDIVIDUALITY.—The Real Idea of man, as distinguished from the outer personality.

IDEA.—A concept. The Ideas of God are the Divine Realizations of His own Being. The real Ideas are eternal.

I AM.—From the universal standpoint, means God; and from the individual, means the Real Man.

INVOLUTION.—Ideas involved in Mind. Involution precedes evolution.

INDUCTIVE REASONING.—Reasoning from effect to cause.

IMAGINATION.—The imaging faculty.

INDUCE.—The act of planting seeds of thought in Creative Mind.

IMPERSONAL RECEPTIVITY.—The Creative Mind is impersonal receptivity, in that It receives all seeds of thought.

INTELLECT.—The reasoning faculty.

ILLUSION OF MIND.—Means looking at a picture in Mind which may be real, only as a picture, but not as substance. As a picture of a person is not the person, so there are many pictures, drawn in Mind, which are real only as pictures. Mine is not an illusion, but might present us with illusions, unless we are very careful to distinguish the false from the true.

INCARNATION.—The Spirit of God in all Creation.

INFINITE.—That which is beyond all comprehension.

IMMUTABLE LAW.—Absolute in its ability to accomplish.

INSANITY.—The loss of the objective faculties.

JESUS.—The name of a man. Distinguished from the Christ. The man Jesus became the embodiment of the Christ as the human gave way to the Divine Idea of Sonship.

KARMA.—The subjective law of cause and effect.

LOGOS.—The word of God.

LAW.—Mind in action.

LIFE.—The animating Principle of Being.

LAW OF ATTRACTION.—Subjective tendencies set in motion which are bound to attract.

LAW OF CORRESPONDENCES.—The subjective image of a desire. In the subjective world there is an exact image of everything that is in the objective world.

LOVE.—The givingness of the self.

LATENT LIFE.—Life that depends upon reality. Distinguished from inherent life.

LOGIC.—Reasoning which keeps faith with itself.

LIBIDO.—The emotional urge within life which causes it to express itself.

LEVITATION.—Where the body is lifted without the aid of any physical medium.

MAYA.—World of mental illusion.

MENTAL CORRESPONDENTS.—The inner image in mind which balances the outer objectification of itself. Every objective thing has an inner mental correspondent.

MASCULINE PRINCIPLE.—The Self-Assertive Spirit, either in God or man.

MATERIAL MAN.—The objective man. Not opposed to Spirit, but the logical outcome of the Self-Knowing Mind.

MENTAL PLANE.—Just between the Spiritual and the physical. The three planes intersphere each other.

METAPHYSICAL PRINCIPLE.—The Universal Creative Mind; as Spirit, It is conscious; as Law, It is subjective.

METAPHYSICS.—That which is beyond the known laws of physics.

MULTIPLICITY.—The many things and people which come from the One. All come from the One, And all live in , and by, the One.

MAN.—The objectification of God in the human form. The idea of God manifested in the flesh. The Sonship of the Father. Generic man is the Type, and the personal man is the concrete expression of the Type.

MONEY.—The idea of Spiritual supply, objectified.

MEDIUM.—One who objectifies subjectivity.

MYSTIC.—One who senses the Divine Presence.

MYSTICISM.—Not a mystery, but a mystic sense of the presence of Ultimate Reality.

MANIA.—An irresistible desire controlling personal action.

MENTAL TREATMENT.—The act, art, and science of inducing thought in Mind, which thought, operated upon by Mind, becomes a manifested condition.

MENTAL EQUIVALENT.—Having a subjective idea of the desired experience.

MENTAL SCIENCE.—The science of Mind and Spirit. A systematic knowledge of the laws of the Mental and Spiritual World.

MIRROR OF MIND.—The subjective world, reflecting the images of thought that are projected into it by the conscious mind.

MIRROR OF MATTER.—The external form of an inner concept.

MATTER.—Any form which substance takes in the world of sense and objectivity.

MANIFESTATION.—The objectification of ideas.

MICROCOSM.—The individual world or universe of man.

MACROCOSM.—The Universal World.

MEMORY.—The subjective retention of ideas.

MESMERISM.—The influence of personality.

MENTAL ATMOSPHERE.—The mental emanation of anything, any person or any place. Everything has some kind of a mental atmosphere.

MIND.—Mind is both conscious and subconscious. Conscious Mind is Spirit, either in God or man. Unconscious Mind is the law of conscious Mind acting and is, therefore, subconscious or subjective.

MENTALITY.—An individual use of Universal Mind. There is One Mind, but within this One Mind are many mentalities. The One Mind is God and the mentalities are people.

MALPRACTICE.—The destructive use of Mind Power. It may be conscious or malicious, innocent, or ignorant.

MENTAL IMAGE.—Subjective likeness.

NEUTRAL.—Not caring which way it works.

NORMAL.—Natural.

NATURAL MAN.—Instinctive or Spiritual Man.

NEUTRALIZING THOUGHT.—The act of mentally erasing thought images.

OCCULT.—Hidden.

OMEGA.—The last.

OBJECTIVE MIND.—The conscious mind.

OBJECTIVE PLANE.—The outer world of expression.

OBJECTIVE SIDE OF THOUGHT.—The conscious side of thinking.

OBJECTIFICATION.—The act of objectifying.

OBSESSION.—Being controlled by thoughts, ideas, or entities.

OMNIPRESENT.—Everywhere present.

OMNISCIENT.—All-knowing.

OMNIPOTENT.—All-powerful.

OMNISCIENT, INSTINCTIVE I AM.—**God** in man and things.

POTENTIAL.—Inherent possibility.

PRACTITIONER.—One who practices mental healing or demonstration.

PERSONALITY.—The objective evidence of individuality. The man as we see him in the relative world.

PROPHET.—One who prophesies.

PSYCHOMETRY.—Reading from the soul side of things.

PRINCIPLE.—Any law of nature.

PERCEPT.—An external object perceived by the mind. Distinguished from a concept which is an inner idea.

PLANES.—Different rates of vibration.

PSYCHIC.—Subjective capacity. All people are psychic, but all are not mediums. A medium is one who objectifies the psychic sense.

PSYCHE.—Soul or subjective.

PRIMORDIAL SUBSTANCE.—The ultimate formless stuff from which all things come.

PEACE.—A state of inner calm.

POISE.—Mental balance.

POWER.—The union of peace with poise.

PERFECTION.—The real state of being.

POVERTY.—A limited thought.

PURPOSE.—Definite intention.

PLASTIC.—Easily molded.

PSYCHOLOGY.—Study of the workings of the human mind.

PARTICULARIZATION.—Concrete forms produced by Spirit.

PRENATAL.—Conditions before human birth.

PSYCHO-ANALYSIS.—A systematic analysis of the subjective thought.

PHILOSOPHY.—A man's idea of life.

PSYCHIC WORLD.—The world of subjectivity.

PSYCHIC PHENOMENA.—Phenomena of the soul or subjective mentality.

PASSIVE RECEPTIVITY.—Willing to receive any and all forms of thought.

REVELATION.—Becoming consciously aware of hidden things.

REASON.—The mental ability to analyze, dissect and figure out the cause of things. The human mind can reason both inductively and deductively. The Divine Mind can reason only deductively.

RICHES.—Idea of abundance.

REALIZATION.—Subjective comprehension of Truth.

RELATIVE.—That which depends upon something else.

REINCARNATION.—Rebirth in the flesh.

RESURRECTION.—Rising from a belief in death.

REALITY.—The truth about anything.

RELIGION.—A Man's idea of God or gods.

RACE-SUGGESTION.—Human beliefs, operating through the mentality of the individual.

SUBSIST.—To live by virtue of spirit.

SPIRITUAL.—The atmosphere of God.

SUGGESTION.—Receiving the thoughts of another. Suggestion accepts the ideas of others and believes in them. It may be conscious or unconscious.

SAINT.—A holy man.

SAGE.—One versed in spiritual truths.

SEER.—One who sees into causes.

SELF-KNOWING MIND.—The conscious mind.

SELF-EXISTENT.—Living by virtue of its own being.

SELF-PROPELLING.—Having power within itself.

SPECIALIZE.—To bring into concrete form.

SILENCE.—The inner realization of the One Life.

SCIENCE.—Knowledge of laws and principles.

SPIRITS.—Personalities.

SUBSTANCE.—The formless back of all forms.

SPIRIT.—God, within Whom all spirits exist. The Self-Knowing One. The Conscious Universe. The Absolute.

SOUL.—The Creative Medium of Spirit.

SUBJECTIVE.—Beneath the threshold of the conscious. The inner side.

SUBCONSCIOUS.—The same as subjective.

SYMBOL.—Mental impressions denoting spiritual or mental truths.

SONSHIP.—Man as the Son of God.

SUBJECTIVE TENDENCY.—The subjective trend of thought.

SPIRITUAL REALIZATION.—The realization of the Divine Presence.

SUBJECTIVE STATE OF THOUGHT.—The sum total of all one's thinking, both conscious and unconscious.

SPACE.—The Cosmic World. The distance between two specific forms. Space is a relative condition within the Absolute.

STREAM OF CONSCIOUSNESS.—The automatic, mental emanation of the subjective state of thought.

SUBJECTIVE SIDE OF LIFE.—The inner side of life, as law.

SUBLIMATE.—To transmute energy into another form of action.

SIMPLE CONSCIOUSNESS.—Consciousness, as in an animal.

SELF-CONSCIOUSNESS.—Personally conscious. Distinguished from Cosmic Consciousness, which is a consciousness of the Unity of the Whole.

SPIRIT OF MAN.—God in man.

SELF-REALIZATION.—A consciousness of the self as a reality.

SPIRITUAL MAN.—Man in a conscious state.

SIN.—Missing the mark. There is no sin but a mistake and no punishment but an inevitable consequence.

SUBJECTIVE CAUSATION.—The mental law set in motion.

SPIRITUAL CONSCIOUSNESS.—The realization of the Divine Presence.

SUBJECTIVITY OF THE UNIVERSE.—The Universal Soul or mental Law.

SUBJECTIVE TO SPIRIT.—The Law is the subjective to the Spirit.

SUBJECTIVE ACTIVITY.—The inner action of the automatic law.

SOUL OF THE UNIVERSE.—The Universal Creative Medium.

SPIRIT OF THE UNIVERSE.—The Self-Knowing Mind of God.

TRIUNE UNITY.—The Trinity.

TREATMENT.—The art, act and science of inducing thought on the subjective side of life. Setting the Law in motion.

TELEKINETIC ENERGY.—Moving ponderable objects without physical contact.

TRANCE.—A subjective state.

TELEPATHY.—Thought transference.

THOUGHT FORMS.—All thought has definite form on the subjective side of life.

THE ONLY.—The One Power.

TIME.—"Sequence of events in a Unitary Whole."

THOUGHT.—The movement of consciousness.

TRUTH.—That which Is.

TRINITY.—The Threefold Universe.

THEOLOGY.—That which treats of the nature of God.

TRANSMUTATION.—Same as sublimation.

UNIVERSE.—The Cosmic World.

UNITY.—The Oneness of God and man.

UNCONSCIOUS MEMORY.—Subjective memory.

UNCONSCIOUS THOUGHT.—Unconscious subjective thought.

UNIVERSAL LAW.—Divine Principle.

UNIVERSAL MIND.—The Creative Medium of Spirit.

UNIVERSAL SPIRIT.—The Conscious Mind of God.

UNIVERSAL SOUL.—The Universal Subjectivity.

UNIVERSAL SUBJECTIVITY.—The Creative Medium or the Universal Mind.

VISUALIZATION.—The art of mentally projecting a thought form into the Universal Creative Medium.

VIBRATION.—Law in execution.

WORD.—The thought of God or man.

THE CALL

This I saw, or else some inner presence made it known to me;
The Universe is filled with life; the air, the sky, the sea
Teem with intelligence, with majesty and might;
And deep within me, some subtle inner sight
Beholds and sees, comprehends and knows the All,
Nor fears nor falters, but answers the Divine Call
To be as one beyond the bounds of time and space,
To overcome the bondage of the human race,
And leap, with trust undaunted, free,
Into the deeps of that Infinite Sea
Whose waters, calm, are ready to receive
Those, who in simple faith, believe.

Creative Mind and Success

TABLE OF CONTENTS

AN INQUIRY INTO THE TRUTH.

An inquiry into Truth is an inquiry into the cause of things as the human race sees and experiences them. The starting point of our thought must always begin with our experiences. We all know that life is, else we could not even think that we are. Since we can think, say and feel, we must be. We live, we are conscious of life; therefore we must be and life must be. If we are life and consciousness (self-knowing) then it follows that we must have come from life and consciousness. Let us start, then, with this simple fact: Life is and life is conscious.

But what is the nature of this life; is it physical, mental, material or spiritual? A little careful thinking based upon logic, more than any merely personal opinion, will do much in clearing up some of these questions that at first seem to stagger us with their bigness.

How much of that which is may we call life? The answer would have to be: Life is all that there is; it is the reason for all that we see, hear, feel—all that we experience in any way. Now nothing from nothing leaves nothing, and it is impossible for something to proceed from nothing. Since something is, that from which it came must be all that is. Life, then, is all that there is. Everything comes from it, ourselves included.

The next question is, how do things come from life? How do the things that we see come from the things that we do not see? The things that we see must be real because we see them. To say they are not real will never explain them nor answer any question about them. God's world is not a world of illusion but one of divine realities. The truth must not explain away things that we see. It must explain what they are. We are living and experiencing varying degrees of consciousness and conditions. Only when the why of this living and of our experiences is

Jesus understood will we know the least thing about the truth. did not say that things are illusions. He said that we must not judge from the standpoint of the seen but must judge righteously or with right judgment; and He meant that we must get behind the appearance and find out what caused it. So let us not in any way fool ourselves nor allow ourselves to believe we have always been fooled. We are living in a world of realities. Whatever we have experienced is a reality as far as that experience is concerned, although if we had had a higher understanding of life, the unpleasant experience might have been avoided.

WHAT LIFE IS.

In he first place, what do we mean by life? We mean that which we see, feel, hear, touch or taste, and the reason for it. We must have come into contact with all we know of life. We have already found what life is or we could not have had any of these experiences. "In the beginning was God" or life. Out of this life which is, everything which is is made. So life must flow through all things. There is no such thing as dead matter. Moreover, life is one, and it cannot be changed except into itself. All forms are forms of this unity and must come and go through some inner activity. This inner activity of life or nature must be some form of self-consciousness or self-knowing. In our human understanding we would call this inner knowing, or consciousness, "thought." The Spirit, or Life, or God, must make things out of Himself through self-recognition, or self-knowing or, as we would call it thinking. Since God is all, there is nothing to hinder Him from doing what He wishes, and the question, "How do things come into being?" is answered: God makes them out of Himself. God thinks, or knows, and that thing which He thinks or knows appears from Himself, and is made out of Himself. There is no other possible explanation for what we see. Unless people are willing to begin here, they will never understand how it is that things are not material but spiritual.

MAN'S PLACE IN CREATION.

But here does man come in? He is. Therefore it follows that he, too, is made out of God, since God, or Spirit, is all. Being made out of God, he must partake of His nature, for we are "made in His image."

Man is a center of God in God. Whatever God is in the Universal, man must be in the individual world. The difference between God and man is one of degree and not of quality. Man is not self-made; he is made out of 'God.

The question might arise, why did God do this? No living person can answer this question. This is something that is known only of the Father. We might suppose that God made man to live with Him and to enjoy with Him, to be one with the Father. It is true, indeed, that those who have felt this most deeply have had a corresponding spiritual power that leads us to suppose that God really did make man as a companion. Man is the individual and God is the Universal. "As the Father hath life within Himself, so hath he given it to the Son to have life within himself." Man's mind is made out of God's mind, and all that man is or ever will be, all that he has or ever will have, must partake of the Divine nature. Man did not make it so, but it is so, and he must accept the fact and see what he can do with it. If he has the same power in his individual life that God has in the Universal, then this discovery will mean freedom from all bondage when he learns how to use his power. As God governs His Universal world so will man govern his individual world, always subject to the greater law and life. This could not be otherwise if we realize what follows from it, for so realizing we find ourselves living in a very different world from the one in which we thought we were living. God governs not through physical law as result, but first by inner knowing—then the physical follows. In the same way, man governs his world by the process which we will call, for want of a better name, the power of his thought.

Man's inner life is one with the Father. There can be no separation, for the self-evident reason that there is nothing to separate him from God, because there is nothing but life. The separation of two things implies putting a different element between them; but as there is nothing different from God, the unity of God and man is firmly established forever. "My Father and I are One" is a simple statement of a great soul who perceived life as it really is and not from the mere standpoint of outer conditions.

Taking as the starting point that man has the same life as God, it follows that he uses the same creative process. Everything is one, comes from the same source and returns again to it. "The things which are seen are not made of the things which do appear." What we see comes from what we do not see. This is the explanation of the whole visible universe, and is the only possible explanation.

As God's thought makes worlds and peoples them with all living things, so does our thought make our world and peoples it with all the experiences we have had. By the activity of our thought things come into our life, and we are limited because we have not known the truth; we have thought that outside things controlled us, when all the time we have had that within which could have changed everything and given us freedom from bondage.

The question, then, naturally arises: Why did God create man and make him a free agent? If God had created us in such a way as to compel us to do or to be anything that was not of our choosing, we should not have been individuals at all, we should be automatons. Since we know that we are individuals, we know that God made us thus; and we are just discovering the reason why. Let any man wake up to this, the greatest truth in all ages, and he will find it will answer all questions. He will be satisfied that things are what they are. He will perceive that he may use his own God-given power so to work, to think and to live that he will in no way hinder the greater law from operating through him. According to the clearness of his perception and the greatness of his realization of this power will he provide within himself a starting point through which God may operate. There will no longer be a sense of separation, but in its place will come that divine assurance that he is one with God, and thus will he find his freedom from all suffering, whether it be of body, mind or estate.

THE BEGINNING OF UNDERSTANDING.

Man is beginning to realize that he has life within himself as the great gift of God to him. If he really has life, if it is the same nature as the life of God, if he is an individual and has the right of self-choice which constitutes individuality; then it follows that he can do with his life what the wants to do: he can make out of Himself that which he wishes. Freedom is his, but this freedom is within law and never outside it. Man must obey law. If he disobeys it, it has to act as law, and so acting has to punish him. This he cannot change but must submit to. Freedom comes to the individual from understanding the laws of his own life, and conforming to them, thereby subjecting them to his use, to the end of health, happiness and success.

Law obtains throughout all nature, governing all things, both the seen and the unseen. Law is not physical or material but mental and spiritual. Law is God's method of operation. We should think of God as the great Spirit whose sole impulse is love, freely giving of Himself to all who ask and refusing none. God is our Father in every sense of the term, watching over, caring for and loving all alike. While all is love, yet, in order that things may not be chaotic, all is governed by law. And as far as you and I are concerned, this law is always mental.

OUR CONDITIONS GOVERNED BY OUR THINKING.

It is easy for the average person to see how it is that mind can control, and to a certain extent govern, the functions of the body. Some can go even further than this and see that the body is governed entirely by consciousness. This they can see without much difficulty, but it is not so easy for them to see how it is that thought governs their conditions and decides whether they are to be successes or failures.

Here we will stop to ask the question: If our conditions are not controlled by thought, by what, then, are they controlled? Some will say that conditions are controlled by circumstances. But what are circumstances? Are they cause or are they effect? Of course they are always effect; everything that we see is an effect. An effect is something that follows a cause, and we are dealing with causation only; effects do not make themselves, but they are held in place by mind, or causation.

If this does not answer your thought, begin over again and realize that behind everything that is seen is the silent cause. In your life you are that cause. There is nothing but mind, and nothing moves except as mind moves it. We have agreed that, while God is love, yet your life is governed absolutely by mind, or law. In our lives of conditions we are the cause, and nothing moves except as our mind moves it.

The activity of our mind is thought., We are always acting because we are always thinking. At all times we are either drawing things to us or we are pushing them away from us. In the ordinary individual this process goes on without his ever knowing it consciously, but ignorance of the law will excuse no one from its effects.

"What," someone will say, "do you think that I thought failure or wanted to fail?" Of course not. You would be foolish to think that; but according to the law which we cannot deny, you must have thought things that would produce failure. Perhaps you thought that failure might come, or in some other way you gave it entrance to your mind.

Thinking back over the reason for things, you will find that you are surrounded by a mind, or law, that casts back at the thinker, manifested, everything that he thinks. If this were not true, man would not be an individual. Individuality can mean only the ability to think what we want to think. If that thought is to have power in our lives then there has to be something that will manifest it. Some are limited and bound by law through ignorance. This law is sometimes called "Karma," it is the law that binds the ignorant and gives freedom to the wise.

We live in mind; and it can return to us only what we think into it. No matter what we may do, law will always obtain. If we are thinking of ourselves as poor and needy, then mind has no choice but to return what we have thought into it. At first this may be hard to realize, but the truth will reveal to the seeker that law could act in no other way. Whatever we think is the pattern, and mind is the builder. Jesus, realizing this law, said, "It is done unto you even as you have believed." Shall we doubt but that this great Way Shower knew what he was talking about? Did He not say, "It is done unto you"? What a wonderful thought. "It is done unto you." Nothing to worry about. "It is done unto you." With a tremendous grasp of the power of true spiritual thought, Jesus even called forth bread from the ethers of life, and at no time did He ever fail to demonstrate that when one knows the truth he is freed by that knowledge.

UNCONSCIOUS CREATION.

The author once attended a patient who was suffering from a large growth. She was operated on and about fifty pounds of water were removed. In a few days the growth had returned. Where did it come from? Not from eating or drinking. Neither did it move from one part of the body to another part, as that would not have increased her weight. It must have been created from elements which she took in from the air. It had to come from something not physically seen, something appearing from nothing that we see. What we call "creation" is the same thing—the visible appearing from the invisible. Was not this phenomenon a creation?

Cases as remarkable as this are occurring every day. We should not deny this fact but try to explain it. In the case of this woman there must have been an activity of thought molded forth into form, else how could this growth have appeared? There is nothing manifest but that there is a cause for the manifestation. Investigation proves that behind every condition, whether of body or environment, there has been some thought, conscious or unconscious, which produced that condition. In the case of this woman the thought was not conscious. But creation is going on all the time; we should realize this and learn how to control it so that there may be created for us the things that we desire and not those that we do not want. Is it any wonder that the Bible says, "With all thy getting get understanding"?

Jesus understood all this, and so it was no more effort for Him to do what He did than it is for us to breathe or to digest our food. He understood, that is all. Because Jesus did understand and did use these great laws with objective consciousness, people thought He must be God. And when to-day something unusual occurs, people think that a miracle has been performed. Jesus was not God. He was the manifestation of God; and so are all people. "I say that ye are gods, and every one of you sons of the Most High."

A thinking person will be compelled to admit, in view of all this, that creation is first spiritual, through mental law, and then physical in its manifestation.

Man does not really create. He uses creative power that already is. Relatively speaking, he is the creative power in his own life; and so far as his thought goes, there is something that goes with it that has the power to bring forth into manifestation the thing thought of. Hitherto men have used this creative power in ignorance and so have brought upon themselves all kinds of conditions, but today hundreds of thousands are beginning to use these great laws of their being in a conscious, constructive way. Herein lies the great secret of the New Thought movements under their various names and cults and orders. All are using the same law even though some deny to others the real revelation. We should get into an attitude of mind wherein we should recognize the truth wherever we may find it. The trouble with most of us is that unless we see sugar in a sugar bowl we think it must be something else, and so we stick to our petty prejudices instead of looking after principles.

FIRST STEPS.

The first thing to realize is that since any thought manifests it necessarily follows that all thought does the same, else how should we know that the particular thought we were thinking would be the one that would create? Mind must cast back all or none. Just as the creative power of the soil receives all seeds put into it, and at once begins to work upon them, so mind must receive all thought and at once begin to operate upon it. Thus we find that all thought has some power in our lives and over our conditions. We are making our environments by the creative power of our thought. God has created us thus and we cannot escape it. By conforming our lives and thought to a greater understanding of law we shall be able to bring into our experience just what we wish, letting go of all that we do not want to experience and taking in the things we desire.

Every person is surrounded by a thought atmosphere. This mental atmosphere is the direct result of thought which in its turn becomes the direct reason for the cause of that which comes into our lives. Through this power we are either attracting or repelling. Like attracts like and we attract to us just what we are in mind. It is also true that we become attracted to something that is greater than our previous experience by first embodying the atmosphere of our desire.

Every business, every place, every person, everything has a certain mental atmosphere of its own. This atmosphere decides what is to be drawn to it. For instance, you never saw a successful man who went around with an atmosphere of failure. Successful people think about success. A successful man is filled with that subtle something which permeates everything that he does with an atmosphere of confidence and strength. In the presence of some people we feel as though nothing were too great to undertake; we are uplifted; we are inspired to do great things, to accomplish; we feel strong, steady, sure. What a power we feel in the presence of big souls, strong men, noble women!

Did you ever stop to inquire why it is that such persons have this kind of an effect over you while others seem to depress, to drag you down, and in their presence you feel as though life were a load to carry? One type is positive, the other negative. In every physical respect they are just alike, but one has a mental and spiritual power which the other does not have, and without that power the individual can hope to do but little.

Which of these two do we like the better? With which do we want to associate? Certainly not with the one that depresses us; we have enough of that already. But what about the man who inspires us with our own worth? Ah, he is the man we will turn to every time. Before ever we reach him, in our haste to be near, even to hear his voice, do we not feel a strength coming to meet us? Do you think that this man who has such a wonderful power of attraction will ever want for friends? Will he ever have to look up a position?

Already so many positions are open to him that he is weighing in his mind which one to take. He does not have to become a success; he already is a success.

Thoughts of failure, limitation or poverty are negative and must be counted out of our lives for all time. Somebody will say, "But what of the poor; what are you going to do with them; are they to be left without help?" No; a thousand times no. The same power is in them that is in all men. They will always be poor until they awake and realize what life is. All the charity on earth has never done away with poverty, and never will; if it could have done so it would have done so; it could not, therefore it has not. It will do a man a thousand times more good to show him how to succeed than it will to tell him he needs charity. We need not listen to all the calamity howlers. Let them howl if it does them any good. God has given us a power and we must use it. We can do more toward saving the world by proving this law than all that charity has ever given it.

Right here, in the manifold world to-day, there is more money and provision than the world can use. Not even a fraction of the wealth of the world is used. Inventors and discoverers are adding to this wealth every day; they are the real people. But in the midst of plenty, surrounded by all the gifts of heaven, man sits and begs for his daily bread. He should be taught to realize that he has brought these conditions upon himself; that instead of blaming God, man or the devil for the circumstances by which he is surrounded, he should learn to seek the truth, to let the dead bury their dead. We should tell every man who will believe what his real nature is; show him how to overcome all limitations; give him courage; show him the way. If he will not believe, if he will not walk in the way, it is not our fault, and having done all we can, we must go our way. We may sympathize with people but never with trouble, limitation or misery. If people still insist upon hugging their troubles to themselves, all the charity in the world will not help them.

Remember that God is that silent power behind all things, always ready to spring into expression when we have provided the proper channels, which are receptive and positive faith in the evidence of things not seen with the physical eye but eternal in the heavens.

All is mind, and we must provide a receptive avenue for it as it passes out through us into the outer expression of our affairs. If we allow the world's opinion to control our thinking, then that will be our demonstration. If, on the other hand, we rise superior to the world, we shall do a new thing.

Remember that all people are making demonstrations, only most of them are making the ones they do not desire, but the only ones they can make with their present powers of perception.

HOW TO ATTAIN STRENGTH.

Let us see that we use the right attitude of mind in all that we do, filling ourselves with such courage and power of strength that all thought of weakness flees before us. If any thought of weakness should come, ask this question: Is life weak? If life is not weak and if God is not discouraged, then you are not, never were, and never will be. I should like to see the sickly, discouraged thought that could withstand this attitude of mind.

No! Life is strong, and you are strong with the strength of the Infinite; forget all else as you revel in this strength. You are strong and can say I AM. You have been laboring under an illusion; now you are disillusioned. Now you know, and knowing is using the law in a constructive way. "I and my Father are One;" this is strength for the weak, and life for all who believe.

We can so fill ourselves with the drawing power of attraction that it will become irresistible. Nothing can hinder things from coming to the man who knows that he is dealing with the same power that creates all from itself, moves all within itself, and yet holds all things in their places. I am one with the Infinite Mind. Let this ring through you many times each day until you rise to that height that, looking, sees.

In order to be sure that we are creating the right kind of a mental atmosphere and so attracting what we want, we must at first watch our thinking, lest we create that which we should not like to see manifest. In other words, we must think only what we wish to experience. All is mind, and mind casts back at the thinker that only which he thinks. Nothing ever happens by chance. Law governs all life, and all people come under that law. But that law, so far as we are concerned, we ourselves set in motion, and we do this through the power of our thought.

Each person is living in a world of his own making, and he should speak only such words and think only such thoughts as he wishes to see manifested in his life. We must not hear, think, speak, read or listen to limitation of any kind. There is no way under heaven whereby we can think two kinds of thought and get only one result; it is impossible, and the sooner we realize it the sooner we shall arrive. This does not mean that we must be afraid to think lest we create the wrong image, but it does mean that the way most people think can produce nothing but failure; that is why so few succeed.

The person who is to succeed will never let his mind dwell on past mistakes. He will forgive the past in his life and in the lives of other people. If he makes a mistake he will at once forgive it. He will know that so long as he desires any good, there is nowhere in the universe anything that opposes him. God does not damn anyone or anything; man damns everyone and everything.

God does not make things by comparing His power with some other power. God knows that when He speaks it done; and if we partake of the divine nature we must know the same thing in our lives that God knows in His.

"I am the master of my fate,
I am the captain of my soul."

WHAT WE WILL ATTRACT.

We will always attract to us, in our lives and conditions, according to our thought. Things are but outer manifestations of inner mental concepts. Thought is not only power; it is also the form of all things. The conditions that we attract will correspond exactly to our mental pictures. It is quite necessary, then, that the successful business man should keep his mind on thoughts of happiness, which produce cheerfulness instead of depression; he should radiate joy, and should be filled with faith, hope and expectancy. These cheerful, hopeful attitudes of mind are indispensable to the one who really wants to do things in life.

Put every negative thought out of your mind once and for all. Declare your freedom. Know that no matter what others may say, think or do, you are a success, now, and nothing can hinder you from accomplishing your good.

All the power of the universe is with you; feel it, know it, and then act as though it were true. This mental attitude alone will draw people and things to you.

Begin to blot out, one by one, all false beliefs, all idea that man is limited or poor or miserable. Use that wonderful power of will that God has given to you. Refuse to think of failure or to doubt your own power.

See only what you wish to experience, and look at nothing else. No matter how many times the old thought returns, destroy it by knowing that it has no power over you; look it squarely in the face and tell it to go; it does not belong to you, and you must know—and stick to it—that you are now free.

Rise up in all the faith of one who knows what he is dealing with, and declare that you are one with Infinite Mind. Know that you cannot get away from this One Mind; that wherever you may go, there, right beside you, waiting to be used, is all the power there is in the whole universe. When you realize this you will know that in union with this, the only power, you are more than all else, you are more than anything that can ever happen to you.

MORE ABOUT THE POWER OF ATTRACTION.

Always remember that Spirit makes things out of itself; it manifests in the visible world by becoming the thing that it wills to become. In the world of the individual the same process takes place. It is given to man to use creative power, but with the using of this power comes the necessity of using it as it is made to be used. If God makes things out of His thought before they come into manifestation, then we must use the same method.

You can attract only that which you first mentally become and feel yourself to be in reality, without any doubting. A steady stream of consciousness going out into creative mind will attract a steady manifestation of conditions; a fluctuating stream of consciousness will attract the corresponding manifestation or condition in your life. We Host be consistent in our attitude of mind, never wavering. lames says, "Ask in faith, nothing doubting, for he that doubteth is like a surge of the sea driven by the wind and tossed. For let not that man think that he shall receive anything of the Lord."

We are all immersed in an aura of our own thinking. This aura is the direct result of all that we have ever said, thought or done; it decides what is to take place in our life; it attracts what is like itself and repels what is unlike itself. We are drawn towards those things that we mentally embody. Most of the inner processes of thought have been unconscious; but when we understand the law all that we have to do is to embody consciously what we wish, and think of that only, and then we shall be drawn silently toward it.

We have this law in our hands to do with as we will. We can draw what we want only as we let go of the old order and take up the new; and this we must do to the exclusion of all else. This is no weak man's job but an undertaking for a strong, self-reliant soul; and the end is worth the effort. The person who can hold his thought one-pointed is the one who will obtain the best results.

But this does not imply the necessity of strain or anything of a strenuous nature; on the contrary, strain is just what we must avoid. When we know that there is but one power we shall not struggle, we shall know, and in calmness we shall see only what we know must be the Truth. This means a persistent, firm determination to think what we want to think, regardless of all outer evidence to the contrary. We look not to the seen but to the unseen. The king of Israel understood this when, looking upon the advancing host of the enemy, he said, "We have no might against this great company, but our eyes are upon Thee"—upon the One Power.

HOW TO ATTRACT FRIENDS.

The man who has learned to love all people, no matter who they may be, will find plenty of people who will return that love to him. This is not mere sentiment, and it is more than a religious attitude of mind; it is a deep scientific fact, and one to which we should pay attention. The reason is this: As all is mind, and as we attract to us what we first become, until we learn to love we are not sending out love vibrations, and not until we send out love vibrations can we receive love in return.

One of the first things to do is to learn to love everybody. If you have not done this, begin to do so at once. There is always more good than bad in people, and seeing the good tends to bring it forth. Love is the greatest healing and drawing power on earth. It is the very reason for our being, and that explains why it is that people should have something or somebody to love.

The life that has not loved has not lived; it is still dead. Love is the sole impulse for creation; and the man who does not have it as the greatest incentive in his life has never developed the real creative instinct. No one can swing out into the Universal without love, for the whole universe is based upon it.

When we find that we are without friends, the thing to do is at once to send our thought out to the whole world,—send it full of love and affection. Know that this thought will meet the desires of some other person who is wanting the same thing, and in some way the two will be drawn together. Get over thinking that people are queer. That kind of thought will only produce misunderstanding and cause us to lose the friends that we now have. Think of the whole world as your friend; but you must also be the friend of the whole world. In this way and with this simple practice you will draw to you so many friends that the time will be too short to enjoy them all. Refuse to see the negative side of anyone. Refuse to let yourself misunderstand or be misunderstood. no not be morbid. Know that everyone wants you to have the best; affirm this wherever you go and then you will find things just as you wish them to be.

The atmosphere created by a real lover of the race is so powerful that although his other shortcomings may be many, still the world will love him in return. "To him who loveth much, much will be forgiven." People are dying for real human interest, for someone to tell them that they are all right. Which person do we like the better: the one who is always full of trouble and faultfinding, or the one who looks at the world as his friend and loves it? The question does not need to be asked; we know that we want the company of the person who loves and loving, forgets all else.

The only reason we think other people are "queer" is because they do not happen to think as we do. We must get over this little, petty attitude and see things in the large. The person who sees what he wants to see, regardless of what appears, will some day experience in the outer what he has so faithfully seen within.

From selfish motives alone, if from no loftier reason, we cannot afford to find fault or to hate or even to hold in mind anything against any living soul. The God who is love cannot hear the prayer of the man who is not love. Love and co-operation will yet be found to be the greatest business principle on earth. "God is Love."

We will make our unity with all people, with all life. We will affirm that God in us is unified with God in all. This One is now drawing into our life all love and fellowship. I am one with all people, with all things, with all life. As I listen in the silence the voice of all humanity speaks to me and answers the love that I hold out to it.

This great love that I now feel for the world is the love of God, and it is felt by all and returned from all. Nothing comes in between because there is nothing but love to come in between. I understand all people and that understanding is reflected back to me from all people. I help, therefore I am helped. I uplift, therefore I am uplifted. Nothing can mar this perfect picture of myself and my relations with the world; it is the truth, the whole truth, and nothing but the truth. I am now surrounded by all love, all friendship, all companionship, all health, all happiness, all success. I am one with life. I wait in the silence while the Great Spirit bears this message to the whole world.

THE CONTROL OF THOUGHT.

The man who can control his thought can have and do what he wishes to have and to do; everything is his for the asking. He must remember that whatever he gets is his to use but not his to hold. Creation is always flowing by and we have as much of it as we can take and use; more would cause stagnation.

We are relieved of all thought of clinging to anybody or anything. Cannot the Great Principle' of Life create for us faster than we can spend or use? The universe is inexhaustible; it is limitless; it knows no bounds and has no confines. We are not depending on a reed shaken by the wind, but on the principle of life itself, for all that we want, have or ever shall have. It is not some power, or a great power, we affirm again; it is ALL POWER. All that we have to do is to believe this and act as though it were so, never wavering, not even once, no matter what happens. As we do this we shall find that things are steadily coming our way, and that they are coming without that awful effort that destroys the peace of the majority of the race. We know that there can be no failure in the Divine Mind, and this Mind is the Power on which we are depending.

Now just because we are depending upon Divine Mind we must not think that we do not have to do our share. God will work through us if we will let Him, but we must act in the outer as though we were sure of ourselves. Our part is to believe, and then to act in faith.

Jesus went to the tomb of Lazarus believing and knowing that God was working through Him. Often we may have to go somewhere or do something and we must know with deep conviction that there will be a power going with us that none can gainsay. When we feel this secure place in our thought, all that we will have to do is to act. There is no doubt but that the creative power of the universe will answer; it always does. And so we need not take the worry upon ourselves, but rather we will "Make known our requests with thanksgiving."

When Jesus said, "All things whatsoever ye pray and ask for, believe that ye receive them and ye shall have them," he was uttering one of those many deep truths that were so clear to Him and that we are just beginning to see. He knew that everything is made out of mind and that without that positive acceptance on the part of the individual there is no mold into which mind can pour itself forth into form. In the mind of God there is the correct mold, the true knowing, but in the mind of man there is not always this true knowing. Since God can do for us only by doing through us, nothing can be done for us unless we are positively receptive, but when we realize the law and how it works, then we will provide that complete inner acceptance. By so doing we permit the Spirit to do the work, to make the gift.

The reason we can make our requests known with thanksgiving is because we know from the beginning that we are to receive and therefore we cannot help being thankful. This grateful attitude to the Spirit puts us in very close touch with power and adds much to the reality of the thing that we are dealing with. Without it we can do but little. So let us cultivate all the gratitude that we can. In gratitude we will send our thoughts out into the world, and as it comes back it will come laden with the fruits of the Spirit.

CREATING ATMOSPHERE.

To the student who has realized that all is mind and that everything is governed by law, there comes another thought: it is that he can create, or have created for him, from his own thinking. He can create such a strong mental atmosphere of success that its power of attraction will be irresistible. He can send his thought throughout the world and have it bring back to him whatever he wants. He can so fill his place of business with the power of success that it will draw from far and near. Thought will always bring back to us what we send out. First we must clear our thought of all unbelief. This book is written for those who believe; and to those who do believe it will come true in their lives.

Without mental clearness on the part of the thinker there can be no real creative work done. As water will reach only its own level, so mind will return to us only what we first believe. We arc always getting what we believe but not always what we want. Our thought has the power to reach, in the outer form of conditions, an exact correspondence to our inner convictions.

By thinking, you set in motion a power that creates. It will be exactly as you think. You throw out into mind an idea, and mind creates it for you and sets it on the path of your life. Think of it, then, as your greatest friend. It is always with you wherever you may be. It never deserts you. You are never alone. There is no doubt, no fear, no wondering; you know. You are going to use the only power that there is in the universe. You are going to use it for a definite purpose. You have already fixed this purpose in your thought; now you are going to speak it forth.

You are speaking it for your own good. You desire only the good and you know that only the good can come to you. You have made your unity with life, and now life is going to help you in your affairs.

You are going to establish in your rooms such an atmosphere of success that it will become an irresistible power; it will sweep everything before it as it realizes the greatness and the All-Mightiness of the One. You are so sure, that you will not even look to see if it is going to happen; you KNOW.

And now your word, which is one with the Infinite Life, is to be spoken in calm, perfect trust. It is to be taken up, and at once it is to be operated on. Perfect is the pattern and perfect will be the result. You see yourself surrounded by the thing that you desire. More than this, you are the thing that you desire. Your word is now establishing it forever; see this, feel it, know it. You are now encompassed by perfect life, by infinite activity, by all power, by all guidance. The power of the Spirit is drawing to you all people; it is supplying you with all good; it is filling you with all life, truth and love.

Wait in perfect silence while that inner power takes it up. And then you know that it is done unto you. There goes forth from this word the power of the Infinite. "The words which I speak, they are spirit and they are life."

THE POWER OF WORDS.

Man's word, spoken forth into creative mind, is endowed with power of expression. "By our words we are justified and by our words we are condemned." Our word has the exact amount of power that we put into it. This does not mean power through effort or strain but power through absolute conviction, or faith. It is like a little messenger who knows what he is doing and knows just how to do it. We speak into our words the intelligence which we are, and backed by that greater intelligence of the Universal Mind our word becomes a law unto the thing for which it is spoken. Jesus understood this far better than we do. Indeed, He absolutely believed it, for He said, "Heaven and earth shall pass away but my words shall not pass away till all be fulfilled."

This makes our word inseparable from Absolute Intelligence and Power. Now if any word has power it must follow that all words have power. Some words may have a greater power than others, according to our conviction, but all words have some power. How careful, then, we should be what kind of words we are speaking.

All this goes to prove that we really are one with the Infinite Mind, and that our words have the power of life within them; that the word is always with us and never far off. The word is within our own mouth. Every time we speak we are using power.

We are one in mind with the whole universe; we are all eternally united in this mind with real power. It is our own fault if we do not use this truth after we see it. We should feel ourselves surrounded by this mind, this great pulsating life, this all-seeing and all-knowing reality. When we do feel this near presence, this great power and life, then all we have to do is to speak forth into it, speak with all the positive conviction of the soul that has found its source, and above all else never fear but that it will be done unto us even as we have believed.

What wonderful power, what a newness of life and of power of expression, is waiting for those who really believe. What may the race not attain to when men wake up to the real facts of being? As yet the race has not begun to live, but the time is drawing near. Already thousands are using this great power, and thousands are eagerly watching and waiting for the new day.

WHY BELIEF IS NECESSARY.

Always when we pray we must believe. Our idea of prayer is not so much asking God for things as it is believing that we already have the things that we need. As we have said before, this already-believing is necessary because all is mind, and until we have provided that full acceptance we have not made a mold into which mind could pour itself and through which it could manifest. This positive belief is absolutely essential to real creative work; and if we do not at present have it, then we must develop it.

All is law, and cause and effect obtain through all life. Mind is cause, and what we term matter, or the visible, is effect. As water will freeze into the form that it is poured, so mind will solidify only into the forms that our thought takes. Thought is form. The individual provides the form; he never creates or even manifests,—that is, of himself; there is something that does all this for him. His sole activity is the use of this power. This power is always at hand ready to be spoken into and at once ready to form the words into visible expression. But the mold that most of us provide is a very poor one, and we change it so quickly that it is more like a motion picture than anything else.

Already we have the power; it is the gift of the Most High in its Finite Expression. But our ignorance of its use has caused us to create the wrong form, which in its turn has caused mind to produce the form which we have thought into it. From this law of cause and effect we may never hope to escape; and while we may think of it as a hard thing, at first, yet, when we understand, we shall see it as absolute justice without which there could be no real self-acting, individual life at all. Because of our divine individuality, even God may have to wait our recognition of Him and His laws.

People in business will do well to remember this and so to form their thought that they will be willing to receive what they send out. No thought of discouragement or disorder should ever be created, but only positive assurance, strong thoughts of success, of Divine activity, the feeling that with God all things are possible, the belief that we are One with that Great Mind. These are the thoughts that make for success.

The realization that we are dealing with one and not with two powers enables us to think with clearness. We are not troubled about competition or opposition or failure because there is nothing but life, and this life is continually giving to us all that we could ask for, wish, or think into it.

We can now see how essential it is that thought should be held one-pointed; that we should think always and only upon what we want, never letting our mind dwell on anything else. In this way the Spirit works through us.

WHY SO MANY FAIL.

The ordinary individual, sitting down to give a treatment to his business, unconsciously does just the thing that he should have avoided; and then he wonders why he did not get the desired results. Most people simply sit and wish for, or long for, something. They may even have a great desire or hope. They may even go so far as to believe that their desire is going to happen. All this is good as far as it goes, but it does not go far enough. What we must do is to provide that already-having-received attitude. This may seem hard at first but we can easily see that it is necessary; and as it is the only way that mind works, this is what we must do.

Power is, and mind is, and life is; but they have to flow through us in order to express in our lives. We are dealing with law; and nature must be obeyed before it will work for us. Just realize that this law is as natural a law as any other of God's laws, and use it with the same intelligence that you would use the law of electricity; then you will get the desired results. We provide the thought form around which the divine energies play and to which they attract the conditions necessary for the fulfillment of the though.

When we give a treatment this is all that we have to do, but before we can do even this we have to clear our minds of all fear, of every sense of separation from the Divine Mind. Law is; but we must enforce it, or use it, in our own lives. Nothing can happen to us that is not first an accepted belief in our own consciousness. We may not always be aware of what is going on within, but practice will enable us to control our thought more and more so that we shall be able to think what we want to think, regardless of what may seem to be the case.

Each person has within himself the capacity of knowing and making use of the law but it must be consciously developed. This is done by practice, and by willingness to learn and to utilize whatever we know so far as we have gone.

The individual who has the most power is the one who has the greatest realization of the Divine Presence, and to whom this means the most as an active principle of his life.

We all need more backbone and less wishbone. There is something which waits only our recognition to spring into being, bringing with it all the power in the universe.

USING THE IMAGINATION.

Just imagine yourself surrounded by mind, so plastic, so receptive, that it receives the slightest impression of your thought. Whatever you think it takes up and executes for you. Every thought is received and acted upon. Not some but all thoughts. Whatever the pattern we provide, that will be our demonstration. If we cannot get over thinking that we are poor then we will still remain poor. As soon as we become rich in our thought then we will be rich in our expression. These are not mere words, but the deepest truth that has ever come to the human race. Hundreds of thousands of the most intelligent thinkers and the most spiritual people of our day are proving this truth. We are not dealing with illusions but with realities; pay no more attention to the one who ridicules these ideas than you would to the blowing of the wind.

In the center of your own soul choose what you want to become, to accomplish; keep it to yourself. Every clay in the silence of absolute conviction know that it is now done. It is just as much done, as far as you are concerned, as it will be when you experience it in the outer. Imagine yourself to be what you want to be. See only that which you desire, refuse even to think of the other. Stick to it, never doubt. Say many times a day, "I am that thing," realize what this means. It means that the great Universal power of Mind is that, and it cannot fail.

MAN'S RIGHT OF CHOICE.

Man is created an individual and as such he has the power of choice. Many people seem to think that man should not choose, that since he has asked the Spirit to lead him, he need no longer act, or choose. This is taught by many teachers but is not consistent with our individuality. Unless we had this privilege, this power of choice, we would not be individuals. What we do need to learn is that the Spirit can choose through us. But when this happens it is an act on our part. Even though we say, "I will not choose," we are still choosing; because we are choosing not to choose.

We cannot escape the fact that we are made in such a way that at every step life is a constant choice. What we do need to do is to select what we feel to be right and know that the universe will never deny us anything. We choose and Mind creates. We should endeavor to choose that which will express always a greater life and we must remember that the Spirit is always seeking to express love and beauty through us. If we are attuned to these, and are working in harmony with the great creative power, we need have no doubt about its willingness to work for us.

We must know exactly what it is that we wish and get the perfect mental picture of it. We must believe absolutely that we now have it and never do or say anything that denies it.

OLD AGE AND OPPORTUNITY.

One of the besetting errors of people is a belief that they are too old to do things. This comes from a lack of understanding what life really is. Life is consciousness and not years. The man or woman who is seventy years old should be better able to demonstrate than the man who is only twenty. He should have evolved a higher thought, and it is thought and not conditions that we are dealing with.

Amelia Barr was fifty-three before she wrote a book. After that she wrote over eighty, all of which had a large circulation. Mary Baker Eddy was sixty before she began her work, and she attended to all of her great activities until she passed from this plane to a higher one. The author of this book once took a man who was over sixty, one who thought his chance for success had gone, and through teaching him these principles in a year's time made him a prosperous business man. He is now doing well and was never before in his life so happy. The last time he was interviewed he said that business was increasing every day and that he had not begun yet. Every day he stands in his store and claims more activity. He speaks the word and realizes increase all the time. If this were not true then life would not be worth the living. What is a few years in eternity? We must get over these false notions about age and competition. In the truth the word competition is never mentioned. The people who think about it have never known the truth.

Life is what we make it from within and never from without. We are just as old as we think we are, no matter what the number of years may have been that we have lived on this planet.

DEMONSTRATING SUCCESS IN BUSINESS.

All demonstrations take place within ourselves. Creation is eternally flowing through all things. The law is always working from that inner pattern. We do not struggle with conditions, we use principles which create conditions. What we can mentally encompass we can accomplish, no matter how hard it may seem from the outside.

All external things are but the outer rim of inner thought activity. You can easily prove this for yourself. If you are in business, say, running an ice cream stand or counter, and are not doing good business, look carefully into your own thought and see what you will find. You will find that it is an established belief there that business is not good. You are not feeling a sense of activity. You will not find within your thought any feeling of success. You are not expecting many customers.

Now suppose someone comes along and says to you: "What is the matter? Why are you not doing more business?" This is about what the answer would be: "People don't seem to want what I have to sell." Or perhaps something like this: "I am too old to compete with modern methods." Or even: "Well, times are hard." All this is negative thought.

Now this man to whom you are talking does not believe a word you have said. He knows that causation is in mind and not in matter, and he says: "The whole thing is in your own mind; the trouble with you is that you don't feel that you are a success."

Perhaps you have heard something of this before; if so you will ask him what he means, or perhaps you think he is talking about something peculiar; but we are taking it for granted that you are so anxious to do something to make your business a success that you will be willing to try anything, so you ask him to explain. He begins by telling you all is Mind; nothing moves but Mind moves it and that you are a center in this Mind. You do not understand how this relates in any way to your business, but he goes on to say that your thought decides whether your business shall be a success or a failure. Here you become indignant, and ask if he means to tell you that you want to fail. Of course he knows you do not, and he explains that while you wish success, you are thinking failure, fearing it, and that there is a law that makes your thought, never asking questions but at once sets about its fulfillment. You become interested and ask how this can be; in return you are asked this question: "How did anything come into being?" This sets you to thinking and of course you realize that there was a time when nothing existed but life; so whatever has come into being must have come from that life, for what we see must come from that which we do not see. You have to admit that. Then what you do not see must be the Cause of everything; and you must also admit that; and that Cause works by Law; this you are compelled to admit. Then this Law, being everywhere, must be in you; this is harder for you to see; but after much thought you begin to realize that it is so. Then you, without knowing where your thought processes were leading you, have conceded that you, yourself, are the reason for what happens in your life, be it success or failure.

God couldn't make you any other way and at the same time make you a self-choosing individual. This is plain.

Now what are you going to do about it? This is what you must do. For every time that you have thought failure you are going to replace it with strong radiant thoughts of success. You are going to speak activity into your business. You are going daily to see nothing but activity and to know that it is Law that you are using, Universal Law, and as such your thought is as sure as the thought of God.

Daily you are going to give to the Great Creative Mind exactly what you want to happen. You will see only what you desire and in the silence of your soul you will speak and it will be done unto you. You will come to believe that a great Divine Love flows through you and your affairs. You will be grateful for this Love.

It fills your life. It satisfies your soul. You are a different man. You are so filled with activity and courage that when you meet people they will wonder at your energy. They will begin to wish simply to come in contact with you. They will feel uplifted.

In the course of a few months you will be a success. People will come to you and say: "How do you do it?" The answer will be the same that was given to you a few months ago.

Let the man who is speaking to the public do the same thing. Let him daily see throngs of people coming to hear him. Let him see nothing else. He will experience what he feels, and sees.

Always remember this. Life is from within outward, and never from without inward. You are the center of power in your own life.

Be sure and not take on false suggestion. The world is full of calamity howlers; turn from them, every one, no matter how great you think they may be; you haven't the time to waste over anything that is negative. You are a success, and you are giving to the Law, every day, just what you want done. And the Law is always working for you. All fear has gone and you know that there is but One Power in all the Universe. Happy is the man who knows this, the greatest of all Truths.

The whole thing resolves itself into our mental ability to control our thought. The man who can do this, can have what he wants, can do what he wishes, and becomes what he wills. Life, God, the Universe, is his.

MONEY A SPIRITUAL IDEA.

Many people seem to think that money must be evil, although I have never as yet seen any who did not want a lot of this evil in their lives.

If all is an expression of life, then money is an expression of life, and as such, must be good. Without a certain amount of it in this life, we would have a hard time. But how to get it; that is the race problem. How shall we acquire wealth? Money didn't make itself, and not being self-creative it must be an effect. Behind it must be the Cause that projects it. That cause is never seen; no cause is ever seen. Consciousness is cause and people who have a money consciousness have the outward expression of it. People who have it as a sure reality in their mind, have it as an expression in their pocket. People who don't have this mental likeness don't have money in their pockets.

What we need to do is to acquire a money consciousness. This may seem very material, but the true idea of money is not material—it is spiritual. We need to make our unity with it. We can never do this while we hold it away from us by thinking that we haven't it. Let us change the method and begin to make our unity with supply by daily declaring that all the Power in the Universe is daily bringing to us all that we can use. Feel the presence of supply. Know that it is yours now.

Make yourself feel that you now have, and to you shall be given. Work with yourself until there is nothing in you that doubts. Money can not be kept away from the man who understands that all is Mind, and that Divine Law governs his life.

Daily give thanks for perfect supply. Feel it to be yours, that you have entered into the full possession of it now.

Refuse to talk poverty or limitation. Stick to it that you are rich. Get the million dollar consciousness. There is no other way, and this will react into everything that you do.

See money coming to you from every source and from every direction. Know that everything is working for your good.

Realize in your life the presence of an Omnipotent Power. Speak forth into It, and feel that It responds to your approach.

Whenever you see anything or anybody whom you think has more than you, at once affirm that you have the same thing. This doesn't mean that you have what is his, but that you have as much. It means that all you need is yours.

Whenever you think about anything big, at once say, "That means me." In this way you learn to unify yourself, in the Law, with large concepts, and according to the way that Law works, it will tend to produce that thing for you.

Never let yourself doubt for even a minute. Always be positive about yourself. Keep watch over the inner workings of your thought, and the Law will do the rest.

ACTION.

The Universe is teeming with activity. There is motion everywhere. Nothing ever stands still. All activity comes from mind. If we want to be in line with things we must move. This doesn't mean that we must strain or struggle, but we must be willing to do our part by letting the Law work through us.

God can do for us only as we will allow Him to do through us. Intelligence gives us ideas and in our turn we work on them. But our work is no longer done in any sense of doubt or fear, for we know that we are dealing with something that never makes a mistake. We proceed with a calm confidence born of the inner trust in a Power that is Infinite. Behind all of our movements, then, is a great purpose, to let the Law work through us.

The Law of Activity must be complied with; we must be willing to take the way of outer activity. Jesus went to the tomb of Lazarus. We may have to go but there will accompany us something that never fails.

This law of activity we must use in our business. So many business places that we go into have such an atmosphere of inactivity, produce such a drowsy feeling, that we at once lose all interest in what is going on. We don't feel like buying. We leave that place without any apparent reason and go into another. Here we feel that all is life, all is motion, all is activity. We feel confident that this is the place we are looking for. We will buy here; we find just what we want; we are satisfied with our purchase and go away cheerful.

Now to create this activity something more than thought is essential. Not that it does not come first, but the one who has this thought of activity will naturally manifest it in vigorous, energetic movement which helps to produce a spirit of activity in his business and in everything he undertakes. Wherever you see a man who does not move, then you will find one whose thought is inactive; the two always go together.

A man in a store or place of business should always be moving his goods. He should always be doing something. People will see this and getting the thought of activity behind it will want to trade there. We are not attracted to a store that always has the same things on the same shelf. The world likes action, change. Action is Life.

Let a clerk in a store think activity and begin to manifest it, even though he may not be waiting on customers, and in a short time he will be waiting on them. Alertness is the word. Always be alert. There must be mental alertness before there can be physical activity.

Act as though things were happening even though they may not appear to be. Keep things moving and soon you will have to avoid the rush. Activity is genius. Half the stores that you go into make you sleepy before you get out, and you feel as though you can't get out fast enough. The other half are alive and those are the ones who are doing the business of the world.

The man who is active in his thought doesn't have to sit by himself to think; he works while he thinks and so complies with the Law which has to work through him. The thought of activity makes him move, and the thought of confidence makes his movements sure, and the thought of Supreme Guidance makes his work intelligent.

We must be careful and not get into ruts; always be doing something new and different, and you will find life becomes a great game in which you are taking the leading part.

Life will never become tiresome to the active mind and body. It is so interesting that we wonder if we will ever get enough of it. Some people get into such lazy mental habits that a new idea cannot find entrance. Great things are done by people who think great thoughts and then go out into the world to make their dreams come true.

If you can't find anything new to do, go home and change the bed around, or the piano; put the cook stove in the parlor and eat on the back step for a time. It will start something moving and changing in you that will never stop. The wide awake person can find so many things to do that he hasn't time even to begin in this life and he knows that Eternity is necessary to carry out the ideals that he already has evolved.

Everything comes from Mind, but Mind acts on itself and we must act on ourselves and on conditions; not as a slave but as a master. Be interested in life, if you want life to be interested in you. Act in Life and Life will act through you. So will you also become one of the great people on earth.

IDEAS OF THE INFINITE.

Suppose that we wish to draw from the Universal Mind some definite idea, some guidance, some information, some leading. How are we going to do this? First we must become convinced that we can do it.

Where do all the inventions come from? Where does Edison get his information about electricity? Where, if not direct from the Mind of the Universe? Everything that has ever come into the race comes direct from Mind. There is nothing else it could come from.

Every invention is but a discovery of something that already is, although we may not have seen it. Where does the harmony of music come from? Where could it originate except in Mind? Does not a great musician listen and hear something that we do not hear? His ear is attuned to Harmony and he catches it straight from Life itself and interprets it to the world. We are surrounded by the music of the spheres but few of us ever catch the sound.

We are so filled with trouble that the Divine Melody is never heard. If we could see, if we could hear, if we could understand, if we only realized the presence of the All, what could we not do?

When a great thought springs up in the mind of an individual, when a great poem is written, when a great work of art is wrought by some receptive artist, it is simply a sign that the veil is thin between; he has caught a glimpse of reality.

But for most of us Inspiration is not to be depended on, and we must take the slower but none the less sure method of receiving straight from the Infinite. The method is a simple one and very effective. When you want to know a certain thing, or how to begin a certain line of action:

First, you must be quiet within yourself. You must not be confused by any outward appearance. Never become disturbed by effects. They didn't make themselves and have no intelligence to contradict you.

Be quiet until you realize the presence of absolute Intelligence all around you, of the Mind that knows. Now get a perfect picture of just what you desire. You cannot get a picture unless you know what it is you want. Put your mind in touch with Universal Mind, saying just what you are waiting for. Ask for it, believe that you are receiving it, and wait. After a few minutes declare that you now know, even though you may not seem to know, yet in the depths of consciousness you have received the impression. Give thanks that you now receive. Do this every day until you get some direction. It is sometimes a good thing to do this just before going to sleep.

Never, after you have done this, deny the knowledge that has been given you. The time will come when some idea will begin to take form. Wait for it and, when it does appear, act upon it with all the conviction of one who is perfectly sure of himself.

You have gotten understanding straight from the source of all understanding, knowledge from the source of knowledge. All can do this if they will be persistent. It is a sure direction and guidance and will never fail us. But we must be sure that we are not denying in other moments what we affirm in the moments of Faith. In this way we will make fewer mistakes and in time our lives will be controlled by supreme wisdom and understanding.

DON'T BE A LEANER.

Never lean on other people. You have strength of your own that is great enough to do all that is necessary. The Almighty has implanted genius within the soul of everyone and what we need to do is to unearth that inner genius and cause it to shine forth. We will never do this while we look to others for guidance. "To thine own self repair, wait thou within the silence dim, and thou shalt find Him there."

All the power and intelligence of the Universe is already within, waiting to be utilized. The Divine Spark must be fanned into a blaze of the living Fire of your own divinity.

Self-reliance is the word to dwell on. Listen to your own voice; it will speak in terms that are unmistakable. Trust in your own self more than in all else. All great men have learned to do this. Every person, within his own soul, is in direct communication with the Infinite Understanding. When we depend on other people we are simply taking their light and trying to light our path with it. When we depend on ourselves we are depending on that inner voice that is God, speaking in and through man. "Man is the inlet and the outlet to all there is in God." God has made us and brought us up to where we recognize our own individuality; from now on we will have to let Him express through us. If it were different we should not be individuals. "Behold I stand at the door and wait." This is a statement of the near presence of power; but we, the Individual, must open the door. This door is our thought and we are the guardian of it, and when we do open the door we will find that the Divine Presence is right at hand, waiting, ready and willing to do for us all that we can believe.

We are strong with the strength of the Infinite. We are not weak. We are great and not mean. We are One with the Infinite Mind.

When you have a real thing to do, keep it to yourself. Don't talk about it. Just know in your own mind what it is that you want and keep still about it. Often when we think that we will do some big thing we begin to talk about it and the first thing we know all the power seems to be gone.

This is what happens. We are all sending out into Mind a constant stream of thought; the clearer it is, the better will it manifest; if it becomes doubtful it will not have so clear a manifestation. If it is confused it will manifest only confusion. All this is according to the Law of Cause and Effect, and we cannot change that Law. Too often, when we tell our friends what we are going to do, they confuse our thought by laughing about it, or by doubting our capacity to do so large a thing. Of course this would not happen if we were always positive, but when we become the least bit negative it will react and we will lose that power of clearness which is absolutely necessary to good creative work.

When you want to do a big thing, get the mental pattern, make it perfect, know just what it means, enlarge your thought, keep it to yourself, pass it over to the creative power behind all things, wait and listen, and when the impression comes, follow it with assurance. Don't talk to anyone about it. Never listen to negative talk or pay any attention to it and you will succeed where all others fail.

CAUSES AND CONDITIONS.

When we realize that life is not fundamentally physical, but mental and spiritual, it will not be hard for us to see that by a certain mental and spiritual process we can demonstrate what we want.

We are not dealing with conditions but with causes. Causes originate only from the unseen side of life. This is not strange as the same might be said of electricity, or even of life itself. We do not see life, we only see what it does. This we call a condition. Of itself it is simply an effect. We are living in the outer world of effects and in the inner world of causes. These causes we set in motion by our thought, and, through the power inherent within the cause, expresses the thought as a condition. It follows that the cause must be equal to the effect and that the effect always evaluates with the cause held in mind. Everything comes from One Substance, and our thought qualifies that Substance and determines what is to take place in our life.

The whole teaching of the Bhagavad Gita is that there is but One and that it becomes to us just what we first believe into it. In other words we manifest the unmanifested. This in no way takes away from the omnipotence of God, but adds to it, for He has created something that is able to do this. God still rules in the Universe, but we are given the power to rule in our lives.

We must realize, then, absolutely that we are dealing with a Substance that we have a right to deal with, and by learning its laws we will be able to subject them to our use, just as Edison does with electricity. Law is but we must use it.

The substance that we deal with, in itself, is never limited, but we often are, because we draw only what we believe.

Because we are limited is no reason why the Universe should have limitation. Our limitation is only our unbelief; life can give us a big thing or a little thing. When it gives us a little thing, it is not limited, any more than life is limited when it makes a grain of sand, because it could just as well have made a planet. But in the great scheme of things all kinds of forms, small and large, are necessary, which, combined, make a complete whole. The power and substance behind everything remain Infinite.

Now this life can become to us only through us, and that becoming is the passing of Spirit into expression in our lives through the form of the thought that we give to it. In itself life is never limited; an ant has just as much life as an elephant though smaller in size. The question is not one of size but one of consciousness.

We are not limited by actual boundaries, but by false ideas about life and by a failure to recognize that we are dealing with the Infinite.

Limitation is an experience of the race, but it is not the fault of God, it is the fault of man's perception. And to prove that this is so, let any man break the bonds of this false sense of life and he at once begins to express less and less limitation. It is a matter of the growth of the inner idea.

People often say when they are told this, "Do you think that I decided to be poor and miserable; do you take me for a fool?" No, you are not a fool, but it is quite possible that you have been fooled, and most of us have been. I know of no one who has escaped being fooled about life; you may not have had thoughts of poverty but at the same time you may have had thoughts that have produced it. Just watch the process of your thinking and see how many times a day you think something that you would not want to happen. This will satisfy you that you need to be watchful, that your thought needs to be controlled.

What we need to do is to reverse the process of our thinking and see to it that we think only positive, constructive thoughts. A calm determination to think just what we want to think regardless of conditions will do much to put us on the highway to a greater realization of life.

Of course we will fall, of course the road is not easy, but we will be growing. Daily we will be giving to the Creative Mind a newer and a greater concept to be worked out into the life around us. Daily we will be overcoming some negative tendency. We must stick to it until we gain the mastery of all our thought and in that day we will rise never to fall again.

We must be good-natured with ourselves, never becoming discouraged or giving up until we overcome. Feel that you are always backed by an Omnipotent power and a kind Father of Love and the way will become easier.

MENTAL EQUIVALENTS.

One of the most necessary things to remember is that we cannot demonstrate life beyond our mental ability to embody. We give birth to an idea only from within ourselves. What we are, we put into our thinking. What we are not, we cannot put into it.

If we are to draw from Life what we want, we must first think it forth into Life. It always produces what we think. In order to have success, we must first conceive it in our own thought. This is not because we are creators, but because the flow of Life into manifestation, through us, must take the form we give to it, and if we want a thing we must have within ourselves the mental equivalent before we get it.

This is what Jesus meant when he said that we must believe when we pray. This belief is providing within us that something which knows before it sees what it asks for.

For instance, suppose a man is praying for activity (our idea of prayer is the accepting of a thing before we get it) in his affairs. First, before this activity can come, he must have it within himself; he must come to see activity in everything; there must be something that corresponds to the thing that he wants; he must have a mental equivalent.

We find that we attract to ourselves as much of anything as we embody within. As water will reach only its own level, so our outward conditions will re-produce only our inner realizations.

A man will always draw to him just what he is. But we can learn to provide within the image of what we desire and so in a definite way use the law to get just what we need. If at first we do not have a great realization of activity we will have to work on what we do have, and as our outer conditions come up to meet the inner cause, we will find that it will be much easier to enlarge the inner receptivity for something greater and more worth while. Of one thing we may be assured—we must all start somewhere, and that somewhere is within ourselves. In this within we must make the affirmation, and there, too, we must do the real work of realization. At the first the way may seem hard, for we are constantly confronted with that which seems to be, and we are not always sure of ourselves nor strong enough to overcome, but we may rest content in the assurance that we are growing. Every day we will be providing a bigger concept of life, and with the inner growth we will have an enlarged power to speak forth into the Creative Mind, with the result that we shall get a fresh impulse and be doing a bigger thing for ourselves. Growth and realization are always from within and never from without.

The old race suggestion of fear and poverty and limitation must be done away with and daily we must clear our thought from all that limits the One from showing forth in our life.

Remember that you are dealing with One power, and not with two. This will make it easier, for you do not have to overcome any condition, because conditions flow from within out, and not from without in.

A man going to a new town will at once begin to attract to him just what he brings in his thought. He should be very careful what he thinks. He should know just what he wants and daily give it over to the Supreme Mind, knowing that It will work for him. Old thoughts must be destroyed, and new must take their places. Every time the old thought comes look it squarely in the face and declare that it has no part in your mind. It has no power over you. You state the law and rely on it to the exclusion of all else. Daily try to see more and to understand more, feel every day that you are being especially looked after. There is no special creation for any individual, but we all specialize the law every time we think into it. For all our thought is taken up and something is always done with it.

A good practice is to sit and realize that you are a center of Divine attraction, that all things are coming to you, that the power within is going out and drawing back all that you will ever need. Don't argue about it, just do it, and when you have finished leave it all to the Law, knowing that it will be done. Declare that all life, all love and power are now in your life. Declare that you are now in the midst of plenty. Stick to it even though you may not as yet see the result. It will work and those who believe the most always get the most. Think of the Law as your friend. always looking out for your interest. Trust completely in it and it will bring your good to you.

ONE LAW AND MANY MANIFESTATIONS.

People often ask if the Law will not bring harm as well as good. This question would never be asked if people understood what Universal Law really means. Of course it will bring us what we think. All law will do the same thing. The law of electricity will either light our house or burn it down. We decide what we are to do with the Law. Law is always impersonal. There is no likelihood of using the Law for harmful purposes if we always use it for the more complete expression of life.

We must not use it for any purpose that we would not like to experience ourselves. This should answer all questions of that nature. Do I really want the thing I ask for? Am I willing to take for myself what I ask for other people? How can we use the Law for evil if we desire only the good? We cannot and we should not bother about it. We want only the good for ourselves and for the whole world; when we have started causation, at once the Law will set to work carrying out our plans. Never distrust the Law and become afraid lest you misuse it. That is a great mistake, all Law is impersonal and cares not who uses it. It will bring to all just what is already in their thought. No person can long use it in a destructive way, for it will destroy himself if he persists in doing wrong. We have no responsibility for any one except ourselves. Get over all idea that you must save the world; we have all tried and have all failed. We may, by demonstrating in our own lives, prove that the Law really exists as the great power behind all things. This is all that we can do. Every one must do the same thing for himself. Let the dead bury their dead, and see that you live. In this you are not selfish but are simply proving that law governs your life. All can do the same when they come to believe, and none until they believe.

TRANSCENDING PREVIOUS CONDITIONS.

What if at times we attract something that we do not want? What about all the things that we have already attracted into our lives? Must we still suffer until the last farthing be paid? Are we bound by Karma? Yes, in a certain degree we are bound by what we have done; it is impossible to set law in motion and not have it produce. What we sow we must also reap, of that there is no doubt; but here is something to think about; the Bible also says that if a man repents his "sins are blotted out, and remembered no more forever." Here we have two statements which at first seem not to agree. The first says that we must suffer from what we have done, and the second that under certain conditions we will not have to suffer. What are those conditions? A changed attitude toward the Law. It means that we must stop thinking and acting in the wrong way.

When we do this we are taken out of the old order and established in the new. Someone will say: If that is true what about the law of cause and effect? Is that broken? No, it is this way: The law is not broken, it would still work out if we continued to use it in the wrong way; but when we reverse the cause, that is, think and act in a different way, then we have changed the flow of the Law. It is still the same Law but we have changed its flow, so that, instead of limiting us and punishing us, it frees and blesses. It is still the law but we have changed our attitude toward it. We might throw a ball at the window, and if nothing stopped it, it would break the glass. Here is law in motion. But if someone catches the ball before it reaches the window, the glass will not be broken. Neither the glass nor the law will be broken. The flow of law will be changed, that is all. So can we, no matter what has happened in the past, so transcend the old experience, that it will no longer have any effect upon us. So if we have attracted something that is not best to keep, we will remember that we do not have to keep it. It was the best that we knew at the time, and so was good as far as it went, but now we know more and can do better.

As law works without variation, so does the law of attraction work the same way. All that we have to do is to drop the undesired thing from our thought, forgive ourselves and start anew. We must never even think of it again. Let go of it once and for all. Our various experiences will teach us more and more to try to mold all of our thoughts and desires, so that they will be in line with the fundamental purpose of the Great Mind, the expression of that which is perfect. To fear to make conscious use of the Law would be to paralyze all efforts of progress.

More and more will we come to see that a great cosmic plan is being worked out, and that all we have to do is to lend ourselves to it, in order that we may attain unto a real degree of life. As we do subject our thought to the greater purposes we are correspondingly blest, because we are working more in line with the Father, who from the beginning knew the end. We should never lose sight of the fact that we are each given the individual right to use the law, and that we cannot escape from using it.

Let us, then, go forward with the belief that a greater power is working through us; that all law is a law of good; that we have planted our seed of thought in the Mind of the Absolute; and that we can go our way rejoicing in the Divine privilege of working with the Infinite.

UNDERSTANDING AND MISUNDERSTANDING.

There are many persons who are constantly unhappy because they seem always to be misunderstood. They find it hard to use the law of attraction in an affirmative way, and they keep on drawing to themselves experiences which they would rather have avoided. The trouble with them is that there is always an undercurrent of thought which either neutralizes or destroys whatever helpful thoughts they have set in motion in their moments of greater strength. Such persons are usually very sensitive, and while this is a quality which is most creative when under control, it is most destructive when uncontrolled, because it is most chaotic. They should first come to know the law and see how it works, and then treat themselves to overcome all sensitiveness. They should realize that everyone in the world is a friend, and prove this by never saying anything unkind to any one or about any one. They must within themselves see all people as perfect beings made in the Divine Image; and, seeing nothing else, they will in time be able to say that this is also the way that all people see them. Holding this as the law of their lives they will destroy all negative thought; and then, with that power which is always in a sensitive person, but which is now under control, they will find that life is theirs to do with as they please, the only requirement being that as they sow so must they also reap. We all know that anything that is unlike good is of short duration, but anything that embodies the good is like God, ever present and Eternal. We free ourselves through the same law under which we first bound ourselves.

The ordinary individual unknowingly does something that destroys any possibility of getting good results in the demonstration of prosperity. He affirms his good and makes his unity with it, and this is right, but he does not stop looking at it in others, which is wrong and is the cause of confusion. We cannot affirm a principle and deny it in the same breath. We must become what we want and we will never be able to do that while we still persist in seeing what we do not want, no matter where we see it. We cannot believe that something is possible for us without also believing the same for every individual.

One of the ways of attainment is, of a necessity, the way of universal love: coming to see all as the true sons of God, one with the Infinite Mind. This is no mere sentiment but the clear statement of a fundamental law and that man who does not obey it, is opposing the very thing that brought him into expression. It is true that through mental means alone he may bring to himself things and he may hold them as long as the will lasts. This is the ordinary way, but we want more than compelling things to appear. What we want is that things should gravitate to us because we are employing the same law that God uses. When we so attain this attitude of mind then that which is brought into manifestation will never be lost, for it will be as eternal as the law of God and cannot be destroyed forever. It is a comfort to know that we do not have to make things happen, but that the law of Divine love is all that we will ever need; it will relieve the overworked brain and the fagged muscle just to be still and know that we are One with the ALL in ALL.

How can we enter in, if at one and the same time we are believing for ourselves and beholding the beam in our brother's eye? Does that not obstruct the view and pervert our own natures? We must see only the good and let nothing else enter into our minds. Universal love to all people and to all things is but returning love to the source of all love, to Him who creates all in love and holds all in divine care. The sun shines on all alike. Shall we separate and divide where God has so carefully united? We are dividing our own things when we do this, and sooner or later the Law of Absolute Justice that weighs out to each one his just measure will balance the account, and then we shall be obliged to suffer for the mistakes we have made. God does not bring this agony on us but we have imposed it on ourselves. If from selfish motives alone, we must love all things and look upon all things as good, made from the substance of the Father.

We can only hope to bring to ourselves that which we draw through the avenue of love. We must watch our thinking and if we have aught against any soul, get rid of it as soon as possible. This is the only safe and sure way. Did not Jesus at the supreme moment of sacrifice ask that the Father forgive all the wrong that was being clone to Him? Shall we suppose that 'we can do it in a better way? If we do not at the present time love all people, then we must learn how to do it, and the way will become easier, when all condemnation is gone forever and we behold only good. God is good and God is Love; more than this we cannot ask nor conceive.

Another thing that we must eliminate is talking about limitation; we must not even think of it or read about it, or have any connection with it in any of our thinking, for we get only that which we think, no more and no less. This will be a hard thing to do. But if we remember that we are working out the science of being, though it may seem long and hard at times we sooner or later do it, and once done it is done forever. Every step in advance is an Eternal step, and will never have to be taken again. We are not building for a day or a year, but we are building for all time and for Eternity. So we will build the more stately mansion under the Supreme wisdom and the unfailing guidance of the Spirit, and we will do unto all, even as we would have them do unto us; there is no other way. The wise will listen, look and learn, then follow what they know to be the only way that is in line with the Divine will and purposes. So shall all see that God is good and in him is no evil.

NO UNUSUAL EXPERIENCE.

In demonstrating the truth of supply we do not have to experience any peculiar emotion or psychic experience. We do not have to feel any thrills or anything of that sort. While it is true that some of these things may come, yet we should remember that what we are doing is dealing with law, and that as law it will obey us, when we comply with its nature and contact it in the right way. What we are doing, is stating something into Mind, and if the impression is clear in our own minds that it is and that it is done we have put all the activity we can put into it, until such a time as something happens in the external for us to work upon. So many people say, "I do wish that I could feel something, when I give a treatment." All this is a mistake and is an attempt to give a physical reason for life. What we do need to feel is that, since God is all and is good, he wants us to have only the good; and feeling this we should take what is already made for us. Our attitude towards such a good Father should constantly be one of thanksgiving. When we begin to prove the power of the truth we will always maintain this attitude. Know that you are dealing with a sure thing and that all you have to do is to know positively into it and wait for the results to come in the outer. Then do what your own good sense tells you to do, for this is the thought of God through you. More and more you will find that you are being led out of difficulty into that freedom which is the Divine birthright of every living soul. Go ahead, then, looking only at the things desired and never at the things not wanted. Victory will always be on the side that the majority of your thoughts rest on in absolute acceptance.

VISUALIZING.

Some people visualize everything that they think of and many think that it is impossible to make a demonstration unless they possess the power to visualize. This is not the case. While a certain amount of vision is necessary, on the other hand it must be remembered that we are dealing with a power that is like the soil of the ground, which will produce the plant when we plant seed. It does not matter if we have never before seen a plant like the one that is to be made for us. Our thought is the seed and mind is the soil. We are always planting and harvesting. All that we need to do is to plant only that which we want to harvest. This is not difficult to understand. We cannot think poverty and at the same time demonstrate plenty. If a person wants to visualize let him do so, and if he sees himself in full possession of his desire and knows that he is receiving, he will make his demonstration. If, on the other hand, he does not visualize, then let him simply state what he wants and absolutely believe that he has it and the result will always be the same.

Remember that you are always dealing with law and that this is the only way that anything could come into existence. Don't argue over it. That means that you have not as yet become convinced of the truth or you would not argue. Be convinced and rest in peace.

WHERE DEMONSTRATION TAKES PLACE.

Does demonstration take place in the patient, the practitioner or in the mind of God? Let us see; We are in the mind of God and so it must take place there. But the patient is also in the mind of God or there would be two minds, and so it must take place in the mind of the patient, also. But that is the mind of God, so what does it matter where it takes place? We do not have to project our thought, because Mind is right at hand and never leaves us at any time. All that we have to do is to know within ourselves, and, when we are absolutely convinced, we will have made the demonstration.

As far as the practitioner is concerned, all that he has to do is to convince himself. Here his work begins and ends. There is a power that will look after the rest. Is this not the supreme attitude of faith in higher power? Of course it is, and the more of that faith that we have, the easier it will be for us and the quicker we will receive an answer to our prayer. If you have a simple, childlike faith it will produce; but it should give us a greater faith when we know something of the way that the law operates. It follows, then, that we should, by understanding, have so great a faith that we shall never fail to get the affirmative answer to all of our thoughts. Each victory will strengthen us until the time will come when we will no longer have to say I hope or believe, but I know.

TREATMENTS.

The way to give a treatment is first of all to absolutely believe that you can; believe that your word goes forth into a real creative power, which at once takes it up, and begins to operate upon it; feel that to this power all things are possible. It knows nothing but its own power to do that which it wishes to do. It receives the impress of your thought and acts upon it.

It is never safe to treat for anything that you do not wish to happen. This means that what you would want for another, you must first be willing to receive for yourself.

Believe then that your word is to be acted upon by an Almighty Power; feel its great reality, in and through all things you speak into it; and declare just what you wish it to do for you, never doubting in your own mind but that it will do just as you have directed.

All that a practitioner has to do is to convince himself, to know, to believe, and that thing will happen to him which he states. One of the first things, then, is to be definite; to have a mental likeness of the thing that you desire; to know exactly what you want. This mental likeness, this absolute acceptance of the fact that it now is, must never be overlooked; without it you will not accomplish.

We sit down of our own souls, at peace with the world, at peace with ourselves; we realize that we are dealing with something that is a reality, something that cannot fail. We try to get a clear concept of the thing; we rest in that realization, while the Universal Creative Power takes it up and acts upon it.

We have stated just what we wanted done unto us; we have believed; we have believed that we have received; never again will we contradict the fact that we have stated. The person who can do this is sure of getting results.

UNDERSTANDING AND GUIDANCE.

The inner man is always in immediate connection with the Infinite of understanding. We are immersed in a living intelligence; we are surrounded by a Power that knows, for "In Him we live and move and have our being."

If our outer thought were never confused, we should at all times draw from this Infinite source of knowledge; we should be guided by It and never make mistakes; our minds would be like the smooth surface of a lake, unruffled by wind and storm.

But with most of us this is not the case; we become confused in the outer so that the surface of the mind is in turmoil, no longer clear and transparent, and we cannot get the clear vision, the real guidance, and we get things wrong because we do not see clearly.

The development of the understanding is learning to draw from the Infinite understanding; we can never do this while we are confused in our thinking.

The first thing to do when we wish a greater understanding is to be still and listen to the inner voice, to withdraw for a few moments into the silence of the soul taking here what we already know, and realizing that a greater intelligence is enlarging it.

Here we indefinitely take the pattern of our thought, the thing that we are working on, and ask for, and receive, new light; we hold this up in Divine Light and try to believe that we are being guided; we state that Supreme Intelligence and Absolute Power are acting upon our thought and bringing it to pass; it is now guiding us and we shall make no mistake; we hold ourselves in the Secret Place of the Most High, and abide under the shadow of the Almighty.

HOW TO KNOW JUST WHAT TO DO.

Often we find ourselves confronted by the problem of how to begin. We are not sure what we want to do; we see no way to begin anything; see nothing to begin on; when we find ourselves in this position, humanly speaking, not knowing where to turn, then of all times we must be quiet and listen; then of all times we must trust that the same power that started all things will also start us in the right road, for without some superior power we shall surely fail.

How often do people in the business world find themselves in this position. They realize that something must be done, but what? How get the idea to work out?

Here we must wait and know that the same power that first thought a universe into being can also think our world and work into being. It knows all things; it knows how to begin and it cannot fail; we wish in some way to connect with this power that will never fail us, so that we may draw from it some idea to begin with.

We must realize that there is something that wants to respond, to make manifest and in this realization wait for the idea; it may not come at first, but we must be patient, never doubting, and waiting thus in faith, it will come.

I once knew a business man who was connected with a firm that had always been very successful, but at that time something had occurred that was causing them to lose out. This had gone on for a year and things were going from bad to worse. Failure seemed inevitable. He became interested in New Thought. He was told he could draw an idea from the Infinite and work it out on the plane of the visible. He told his partners that he wished to go home for a few days and that when he came back he would have worked out an idea which would put the business on a successful basis. They laughed at him, as people generally laugh at something they do not understand, but having no other plan they gave their consent. He went home and for three days sat in deep thought, claiming Supreme guidance and absolute leading of the Spirit. During this time a complete plan formulated in his mind as to the exact method to pursue in the business. He returned and told his plan to his partners. Again they laughed, saying it could not be done in business; could not be done any way; it would not work. But again they consented, knowing it was this or failure.

He then went to work carrying out all the details of his thought, following each leading that had come to him during those three days, and within a year he brought the failing business to a standard that transcended anything they had ever before experienced, He proved the law and became such an expert, that he gave up his business and devoted his entire time to helping other people do the same for themselves as he had done.

What this man did any one can do if he will follow the same course and refuse to become discouraged. There is a power that simply awaits our recognition of it, to spring into our thought as an unfailing leading, an unerring guidance. To those who lean on the ever outstretched arm of the Infinite, life is big with limitless possibilities.

We must wait and listen, then go about our outer business with an inner conviction that we are being led into a more perfect expression of life. All can do this.

FOLLOWING UP A THOUGHT.

When we feel that we do have the right leading; when that something inside us tells us that we are led; then, no matter what it appears like, we must follow it up. Something beyond our intelligence is doing the thing through us and we must do nothing to contradict it.

Perhaps it will cause us to do something that seems to go contrary to the experience of the race. This makes no difference. All advance in invention and all advance along any line has always gone ahead of what the experience of the race thinks is possible.

Great men are the ones who get a vision and then go to work to make it come true, never looking to one side but with one-pointedness and calm determination, stick to the thing until it is accomplished.

It may take much patience and a great deal of faith, but the end is as sure as is the reality of a Supreme Being itself.

Never hesitate to trust in that inner leading, never fear but it will be right. We are all in the midst of Supreme Intelligence; It presses against the doors of our thought, waiting to be known. We must be open to It at all times, ready to receive direction and to be guided into greater truths.

THE SINGLE STREAM OF THOUGHT.

Ate are all in Mind and what we think into it is taken up and done unto us.. This means that as we think it will be done. We cannot think one way one day and change our thought the next and hope to get the desired results. We must be very clear in our thought, sending out only such thoughts as we wish to see manifested in our condition.

Here is something worth remembering. Unless we are working with people who think as we do, we had better be working alone. One stream of thought, even though it may not be very powerful, will do more for us than many powerful streams that are at variance with each other. This means that, unless we are sure that we are working with people who harmonize, we would better work alone. Of course we cannot retire from business simply because people do not agree with us, but what we can do is to keep our thoughts to ourselves. We do not have to leave the world in order to control our thought; but we do have to learn that we can stay right in the world and still think just what we want to think, regardless of what others are thinking.

One single stream of thought, daily sent out into Creative Mind, will do wonders. Within a year the person who will practice this will have completely changed his conditions of life.

The way to practice this is daily to spend some time in thinking and in mentally seeing just what is wanted; see the thing just as it is wished and then affirm that this is now done. Try to feel that what has been stated is the truth.

Words and affirmations simply give shape to thought; they are not creative. Feeling is creative and the more feeling that is put into the word the greater power it will have over conditions. In doing this we think of the condition only as an effect, something that follows what we think. It cannot help following our thought. This is the way that all creation comes into expression.

It is a great help to realize mentally that at all times a great stream of thought and power is operating through us; it is constantly going out into Mind, where it is taken up and acted upon. Our business is to keep that stream of thought just where we want it to be: to be ready at any time to act when the impulse comes for action. Our action must never be negative, it must always be affirmative, for we are dealing with something that cannot fail. We may fail to realize, but the power in itself is Infinite and cannot fail.

We are setting in motion in the Absolute a stream of thought that will never cease until it accomplishes its purpose. Try to feel this, be filled with a great joy as you feel that it is given to you to use this great and only power.

Keep the thought clear and never worry about the way that things seem to be going. Let go of all outer conditions when working in Mind, for there is where things are made; there creation is going on, and it is now making something for us. This must be believed as never believed before; it must be known as the great reality; it must be felt as the only Presence. There is no other way to obtain.

Though all the Infinite may want to give, yet we must take, and, as far as we are concerned, that taking is mental. Though people may laugh at this, even that does not matter, "He laughs best who laughs last." We know in "What we believe," and that will be sufficient.

ENLARGING OUR THOUGHT.

We can never stand still in our thought. Either we will be growing or else we will be going back. As we can attract to ourselves only what we first have a mental likeness of, it follows that if we wish to attract larger things we must provide larger thoughts. This enlarging of consciousness is so necessary that too much cannot be said about it.

Most people get only a short way and then stop: they cannot seem to get beyond a certain point; they can do so much and no more. Why is it that a person in business does just about so much each year? We see people in all walks of life, getting so far, never going beyond a certain point. There must be a reason for everything; nothing happens, if all is governed by law, and we can come to no other conclusion.

When we look into the mental reason for things we find out why things happen. The man who gets so far and never seems to go beyond that point is still governed by law; when he allows his thoughts to take him out into larger fields of action, his conditions come up to his thought; when he stops enlarging his thought he stops growing. If he would still keep on in thought, realizing more and still more, he would find that in the outer form of things he would be doing greater things.

There are many reasons why a man stops thinking larger things. One of them is a lack of imagination. He cannot conceive of anything more to follow than that which has already happened. Another thought works like this: "This is as far as any one can go in my business." Right here he signs his own death warrant. Often a person will say, "I am too old to do bigger things." There he stops. Some one else will say, "Competition is too great"; and here is where this man stops; he can go no further than his thought will carry him.

All this is unnecessary when we realize that life is first of all Consciousness, and then conditions follow. We see no reason why a man should not go on and on, and never stop growing. No matter what age or what circumstance, if life is thought, we can keep on thinking bigger things. There is no reason why a man who is already doing well should not be able mentally to conceive of a still better condition. What if we are active? There is always a greater activity possible. We can still see a little beyond what has come before. This is just what we should do, see, even though it be but a little beyond our former thought. If we always practice this, we will find that every year we shall be growing, every month we shall be advancing; and as time goes on we shall become really great. As there is no stopping in that power which is Infinite, as the Limitless is without bounds, so should we keep on trying to see more and greater possibilities in life.

We should definitely work every day for the expansion of thought. If we have fifty customers a day we should endeavor to believe that we have sixty.

When we have sixty we should mentally see seventy. This should never stop; there is no stopping place in mind.

Let go of everything else, drop everything else from your thought, and mentally see more coming to you than has ever come before; believe that Mind is establishing this unto you, and then go about your business in the regular way. Never see the limitation; never dwell upon it, and above all things else never talk limitation to any one; this is the only way, and there is no other way to grow a larger thought. The man with the big thought is always the man who does big things in life. Get hold of the biggest thing that you can think of and claim it for your own; mentally see it and hold it as a thing already done, and you will prove to yourself that life is without bounds.

ALWAYS BE GATHERING.

There is no reason why a person should ever stop.

This does not mean that we should be miserly, trying to accumulate more and more to hold, but that our thought should so enlarge that it can not help gathering more and more, even though, on the other hand, or with the other hand, we are ever distributing that which we gather. Indeed, the only reason for having is that we may give out of that which we have.

No matter what big thing happens to us we should still be expecting more and more. Even when we think that we have at last arrived; right at the moment when it seems as though life had given us all that we could stand; right here let it be but a beginning for still greater things.

No matter how large the picture that you hold in mind, make it larger. The reason why so many people come to the point where they stop is that they come to a point where they stop growing in their own minds. They come to a point where they can see no more, thinking that because they have really done a big thing they should stop there. We must watch our thought for signs of inactivity. Nothing in the universe ever stops. Everything is built on a boundless basis, drawn from a limitless source, come forth from an Infinite sea of unmanifest life We speak forth into this life and draw back from it all that we first think into it. Life is always limitless, and the only thing that limits us is our inability to conceive mentally, and we should draw more and more from that limitless source.

MENTAL LIKENESS.

We can draw from the Infinite only as much as we first think into it. It is at this point that so many fail, thinking that all they need to do is to affirm what they want and it will follow. While it is true that affirmations have real power, it is also true that they have only that which we speak into them.

As we cannot speak a word that we do not know, so we cannot make an affirmation that we do not understand. We really affirm only that which we know to be true; we know that to be true which we have experienced within ourselves. Although we may have heard or read that this or that thing is true, it is only when there is something within our own souls that corresponds or recognizes its truth, that it is true to us. This ought never to be lost sight of: we can effectively affirm only that which we know, and we know only that which we are. It is herein that we see the necessity of providing within a greater concept of life; a bigger idea of ourselves and a more expanded concept of the Universe in which we live, move and have our being. This is a matter of inner growth together with the enlarging of all lines of thought and activity.

If we want to do a thing that is really worth doing, we must mentally grow until we are that thing, which we want to see made flesh. This may take time, but we should be glad to use all the time necessary to our own development.

But few people in limitation have a mental likeness of plenty. This likeness must be provided. The thought mast be large enough to cover the whole of the thing desired; a small thought will produce only a small thing. The very fact that all is Mind proves this to be true. All is mind and, because it is, we can draw from that mind only that which we first think into it as a reality. We must become the thing we want. We must see it, think it, realize it, before the creative power of Mind can work it out for us. This is an inner process of the expansion of consciousness. It is a thought, growing and realizing within. All can do this who wish and who will take the time and trouble, but it will mean work. The majority of people are too lazy to make the effort.

Daily we must train our thought to see that only which we wish to experience, and since we are growing into what we are mentally dwelling upon, we should put all small and insignificant thoughts and ideals out of our thinking and see things in a larger way. We must cultivate the habit of an enlarged mental horizon, daily seeing farther and farther ahead, and so experiencing larger and greater things in our daily life.

A good practice for the enlargement of thought is daily to see ourselves in a little bigger place, filled with more of activity, surrounded with increased influence and power; feel more and more that things are coming to us; see that much more is just ahead, and so far as possible, know that we now have all that we see and all that we feel. Affirm that you are that larger thing; that you are now entered into that larger life; feel that something within is drawing more to you; live with the idea and let the concept grow, expecting only the biggest and the best to happen. Never let small thoughts come into your mind, and you will soon find that a larger and greater experience has come into your life.

KEEPING THE THING IN MIND.

Never let go of the mental image until it becomes manifested. Daily bring up the clear picture of what is wanted and impress it on the mind as an accomplished fact. This impressing on our own minds the thought of what we wish to realize will cause our own minds to impress the same thought on Universal Mind. In this way we shall be praying without ceasing. We do not have to hold continually the thought of something we want in order to get it, but the thought that we may inwardly become the thing we want. Fifteen minutes, twice each day, is time enough to spend in order to demonstrate anything, but the rest of the time ought also to be spent constructively. That is, we must stop all negative thinking and give over all wrong thought, holding fast to the realization that it is now done unto us. We must know that we are dealing with the only power there is in the Universe; that there is none other beside it, and that we are in it partaking of its nature and its laws. Always, behind the word that we send forth, must be the calm confidence in our ability to speak into the power, and the willingness of Mind to execute for us. We must gradually grow in confidence and in trust in the unseen world of spiritual activity. This is not hard, if we but remember that the Spirit makes things out of Itself by simply becoming the thing that it makes, and since there is no other power to oppose it, it will always work. The Spirit will never fail us if we never fail to believe in its goodness and its responsiveness.

Life will become one grand song, when we realize that since God is for us, none can be against us. We shall cease merely to exist; we shall live.

DESTROY ALL THOUGHTS THAT
WE DO NOT WISH TO EXPERIENCE.

We must resolutely set our faces to the rising consciousness of the Son of Truth; seeing only the One Power we must destroy the adversary and leave the field to God or Good. All that is in any way negative must be wiped off the slate and we must daily come into the higher thought, to be washed clean of the dust and chaos of the objective life. In the silence of the soul's communion with the Great Cause of All Being, into the stillness of the Absolute, into the secret place of the Most High, back of the din and the ceaseless roar of life, we shall find a resting place and a place of real spiritual power. Speak in this inner silence and say, "I am one with the Almighty; I am one with all life, with all power, with all presence. *I am, I am, I am.*" Listen to the silence. From out of the seeming void the voice of peace will answer the waiting soul, "All is well."

Here we make known all our needs and wants, and here we receive first hand from the Infinite all that we shall ever need to make life healthy, happy and harmonious. Few enter here, because of the belief that conditions and circumstances control. Know that there is no law but God's law; that the soul sets its own law in the Infinite and that our slightest wish is honored of the Father Mind.

Daily practice the truth and daily die to all error-thought. Spend more time receiving and realizing the, presence of the Most High and less time worrying. Wonderful power will come to the one who believes and trusts in that Power in which he has come to believe. Know that all good and all God is with you; All Life and All Power; and never again say, "I fear," but always, "I trust, because 'I know in whom I have believed.'"

DIRECT PRACTICE FOR PROSPERITY.

Suppose that you are doing a mail order business and sending out cards to the whole country. Take the cards into your hands, or simply think of them and declare into the only Mind that they will accomplish that for which they are sent out; know that every word written on them is truth and carries its own conviction with it; see them each reaching that place where it will be received with gladness and read with interest; declare this to be so now; feel it to be the truth; mentally assert that each card will find its way to the exact place where it will be wanted and where it will benefit the receiver; feel that each card is cared for by the Spirit; that it is a messenger of truth and power and that it will carry conviction and realization with it. When the word is .spoken always feel that Mind at once takes it up and never fails to act upon it. Our place in the creative order is to know this and to be willing to do all that we can without hurry or worry, and, above all else, to trust absolutely in the Spirit to do the rest. He who sees most clearly and believes most implicitly will make the greatest demonstration. This one should be you, and will be you as soon as the false thought is gone and the realization that there is but the one power and the one presence comes. We are wrapped in an Infinite Love and Intelligence and we should cover ourselves with it and claim its protection from all evil. Declare that your word is the presence and the activity of the Power of all that is and wait for the perfect concept to unfold.

RACE CONSCIOUSNESS.

One of the things which greatly hinders us from demonstrating a greater degree of prosperity we may call race thought or race consciousness. This is the result of all that the race has thought or believed. We are immersed in it, and those who are receptive to it are controlled by it. All thought seeks expression along the lines of least resistance. When we become negative or fearful we attract that kind of thought and condition. We must be sure of ourselves; we must be positive; we must not be aggressive, but absolutely sure and poised within. Negative people are always picking up negative conditions; they get into trouble easily: Persons who are positive draw positive things; they are always successful. Few people realize that the law of thought is the great reality; that thoughts produce things. When we come to understand this power of thought, we will carefully watch our thinking to see that no thought enters that we should not want made into a thing.

We can guard our minds by knowing that no negative thought can enter; we can daily practice by saying that no race thought of limitation can enter the mind; that Spirit forms itself around us and protects us from all fear and from all limitation. Let us clothe ourselves in the great realization that all power is ours and that nothing else can enter; let us fill the atmosphere of our homes, and places of business with streams of positive thought. Other people will feel this and will like to be near us and enter into the things that we enter into. In this way we shall be continually drawing only the best.

DEVELOPING INTUITION.

If a person always lived near to mind he would never make any great mistakes. Some seem to have the faculty of always knowing just what is best to do; they always succeed because they avoid making errors. We can all so train ourselves that we will be guided by the Supreme Mind of the Universe; but we can never do this until we believe that we can receive direct from the source of all knowledge. This is done by sitting in the silence and knowing that the Spirit is inwardly directing us. We should try to feel that our thought is being permeated by the thought of the Spirit. We should expect it to direct but should never become discouraged if at once a direct impression is not received. The work is going on even if it is not seen or even felt. Thought is forming in our mind and in time will come forth as an idea. When the idea does come always trust in it even though it may not seem to be quite as we had expected. The first impressions are usually the most direct and the clearest; they are generally direct from the Mind of the Universe and should be carefully worked out into expression.

We declare as we sit in the silence that the Spirit of all knowledge is making known within us just what we should do; that it is telling us just what to say or where to go. Have absolute reliance on this as it is one of the most important things to do. We should always get that inner assurance before undertaking any new enterprise; being sure that we have really put the whole thing into the hands of life and that all that we have to do is to work it out in the outer. We shall learn to avoid mistakes when we learn to be directed by that inner voice that never makes mistakes. We should declare in the silence that intelligence is guiding us and it will do so.

PRESENCE OF ACTIVITY.

Suppose that your place of business does not seem to manifest any activity; that is, suppose that customers do not come. To the person in the business world the presence of customers generally means activity. Suppose that you have come to believe that the principle will work in the smallest as well as in the greatest things. What you want now is a greater activity. How are you going to see activity when there is none?

Here is a great question in Truth. Must we overlook that which we see, and that which we have experienced? Yes, absolutely; there is no other way. If we keep on seeing the thing as it appears we will never be able to change its appearance. What we must do, then, in spite of the seeming inactivity, is still to know and mentally to see and declare that we are in the midst of activity. Feel this to be true; mentally see the place crowded; know that it is packed full of customers all the time; declare that your word draws them in; have no sense of strain about it whatever; simply know that you are dealing with the only power that there is; it will work; it must work. Realize when you have spoken the word that a greater power has taken it up and that it is being established unto you. Have no idea of limitation; speak forth into mind with perfect trust. If you have the ability mentally to see the place full, combine this with the word, and daily visualize it as being filled. Always combine faith in the higher power with all that you do; feel that you are being especially looked after. This is true. When a soul turns to the Universe of unmanifest life, at the same time It turns toward him. Jesus told this in the story of the Prodigal Son; the Father saw him afar off. Always there is that inward turning to us of the Parent Mind when we turn to It and place ourselves in closer contact with Life.

We must keep our mind clear so that when the Spirit brings the gift we will be open to receive it. Even God cannot force things upon us. We must receive even before we see.

"For the feeble hands and helpless,
Groping blindly in the darkness
Touch God's right hand in that darkness
And are lifted up and strengthened."

[paragraph continues] Always, when we believe, we will have that belief honored of the Spirit of Life. Mentally seeing just what we want; still seeing even though the heavens fall, we shall succeed in proving that the law of life is a law of liberty. God made man to have all that the Universe contained and then left him alone to discover his own nature.

Stop all striving and all struggle and within your own soul know the truth and trust absolutely in it. Daily declare that you are being guided and protected and that the power of the Spirit is bringing all to pass, and wait in perfect peace and confidence. Such an attitude of mind will overcome anything and will prove that spiritual thought force is the only real power in the Universe.

DRAWING YOUR OWN TO YOU.

Suppose that you wish to draw friends and companions to you; that you wish to enlarge your circle of friendships. This, too, can all be worked out by law, for everything can be worked out by the same law, the reason being that all is One and that the One becomes the many in expression. There are too many people in the world who are lonesome because they have a sense of separation from people. The thing to do is not to try to unify with people, but with the Principle of Life behind all people and things. This is working from the center and not the circumference; in this One Mind are the minds of all people. When you unite your thought with the whole you will be united with the parts of the whole. The first thing to do, then, is to realize that Life is your friend and companion; feel the divine companionship; feel that you are one with all life; declare that, as this thought awakens within your mind, so does it awaken within the mind of the whole race; feel that the world is being drawn to you; love the world and everyone who is in it; include all, if you would be included in all. The world seeks strength; be strong. The world loves love; embody it; see the good in all people; let go of all else. People will feel your love and will be drawn into it. Love is the greatest power in the Universe; it is at the base of all else; it is the cause of all that is. Feel your love to be like a great light lighting the pathway of the whole world; it will come back to you bringing so many friends that there will not be time enough to enjoy them all. Become a real friend and you will have many friends.

Be sufficient unto yourself and at the same time include all else, and people will feel your strength and will have a desire to come into the radiance of it. Never become unhappy or morbid; always be cheerful and radiate good nature and happiness; never look depressed or down in the mouth; the world is attracted to the strongest center of cheer and good fellowship. Never allow your feelings to be hurt. No one wants to hurt you, and none could, even though they did want to; you are above all that. Wherever you go know that the Spirit of Truth goes before and prepares the way, bringing to you every friend and influence that will be necessary to your comfort and well being. This is not selfishness but good sense and will surely bring to you a harvest of friends and companions.

Declare unto Mind that you are now linked with all people and that all people are linked with you: see yourself surrounded with hosts of friends; mentally feel their presence and rejoice that all good is yours now. Do this no matter what seems to happen, and it will not be long before you will meet wonderful friends and will be brought into touch with the great of the world.

THE FINAL WORD.

In the last analysis, man is just what he thinks himself to be; he is big in capacity if he thinks big thoughts; he is small if he thinks small thoughts. He will attract to himself what he thinks most about. He can learn to govern his own destiny when he learns to control his thoughts. In order to do this he must first realize that everything in the manifest universe is the result of some inner activity of Mind. This Mind is God, producing a universe by the activity of His own divine thoughts; man is in this Mind as a thinking center, and what he thinks governs his life, even as God's thought governs the Universe, by setting in motion all the cosmic activities. This is so easy to understand, and so plain as to use that we often wonder why we have been so long finding out this, the greatest of all truths of all the ages. Believing; thinking what is believed to be true; thinking into Mind each day that which is wished to be returned; eliminating negative thoughts; holding all positive thoughts; giving thanks to the Spirit of Life that it is so trusting always in the higher law; never arguing with one's self or with others; using; these are the steps which, when followed, will bring us to where we shall not have to ask if it be true, for, having demonstrated, we shall know.

The seed that falls into the ground shall bear fruit of its own kind; and nothing shall hinder it.

"He that hath ears to hear, let him hear."

Creative Mind

TABLE OF CONTENTS

INTRODUCTION.

The hand of eternal progress is brushing the cobwebs from the corridors of time and is again revealing to the human race the mysteries of being. As there is "nothing new under the sun," the searchlight of Truth is bringing to light only what has been known to the few in all generations. The time has now come when the few must become the many. The whole world, from the least to the greatest, must know the Truth, so that man may understand the great laws that govern his life. He must learn to control his own destiny, to heal his own body and bring happiness to his own soul. Ignorance must vanish and understanding must be ushered in. Man is no longer to be governed by anything outside himself. Creeds, doctrines, churches, institutions, organizations, governments are all being changed to give place to the realization of the individual. There is a power in and through all that is working this great transformation. All that will not measure up to the standard must fall by its own weight; all that is in line with the Truth must still prosper. The time is at hand; we are in the greatest age of all history; we are in the age of the unifying of all people and all things into the "Ever Present One." "The temple not made with hands" is now being silently builded by the emancipated souls of this planet.

This little book is an attempt to explain what each soul must discover for himself, that he stands in the midst of an eternal creative power which presses itself around his own thought, and casts back to him glorified all that he thinks. If it awakens within the consciousness of one single individual the realization that the mind of the Universe (which is the only mind that there is) is his own mind; that the creative power of this mind is his also; that the manifestation of this mind is his own individuality; that the love and power and peace of this mind is within himself, it will not be written in vain. May it then do much in simplifying and bringing to light some of the deeper mysteries and meanings of life.

Ernest Shurtleff Holmes
October 1, 1918.

IN THE BEGINNING.

"In the beginning, God!" Clear and expressive are these words. In the beginning, God only. No manifest universe! No system of planets! Nothing of form or life, of brute or man! God was the Spirit of All that was to be, but He had not yet moved upon the waters. Then this All-Being moved, or began to create. Where did Spirit move, upon what did It move to create; where did It get a pattern; what means or power did It employ; through what agencies did It work? In short, what is the world, ourselves included, made out of, and how did we and all else come into being? These questions correctly answered would solve the problem of being and set men free. Let us consider.

The Spirit was all; there was nothing else but Itself. All-Inclusive, Everywhere, Infinite. This All-Spirit could not have had the impulse to move unless It were self-conscious, therefore the Spirit is the Power that knows Itself; It is accordingly All-Knowing as well as All-Present. Being one, undivided, whatever It knows, It knows all over instantly. We find then that the Spirit operates through self knowing. It moves, and that inner movement must be one of Infinite Power, moving upon Itself—since It is all—and with a definite purpose. The Spirit, then, moves upon Itself, and makes out of Itself all that is made. In other words, what we see comes from what we do not see, through some inner intelligence at work, which knows there is no power but Itself. "The things that are seen are not made of the things that do appear." The only possible operation of intelligence is thought, or "The Word." So all things were made by the Word, and "Without the Word was not anything made that hath been made." How simple the process of creation when we understand it. The Spirit speaks—and since there is nothing but the Spirit and it is All-Power, it has only to speak and it is done; "The Word was with God and the Word was God."

From the Word, then, comes forth all that appears. Each life, human or divine, each manifestation is a different kind of word coming into expression. The great fact to dwell upon is that Spirit needs nothing to help It; It is self-conscious and has all power and all ability to do whatever It wishes to accomplish. It operates simply by speaking.

It is hard to get a clear concept of this great Ceaseless Cause, this something from which all things come; at times we get into a maze of confusion when we attempt to realize what the Spirit means. It is then that we should think of It as the great reason behind everything. Being all-knowledge It must know Itself, and must know everything It creates; so It knows us and It knows everyone. Since It is All-Presence we can contact anywhere and will never have to go to some particular spot to find It. As It is All-Knowing and operates through the power of the Word, It know everything we think. Just how It creates we cannot know and need not attempt to understand, for whatever this process of creation is, we find it is always an inner thought process. We should keep this in mind—the Spirit makes all things out of Itself. Everything comes into being without effort, and when we exert ourselves we are not in accord with the Creative Spirit in the way in which It works. The impulse of the Spirit to move must be caused by a desire to express what It feels Itself to be—Beauty, Form, Color, Life, Love and Power. All things else we find in the manifest universe are attributes of the Spirit, and are caused to spring into being through the Word, because the Spirit wants to enjoy Itself.

We find, then, that the Word, which is the inner activity of thought, comes first in the creative series, and all else comes from the effect of the Word operating upon a universal substance. If the Word precedes all else, then the Word is what we are looking for, and when we get it we shall have what the world has sought from time immemorial. We must, if we wish to prove the power of the Spirit in our lives, look not to outside things or effects, but to the Word alone. The human eye sees and the human hand touches only that which is an effect. Unseen law controls everything; but this Law also is an effect; Law did not make itself; the Law is not intelligence or causation. Before there can be a Law there must be something that acts, and the Law is the way it acts; it is intelligence. "In the beginning was the Word." This Word or the activity of the Spirit, is the cause of the law, and the law in its place is the cause of the thing, and the thing is always an effect; that is, it did not make itself; it is a result. The Word always comes first in the creative series; "The Word was with God and the Word was God" and the Word still is God.

When we realize that man is like God (and he could not be otherwise, being made out of God), we will realize that his word also has power. If there is but One Mind then it follows that our word, our thought is the activity of that One Mind in our consciousness; the power that holds the planets in their place is the same power that flows through man. We must place the Word where it belongs, whether it is the word of God in the Universe or the word of man in the individual; it is always first, before all else, in the beginning. The real sequence is this: Cause, Spirit, Intelligence, God; the Word, the activity of Intelligence; the effect, or the visible thing, whether it is a planet or a peanut. All are made out of the same thing.

What we need to do is to learn how to use the word so that all will come to see that they are creative centers within themselves.

A PRINCIPLE THAT CAN BE PROVEN.

Knowing that Mind is, we have a principle that is absolute; it is exact; it is going to correspond to our thinking about it. The first great necessity is to believe this; without belief we can do nothing. This is the reason Jesus said "It is done unto you even as you have believed." Always it is done unto people as they believe, and there is Something that does it which never fails.

We must believe that our word is formed upon and around by this creative Mind; for instance, we wish to create activity in our business; we believe that our word is law about that thing, and there is something that takes our thought and executes it for us. If we have accepted the fact that all is mind and that the thought is the thing, we shall see at once that our word is the power behind the thing, and that it depends upon the word or thought that we are sending out. (See Creative Mind and Success by the author.)

So plastic is mind, so receptive, that the slightest thought makes an impression upon it. People who think many kinds of thought must expect to receive a confused manifestation in their lives. If a gardener plants a thousand kinds of seeds, he will get a thousand kinds of plants; it is the same in mind.

THE WORD GOING FORTH.

Since this is true, everything depends upon our mental concepts. "As a man thinketh in his heart, so is he"; the Bible reiterates this statement telling us many times of the creative power of thought; Jesus taught nothing else; He said "the words which I speak unto you, they are Spirit and they are life."

The Centurion coming to Jesus recognized the power of the word spoken by the latter. He said, "I also am one in authority"; but his authority was on the physical plane, and he saw that Jesus had authority on a Spiritual plane, for he said, "Speak the word only."

The Bible also tells us that the word is not afar off but in our own mouth. It is neither here nor there; it is within every living soul. We must take the responsibility for our own lives. All must awake to the facts that they have absolute control over their lives, and that nothing can happen by chance. Then they will have a broader concept of God, a greater tolerance for their neighbor, and a greater realization of their own divine nature. What a relief from strenuous labor; no more struggle or strife. "Be still and know that I am God, and beside me there is none other." The Spirit being all there is, we cannot conceive of anything that can hinder its working. When the Spirit has spoken, the Word becomes Law, for before the Law is the Word; It precedes all else. First is Absolute Intelligence, All-Power, All-Presence, All-Causation; then the movement upon itself through the power of the Word; then the Word becoming Law; the Law producing the thing and holding it in place.

So long as the Word exists the thing will exist, for since the Word is All-Power there is nothing beside It. "I Am that I Am, and beside me there is none other." This "I Am" is Spirit, God, All. There is no physical explanation for anything in the universe; all causation is Spirit and all effect spiritual. We are not living in a physical world but in a spiritual world peopled with spiritual ideas. We are now living in Spirit.

God, or Spirit, governs the universe through great mental laws that work out the divine will and purpose, always operating from Intelligence. This Intelligence is so vast, and the power so great that our human minds cannot even grasp it; all that we can hope to do is to learn something of the way in which it works, and by harmonizing ourselves with it, to so align ourselves with Spirit that our lives may be controlled by the great harmony that obtains in all the higher laws of nature, but has been very imperfectly manifested in man. This brings us to the second point of consideration.

WHY, AND WHAT IS MAN?

We find in the physical universe that automatic laws govern everything; for instance, the tree cannot say "I will not," because of the law that holds it in place; it grows without any volition of its own. So it is with all nature; but when we come to man we find a different manifestation of the Spirit, a being who can say "I choose." In all creation, man alone is an individual; man alone is free; and yet man alone wants, is sick, suffers, and is unhappy. "Man marks the earth with ruin"; why? because he has not found his true nature. The very thing that should free him, and eventually will do so, now limits him. God could not make an individual without making him able to think, and he cannot think without bringing upon himself the results of his thought, good or bad. This does not mean using two powers, but using the One from two standpoints. Nothing in itself is either good or bad; all things exist in mind as a potentiality; mind is eternally acting upon thought, continually producing its own images from mind, and casting them out into manifestation. Man must be the outcome- of the desire of the Spirit to make something which expresses the same life that It feels. Man is made to be a companion of the Infinite; but to arrive at this exalted plane of being, he must have his freedom, and be let alone to discover his own nature; to return love to his Creator only when he chooses to do so. At the doorway, then, of man's mind this wonderful God has to wait. "Behold, I stand at the door and knock"; the opening must be on the part of the individual.

Man lives in a mind that presses in upon him from all sides with infinite possibilities, with infinite creative power. The divine urge of infinite love crowds itself upon him, and awaits his recognition. Being the image of this Power, his thought also must be the Word or cause it the life. At the center of his being is all the power that he will need on the path of his unfoldment; all the mind that man has is as much of this Infinite Mind as he allows to flow through him. We have often thought of God as far off, and of man as a being separate from the All Good; now we are coming to see that God and man are one, and that that One is simply awaiting man's recognition, that he may spring into being and become to man all that he could wish or want. "As the father has inherent life in himself, so hath he given to the Son to have life within himself." It could not be otherwise; we are all in Mind and Mind is always creating for us as we think; and as we are thinking creatures, always thinking, our happiness depends upon our thought. Let us consider the law of our life.

THE LAW OF OUR LIVES.

Spirit creates through law. The law is always mind in action. Mind cannot act unless intelligence sets it in motion. In the great universal mind man is a center of intelligence, and every time he 'thinks he sets mind into action. 'What is the activity of this mind in relation to man's thought? It has to be one of mental correspondence; that is, mind has to reflect whatever thought it casts into it. Wonderful as Universal Mind is, it has no choice but to create whatever thought is given it; if it could contradict that thought, it would not be a unit, since this would be recognizing something outside itself. This is a point in Truth which should not be overlooked. The *one mind* knows only its own ability to make whatever is given It; It sees no other power and never analyzes or dissects; It simply *knows*, and the reason why people do not understand this is that they have not realized what mind is. The ordinary individual thinks of mind only from the limitation of his own environment. The concept he has of mind is the concept of his own thinking, which is very limited.

We are surrounded by an All Seeing, All Knowing Mind, which is One and runs through all. The belief in the dual mind has destroyed practically all philosophies and religions of the ages, and will continue to do so until the world comes to see that there is but One. Whatever name is given it there is but One. It is this One that creates for us, whatever we believe. Our thought operative through this One produces all our affairs. We are all centers in this Mind, centers of creative thought activity. There is nothing which appears in the manifest Universe other than an objectified thought, whether it be a bump on your head, a growth on your foot or a planet. It could not be there were it not made out of Mind, for mind is all there is to make anything out of. Whatever is made is made out of it. Nothing exists or can exist without a source from which it springs.

We are not dealing with a negative as well as a positive Power—not two powers but one; a power that sees neither good nor evil, as we see it. It knows only that it is all, and since it is all, it creates whatever is given it. From our limited standpoint we often think of good, and evil; not realizing that, as yet, we do not know the one from the other. What we call good to-day, we may call evil to-morrow, and what we think to be evil to-day, we may to-morrow proclaim as the greatest good we have known. Not so with the great Universal Power of Mind; It sees only Itself, and Its infinite ability to create.

To the thinking person this will mean much; he will see that he is no longer living in a limited universe, a world of powers, but that he is immersed in an Infinite Creative Medium which, because of Its Nature, has to create for him whatever he believes. Jesus understood this, and in a few simple words, laid down the law of life: "It is done unto all people as they believe." This is a great thing to keep in mind. It is done unto us; we do not have to do it, for it is done unto us of a power that knows itself to be all there is. Could we even believe that some material mountain would be moved, the power is there to do it. Without this belief there is no real impulse for the Creative Mind, and we do not get an affirmative answer. We must realize more clearly that this Great Power has to operate through us.

MAN'S PART.

Creative mind cannot force itself upon us because we have the power of self-choice. It recognizes us when we recognize it. When we think that we are limited or have not been heard, it must take that thought and bring it into manifestation for us.

When we look about us and see nature so beautiful, lavish and so limitless, when we realize that something, some power, is behind all, and sees to it that plenty obtains everywhere, so that in all things manifest there is more than could be used; and when on the other hand we see man so limited, sick, sad and needy, we are disposed to ask this question: "Is God good after all? Does He really care for the people of His creation? Why am I sick? Why am I poor?" Little do we realize that the answer is in our own mouths, in the creative power of our own thought. The average person when told the Truth will still seek some other way.

God has already done for us—in a mechanical way—all that He can do; and having been given the ability, we will have to do for ourselves the rest. Yet the Great Power is always near, ready at any time to help, but we must use it according to its own nature in harmony with its laws. Man should learn that he himself is the center of this Divine activity. Realizing this, he must seek more and more to utilize his own Divine nature, and by so doing he will come more fully under the protection of the great laws that govern all life, manifest and unmanifest. Whatever man is, he must find that because he is made out of God, he must be of the same nature. This Infinite One cannot know anything outside of itself; anything that would be a contradiction of its Divine nature; man's ignorance of his real nature binds him with his own freedom, until he comes to see things as they really are, and not as they appear to be.

In the Infinity of mind, which is the principle of all metaphysics and of all life, there is nothing but mind, and that which mind does. That is all there is in the Universe. That is all there ever was or ever will be. This mind is acted upon by our thought, and so our thought becomes the law of our lives. It is just as much a law in our individual lives as God's thought is in the larger life of the Universe.

For the sake of clearness, think of yourself as in this Mind, think of yourself as a center in it. That is your principle. You think, and Mind produces the thing. One of the big points to remember is that we do not have to create; all that we have to do is to think. Mind, the only Mind that there is, creates.

Few people seem to understand the nature of the law and so think that they have got to do something, even if it is only holding a thought; thinking or knowing is what does the thing. It will make it much easier for us when we realize that we do not have to make anything, just to know; that there is something back of the knowing which does the work for us.

That person gets the best results who realizes that he can use this divine principle; he who can get the clearest concept of his idea, and who can rely on mind to do for him, keeping everything out of his thought that would contradict the supremacy of Spirit or Mind.

By simply holding a thought we could not make anything but by knowing in mind what cannot we do?

BONDAGE AND FREEDOM.

Never get away from the fact that you are surrounded by such a power; it is the principle of demonstration. It knows every thought. As we send forth our thought into it, it does unto us. The person who is ignorant of this law must by that ignorance be bound by his thought, by his human beliefs. One who understands will begin to break these ties that bind him; one by one he will destroy every negative thought until at last he is able to think what he wants to think; and so he frees himself by the use of the same power that at one time bound him. We must destroy all thought that we would not see manifest and hold to that which we would see, until we receive the affirmative answer.

Never struggle, Mind makes things out of Itself, there is no effort made. Don't think that there is so much to be overcome. Have only a calm sense of perfect peace as you realize that God is all, and that you are using the perfect law and that nothing can hinder it from working for you. Many people are learning to do this, and no one has yet failed to demonstrate who has been steadfast, using the law in a consistent and persistent trust.

All that we have to do is to provide the right mental and spiritual attitude of mind and then believe that we already have, and the reward will be with us. We shall see it.

The time will come when we will not have to demonstrate at all because we will be always living so near to the law that it will do all for us without much conscious thought on our part.

So when you say, "I am poor, sick or weak; I am not one with the Creative Mind," you are using that creative power to keep yourself away from the Infinite; and just as soon as you declare that you are one with God, there is a rushing out to meet you, as the Father rushed out to meet the prodigal son. "The Spirit seeketh," but as long as your mind thinks in the terms of conditions you cannot overcome. The difficulty comes from our inability to see our own Divine nature, and its relation to the Universe. Until we awake to the fact that we are one in nature with God, we will not find the way of life; until we realize that our own word has the power of life we will not see the way of life; and this brings us to the consideration of the use of the Word in our lives.

THE WORD.

"The Word was with God and the Word was God." "The Word is nigh thee, even in thy own mouth that thou shouldst know it and do it." What does this mean? It clearly states that whatever power there is in the Word (and it says it is All Power) is also in our own mouths. There is no avoiding the fact that the Bible claims for man the same power in his own life and his own world that it claims for God. In the lives of the majority, men do not realize that the Word is in their own mouths. What Word? Little do we realize that this Word which they are so earnestly seeking is every word they hear, think or speak. Do we who are endeavoring to realize the greater truths of life always govern our words? If any word has power, it follows that all words have power. It is not in the few moments of spiritual meditation that we demonstrate, but we bring out the possibilities of the hidden word when we are allowing our thoughts to run in any direction; not in the short time spent in silence, but in the long hours stretching themselves into days, months, and years, are we always using the word. An hour a day spent in silent meditation will not save us from the confusion of life; the fifty-one per cent. of a man's thinking is what counts. It is easy when we are alone to brave the storms of life; surrounded by our own exalted atmosphere we feel the strength of the Infinite; we rise in Spirit, we think we are experiencing the ultimate of truth, that all things are ours. These moments in a busy life are well spent, but must unavoidably be brief. But what of the rest of the day; what of the busy street, of the market place, and of all the daily contact with life? Do we then obtain? Do we keep on in the same even way? Or do we fall before the outer confusion of our surroundings? We are still creating the word and setting it afloat in the great ethers of life. Are these words creating for us? Yes!

How necessary, then, to "keep the independence of the solitude"; how seldom we do this!

"God sent an angel to speak to me—
A word He was fain I hear;
And the angel brought the message
And whispered it in my ear.

"God knew I needed the word He sent—
I had lost the zest of fight;
And the right was all but beaten;
The wrong it was all but right.

"Simple the word that He sent me—
But it soothed a spirit raw
With the pain of too much striving—
'Twas 'Love fulfills the law.'"

Few people indeed in the day in which we live are well poised. Where do we find the man who can live above his surroundings, who in his own thought can dominate all conditions, and in the midst of the crowd keep his own even way, and his own counsel? When we do meet with such a person we will know him; for we shall find on his face the image of perfect peace.

We shall detect in his bearing the ease and independence that comes only to the man who has found himself and who is centered not in the outer but in the inner world.

Such a character as this has the power to attract to himself all of the best in the world; he is a center toward which all else must gravitate. The atmosphere which he creates and with which he surrounds himself is one of absolute calm and peace. The world at once sees in this man a master, and gladly sits at his feet. And yet this man who has risen above the thought of the world cares not that other people should sit at his feet. He knows that what he has done all may do, and he well knows that all the teaching in the world will not produce another such as he. He knows that it is not from the teaching but from the being that true greatness springs. So this man does not go around teaching or preaching; he simply is.

THE MAN WHO HAS ARRIVED.

The man who has arrived will realize that he has done so in the midst of an outer confusion; he will be the one who has gone into the silence for strength, and has come out into the world equipped with power from on high; but that light which he has received must be kept burning.

Not alone in the silence but in the busy throng must all of us find the way of life. Our every thought creates. For the majority of us these thoughts come in every-day affairs, some of which are very trivial, but these too will be demonstrated.

We have missed the whole point, unless we have learned so to control our thought that time and place make no difference.

THE POWER WE HAVE WITHIN US.

We have within us a power that is greater than anything that we shall ever contact in the outer, a power that can overcome every obstacle in our life and set us safe, satisfied and at peace, healed and prosperous, in a new light, and in a new life.

Mind, all Mind is right here. It is God's Mind, God's creative Power, God's creative Life. We have as much of this Power to use in our daily life as we can believe in and embody.

The store house of nature is filled with infinite good awaiting the touch of our awakened thought to spring forth into manifestation in our life; but the awakening must be on our part and not on the side of life. We static! at the gateway of limitless opportunity in the eternal and change-less NOW. Now is the day in which to begin the new life that is to lift us up to the greater expression of all that is wonderful. The word that we speak is the Law of our life and nothing hinders but ourselves. We have through ignorance of our real nature misused the power of our word, and behold what it has brought upon us, "the very thing that we feared." But now it shall produce a new thing, a new heaven and a new earth.

INDIVIDUAL IDEAS.

We find that in the Universe every separate idea has a word, a mental concept behind it, and as long as that word remains the thing is held in place in the visible world; when the concept is withdrawn the idea in the visible melts away, disappears; it ceases to vibrate to the word, which is the law behind it, for when the word is withdrawn the condensation of the ether that forms the word melts again into the formless. There was a time when the world was without form, and from the word alone all things were made that are made. When our word says that there is no longer life in our bodies, the life principle withdraws and our bodies return to the substance from which they came. Here is the great mystery of life, that we are able to use this creative word for whatever purpose we may desire, and that word becomes the Law unto the thing for which it was spoken.

And so in our lives we might say that without our word was not anything made that was made. For we are given the power to sit in the midst of our lives and direct all their activities. There is no struggle and no strife necessary. All that we have to do is to know. We must awake and with the glorified consciousness of an emancipated soul use our God-given power.

THE REASON FOR THE UNIVERSE.

This Universe is the reason, first of an Infinite Intelligence which speaks or thinks, and as this thought becomes active within itself, it creates from itself, at the power of its own word, the visible Universe. We are living in a Universal activity of mental law, we are surrounded by a Mind which receives every impression of our thought and returns to us just what we think. Every man, then, is living in a world made for him from the activity of his thought.

It is a self-evident proposition that Mind must create out of Itself; and this Self being Limitless, it follows that its creative power is without limit.

MIND IN ACTION.

Everything that we see is the result of mind in action. We all have a body and we have what is called a physical environment; we could have neither if it were not for mind. The law implanted within us is, that we need nothing except ourselves and this All-Wise Creative Mind to make anything; and that just so far as we depend upon any condition, past, present or future, or upon any individual, we are creating chaos, because we are dealing with conditions and not with causes. Every living soul is a law unto himself, but of this great truth few people are conscious. It seems difficult for the race, which feels itself to be so limited, to comprehend the fact that there is a power that makes things directly out of itself, by simply becoming the thing that it makes, and that it does this by self knowing. But we will not demonstrate until we see at least some of this, the greatest truth about life.

We should realize that we are dealing with the principle that is scientifically correct. It will never fail us at any time but is eternally present. We can approach the Infinite Mind with a depth of thought and understanding, knowing that it will respond, knowing that we are dealing with reality.

Jesus, who saw this very dearly, laid down the whole law of life in a few simple words: "It is done unto you as you believe." We do not have to do it, it is done unto us, it is done by a power that is all. Could we believe that a material mountain would be moved, it would be done unto us. But unless we do believe there is no impulse for the creative power and we do not receive. Life externalizes at the level of our thought.

ACTION AND REACTION.

There is something that casts back at us every thought that we think. "Vengeance is mine, I will repay, saith the Lord," is a statement of eternal truth and correspondences against which nothing can stand, and whatever man sets in motion in mind will be returned to him, even as he has conceived within himself and brought forth into manifestation. If we wish to transcend old thoughts we must rise above them and think higher things: We are dealing with the law of cause and effect and it is absolute; it receives the slightest as well as the greatest thought and at once begins to act upon it. And sometimes even when we know this we are surprised at the rapidity with which it works. If we have been misusing this law we need not fail; all that we have to do is to turn from the old way and begin in the new. We will soon work up out of the old law into the new which is being established for us. When we desire only the good the evil slips from us and returns no more.

ARRIVING AT A HIGH CONSCIOUSNESS.

The best way to arrive at the highest consciousness is to have a great faith in the willingness and the ability of Life to do all for us, by working through us. We must believe in the inherent goodness and all-powerfulness of the Spirit of Truth. And so every path leads us back to the one point and we must learn to realize the near presence, the great reality. There, through the door of our own thought, we enter into the Universal Consciousness, into a complete realization of life and truth, of love and beauty; and as we sit in the silence of our own souls and listen, it will be the greatest thing that we will ever do. In that completeness we are lost and yet we are found. This is what is meant that a man must lose his life in order to find it. We are lost to the human and found in the divine. We realize that we are One with Cause.

OUTER SUGGESTIONS.

Nearly all people are controlled by outer suggestions, and not by inner realizations. Ordinarily man thinks only what he sees others do, and hears others say. We must all learn so to control the inner life that outside things do not make an impression upon our mentalities. As we are thinking beings, and cannot help thinking, we cannot avoid making things happen to us, and what we need to do is so to control our thought processes that our thinking will not depart from the realization of that which is perfect.

Man is governed by a mind which casts back to him every thought he thinks; he cannot escape from this and need not try; it would be useless. The laws of mind are simple and easy to understand. The trouble with us has been that we have laid down great obstructions, and then have tried to overcome them. Stop trying, stop struggling, begin to be calm, to trust in the higher laws of life, even though you do not see them; they are still there.

Did you ever see the law that causes a plant to grow? Of course you did not, and yet you believe in this hidden law of growth. Why do you believe? Simply because every year, out of the seed time comes a harvest. Shall we not have as great faith in the higher laws of being? To those souls who have dared to believe has come as definite an answer as came to those who believed in receiving a harvest from the planted seed. This law is, and if we would see results we must use it; that is, we must provide the mental receptivity that will prepare us to accept the gift when the Spirit makes it. This receiving is a mental process, a process in which we lose all sense of limitation.

If you wish to demonstrate prosperity, begin to think and talk about it, and to see it everywhere. Do nothing that contradicts this thought either mentally or physically. The world is full of good; take it and forget all else. Rise above depression and be glad that you are saved from adversity; the human mind needs to be cleansed from the morbid thoughts that bind through its false beliefs.

No living soul can demonstrate two things at the same time, if one contradicts the other. There is no way except to let go of all that you do not wish to come into your experience, and, in mind, take all that you do wish.

See, hear, talk about, and read only what you wish, and never again let a negative thought come into your mind.

God knows good only, and when we are in line with good He knows us; when we are out of harmony with good, we say, "God has forgotten us." On the one hand we have an Infinite Intelligence which has brought us up to where we are to-day; and having done all that it can for us now lets us alone to discover our own nature. On the other hand we have the Infinite Law—which is an activity of God—and we can use it for what we will, only with this provision, that, in so far as we use it for the good of all, are we protected.

The law obtains through all nature that as a man sows, so must he reap. Now the Father has brought us to where we can understand life, and we must go as we choose. If we are in harmony with the great forward movement of the Spirit, there is nothing that can hinder our advancement; if we oppose it, somewhere along our pathway it will crush us. As with individuals so with nations; in so far as they work with a right spirit they prosper; when they begin to fail in the use of this law they begin to fall. He who understands will take the position of one who wishes to work in union with the Power of Good; and to such an one will come all the power that he can conceive of and believe in; his word becomes in expression as the very word of God, and he must realize it to be all powerful. So the one who is truly united with Good will wish to express only the truth for all; and in doing so he is working along the lines of the unfoldment of the Spirit, and though he may seem to fail, from the ordinary standpoint, yet his success is assured; for he is at one with the only ultimate power before which, in time, all else must fall.

THE USE OF THE GREATER CONSCIOUSNESS.

In practice the emancipated soul must always realize that he is in union with the Father; what the Father does, he can do in his own life; what God is, he can become. His word must be spoken with absolute authority; he must know; there should be no uncertainty. The word is the only power; everything must come from it, and nothing can stand against it; it is the great weapon which he is to use against all evil and for all good. It is his shield against all adversity and his sure defense against all seeming limitation.

The secret place of the Most High is in his own soul, where God dwells in eternal peace and infinite calm. Here he walks the waters of life undisturbed by the waves and the storm. Divine companionship is his for all eternity. Peace which transcends all human confusion comes, and he realizes that indeed he is honored of the Father. His word is flung out and will work and none can hinder it; the sense of sureness is complete. Heaven and earth may pass away, but the word goes on and on accomplishing that thing for which it was sent; and all power is given to it on earth and in heaven. If he speaks to the sick and they receive, it will heal them. If he says the word of prosperity it will manifest, and nothing can hinder it; the world will abound with good, and his cup run over with life.

What more can we ask! What greater realization of life than to know that God is with us! From this great realization comes peace, a peace which the world little understands, and a calm which is as deep as the infinite sea of love in which he realizes himself to be immersed. Peace brings poise, and the union of these two gives birth to Power. No person can hope to arrive while he believes in two powers; only as we rise to the realization of the One in and through all can we attain. When we speak the word there must be no confusion but only that calm reliance which knows that "Beside me there is none other." Realize that Spirit is All Causation, and that all things are made out of it, by the operation of the word through it, and that you can speak the word that is one with the Spirit and there will be no more confusion. "As the Father has inherent life in himself, so has he given to the Son to have inherent life within himself." "Speak the word only and it shall be done." "The word is in your own mouth that ye should know it and do it." "Stranger on earth, thy home is heaven; Pilgrim, thou art the guest of God."

THE GREATER CONSCIOUSNESS.

Man is surrounded by a great universal thought power which returns to him always just as he thinks. So plastic, so receptive is this mind, that it takes the slightest impression and moulds it into conditions. There are two things in man which his thought affects, his body and his environment. At all times he is given absolute control over these two things, and from the effect of his thought upon them he cannot hope to escape.

At first, being ignorant of this fact, he binds himself by a misuse of the laws of his being; but as he begins to see that he himself is responsible for all that comes to him on the path of life, he begins to control his thought, which in its turn acts on the universal substance to create for him a new world.

The great soul is learning more and more to dare to fling out into mind a divine idea of himself, and to see himself perfect and whole.

If he has a divine thought he will get a divine thing, if he has a human thought he will get a human thing; he will receive whatever his innermost thought embodies. And so we find in the Bible twice repeated these words: "To the pure Thou wilt show Thyself pure and to the froward Thou wilt show Thyself froward." It is done unto all as they believe.

We often wonder why it is that we are not making better demonstrations. We look about and observe that some are getting wonderful results, they are speaking the word and people are being healed. We see others struggling along with the word, and nothing seems to happen; and when we inquire into the reason for all this we find it to be very plain indeed. All is mind and we are mental, we are in mind and can only get from it what we first think into it. We must not only think but we must know. We have to provide within ourselves a mental and spiritual likeness for the thing desired. The reason why so few succeed, then, must be because they have not mentally really believed to the exclusion of all that would deny the thing which they believe in. And the reason why others do succeed must also be because they have absolutely believed and allowed real power to flow through and out into expression. They must have a real concept of life. Hold an object in front of a mirror and it will image in the mirror the exact size of the object. Hold a thought in mind and it will image in matter the exact likeness of the thought. Let us take this image which we hold before a mirror and change it ever so slightly and there will be a corresponding change in the reflection. It is just the same in the mental world; whatever is imaged is brought forth from mind into manifestation.

We must not deny that which we affirm. We must reason only from that cause which is spiritual and mental and weed out all thought that would deny its power in our lives. There seems to be something in the race thought that says man is poor; man is limited; that there is a lack of opportunity; that times are hard; that prices are high; that nobody wants what I have to offer. No person succeeds who speaks these ideas. When we express ourselves in this way we arc using a destructive power. All such thoughts must go, and we must all realize that we are an active center in the only power there is.

We must get the perfect vision, the perfect conception; we must enlarge our thought until it realizes all good, and then we must swing right out and use this Almighty Power for definite purposes. We should daily feel a deeper union with Life, a greater sense of that indwelling God, the God of the everywhere, within us. When we speak into this Mind we have sown the seed of thought in the Absolute and may rest in peace. We do not have to make haste, because it is done unto all as they believe. "In that day that they shall call upon me I will answer."

People will often ask, "What is the best method for demonstration?" There is but one answer to that question; the Word is the only possible method of demonstrating anything; the word really felt and embodied in our thought. Then the word becomes flesh and dwells among us and we behold and experience it. We will ask for no other way when we understand this.

The person who does not understand these laws will be likely to say that this is presumptuous; that it is even sacrilegious; but this comes only from a lack of understanding of the fact that all is governed by law, and that all law is impersonal and universal. We have just as much right to use spiritual law as to use so-called physical laws. Strictly speaking there is no such a thing as a physical law, as all things are spiritual and all law is a law of the activity of the Spirit. The greatest use of these laws will always come to that soul who is the most deeply spiritual, as such an one comes the nearest to using law as God uses it. So to the really great soul there must come a very close relationship with the Invisible God; this relationship cannot be expressed in words but only in inner feeling which transcends the power of words to express. God must become the great reality, not simply as the principle of life, but more as the great Mind which knows, and which at all times understands and responds. To say that God does not understand our desires would be to rob the divine mind of all consciousness and place God lower in the scale of being than we ourselves are. On the other hand we must be careful not to believe that God thinks evil and understands that which is not perfect, as then we would have an imperfect being for the First Cause.

We should more and more learn to think of things in the absolute, that is, to think of things as not limited by conditions. Realize at all times that the Spirit makes things out of Itself, and needs no beginning except its own self-recognition. Then we must cognize our relation to this great power as one of absolute correspondence; what we think into it, it takes up and does for us as we think. It should not be an effort so to think; we should do so with ease, without strain. The law must return to us; we have no responsibility except to provide the proper channel. It can return only in the exact way that we think. If we think struggle is the reality, we shall gain our demonstration, but struggle will have to be the result. There is a law of reflection between Mind and the one who thinks; and it is not only what a man thinks but also how he thinks that "shall be done unto him."

If you believe absolutely that you can do a certain thing, the way will always be opened for you to do it; if also you believe that time will have to elapse, then you are making that a law, and time will have to elapse. If on the other hand you believe that mind knows just how and never makes mistakes, but lets it be done unto you, then it will be done. Confusion brings more confusion; peace begets more peace; we cannot imagine the Great Spirit hurrying or worrying, fretting or trying to make anything happen. The only reason we worry and fret is because we have thought there was some other power which could bring confusion. Such is not the case. There is but one, and we are always using that one but using it according to our belief. This is our divine birthright, nothing hinders but ourselves. Remember that since all is mind, you cannot demonstrate beyond your ability to comprehend mentally, that is, beyond your ability to know about a certain thing. For instance, suppose you wish to heal some one who is sick; your ability to do this will depend entirely upon your ability to see perfection mentally, coupled also with the realization that your word destroys everything unlike itself. If you try to see perfection for a few minutes only, it will never heal. Your thought goes on at all times, and in the moments when you least realize it, conditions are being moulded for you. It is not enough to declare consciously for the truth. The truth must be lived or no good results will be forthcoming.

THE PERFECT UNIVERSE.

The one who desires to heal must stop seeing, reading about, discussing, or listening to conversation about sickness. There is no other way under the sun except as we let go of that which we do not desire, and take that which we wish to have. There is too much of this deceiving ourselves into thinking that we can do two ways at once. We may deceive ourselves and possibly other people, but the law remains the same, a law of mental correspondences, and nothing else. We cannot go beyond our ability to realize the truth; water rises only to its own level. In our patients as well as in ourselves and our environment we will reflect what we are, not at our best in the few moments of silence, but in the long run of ordinary life and thought.

To acquire the larger consciousness is no easy task. All that we have believed in which contradicts the perfect whole must be dropped from our thought, and we must come to realize that we are now living in a perfect universe, peopled with perfect spiritual beings, each of which (coupled with the Great Divinity) is complete within himself. We must see that we are one in the great one, and then we will not separate or divide, but unite and add to, until in time we will find that we are living in an entirely different world from that in which we had once thought we were living. Of course this will meet with much opposition from those unenlightened souls whom we must contact in the world. But what of that? Remember, the great man is the one who can keep in the crowd the calm, even thought, the deep, divine reliance on principle. And more, this is the only way to help or to save the world. In time all people will come to the same understanding. You are lifting up the standard of life, and those who are ready will follow. You have no responsibility to save the world except by exemplifying the truth. The world must save itself.

All are alike; there is no difference between one person and another. Come to see all as a divine idea; stop all negative thought; think only about what you want, and never about what you do not want, as that would cause a false creation. Too much cannot be said about the fact that all are dealing with only one power, making and unmaking for man through the creative power of his own thought. If . there is something in your life that you do not want there, stop fighting it—forget it!

ABOUT STRUGGLE—KARMA.

There is too much struggle coming into the metaphysical thought. Often we hear some seeker after truth say, "I have a big fight ahead." O foolish and untaught, how can you hope to enter in! The kingdom comes not from without, but from within, always. Stop all struggle and wait upon the sure principle that creates whatever it wills because there is nothing to oppose it. As long as we think that opposition exists we are blocking the way for the clearer vision. Those that take up the sword must perish by it; not because God is a jealous God, but because that is the way the law must work.

Cause and effect must obtain everywhere. Do not even fuss about your Karma; too often we hear people say, "This is my Karma." This may be true enough, but how many people know what they mean when they use the word Karma? Do you realize that your Karma is nothing but your false thinking, and that the only way to escape it is to think the truth, and that brings in the higher law? When the greater comes in the lesser leaves because there is no longer anything to give life to it. The past is gone when we learn to forgive and to forget.

This erases from mind all that is held against us, and even our sins "Are remembered no more against us forever." Fate is in our own hands, and when we will rise to that pure atmosphere where we see things in their completeness, and know that an All-Wise Power is behind it all, we will see that the Infinite Mind could wish for us only that which expresses itself in limitless terms. The whole trouble has been that we reason as men and not as Gods. "I say ye are Gods and every one of you Sons of the Most High."

The great law of life is thinking and becoming; and when we think from the lofty heights of the Spirit we will become great, and not until then. Do not try to convince any one of the truth; that will bring confusion. Truth is, just as much as God is; and the whole world is coming gradually into the realization of it. Keep the truth within your own soul, lift your own self above the confusion of life, and then people will believe. So all our thought is to be created in the realization of the One becoming the many, without struggle, without fear; stripped of all that denies the truth.

How limited we are, how little our thought! How the human race rises in the morning, plods off to the day's work, plods home at night, sore and tired, eats and sleeps, works and dies. As has been said of man, "Man works hard to get money to buy food to get strength to work hard to get money to buy food to get strength to work hard to get money, etc." This was never intended; it is the curse imposed on the man who believed in two powers, one of good and one of evil. To us there has come a greater vision, and to those who believe and act as though it were true it is proving itself.

We must turn from all human thought and experience. We are not down trodden, depraved and miserable sinners, born in sin and conceived in iniquity and shame, some to go to heaven and some to hell and all to the eternal glory of God. This is a lie, it always was and always will be. But as long as we believe in a lie it seems to be present with us.

Man is born of the Spirit of God Almighty, is pure, holy, perfect, complete and undefiled; is at one with his eternal principle of being. Many people are finding this out and as a monument to its truth millions are daily proving it for themselves.

Somewhere down the path of human experience we will all awake to the realization that we ourselves are heaven or hell.

We live in Spirit awaiting the touch of thought that believes. All people look, a few see.

PRACTICE.

The one who wishes to practise metaphysics must first, last, and all the time realize that he himself is a center of the divine. activity; he must know that whatever God is in the Universal, he is in the world in which he lives. He must know that all things are made out of Spirit, which is First Cause; nothing comes before Spirit. Operating upon itself out of itself, it makes what it will out of its own perfect desire. He must think of the Spirit as the Father of his own life, eternally bound to him, eternally binding him to it.

He must know that the Spirit not only can manifest through him, but that it wishes to do so; "The Father seeks such to worship Him." The practitioner who understands the truth knows that as long as God exists, he will exist; that he could no more become non-existent than God could. Walking, talking, moving in God, he must not only see the Divine Being as the great unknown Cause, but he must go a step further and see God as the great self-knowing, understanding power of Infinite Intelligence, thinking through his own thought and willing into his own life all power and all good. More than this, God must become within his own soul the greater self, the inner life, the inner light that is to light his path with sure step to the attainment of the greater ideals. God is to become the great friend of his life, understanding him, and helping him at all times to understand all things.

No more books, no more teachers, no more preachers, creeds or candlesticks will he ever need. The old methods must vanish into their native nothingness, as the great realization that God is all in his life dawns upon his awakened thought.

"Naught is the squire, when the king's at hand;
Withdraw the stars, when dawns the sun's brave light."

He must know that not height, nor depth, nor any other thing, can come between the soul and its perfect Creator. Too long have we listened to people; now our own soul shall speak in a language that is unmistakable; now shall we ourselves become masters of all life and interpreters of all mysteries. Now my Father and I are one.

As the word of God goes forth and sets in motion the all law, so must we realize because we are one with the word that our own thought has the power of expression. The one who wishes to heal must come to see all evil as impersonal, fastening it to no one, but realizing that it is simply false thought; the healer knows that the word which he is to speak will destroy this false impression; and by erasing it, it will vanish.

There should be absolutely no sense of responsibility beyond speaking the word in positive faith, knowing. All struggle belongs to the Old Order; in the New peace takes the place of confusion, faith answers the cry of doubt and fear, and the Word is supreme.

We must know that our word is law, and cannot be set aside by the false thought of the world. Every time that we state a truth, we must know that that truth destroys all that is unlike itself and frees the thought of the one whom we wish to help and to heal.

This word must become the new Law which frees. People are sick because they think sickness and will be healed only when they turn from this kind of thought and begin to think in terms of health.

THE SAME POWER USED IN TWO WAYS.

There is only One power, but we use it in two ways, either to destroy or to save. The blessing and the curse are one and the same thing; the power of mind used either affirmatively or negatively; the word used in fear and doubt or in faith and assurance.

You do not have to understand material philosophy or be learned in the books of the human race. All these things may be good in their place, but to one who understands the greater laws of life they are as simple babblings—

"An infant crying in the night,
An infant crying for the light.
And with no language but a cry."

We no longer cry, we Know. We no longer ask if there be a God, or if we dare to speak to Him lest we die; we do not analyze, dissect, affirm, or deny, We know.

We trust our own word because first we "Know in whom we have believed." The sooner the one who is striving to attain will realize that truth must become revealed through his own soul, and not that of another, the sooner he will attain. We must then become immune from the race suggestion of an hypnotic power that sets itself up as an authority. There is no other authority than your own soul, as "There is no law but that your soul has set." Leave authorities to smaller minds, and to those who need a leader because of this their own self-confessed weakness, and be Free. Dare to "Stand amidst the eternal way" and proclaim your own Atonement with all the power that there is, was, or ever will be.

Practically the whole human race is hypnotized, thinking whatever it is told to think. We get our concepts from our physical environment, we say, "See sin, sickness and death, misery, unhappiness and calamity." And this concept we are giving to the creative, impersonal Mind, and so we are making a law for ourselves that will produce what we believe in. Do we really know what law means? It means that which will exact the utmost farthing from our thought.

Like produces like, attracts like, creates like. If we could see our thought and take a picture of it and of our conditions we would see no difference between the two, for they are really but the inside and the outside of the same thing.

We cannot make affirmations for fifteen minutes a day and spend the rest of our time denying the thing which we have affirmed, and affirming the thing which we have denied, and obtain the results which we seek. We send out the word and it sets the power in motion; then we think the opposite thing which neutralizes the first word, and zero is the result.

We cannot demonstrate one iota beyond our mental ability to conceive and steadfastly to embody. Infinite as Creative Power is, receptive and quick as it is, it can only become to us what we first think into it. God can do for us only what He can do through us.

Dare to say, "Behold I am he. Great men have come and gone, and behold a greater now stands here where I stand, and I am that one." The world will laugh and perhaps scorn. The Christian world will hold up its hands in holy horror, lest you blaspheme; the unchristian world will smile knowingly. Neither the one nor the other will understand, but the understanding of either counts for nothing. You are now free, and your freedom will yet save the world from itself. The great soul finds within himself the Divine companionship which he needs. He finds within himself the "Peace which passeth all understanding" and the power to do all things. All Power! He speaks, his word is Law and it is done unto him of all the power there is. His word knows itself to be the law of life unto all for whom it is spoken and who receive it.

HEALING THE SICK.

We shall be called upon to heal all manner of disease, to comfort the sorrowing and to bring peace to the distressed. First we must heal ourselves. When we are healing others we are also healing ourselves. A healer's work takes place within himself. This idea of "sending out thought" and "holding thought" is all a mistake. Think, come into being not only by "taking thought" but by knowing that the Word is infinite. This word is in your own mouth, and there alone can it be spoken. Here your responsibility begins and here it ends, in your own mouth. You must feel no responsibility for the recovery of your patient, for it brings confusion and disturbance to be always wondering if it is working. It must work, if you have the sure faith, and your patient is receptive. You are dealing with the same power that said, "Let there be light" and there was light.

If your patient is suffering from a belief that he is dying of some dread disease, you must know that when you speak the word it will destroy this false belief and set him free. There must be no doubt about the power in the word which you speak. It should be said in perfect calm, in peace, and with absolute faith that it will work. This word then establishes the law of life unto the patient, it casts out all fear, it destroys all false sense of a material life and realizes that all is an expression of a perfect God; and so leaves nothing that can sin, be sick, suffer or die. When you are as sure of this as that von breathe, when you truly know within yourself, your patient will be healed, provided he also believes. If he does not believe it is not your fault, and you will have done for him all that can be done.

DENIALS.

Some people teach the use of denials. This must be settled by each individual for himself. Here and at all times we must settle every question from within and not from without. No living soul can say how another should or should not work. Beware of the danger of a self-appointed authority; this danger is as apt to come into New Thought as it was in the Old. No one is your authority on anything. Let us look into the philosophy of denials. We find that many people teach and practise them, and we do not wish in any way to criticize them. Their reasoning is this: "All disease is an image of thought held in mind until it appears in the body." It is true that without the ability to think man could not be sick. If he thinks a sick thought it will make him sick; when he changes his thought and thinks health, he is healed. It is taught that since sickness is negative thought, it must be counteracted by a positive thought, and that the best way is to deny the sick and affirm the positive thought; for instance, "There is no matter, and nothing can be the matter. This man has no material stomach, he is spiritual and not material; his lungs are not made of matter, they are spiritual ideas; I deny that man can be sick or suffer or die." All this may be accurate; man is a spiritual idea, and so must be perfect in his real nature; but there is a question if this is the better way. When we look into the creative way of the spirit we find it impossible for denial to enter, as the Spirit recognizes no opposite to its own nature.

It knows that "I Am and beside me there is no other." The Spirit does not deny anything, it simply affirms itself to be that which it desires to be. Seeing and recognizing no opposite to itself, it finds no need of denial, indeed, this thought need not enter the mind; if we are working with the Spirit we need not deny but state the affirmative attitude of mind, realizing that we are dealing with the only power that exists. There is a subtle danger in using denials; we may deny to such an extent as to erect a barrier or build a mountain to overcome. Once realize that God makes things out of Himself simply by speaking, and you will never again use denials in treating. All that needs changing is the false thought, and by affirming that your word destroys everything but itself you will embody all that a denial could. In those systems that teach denials we find that the more enlightened ones are gradually using the affirmative method, and as this is the growth of experience there can be no doubt that it is the better method. Of one thing we may be sure, the Spirit never denies. It simply knows that I am.

THE USE OF AFFIRMATIONS.

The affirmation is the great weapon of the healer; it is in alignment with the way of the original creative spirit and is the true use of the Word of All Power. We need only to say that our word is the law unto the case and calmly state what we want to be done, and then say and do nothing that contradicts it and wait for the fulfillment of that word. There is a power that operates on what we say, and it is done unto us, and we need have no fear about the results.

If I am treating Mary Jones I need only say I am helping her, and go to work within myself to realize that she is now a perfect being, made in the image of God. I must know that I am destroying all imperfection; when I know within myself that I am speaking the truth and realize that she is perfect, the healing is done as far as I am concerned. If she receives she is healed; I am not responsible for her receptivity. Know that there is a power that corresponds to your own mental attitude and you will see that the way you are believing is what makes things happen the way they do. Always believe in what you are doing; never see the negative side of life, never talk about it, or listen to talk of other people, and never think about or see imperfection; and you will have no trouble in making demonstrations.

THE HIGHEST ATTITUDE OF MIND.

The highest attitude of mind, from which all else springs, is one of perfect calm and absolute trust in the Spirit. The one who can with perfect confidence look into the future and with perfect ease of mind rest in the present, and who never looks backward, but who has learned to be still in his own soul and wait upon the Spirit, he is the one who will the most completely demonstrate the supremacy of spiritual thought over all so-called material resistance. "Be still and know that I Am God."

NON-RESISTANCE.

"Resist not evil and it will flee from you." Here is a statement of one of the great laws of our being. When we resist we make a mental image of the thing we are fighting, and that tends to have it created for us. When we learn to look only at what we watt and never at what we do not want, we will no longer resist anything. "Suffer it to be so now." You need not try to change the world. Let it alone; all people are doing the best they can. No one needs to be saved but yourself, and the sooner you realize this the sooner you will attain. Get over that "holier than thou" attitude. It is an illusion that many people suffer from, especially in the religious world. The world is all right; it is not going to Hell; it is on the way to Heaven. It is getting good so fast that in the process many things are being overturned and confusion appears to be on the surface. A great change is taking place, and on the surface the results are as yet a little mixed, but underneath, the power is at work destroying all unlike itself. In time all will come to see this. What a load of responsibility we assume that we were never meant to carry.

Remember that in the Divine plan no mistakes are made and that if God could have done it in a better way he would have done it differently. No souls are lost, for all "Live and move and have their being in Him" and "God is not a God of the dead but of the living, for in His sight all are alive." Too long have we believed in the negative simply because we have allowed ourselves to become hypnotized by a few strong-minded people, and by those who have imposed upon the race a mass of false philosophy.

BE ALIVE.

There is no place in the New Order for "dead ones." The true metaphysician is alive to all that is useful. Filling his place in the events of the human race, he takes part in all its labor and in all its fun. Pessimism must be relegated to the scrap heap. There is no place among the living for the dead. "Let the dead bury their dead." "Follow thou me." Do not hesitate to enter into the game of life, but do so with a zest and an enthusiasm that overflows with life. Fill yourself with the radiance of a life running over with power and usefulness. Then shall the world see your light.

People in the New Thought above all others should enter into the business world, into educational vocations, into politics, into every walk of life, and there prove before a waiting world, tired of itself, that a "man's a man," with this difference: not a "son of man" but a "Son of God."

BE HAPPY.

How can we hope to make the world see the right way unless we overflow with joy? The world has now too many sad faces. We see them everywhere, that resigned look that seems to say, "One rebuff more or less makes no difference; I am already so sad that nothing matters; I can bear it." This was all right when we thought everything was all wrong, but now we know that "all's well with the world" we must get over this depression which robs us of the power of attraction of the good things of life, and "enter in."

The man who is always glad will surround himself with people who are happy, and life will be a continual enjoyment, This robs no one; it does not make a race of irresponsible people; it makes a world of joy, a world that is good to live in.

No one wants to associate with the dead. People are looking for a more abundant expression of life, not for depression and fault-finding. Find fault with no one, and more than this find no fault with yourself. Get over the thought of condemning people and things. People and things are all right; let them alone and enjoy life. Your very atmosphere will cheer and uplift the people who contact you, and a new life will enter into them. Overflow.

"As it's given me to perceive,
I most certainly believe
When a man's glad plumb through,
God's pleased with him same's you."

LIVE IN THE PRESENT.

Life is for us to-day. There will be no change for to-morrow unless we do the changing to-day. To-day we are setting in motion the power of to-morrow. To-day is God's day, and we must extract from it what of life we are to live. To-morrow in the divine course of events will care for itself. The soul that learns to live in the great gladness of to-day will never weary of life but will find that he is living in an eternal here and now. Now, all good is his; now, all life, truth and love are his; now, he has entered in, and the good things of life are his to-day.

"Lord, for to-morrow and its needs I do not pray,
Make me to do thy will just for to-day."

Let your soul sing to-day and the song that comes to-morrow will be all the sweeter, will ring out over the vistas of time with an unmistakable clearness. Here is a soul who knows himself and has found life. within himself, who has met God to-day. No more waiting, no more longing, no more weary roads to travel. He has arrived. The goal is won and peace has come at last. To-clay.

SEE THE GOOD IN ALL THINGS.

Learn to see God in all manifestation, in all people, through all events. The ordinary person sees only the lump of matter. Not so with the awakened soul. He sees in all things the Divine Mind at work molding out into expression what it feels itself to be of life, of color, of form and beauty. There are some illusioned ones who claim that what we see is all false, and that the so-called material universe is an unreality. What a mistake! What we see is the body of God, full, free, complete, whole.

"A primrose by the river's brim,
A yellow primrose was to him,
And it was nothing more."

He never saw the idea behind—it was seen only as matter, matter, matter; yet what he could have seen was God's thought of himself coming out into wonderful beauty, and color, and form; The Infinite One manifesting in an infinite variety of forms. What do you see when you look upon the human form, the crowning glory of God's perfect creation? Matter, matter, matter? Flesh, blood and bones? Indeed, these may be passing into expression, but what of the idea, what of the reality of the body? This body of ours is as real as God is real. It would not be if it were an illusion. The very touch of the flesh should send a thrill through the whole body, bringing up its vibration to a higher pitch, to a finer form. The body is not one "mass of pollution," it is the temple of the living God and should be so thought of. Too long have we condemned it, and now we must free it by reversing the process. Of all things on earth the human body is the most beautiful, the most wonderful and the most God-like.

"If you do not love your brother whom you have seen, how can you love God whom you have not seen?" Human magnetism is not hypnotism, it is the divinity of man in expression; and when we learn to convert human passion into divine love, to transmute the lower into the higher, we shall have with us a power of attraction against which nothing can stand.

"He who hath ears to hear, let him hear."

When we behold a beautiful sunset we should see the wonderful thought of God, the radiance of his presence. In the strength of the hills we should see the strength of the Spirit; and seeing all things as spiritual ideas, we should learn to love them, because God has made them and given them to us to use. The soul who in ecstasy can rush up to a tree and embrace it realizes more of God than all the bigoted priests who have ever lived. The one who can sniff the ocean breeze with delight feels the presence of the divine being more keenly than does the one who kneels in despair before an awful God of Justice.

Learn then how to appreciate Nature and Nature's God. Spend much time in the out of doors; look up at the stars; let them be your companions; tread the pathless ways of the trees and the giant forests and see God in everything that you look upon, the God of the everywhere.

BE EXPECTANT.

Expect the best to happen. Don't sit around waiting for trouble; have absolutely nothing to do with it. It is no part of the divine plan. It is an illusion of the material sense. One who has learned to trust will not be surprised even when he finds things coming from the most unexpected sources. All things are man's to use and then let go of. What more can we ask? We want nothing that we have to keep; things are to use not to hold. Expect that everything is to come your way. Be content and cheerful if you wish to attract from out the store of the infinite. Open up your whole consciousness to the greater possibilities of life. Line up with the big things. When you speak the word expect it to happen. Know that it must be as you say. This will not be fooling yourself, it will simply be using the law as it is meant to be used.

EXPANDING OUR THOUGHT.

All things come to us through the use of our thought. If we have a small concept of life we will always be doing small things. First in the creative series is the Word, but the Word carries us no further than our consciousness back of it. Unless we are constantly expanding our thought we are not growing. Growth is the law of life and it is necessary. We cannot stand still. If you want to do a new thing, get a new thought and then you will have the power of attraction which has the possibility of drawing to you the circumstances which will make for the fulfillment of your desires. Get over the old idea of limitation.

Overcome all precedents and set yourself in the new order of things. If you want to build a railroad, you will never do it unless you get over the idea that the most you can hope for in life is to sell peanuts. Let the people sell peanuts for a living who think in the terms of peanuts. Get out of the rut. God has created you for a glorious future; dare to fling out into mind the greater assurances about yourself.

THE POWER OF A TREATMENT.

A treatment has as much power as we put into the word which we speak when we are giving it. This does not mean screwing up our mind or using our will power, or using force from the material standpoint. It means simply knowing that what we say will be done unto us of a Power which can do anything that is given It to do. We must know that our word breaks down every material law and sets the patient free to express God. We must know that the word would endure even though all else should fail. "Heaven and earth will pass away but my word will accomplish." In calm confidence and perfect faith, speak and wait upon the perfect law. Get that mental attitude that never wavers. Be sure and it will be done.

REPEATING THE TREATMENT.

One treatment would heal anything if it were not for the fact that people are constantly receiving false suggestions from the outer life. As it now stands we should treat until we get results, always expecting that it will happen at once. Every treatment should be complete, and at the close we should always realize that it is done.

The word spoken once from the mind that knows is immediately taken up by the Mind in which we live, and this Mind begins to create around the word, which is the seed, the thing thought of. We must speak that word with authority. There can be no wondering if it is going to work. When we plant a seed in the ground and water and care for it, we never doubt but a plant will spring into being. So it is with the word. It is acted upon by some power which we do not see, but that the power is there there is no doubt, since all who go about it get results. As Thomas Edison says of electricity, "It Is; use it;" so we say of mind, "It Is; use it." Always remember that your every thought is the way that you are treating, since it is the way that you are thinking.

IMPERSONAL HEALING.

The very presence of one that understands the truth will have a great power of healing. The reason for this is that we are all in Mind, and we have with us at all times our thought, and since all manifestation is the result of mind in action, and we are thinking beings and are always causing mind to act, the very presence of our thought will have some power to act upon whatever we are thinking about. We are dealing with a power which in itself is limitless. We limit it, and so it cannot become to us the bigger thing. Of itself the power is the same that made the worlds, and it cannot realize any sense of limitation. "They could not enter in because of their unbelief and because they limited the Holy one of Israel." Stop limiting things. Things are as big as we make them, no more, no less. There is room at the top. Get on top of everything, and dare to dominate the earth. All things are given us to use; make use of them. Everything is limitless, and we must see the truth that the fault is not in the Law but in ourselves when we fail. Not with God but with man. Dare, Dare, Dare.

Think of the bigness of things in the universe, think of the number of grains of sand, the profusion of all life, and never again limit anything. All is yours to use. Jesus would never have become the Christ unless he had had the courage to say, "Behold, I Am He." You will never attain until in some degree you are able to say the sane thing of yourself.

We must learn to reach out and take what is meant for us, the greater life, the all good. People say, "Yes, but how do you do it?" Simply know that God makes things out of Himself by speaking the word, and that in your own life you can do the same. All people can think, and all people can speak, at least mentally; this is all that you need to begin on. The word is at the center of all creation and is first cause, the starting point of all that you see. The word is in your own mouth, and all that you have to do is to speak it. The trouble is that we are speaking the word, and in the next breath we are denying its power by seeing something that contradicts It. If the word is the way that God creates, it is the right way. If it works for God, shall it not work for us? As yet our word is more or less imperfect; but more and more it will become perfect, and so the outer condition will be brought up to the inner word. All words have as much power as we put into them when we speak. "The word is already in our own mouths." That word is all that you will ever need to bring happiness, health and success to you.

Do you wish to live in a perfect world peopled with friends who love you, surrounded by all that is beautiful and pleasing? Do you wish to have the good things of life? There is but one way and that way is as sure as that the sun shines. Forget all else and think only upon what you want. Control all thought that denies the real, and as the mist disappears before the sun so shall all adversity melt before the shining radiance of your own exalted thought.

The prodigal son remained a prodigal only so long as he chose to do so. When the thought came to him to return he was greeted by the Father with outstretched hands. So shall we find that when we turn to that world which is perfect there will be something that will turn with us, and we shall behold the new heaven and the new earth; not in some far off place somewhere beyond the clouds, but here and now shall we become free.

We must do away with all that hinders the true growth, all the little thoughts that hinder us from becoming. Human strife comes from the thought that there is not enough to go around. Forget it; we cannot use even what we see, and what we do not see is infinite. You will rob no one by becoming prosperous, and the laws that underlie this state of being are simple and easy to understand, and not hard to attain for the one who is willing to let go of the negative state of being.

PROSPERITY.

Here are a few simple rules for prosperity that are as sure of working as that water is sure to be wet. First remember that nothing happens by chance. All is law and all is order. You create your own laws every time you think. There is something, call it what you will, but there is a Power around you that knows and that understands all things.

This Power works like the soil; it receives the seed of your thought and at once begins to operate upon it. It will receive whatever you give to it and will create for you and throw back at you whatever you think into it.

This means that the practitioner should be very careful how he is thinking at all times. Not alone in the moments of the deeper silence are we treating our patients, but perhaps more than this we are treating them in an impersonal way at all times. When we take a patient into our thought for a treatment there will be a constant stream of consciousness flowing out to him, during all the time that he is in our care. We should be very careful of our thoughts as we realize the deep truths of mental action and reaction.

WHAT IS THE SPIRITUAL MIND?

What is true spirituality? Many people have asked this and as many have answered it. I do not pretend to know more about this all important topic than others, but to the thinking person who has come to realize that all is love, yet at the same time all is governed by law, there must be a different answer given than the one we ordinarily hear. The average religious person thinks that spirituality must manifest in some unnatural way, such as giving up all personal pleasure and becoming resigned to whatever happens; that we must give up most of what life holds here; that in some far-off future perhaps we may attain. This was not the case with the man Jesus. We have more accounts of his being at feasts and weddings and similar gatherings than at other places. His first miracle was performed at a wedding feast, and we must remember that here he even turned water into wine for the pleasure of the guests of the house. Perhaps we have made a mistake about what true spirituality means.

Other people think we must live some kind of an excluded life in order to obtain. Perhaps this may be true of the weak ones. But what of the wood? What of the busy street? Is it not to be saved also? Jesus spent much time with the common people as well as with the rich. And it is certain that he also spent much time alone with the Spirit.

What is the Spirit, anyway? We all answer, "Why of course, it is God." Where is the Spirit? It is present at all times and in all places. True spirituality must simply mean coming to realize the presence of this Spirit. It must be coming to rely upon it more than anything else. The one then who is the most spiritual is simply the one who relies the most; that is all. No matter where he is, he must rely, he must trust, he must believe. We do not have to give up anything but negative thought and act. We do not want to do anything that contradicts the forward march of the unfoldment of the Spirit, so all that we think and do must be in line with that which is right. But who shall say what is and what is not right? Remember this forever, only your own soul shall say what is right and what is wrong. "To thine own self be true, and it shall follow as the night the day, thou canst not then be false to any man." Look to no one for guidance. This is the "blind leading the blind." The Almighty has put the truth into your own soul; look there and there alone for it. Many people seem to think that for a man to look spiritual he must have no color in his face, have some kind of far-away truth; he must be peculiar either in looks, or in the way he dresses.

To one who knows the truth, both praise and blame sound alike, but from the human standpoint at least a person cannot help being amused at the way in which the world judges true spirituality. My idea of true spirituality is that a man should live a perfectly normal life, entering into and enjoying all in life that is clean and good. He should place himself absolutely under the divine guidance. Other than this he will seem just like other people, neither better nor worse. Get over all kinds of unnatural thought and remember that all is good. Neither criticize nor condemn people or things. You are spiritual in so far as you trust in the Spirit, at all times, in all places, under all conditions. In order to do this you do not have to seclude yourself from the world. To do so is an open confession of your own weakness and lack. There are moments when it is best to be alone with the Power. From these moments we gather strength. To keep that strength to ourselves is pure selfishness. Walk, talk, live with the human race, hand in hand with all people and unified with all events, live and love and learn. Be natural and normal. If you seek to enter some other way it must all be done over again, for no one lives or dies unto himself but unto all people.

THE CHURCH OF GOD.

The Church of God is not built with hands, it is eternal in the heavens; it is not lighted with candles; its dome is heaven and it is lighted by the stars of God's illumined thought, and each member in his separate star "shall draw the thing as he sees it, for the God of things as they are." Here all people recognize the God within their own souls and ask for and see no other God. When you can look upon all creation as the perfect work of a perfect God, you will become a member of this church. I doubt very much if the church universal admits members from the church individual. When you can see in the saint and the sinner one and the same person, when you can realize that the one who kneels before the altar and the one who lies drunk in the street is the same one, when you can love the one as much as you do the other, no doubt you will be able to qualify. As it now is we have too many preachers who do not understand, that have no purpose; too many prayers, too many creeds, too many teachers, that have no message; too many churches, too many "learned" people, and too few thinkers. "The Kingdom of Heaven cometh not by observation." It is the "Still, small voice" within the soul that speaks. The expanded thought will never wish to join or be joined to. Nothing human can contain it. It feels the limitation of form and ceremony and longs for the freedom of the Spirit, the great out of doors, the Great God of the everywhere. Alone in the desert, the forest or by the restless ocean, looking up at the stars, man breathes forth these words, "With only my Maker and me."

THE PATH TO PROSPERITY.

The healing of conditions is no different from other healing. All healing is the constructive use of a mental law which the world is gradually beginning to understand something of. Again we must reiterate the principle of all life. We are surrounded by a thinking medium from which all things come. We think into it; it does the rest. Since we are thinking beings and cannot stop thinking, and since Creative Mind receives our thought and cannot stop creating, it must always be making something for us. What it will make depends absolutely and only upon what we are thinking, and what we will attract will depend entirely upon our holding thought to the complete exclusion of all that would contradict it. It is not enough that we should sit down and say, 'I am one with Infinite Life." This must mean more than mere words; it must be felt, it must become an embodiment of a positive mental attitude. It is not claiming something to be true which is going to happen; it is not sending out an aspiration, or a desire, or a supplication, or a prayer; it must be the embodiment of that which knows that now it is. This is more than holding a thought. Our ability to attract will depend upon the largeness of our thought as we feel that it flows out into a great Universal Creative Power. We are dealing with the form in thought, and not with the form in matter. We have learned that when we get the true form in thought and permeate it with the spirit of belief we will see the thought made flesh without any further effort on our part.

Thought can attract to us only that which we first mentally embody. We cannot attract to ourselves that which we are not. We can attract in the outer only that which we have first completely mentally embodied within, that which has become a part of our mental make-up, a part of our inner understanding.

A man going into business will attract to himself that which he thinks about the most. If he is a barber he will attract people who want to be shaved or have their hair cut. If he sells shoes he will attract people who want to buy shoes. (See Creative Mind and Success, by the author of the present volume.) So it is with everything; we will not only do this, but we will also attract as much of anything as we mentally embody. This is apt to be overlooked in the study of metaphysics. It is not enough to say that we attract what we think; we become what we think, and what we become we will attract.

Do not become merely sentimental about this. Your life is governed by more than a sentiment; it; is governed by law, something that cannot be broken, something that picks up every mental attitude and does something with it.

This fundamental proposition of the law should then work out into our conditions. Always remember that it does just as we think. It does not argue, it simply does the thing as we think it. Now how are we thinking? Never ask a patient how he is feeling; ask, how are you thinking to-day? This is the only thing that matters. How are we thinking about life and our conditions? Are we receiving the race suggestion; are we saying that there is not enough to go around? If we are saying this, it is our belief, and there is something that will see that it becomes a part of our expression. Most people, through ignorance of the higher laws of their being, are suffering from the thoughts imposed upon them from a negative and doubtful world. We who are claiming the use of the greater law must emancipate ourselves from all sense of limitation. We are not to be governed by the outer confusion but by the inner realization. We are to judge life not from the way that things in the past have been done, but from the way that the Spirit does things.

THE WAY OF THE SPIRIT.

Again let us say that the Spirit creates by becoming the thing that it thinks. There is no other possible way in which it could work. Since it is all and there is no other, the thought of opposing forces never enters into its mental working; when we are judging from the outer we are not working in line with the power that we should be using. We must come to see that there is only One Power and that we are touching it at all points, for there is not a power of poverty and a power of prosperity. There is the one becoming the many; it makes and it unmakes that a higher form may appear to express through it. All that is not in line with its forward movement will soon pass away, for it recognizes no opposite. As far as we are concerned what we are and what we are to become depends only upon what we are thinking, for this is the way that we are using creative power. The sooner we get away from the thought that we have to create, the sooner we will be able to work in line with the Spirit. Always man uses; he never creates anything. The united intelligence of the human race could not make a single rose-bud; it does not know enough. But our slightest thought adrift in mind causes the same power that makes all things to create for us. The great error of the race is, and always has been, that men have thought to give a physical reason for things. When that reason has not answered the problems of life they have sought out some other reason just as physical. The fact that they are all wrong is shown in that every generation has found a different reason. When truth is found it will also be found that it never changes to suit the whims of the human fancy. This is proven by the fact that whatever of the real truth the race has discovered has never been changed. The truth that was revealed to the prophets of old has never changed; it is the same to-day as it was thousands of years ago. Whoever touches truth, no matter in what generation, will always get the same answer. The great truth that was revealed from Moses to the time of Jesus is the same truth that is still revealed to all who will accept it; it is simply this: we are now living in a Spiritual Universe governed by mental laws of cause and effect. Moses saw it mostly from the standpoint of the Law of cause and effect, an eye for an eye. What does this mean? It means, as Jesus said, "As a man sows, so shall he reap." Moses saw the law. Jesus saw not only the law ("I am come not to destroy but to fulfill"), but he saw behind the law the reason for it, and revealed behind all law the Great Law-giver, a God of love working out the great inner concepts of His own being in harmony and in beauty, filled with peace, causing the sun to shine alike upon the just and the unjust. Jesus did not try to overcome the use of law; He understood all law and He well knew that all law was at His command; He did not break the law, He fulfilled it. So we must find that all is at our command through these same laws. The man who understands law and complies with it will have no difficulty in demonstrating that it is as true for him as it ever was for any one else. What, then, are the laws underlying prosperity? The first is this, and we must not try to escape it: "Thou shalt have no other Gods before me." This Me is Spirit. We are, then, to trust only in the activity of Spirit for what we need. But the world will say. "Human things come through human agencies." This may be true, but we must realize that the power we are dealing with also has within its own mind all people and all things. We do not have to treat people; what we have to do is to embody principle. Principle may use people, but that is no part of our responsibility. Ultimately all is Spirit, and Spirit which is the beginning is also the end of all manifestation. "I am the Alpha and the Omega." Our life, then, is to be governed by Spirit. We need look no further. It will do for us all that we will ever ask, provided we believe. Why, then, has it not done so? The answer is that it has already done so, but we have not received it. The Spirit may offer, but we must accept the gift before it can be made. "Behold, I stand at the door and knock." We must understand that this receiving is a mental process; it is one of mentally taking.

The way, then, that we are using mind through our thought is the way that we are treating ourselves for prosperity. So simple, and yet we have not understood it! If a man says, "I have not." he will not receive; if he says, "I have," he will receive. "To those who have shall be given, and to those who have not shall be taken away even that which they have." This is a veiled statement of the law of cause and effect. When you send out into mind the thought that you have not, it accepts the idea and takes away from you even that which you have. Reverse the process and say, "I have," and it will at once set to work to create for you even more than you now possess. You will readily see then that you are not dealing with two powers but with one, and that it operates through your own thought, doing unto all even as they believe.

THE LEVEL OF CONSCIOUSNESS.

Since all is mind, and it is done unto us as we mentally think, all life is simply a law of thought—activity of consciousness. In our life the power flows through us. If we provide a big receptivity, it will do a big thing; if, on the other hand, we only believe in a small way, the activity must be a small one. The Spirit can do for us only what it can do through us. Unless we are able to provide the consciousness, it cannot make the gift. Few people have a great consciousness, and this explains why so few excel. The power behind all things of itself is without limit; it is all-power; in us it has to become what we make it. We carry within our own soul the key to all expression, but few enter in. The door is not seen with the physical eye, and as yet but few have gained the ability to see; the majority merely look. Realizing, then, that while the power is limitless it must become operative through our own thought, we shall see that what we need is not some greater power, but that what we really need is a greater consciousness, a deeper realization of life, a grander concept of being. We must unify ourselves with the great whole. The man who dares to fling his thought out into universal intelligence with the positive assurance of one who knows and dares to claim all there is will find that it will be done. God will honor his request. On the other hand, the one who fears to speak lest God will smite will find himself smitten of the law, not because God is angry, but because it is done as he believes.

We have a right to have and should expect to have in this world all that will make for the comfort and for the luxuries of life. What matter how much we have, if we rob no other soul to get it? Shall not the Power that so lavishly spreads Itself out into nature give to us Its highest expression, all that we can ask? We dishonor God when we claim less than all. Until we can expand our thought so that we shall be able to say also, "I am," we need not expect to get great results.

The soul that knows its own Divinity is the great soul; before it all else must bend; to it all else must gravitate. Enlarge your thought processes. Away with the little personal thoughts of things, and dare to think in universal terms about all things. The universe is running over with good, it is for you, but you must believe and then take it. Do you dare to believe that your own word is invincible? When you speak it how do you feel? Is it limitless, is it all power, is all power given to you in heaven and on earth. are you one with the only power that there is? Until you can say yes to all these questions and not simply believe them but know them, you can not hope to attain. It is useless in making a demonstration to beg for things; as well beg that water should be wet or that fire should be hot. Things are, we must take them. Your word has only the power that you put into it, no more and no less. We are all held accountable for every word that we speak because all is the action and the reaction of mind. Man is his own heaven and his own hell.

We start a new enterprise and wonder what the chances of success are; have we realized that the outer is simply the inner manifested? When we go to a new place we shall find there only what we have taken with us. If we have taken success we will find success; if, on the other hand, we have taken failure we will find failure. This is the law; none can avoid it, none need try. Every living soul is a law unto his own life. "There is no law but my own soul shall set." Nothing can come upon the path of the soul but that thing that the soul attracts.

PRACTICE FOR PROSPERITY.

Prosperity is in our own hands to do with as we will, but we will never reach it until we learn to control our thought. We must see only what we want and never allow the other things to enter. If we wish activity we must be active in our thought, we must see activity and speak it into everything that we do. The spoken word shall bring it to pass. We speak the word, it is brought to pass of the Power that we speak it into. We can only speak the word that we understand, the activity will correspond to our inner concepts. If they are large the results will be large. The thing to do is to unify ourselves with all the biggest ideas that we can compass; and realizing that our ideas govern our power of attraction, we should be constantly enlarging within ourselves. We must realize our at-one-ment with All Power and know that our word will bring it to pass. We speak the word, it is brought to pass of As consciousness grows it will manifest in enlarged opportunities and a greater field of action. Most people think in the terms of universal powers. Feel that you are surrounded by all the power that there is when you speak and never doubt but that what you say will spring into being.

We should speak right out into mind all that we desire, and believe that it will be done unto us. Never take the time to listen to those who doubt. We observe that their philosophy has done but little to save the world or themselves. here again let the dead bury the dead and see to it that you maintain in your own thought what you want, letting go of all else. Think only what you want to happen and never let yourself get mentally lazy and sluggish taking on the suggestions of poverty and limitation. See your-self as being in the position that you desire, mentally dwell upon it and then speak with perfect assurance that it is done; and then forget it and trust in the law. This will answer all needs. If you want to do this for someone else, all that you will need to do is to think of them and go through the same process of mind action. You will be sending out the truth for them, and mind being always active will not contradict what you have said.

Remember that you cannot hope to get results unless you keep but the one idea and do not mix thoughts in your mind. All is yours, but you must take it. The taking is always a mental process; it is believing absolutely. This is divine principle.

CONCLUSION.

Principle itself is simplicity, yet it is infinite—it is Infinite Mind and manifestation of Mind. We live in a Spiritual universe governed through thought, or the word which first becomes law; this law creates what we call matter. Jesus Christ discerned the truth about spiritual principles more than any other man who ever lived, and he proclaimed the eternal reign of law and understanding, absolute, complete, perfect; and he found that law to be operative through his own thought and the power of his own word. And when you and I shall cease looking outside ourselves to any person and shall realize that whatever truth and whatever power we shall have must flow through us; when we begin to interpret our own natures, we shall begin to understand God and law, and life, and not until then.

We live and move and have our being in what we call an Infinite Mind, an Infinite Creative Mind, also infinitely receptive, operative, omnipotent, and all-knowing; and we have learned that this mind presses against us on all sides, flows through us, and becomes operative through our thinking. The human race, ignorant of the laws of this mind, ignorant of the power of its own thought, has through its ignorance misused and abused the creative power of its thought, and brought upon itself the thing it feared. This is true because all thought is law, and all law is mind in action, and the word which you speak to-day is the law which shall govern your life to-morrow, as the word which you spoke, ignorantly or innocently, consciously or unconsciously yesterday, is absolutely governing your life to-day. As metaphysicians, then, we are not dealing with a material, nor denying a manifest universe, but we are claiming that the manifestation is the result of the inner activity of the mind; and if we wish for a definite manifestation, we must produce a definite inner activity. You and I, then, are not dealing with conditions, but with mental and spiritual law. We are dealing with the power of thought, the power of mind, and the more spiritual the thought the higher the manifestation. The more our reliance upon what we call God, the greater the power.

It is the new education because it strips all the false from the old belief and reveals the individual. It is the new age, because as sure as God is, it will usher in and express the perfect life, the revelation of this truth, and our ability to use it; and it is your own fault when you know this and do not prove it.

If, knowing the infinite power flowing through you, you still remain sick and unhappy, miserable and poor, my friend, it is your own fault. Do not blame God, do not blame man, and do not say it is of the devil. It is your own fault. Every time you say I Am, you are recognizing the eternal infinite presence of omnipotent power within your-self, which is God operating through your thought, and that is why you bring upon yourself the thing you fear, and why you bring to yourself the thing you want.

When fifty-one per cent. of your thinking is health and life and power, that day the fifty-one per cent. will swallow up, erase, kill out the rest. The day you, as an individual, through fifty-one per cent. of your thought, pass beyond the perception of limitation, you will draw out of the universe everything you desire; poverty will desert you and you will be emancipated forever. The day you think fifty-one per cent. of happiness, misery shall depart and never return. Is it not then worth your time and your effort, and should it not be the greatest purpose in the life of any awakened soul so to depict this principle as to emancipate himself?

The way can be shown, but each individual must him-self walk the way. We are so bound by suggestion and hypnotized by false belief, so entangled by the chaotic thinking of the world, thinking which is based upon the principle of a dual mind, that we become confused and are not ourselves. Wake up! Your word is all-powerful, your consciousness is one with Omnipotence. Your thought is infinite. Your destiny is eternal and your home is everlasting heaven. Realize the truth—I am living in a perfect universe, it always was perfect and always will be perfect. There never was a mistake made, there are no mistakes being made, and there never will be. I live in the great and eternal universe of perfection from cause to effect, from beginning to end, and "The world's all right, and I know it."

Majestic and calm, waiting with eternal and divine patience, the Great Principle of Life is ready to give to us all that it has. And while we listen and wait we will cast from us everything that hinders its complete expression through us, we will let go of all struggle and all strife and be at peace with Life.

Perfect peace to the soul as we rest in the realization of our unity with all that there is, was or ever will be. One with the Infinite Mind. All the power of the Spirit is working through our thought as we believe and receive. Now we will ask for and take that thing which we desire; it is done, it is complete, now and forever. Perfect life, perfect healing, perfect harmony, Divine guidance, Infinite strength and joy forever.

QUESTIONS AND ANSWERS.

What is the Truth?

The Truth is that which is. It is all that is. As there cannot be something and nothing, so the Truth, being that which is. must at the same time be all that there is.

Where is the Truth?

If the Truth is All, it must be everywhere; being all, there is no other substance to divide it with; being undivided, it is everywhere present. All Truth, which means all power, must be present at all points, or at any given point, at any and at all times.

Has the Truth changed?

A substance cannot change unless there is something for it to change into. Since the Truth is all, it cannot change, for there is no other thing for it to change into; whatever is the Truth, then, has never changed.

Is the Truth, or that which is, one or many?

It must be one, since it is all.

Is the Truth conscious?

Yes, man is conscious. He could not be so unless Truth or Life were conscious. Man's self-consciousness proves the self-consciousness of Life or Truth or Spirit. Like produces like.

What comes out of life?

Everything that is comes out of life. If life is all then it follows that all that is is some form of life.

How does Life make things?

Being all, it must make things out of itself. It must operate upon itself, through itself, and out of itself must make all that is made. Being conscious, it must know that it is doing this.

What would we call this inner movement of Life?

The inner movement of Life or consciousness we would call thought or the self-knowing of Life or Spirit.

Then the universe and all that is a part of it comes from thought?

Yes, everything comes from thought.

Do we not see a visible world that seems to change, and if we do, how is it that it could come from something that never changes?

Yes, we do see a changing world, but back of it is a changeless substance. The thing that changes is the thought or form; the substance from which this form comes never changes. It is one and undivided, and takes form through thought in all things. We prove this when we resolve all things into one source. All material things, so called, can be reduced into formless 'substance, the sole activity of which must be thought or the movement of intelligence upon itself.

What causes form to change?
The intelligence behind it.

Is there nothing in the universe, then, but Life, thought and form?
These are all.

If this is true, what is physical law?
Physical law is simply the result of the inner movement of Life.

If things and laws are the result of the inner movement of Life, then does it not follow that thoughts are things?
Yes, all things are simply thought forms.

How long does thought last as form?
As long as the thought is held in Life or Mind.

Does the thought of Life, Mind or Good ever change?
From all that we can know the thought of God seems to change. That is, planets change, take form and again become formless. When we realize that all this can take place without ever changing the substance behind it, we see no reason why God's thought could not change and ever build up a higher form. Indeed, this is one of the teachings of Ancient Wisdom, that while reality never changes, the form that it takes is ever changing.

What is man's place in the creative order?
Man is a thinking center in Mind, reproducing in a smaller scale all there is in the Universe.

Does this not make man's thought creative?
In a certain sense it does. What we call creation is not making something out of nothing, but it is thought taking form. And as man thinks, and as thought must take form, then it must follow that man's thought must take form in mind and so become creative.

What is man's thought?
It is the activity of that something within that can say, "'I Am.''

What is the difference between God and man?
The very fact that man can say, "I Am," proves that he is. Since he is he must be made out of life and must be some part of all that there is. This being

so, man must be a part of God's consciousness. The difference would be in degree only. He must be as much of Life as he recognizes himself to be.

Is all of man's thought creative?
Yes, all or none. If one thought produces, then all must.

If this be true, how is it that man seems to be so limited?
Because he has thought limitation, and thoughts are things and will always make the thing thought of. In reality the very fact that man's thought can limit him also proves that it could free him from all limitation by simply changing his thought.

But why is man so made that he can think two ways?
This is a question that can be answered only in one way. Unless a man can think as he wants to think he would not be a man at all but simply a piece of mechanism. Man is an individual and that means self choice, backed by a power that will produce the thing chosen. In discovering himself man chooses many things, uses them and passes to a higher choice, ever ascending in the scale of being. As fast as he chooses, he experiences that thing which he thinks about.

What is evil?
Evil is the result of a lack of clear seeing, based upon a belief in two powers, and limitation and what we call sin is the result of man's struggle to find himself.

If this be true, why could we not at once begin to change our whole life by first changing our thought?
We could. We would not be changing real substance, but we would be changing the form that it takes through our thought. All that we can change is the form of thought through which experiences come to us.

What is the limit of man's creative use of Mind?
Man is limited by nothing but his own thinking, by his mental ability to conceive.

What is meant by mental conception?
All things are produced by thought. The thing produced from mind is first formed in thought; thought molds mind into form.

But do we not have to act?
We cannot think without acting; an inactive body is the result of an inactive mind.

In using our creative powers, how far do we have to consider the conditions under which we live?
We do not have to consider them at all. Conditions are the result, the effect and not the cause; we create them as fast as we think.

How would a person start to change conditions?

By first changing thought and by realizing that we are not dealing with an illusion, but with the great reality. Then by acting as though we already have what we think.

How long would it take to do this?

As long as it would take to let go of all negative thought and embody all positive thought. This would depend entirely upon the individual and his mental ability to control thought.

What would hinder us the most?

Ourselves; no one gives to us but ourselves and no one takes from us but ourselves.

Can no one else help us?

Only to a limited degree. While we may be helped by those who understand the law, for a time, yet sooner or later we must ourselves take the creative responsibility of our own lives. Others may think for us for a few moments a day, but we think for ourselves all the time.

But does not God help us?

Yes, God helps all, but must do it through law. "All's love yet all's law."

How should we pray?

By giving thanks that we already have that thing that we pray for; by completely believing and by never doubting. "When ye pray believe that ye have received and ye shall receive." We must be sure that in no way shall we think, act or talk or read about limitation. We must all be a law unto ourselves.